Here are your
1992 SCIENCE YEAR
Cross-Reference Tabs

For insertion in your WORLD BOOK

Each year, SCIENCE YEAR, THE WORLD BOOK ANNUAL SCIENCE SUPPLEMENT, adds a valuable dimension to your WORLD BOOK set. The Cross-Reference Tab System is designed especially to help you link SCIENCE YEAR'S major articles to the related WORLD BOOK articles that they update.

How to use these Tabs:

First, remove this page from SCIENCE YEAR.

Begin with the first Tab, **AIR POLLUTION**. Take the A volume of your WORLD BOOK set and find the **Air pollution** article. Moisten the **AIR POLLUTION** Tab and affix it to that page.

Go on to glue all the other Tabs in the appropriate WORLD BOOK volumes. Your set's E volume may not have an article on **Endangered species.** If it doesn't, put the **ENDANGERED SPECIES** Tab in its correct alphabetical location in that volume — near the **Encyclopedia** article.

1992
Science Year

The World Book Annual Science Supplement

A review of Science and Technology
During the 1991 School Year

World Book, Inc.

a Scott Fetzer company

Chicago London Sydney Toronto

The Year's Major Science Stories

From the discovery of bizarre geologic features on Venus to the ecological devastation of the Persian Gulf War, it was an eventful year for science and technology. On these two pages are the stories that *Science Year* editors picked as the most memorable, exciting, or important of the year, along with details about where you will find information about them in the book.

The Editors

▲
Yosemite Fires
Fires swept through thousands of hectares of forestland in Yosemite National Park in August 1990. In the Special Reports section, see FIRE AND NATURE.

Chernobyl Fifth Anniversary
The fifth anniversary in 1991 of the April 1986 disaster at the Soviet Union's Chernobyl nuclear power plant sparked renewed debate about the safety of nuclear energy. In the Special Reports section, see THE NEW NUCLEAR REACTORS.
▼

▲
New Views of Venus
The *Magellan* spacecraft in September 1990 began mapping the surface of Venus, providing radar images of a world of complex geologic activity. In the Special Reports section, see EXPLORING THE SURFACE OF VENUS.

ISBN 0-7166-0592-9

ISSN 0080-7621
Library of Congress Catalog Number: 65-21776
Printed in the United States of America.

Devastating Cyclone
A cyclone and widespread flooding in Bangladesh killed at least 125,000 people in April 1991. In the Science News Update section, see METEOROLOGY.

Ecological Damage of War
The war in Kuwait in early 1991 blackened skies and shores throughout the Persian Gulf area. In the Science News Update section, see ENVIRONMENT (CLOSE-UP).

Ozone Hole
The seasonal thinning of Earth's protective layer of ozone above Antarctica reached record levels in autumn 1990. In the Science News Update section, see ENVIRONMENT; METEOROLOGY. ▶

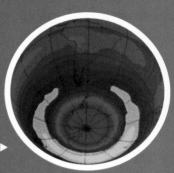

◀ **Hubble Update**
Despite flaws in its mirror, the *Hubble Space Telescope* in 1990 began providing sharp and detailed views of the universe. In the Science News Update section, see SPACE TECHNOLOGY (CLOSE-UP).

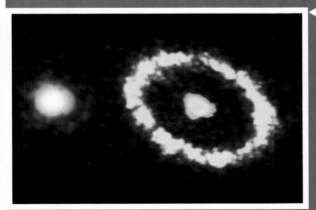

Volcanic Eruptions
Eruptions in Japan and the Philippines in June 1991 displayed the awesome force of volcanoes. In the Special Reports section, see VOLCANO WATCHING. In the Science News Update section, see GEOLOGY. ▶

Contents

See page 12

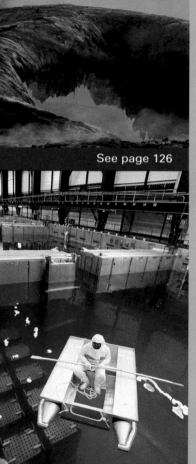

See page 83

See page 126

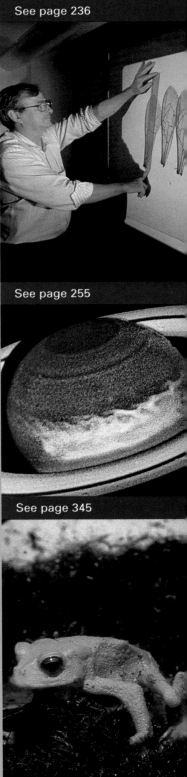

See page 236

See page 255

See page 345

Staff

Editorial Director
A. Richard Harmet

Editorial
Managing Editor
Darlene R. Stille

Associate Editor
Jinger Hoop

Senior Editors
David L. Dreier
Mark Dunbar
Lori Fagan
Carol L. Hanson
Barbara A. Mayes
Karin C. Rosenberg
Rod Such

Contributing Editors
Sara Dreyfuss
Joan Stephenson

Editorial Assistant
Ethel Matthews

Cartographic Services
H. George Stoll, Head
Wayne K. Pichler

Index Services
Beatrice Bertucci, Head
Dennis P. Phillips
David Pofelski

Art
Art Director
Alfred de Simone

Senior Artist, Science Year
Cari L. Biamonte

Senior Artists
Lisa Buckley
Melanie J. Lawson

Photographs
Photography Director
John S. Marshall

Senior Photographs Editor
Sandra M. Dyrlund

Photographs Editor
Geralyn Swietek

Research Services
Director
Mary Norton

Library Services
Mary Ann Urbashich, Head

Product Production
Director of Manufacturing
Sandra Van den Broucke

Pre-Press Services
Jerry Stack, Director
Madelyn S. Underwood
Randi Park
Barbara Podczerwinski

Proofreaders
Anne Dillon
Marguerite Hoye
Daniel Marotta

Publisher
William H. Nault

Editorial Advisory Board

Contributors

Adelman, George, M.A., M.S.
Editor,
Encyclopedia of Neuroscience.
[*Neuroscience*]

Amato, Ivan, M.A.
Staff Writer,
Science Magazine.
[Special Report, *Microscopic Machines;*
Chemistry (Close-Up)]

Arbeiter, Larry, B.S.
Director,
University of Chicago News Office.
[Special Report, *Questions of Gravity*]

Asimov, Isaac, Ph.D.
Science Writer.
[Special Report, *Science and the Voyage
of Columbus*]

Barnett, Robert A., B.A.
Free-Lance Writer.
[*Nutrition*]

Beatty, J. Kelly, M.S.
Senior Editor,
Sky & Telescope Magazine.
[*Space Technology* (Close-Up)]

Bower, Bruce, M.A.
Behavioral Sciences Editor,
Science News Magazine.
[*Psychology*]

Brett, Carlton E., Ph.D.
Professor,
Department of Geological Sciences,
University of Rochester.
[*Paleontology*]

Brohan, Mark, M.A.
Editor,
Bank Network News.
[Science You Can Use: *Cash by
Computer: Automated Teller Machines*]

Cain, Steve, B.S.
News Coordinator,
Purdue University School of Agriculture.
[*Agriculture*]

Covault, Craig, B.S.
Space Technology Editor,
Aviation Week & Space Technology
Magazine.
[*Space Technology*]

Decker, Barbara B., B.A.
Free-Lance Writer.
[Special Report, *Volcano Watching*]

Decker, Robert, Ph.D.
Visiting Professor of Geophysics,
University of Hawaii at Hilo.
[Special Report, *Volcano Watching*]

Delson, Eric, Ph.D.
Professor of Anthropology,
Lehman College.
[*Anthropology*]

Denkin, Nathan M., Ph.D.
Technical Staff,
AT&T Bell Laboratories.
[Science You Can Use: *Information on a
Light Beam*]

Elfring, Chris, M.S.
Senior Staff Officer,
National Academy of Sciences.
[Special Report, *Fire and Nature*]

Engelman, Robert
Science Correspondent,
Scripps Howard News Service.
[*Environment*]

Ferrell, Keith
Editor,
OMNI Magazine.
[*Computer Hardware; Computer
Software*]

Fisher, Arthur, M.A.
Science and Technology Editor,
Popular Science Magazine.
[Special Report, *The New Nuclear
Reactors*]

Gordon, Arnold L., Ph.D.
Professor,
Columbia University.
[Special Report, *Currents and Climate*]

Graff, Gordon, Ph.D.
Free-Lance Science Writer.
[*Chemistry*]

Hay, William W., Ph.D.
Professor of Geology,
University of Colorado, Boulder.
[*Geology*]

Haymer, David S., Ph.D.
Assistant Professor,
Department of Genetics,
University of Hawaii.
[*Genetics*]

Hecht, Jeff, B.S., M.Ed.
Correspondent,
New Scientist Magazine.
[*Materials Science*]

Hellemans, Alexander, B.Sc.
Free-Lance Science Writer.
[*Physics, Fluids and Solids*]

Hester, Thomas R., Ph.D.
Professor of Anthropology and
Director,
Texas Archeological Research
Laboratory,
University of Texas, Austin.
[*Archaeology, New World*]

Howell, T. Howard, D.D.S.
Assistant Professor of Periodontology,
Harvard School of Dental Medicine.
[*Dentistry*]

Johnson, Cecil E., Ph.D.
Professor Emeritus,
Riverside City College.
[Science You Can Use: *The Biology of a
Compost Heap*]

Jones, William Goodrich, A.M.L.S.
Assistant University Librarian,
University of Illinois at Chicago.
[*Books of Science*]

Katz, Paul, M.D.
Professor and Vice Chairman,
Department of Medicine,
Georgetown University Medical Center.
[*Immunology*]

King, Elliot W., M.S. , M.A.
Editor,
Optical and Magnetic Report.
[*Electronics*]

King, Lauriston R., Ph.D.
Deputy Director,
Office of University Research,
Texas A&M University.
[*Oceanography*]

Kleinstein, Robert N., Ph.D.
Professor of Optometry,
University of Alabama at Birmingham.
[Science You Can Use: *Sunglasses
Wear New Rating Labels*]

Kowal, Deborah, M.A.
Free-Lance Medical Writer.
[*Public Health*]

Lechtenberg, Victor L., Ph.D.
Executive Associate Dean of
Agriculture,
Purdue University.
[*Agriculture*]

Lilly, Douglas K., Ph.D.
Director,
Center for the Analysis and Prediction of Storms,
University of Oklahoma.
[*Meteorology*]

Lunine, Jonathan I., Ph.D.
Associate Professor,
University of Arizona
Lunar Planetary Lab.
[*Astronomy, Solar System*]

Luoma, Jon R., B.A.
Free-Lance Writer.
[Special Report, *The Technology Behind Recycling*]

March, Robert H., Ph.D.
Professor of Physics,
University of Wisconsin.
[*Physics, Subatomic*]

Marschall, Laurence A., Ph.D.
Professor,
Department of Physics,
Gettysburg College.
[*Astronomy, Extragalactic; Astronomy, Extragalactic* (Close-Up)]

Meltzer, David J., Ph.D.
Associate Professor of Anthropology,
Southern Methodist University.
[Special Report, *Who Were the First Americans?*]

Merz, Beverly, B.A.
National Editor,
Science and Technology,
American Medical News.
[*Medical Research; Medical Research* (Close-Up)]

Meyer, B. Robert, M.D.
Chief, Division of Clinical
Pharmacology,
North Shore University Hospital.
[*Drugs*]

Patrusky, Ben, B.E.E.
Free-Lance Science Writer.
[Special Report, *Drug-Bug Warfare*]

Pennisi, Elizabeth, M.S.
Chemistry/Materials Science Editor,
Science News Magazine.
[*Zoology; Zoology* (Close-Up)]

Raloff, Janet, M.S.J.
Environment/Policy Editor,
Science News Magazine.
[*Environment* (Close-Up)]

Salisbury, Frank B., Ph.D.
Professor of Plant Physiology,
Utah State University.
[*Botany*]

Saunders, R. Stephen, Ph.D.
Project Scientist, Magellan,
Jet Propulsion Laboratory.
[Special Report, *Exploring the Surface of Venus*]

Schroeder, Don, B.S., B.A.
Assistant Technical Editor,
Car and Driver Magazine.
[Science You Can Use: *Antilock Brakes: A Potential Lifesaver*]

Snow, Theodore P., Ph.D.
Professor of Astrophysics,
University of Colorado, Boulder.
[Special Report, *Mysteries of the Milky Way; Astronomy, Galactic*]

Tamarin, Robert H., Ph.D.
Professor and Chairman of Biology,
Boston University.
[*Ecology; Genetics* (Close-Up)]

Tobin, Thomas R., Ph.D.
Assistant Professor,
ARL Division of Neurobiology,
University of Arizona.
[*Zoology*]

Visich, Marian, Jr., Ph.D.
Associate Dean of Engineering,
State University of New York.
[*Energy*]

Wallace, Joseph, B.A.
Free-Lance Writer.
[Special Report, *The "Forests" in Our Cities*]

Wenke, Robert J., Ph.D.
Professor,
Department of Anthropology,
University of Washington.
[*Archaeology, Old World*]

Wintsch, Susan J., M.A., M.S.
Free-Lance Writer.
[Special Report, *How Smart Are Dolphins?*]

Special Reports

Fifteen articles give in-depth treatment to significant and timely subjects in science and technology.

See page 30

See page 62

See page 97

See page 190

BY ISAAC ASIMOV

Science and the Voyage of Columbus

A noted science writer presents a fascinating argument that Columbus' discovery of new continents may have made possible the rise of Western science.

Modern science had not yet been developed when Christopher Columbus set sail on his historic voyage across the Atlantic Ocean in 1492. In Columbus' lifetime, people believed the Earth was 6,000 years old, that the sun moved about Earth, and that lead somehow could be changed to gold through mysterious processes known as alchemy. They knew nothing about the nature of the stars, about the causes of disease, about how the human body had developed, or how it worked. Yet in the 1400's, despite the primitive state of scientific knowledge, two different nations at opposite ends of the Eurasian continent engaged in massive projects of exploration that were as difficult for those times as the reach for the moon was in ours.

One nation was China, which was then the largest and richest nation in the world, with a population of 80 million. It was the most advanced nation technologically and had the most intricate society. The Chinese had long before 1492 discovered the magnetic compass, gunpowder, and printing. Europe was small, poor, and primitive by comparison.

In the early 1400's, China sent out fleets of ships that crisscrossed the Indian Ocean and established dominance over what is now Indonesia, Sri Lanka, and other places in the Far East. Chinese influence reached as far westward as the Red Sea and the centers of Muslim power in the Middle East. But then the Chinese lost interest and ceased exploring.

In the late 1400's, Portugal also embarked on adventures of exploration. It was a tiny country with only 1 per cent of the population of China and was much less technologically advanced. Nevertheless, Portugal gave the world a lesson in determination that has never been forgotten. Portugal sent ship after ship down the coast of Africa and, unlike China, it did not lose interest. It was Portugal that established a vast overseas empire. China never reached Portugal, but Portugal reached China and India, and Japan, and Indonesia.

Why did little Portugal succeed, where giant China failed? For one thing, China was too conscious of its own power, achievements, and wealth of spices and silks. There was nothing in the rest of the world that the Chinese wanted or needed. So there was no use sending out ships to explore barbaric and useless places.

On the other hand, ever since the Crusades in the 1100's and 1200's, when European knights ventured to Palestine to seize the Holy Land from the Muslims, Europeans had been aware of how far behind the Eastern civilizations they were. They desperately wanted the sugar and spices, the silks and satins, gold and ivory that they could only get from the East. So there was no chance that the Portuguese and other Europeans would stop exploring. What's more, the Europeans, aware of their inferiority, labored to correct it with amazing energy. When knowledge of the magnetic compass, gunpowder, and printing reached Europe from the East, Europeans developed these technologies far beyond what the complacent Chinese felt it necessary to do. And the curiosity and energy of the

The author:
Isaac Asimov is a well-known author of many books and articles about all areas of science.

backward Europeans eventually worked to their advantage and led to the development of modern science.

We have become accustomed to periods of time being defined by scientific questions or advances. In the atomic age, which began in the 1940's, the great scientific questions involved the structure of the atom. In the space age, which began in the late 1950's, much scientific research was directed at how to build better rockets and spacecraft. In the Age of Exploration, which began in the 1400's, the great scientific question involved the size of the Earth.

At that time, all educated people understood that the Earth was a sphere. This had been known ever since the time of the ancient Greeks, 1,800 years earlier. The problem in 1492 was this: How large was the sphere of the Earth?

A Greek mathematician living in Egypt had worked out the size of the Earth around 200 B.C. Eratosthenes, librarian at Alexandria, used an ingenious method of measuring the angle of sunlight striking Earth's surface at two places. He calculated that the distance between the places was about $\frac{1}{50}$ the diameter of Earth. From this, he figured Earth to have a circumference of about 40,230 kilometers (25,000 miles). He was right within just a few miles. Earth's circumference is 40,008 kilometers (24,860 miles). But other philosophers later came up with circumferences of about 29,000 kilometers (18,000 miles), and in Columbus' time there was no certainty as to which estimate was right.

One crucial question related to the size of Earth was: How wide is the Atlantic Ocean? This was important to traders. Bringing goods to Europe from the East over land routes was costly and dangerous. Portuguese traders reached the East by sailing around Africa, but this was a long, long voyage. Every once in a while, someone would suggest a shortcut. Why not sail due westward and reach the East by crossing the width of the Atlantic Ocean? If the Earth were 40,230 kilometers in circumference, then it would mean ships would have to sail westward at least 19,300 kilometers (12,000 miles) to reach the East. No ship of Columbus' time could make a voyage of that length over open water. However, what if the Earth were only 29,000 kilometers in circumference? In that case, the westward voyage might be only 8,000 kilometers (5,000 miles). In fact, some thinkers of the time reasoned that it might be even shorter. In the late 1200's, Italian explorer and merchant Marco Polo had traveled overland to China. In his discussion of its geography, he described China as extending farther eastward than it really did. Paolo Toscanelli, a Florentine astronomer, geographer, and physician, pieced together the calculations of the ancient Greek philosopher Ptolemy with accounts of Marco Polo and other explorers and concluded that if one sailed westward from Europe, then the East would be reached after a voyage of only about 4,800 kilometers (3,000 miles).

Christopher Columbus accepted the estimate of a smaller-sized

Earth and a shorter sailing distance across the ocean. Columbus failed to persuade the king of Portugal and his advisers that the Earth was this small. But he succeeded with the king and queen of Spain. They agreed to support his exploration project, and on Aug. 3, 1492, Columbus sailed westward with three ships—the *Niña*, the *Pinta*, and the *Santa María*. On October 12, after seven weeks on the open ocean, he reached land. Returning to Spain, he announced that he had reached the Asian East, then called the Indies.

Of course, Columbus was wrong. The Earth was not 29,000 kilometers in circumference, but more than 40,000 kilometers, and Asia did not extend as far eastward as Marco Polo had said. What Columbus did reach was not the East, but vast continents of whose existence the Europeans were completely ignorant, continents we now call North and South America. It was fortunate for Columbus that they existed, for otherwise he would have sailed westward to destruction by storms or by starvation, because Asia was, indeed, a sailing distance of more than 19,000 kilometers from Europe.

Columbus never appreciated his good fortune. To the end of his life, he was certain that he had reached Asia, even though increasing numbers of other navigators grew convinced that what had been discovered was a New World. One of the explorers who most strongly insisted on this was the Italian navigator Amerigo Vespucci. That is why the continents are now considered American and not Columbian.

The matter of Asia versus a New World was not completely settled until 1521, when what was left of an expedition under the command of Portuguese navigator Ferdinand Magellan returned to Spain after making the first voyage around the globe, a journey that took three years. In the process, only 1 of Magellan's 5 ships and only 18 of his men completed the voyage. Magellan himself died in combat in the Philippines. But Magellan, unlike Columbus, did reach Asia, and with his voyage the matter of the size of the world was settled once and for all.

Voyages over the open sea, such as those that Columbus and Magellan undertook, would not have been possible without the magnetic compass.

The development of sturdy ships called carracks, of which Columbus' ship the *Santa María, right,* was an example, allowed European navigators to make long voyages around the coast of Africa to China for silks, spices, and other riches, *background.*

17

The Great Question of 1492: How Big Is Earth?

Educated Europeans in the 1400's knew that Earth is shaped like a sphere. They learned this from the writings of the ancient Greek philosophers. Even though a Greek had estimated correctly the size of the Earth, Europeans in 1492 did not agree on its size.

Eratosthenes' estimate

Greek philosopher Eratosthenes in about 200 B.C. made an almost accurate estimate of the size of Earth. He based his ingenious calculations on the assumption that all the sun's rays striking Earth are parallel.

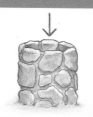

It was a known fact that on June 21 the sun's rays shined directly down on the bottom of a well at the Egyptian town of Syene. If the sun's rays are parallel to each other, Eratosthenes reasoned, they should strike Earth at an angle at Alexandria, due north about 5,000 stadia, the unit of measurement at that time.

On June 21, he measured the angle of the sun's rays at Alexandria by setting a stick in the ground and drawing an imaginary line from the end of the shadow cast by the stick to the top of the stick. The angle this formed, and thus the angle of the sun's rays, was about 7 degrees.

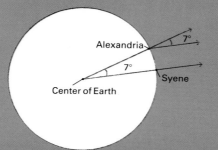

Eratosthenes knew that Alexandria and Syene were on the same meridian, an imaginary line going around the globe. He also knew that Earth is round; its circumference forms a circle of 360 degrees. He reasoned that plumb lines dropped from the two towns to the center of the Earth would, like the sun's rays, form a 7 degree angle.

> 7° = about 1/51 of 360°
> 5,000 stadia = 1/51 Earth's circumference
> 5,000 stadia X 51 = 255,000 stadia*
> *(about 40,230 kilometers or 25,000 miles)

Eratosthenes worked out a formula. He determined that the distance from Alexandria to Syene was about 1/51 the circumference of Earth. So multiplying the distance in stadia gave him a circumference of 25,500 stadia, which scholars believe is about 40,200 modern kilometers (25,000 miles).

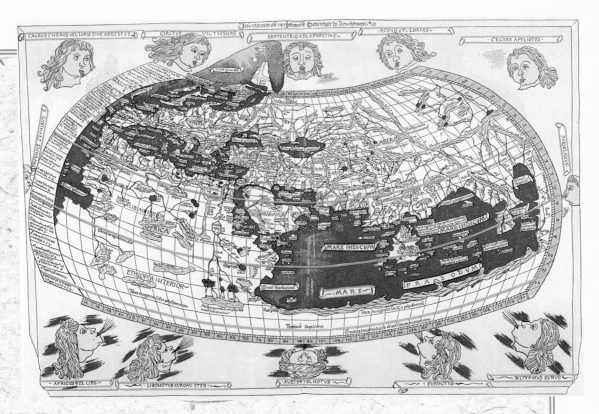

Ptolemy's map

The Greek philosopher Ptolemy in the A.D. 100's had created a map of Earth's surface, which Europeans in the 1400's believed was essentially correct. But Ptolemy had no idea that two great continents lay in the Atlantic Ocean between Europe and Asia.

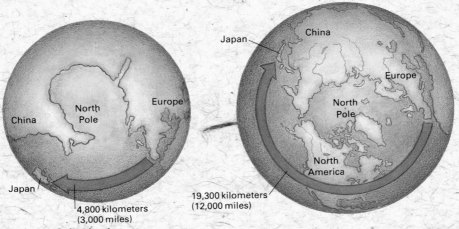

19,300 kilometers (12,000 miles)

4,800 kilometers (3,000 miles)

Columbus' error

Columbus believed Earth's circumference was 29,000 kilometers, *above left*, and the distance across the ocean to China, 4,800 kilometers rather than 19,000 kilometers, *above right*. If Columbus had not found land, he and his ships would have perished.

There are no landmarks in the open sea, so it is very difficult to tell in what direction you are going. The North Star always indicates the north, but the stars are not visible by day, and sometimes, thanks to clouds, they are not visible by night, either. The needle of a magnetic compass, however, always points north by day or by night, in fair weather and in storms. No one in Columbus' time understood why the needle should always point north, but it did, and that was enough. Thanks to the compass, Columbus, by keeping north always on his right hand, could steer his ships westward without getting lost and sailing in circles. We now know that Earth has a magnetic north pole and that a magnetized needle will point toward it.

There was a catch, though. The compass did not point exactly to the north. It was a little off. This is because the magnetic north pole is a shifting point and is always a few hundred kilometers from the geographic North Pole. But navigators knew how to make allowance for this difference, called *variation*.

However, no navigator had sailed as far in an east-west direction as Columbus had, and Columbus noticed something very peculiar about the compass. When he started his voyage, it pointed a little bit east of the North Star, but as he traveled onward, it shifted until it finally pointed a little bit west of the North Star. No one had ever before observed this shifting of the direction of the needle, and Columbus kept it secret from his men. He was afraid that if they found out that the compass wasn't working perfectly, they would fear to go on any farther and would try to make Columbus turn back. We now know that there was nothing wrong with Columbus' compass. The variation of a compass needle is different at different places on Earth and at different times of the year. Mariners' charts now contain information about variation. Columbus' observation of variation was, by the way, the first known scientific finding ever made during a sea voyage.

The compass told Columbus the direction he was traveling in, but not how far or how fast he was going. In order to locate a ship's position in the open ocean, the navigator must know its latitude and its longitude. Latitude and longitude are imaginary lines on the globe. Lines of latitude run around the globe parallel to the equator. Lines of longitude run north and south. Together, lines of latitude and longitude form a grid on which a ship's position can be pinpointed. Latitude can be determined by measuring the highest point in the sky reached by the sun in the course of the day, and there were instruments available during the time of Columbus to determine this. So Columbus knew roughly how far north of the equator he was.

There was, however, no way of determining longitude. For that, an accurate clock is needed, because longitude is calculated in terms of time. This is possible since any point on Earth's surface completes a 360-degree rotation in 24 hours as the Earth spins on its axis. One hour is equal to 1/24 of 360 degrees, or 15 degrees. Each degree is

How Columbus Navigated

In the late 1400's, little was known about celestial navigation, or navigating by the positions of the stars. And there were few instruments to help captains determine where they were on Earth. Instead, navigators estimated their position using a technique called dead reckoning.

Columbus relied on a ship's compass to tell him the direction in which he was sailing. This was a round card, *above,* mounted on a spindle in a bowl. Underneath the card was a magnetized needle that always pointed north. On the bowl was a mark called the lubber's line. The direction of the ship was indicated by the point on the compass card that lined up with the lubber's line.

Columbus estimated his ship's speed by watching bubbles or seaweed float by and timing its passage with a half-hour glass.

Using his compass directions and his speed estimates, Columbus plotted what he thought were his daily positions on a chart.

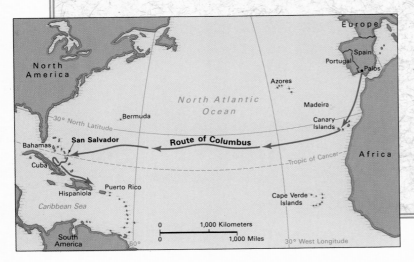

Although Columbus believed by his dead reckoning that he had reached the Indies, he had actually sailed to the island of San Salvador in the Caribbean Sea.

Astronomy in Columbus' Time

Astronomy was one of the most advanced sciences throughout many cultures in both the Old World and the New World.

In the New World that Columbus "discovered," the Maya were skilled astronomers and mathematicians who had recorded predictions about eclipses and the orbit of Venus, *right*. At Chichén Itzá in the Yucatán, they had built a large stone building, *below*, that archaeologists think might have been an astronomical observatory.

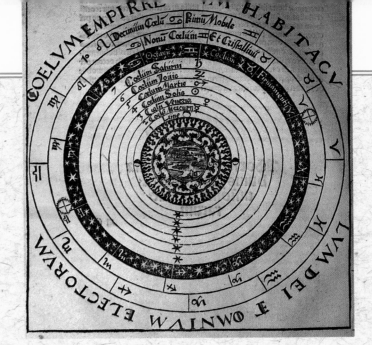

European scholars relied on the astronomical views of the ancient Greeks, portrayed in Ptolemy's diagram of the universe, *right,* which depicted Earth at the center of the cosmos, orbited by the sun and the planets.

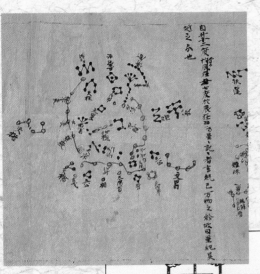

The Chinese were the most advanced in astronomy in 1492. They had been observing the heavens for hundreds of years and had produced complex maps of the stars, *left.* At the Pekin Observatory, *below,* the Chinese by the late 1600's had set up sophisticated instruments for tracking the movements of celestial bodies.

Some Unscientific Ideas

The age of modern Western science had not yet dawned in Europe when Columbus set sail.

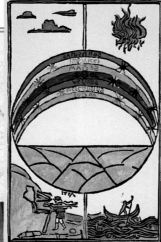

The physical world
European ideas about the physical world were based on the theory that all substances were made of four "elements," earth, air, fire, and water. Different materials were made of various combinations of the four elements.

In their "laboratories," equipped with furnaces for heating up chemical mixtures, alchemists tried unsuccessfully to refine base metals to a pure "essence," which they thought was gold. From these futile experiments, however, alchemists began to lay the foundations for later understanding of the properties of chemical compounds.

The state of medicine
Very little was known in 1492 about the human body or what caused diseases. Physicians believed that human personality and human ills were all the result of four "humors," called phlegm, blood, black bile, and yellow bile.

   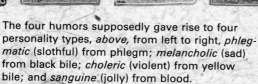

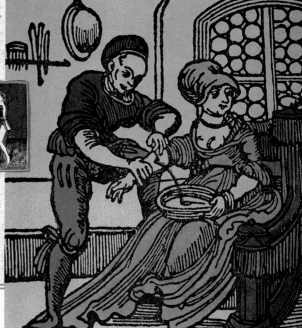

The four humors supposedly gave rise to four personality types, *above,* from left to right, *phlegmatic* (slothful) from phlegm; *melancholic* (sad) from black bile; *choleric* (violent) from yellow bile; and *sanguine* (jolly) from blood.

What People Died of in 1492

Infants and Children
One-third to one-half of everyone born died in infancy or childhood.

What infants and children died of:
- Malnutrition
- Measles
- Other childhood diseases
- Pneumonia
- Plague

Adults
No one can say for certain what the average life span of an adult was in 1492, because there were no accurate records. But before the invention of antibiotics, the average U.S. life span around 1900 was about 47 years.

What adults died of:
- Diphtheria
- Childbirth (deaths ranged from an estimated 12 to 16 %)
- Bacterial infections of wounds
- Tuberculosis
- Smallpox
- Plague

Diseases Europeans brought to the New World:
- Smallpox (1518, first recorded epidemic)
- Measles (1530)
- Typhus (1540's)
- Influenza (1558)
- Diphtheria
- Mumps

The standard cure for almost anything was bloodletting, *left.* Physicians thought the humors were carried by the bloodstream, and that an imbalance in the humors caused symptoms of disease. A surgeon or a barber opened a vein to let out the excess or "bad humors." This was accepted medical theory and practice until the mid-1800's.

further divided into minutes and seconds. Every hour, 15 degrees of longitude pass beneath the sun. Knowing this and the ship's speed, a navigator can plot an east-west position. But this requires a clock, one that can tell time to the nearest second. No such thing existed in Columbus' time. As a result, ship captains in the 1400's had to estimate how fast they were traveling, use a compass to determine their direction, then plot on a chart where they thought they were on the face of the ocean. This is called dead reckoning.

Skilled captains could be quite accurate in their dead reckoning, which is why such captains were always much in demand. However, even the best captain could have his ship struck by a storm and driven in an uncertain direction at an uncertain speed. When things settled down, the ship might have been completely lost at sea. It was not till the middle 1700's that accurate clocks were built for use on shipboard, and with that, ships stopped getting lost.

Another problem involved in the long voyages that were made during the Age of Exploration was medical. Ships had to carry food for the sailors, but in the days before refrigeration, only certain types of food could be stored over long periods without going bad. Hard, dry bread and meat that had been dried and salted were the chief items of nourishment. It grew very boring having to eat this for weeks at a time, but people assumed that food was food. Nothing at all was known about vitamins, minerals, or other essential elements of good nutrition that had to be present in food. And so the Age of Exploration made common one disease of malnutrition: scurvy.

The first reports of scurvy came from Portuguese navigator Vasco da Gama, who completed the first sea voyage to India in 1497. During that long journey, a number of his sailors fell sick with bleeding gums, anemia, painful joints, and wounds that would not heal. Eventually, 100 of his 170 sailors died of scurvy. We now know scurvy results from a lack of vitamin C, which can be found in fresh fruits and vegetables but not in dried bread and meat.

Scurvy became the scourge of long sea voyages and, until the mid-1700's, no one knew how to prevent it or how to cure it. It was not until 1753 that the importance of diet in preventing scurvy came to be understood. Scottish physician James Lind discovered that citrus fruit would cure scurvy. British sailors were then fed limes (even though no one understood why limes helped), and they are still called limeys, as a result.

The Age of Exploration also opened the world's regions to each other. Europeans obtained new kinds of foods from the New World, such as potatoes, yams, and corn. They picked up the curse of tobacco as well. Diseases also were spread back and forth. There is a controversial claim that the Indians may have given Europeans syphilis, while Europeans brought to the New World smallpox, plague, measles, mumps, and a host of other infectious diseases.

The most important consequence of Columbus' voyage and the others that followed, however, was this: It made possible the Scientific Revolution of the 1500's. How this was so needs to be explained.

European scholars at the time of Columbus relied almost entirely on the teachings and writings of the ancient Greeks. The Greeks had not only developed literature, art, and politics to a high pitch, but they had been the great scientists (philosophers) of the ancient world.

The most important of the Greek scientist-philosophers was Aristotle, who in the 300's B.C. wrote books on every known aspect of physics and biology. Soon afterward, Euclid summarized all of Greek mathematics known up to his time. The Greek astronomers assumed that the sun and known planets moved in circles about the Earth, and they worked out their motions in great detail. The Greek astronomer Claudius Ptolemaeus (better known as Ptolemy), in the 100's, summarized all that the Greeks had learned in astronomy. In the next century, the great physician Galen summarized all of Greek medicine up to his time.

Then Greek culture went into decline in the A.D. 100's and 200's, and so did Greek science. No one else took it up. The ancient Romans by this time had set up a magnificent empire, but they were interested mainly in law, politics, architecture, and military conquest. They were not interested in science. By the time the Roman Empire had disintegrated in the 400's, science was virtually dead in Europe.

Thereafter, the early Middle Ages, often called the Dark Ages, enveloped Europe. But, in the Middle East, Muslims rediscovered the old Greek texts on science and translated them into Arabic. The Muslims built on the Greeks' knowledge, and were certainly far more scientifically advanced than the Europeans of that time.

Beginning in 1096, European Christians began the first of eight major Crusades to recapture the Holy Land from the Muslims. Thanks to these Crusades the people of western Europe came into contact with the Muslims and discovered the old Greek texts now in Arabic. Europeans, with Muslim help, began to translate them into Latin so that scholars in the West could read them.

The result was that, between 1100 and 1500, Europeans were immersed in these texts and felt that the ancient Greeks had been far ahead of them scientifically. Europeans believed that all scientific questions could be answered by studying Aristotle's physics, Ptolemy's astronomy, Euclid's mathematics, and Galen's medicine.

To many European scholars, it seemed that nothing could be right unless Aristotle and the other Greeks said it was right. And as long as Europeans worshiped the past in this fashion, there scarcely could be any progress. But what could possibly destroy this worship? It would have to be something very dramatic that would highlight the fact that the Greeks did not know everything and that Europeans were capable of forging forward on their own.

This was precisely what Columbus' voyage did. If he had actually reached Asia, it would not have been so important. Even Aristotle would have agreed that, in theory, it was possible to sail westward from Europe to Asia. But Columbus discovered completely new continents that Aristotle had never mentioned. Explorations of the New World were soon well known to every European, and this was an area in which European accomplishments far exceeded those of the Greeks. It was no longer necessary to worship the ancients.

For the first time, it became possible to suspect that Greek science was incomplete or that the Greeks might actually be wrong. At the time of Columbus' first voyage, the future great astronomer Nicolaus Copernicus was studying mathematics in Poland. Only 15 years later, in 1507, it occurred to him that Ptolemy was wrong in assuming that the Earth was the center of the solar system. Copernicus found that it would be easier to calculate the changing positions of the planets if he assumed Earth went around the sun rather than vice versa.

Copernicus spent years working out this new sun-centered theory, but never dared to publish it because he knew it would make trouble for him at the hands of those who would not abandon the Greeks, particularly authorities of the church. In fact, it was not until 1543, the year of his death, that he finally published it, and the story is that he got the first copy of his book as he lay dying. This book marked the beginning of modern astronomy.

It was not a smooth beginning, however. Copernicus' notions did make trouble for other people who adopted them. It took more than 100 years for "establishment" scholars to completely accept them.

Meanwhile, a Flemish biologist named Andreas Vesalius was becoming an expert on Galen. Like others of his time, Vesalius studied anatomy by reading what Galen had to say 1,300 years earlier, even though Galen had never been allowed to study the human body through dissection. But the times were changing, and European scholars were growing more courageous. Vesalius began to dissect human corpses and to study what he actually saw and not what Galen said he would see. In 1543, he published a great book on the subject, which marked the beginning of modern anatomy.

Modern astronomy, geography, physics and other sciences were born in the 1500's, after Galileo, *above* (right), and other European scholars began to question erroneous teachings of the ancient Greeks.

Publishing this book, however, ended Vesalius' career. The church accused him of heresy and other crimes and forced him to do penance by making a pilgrimage to the Holy Land. He did this, but died on the way home.

The publication of Copernicus' book on astronomy and Vesalius' book on anatomy, both in 1543, is considered the beginning of the Scientific Revolution. But even after Ptolemy was shaken by Copernicus and Galen was altered by Vesalius, there still remained Aristotle, whose descriptions of physical law seemed strong and formidable. Aristotle went into great detail on how it was that motion came about. He reasoned that every type of object had its natural place in the universe and, if displaced, tried to restore itself to that natural place. Thus, the natural place of a rock was the surface of Earth. If a rock is thrown into midair, it therefore falls to the Earth. What's more, the heavier it is, said Aristotle, the faster it falls. After all, he reasoned, we can all see that a pebble falls more rapidly than a feather does.

In 1589, a 25-year-old Italian astronomer and physicist named Galileo began to study the way in which objects fall. This was not quite a century after Columbus' voyage and not quite half a century after the beginning of the Scientific Revolution. Galileo used balls of various sizes in his experiments. But instead of just letting balls fall, Galileo let them roll down a slant. That slowed them up and gave him a chance to measure the time it took balls of different masses to move a given distance. His measurements showed that different balls accelerate at the same speed regardless of their mass. We now know it is air resistance that prevents light objects from falling as rapidly as heavier ones. In a vacuum, a feather would fall at the same rate as a pebble. In the Special Reports section, see QUESTIONS OF GRAVITY.

Galileo is considered the founder of experimental science. His experiment was easily repeated by anyone who tried, and so his conclusions were accepted as being right. What was important, however, was not that Galileo was right, but that Aristotle was wrong. At last, Europeans could be freed from intellectual slavery to the Greeks.

Of course, Galileo got into trouble with his newfangled notions and with his acceptance of the ideas of Copernicus. In 1633, the Inquisition forced Galileo to deny that the Earth revolved around the sun. But the Inquisition's handling of him was the last victory of those who believed in all things Greek. Thereafter, science advanced and, while there have always been those who objected to new views, they could do nothing to stem the advance.

If anything were needed to show the power of the new science, it came later in the 1600's with the English mathematician and physicist Sir Isaac Newton. He invented calculus and the reflecting telescope and showed that sunlight consists of a spectrum, or rainbow, of different colors. His greatest feat, however, was to work out a theory of gravitation and the laws that govern the motion of objects on Earth and in space. He put it all into a book called *Principia Mathematica*, which he published in 1687. It made complete sense out of physics and astronomy and is considered to be one of the greatest scientific works ever written. To be sure, Newton's work has been modified since he published that book, but its basic value remains.

So we can trace the advance of modern Western science from Newton back to Galileo, back to Copernicus and Vesalius, and from them back to Columbus. Would European thinkers have had the courage to establish European science if it were not for the great navigators of the 1400's and for Christopher Columbus and his astonishing discovery in particular? We can't really say, for we can't go back and run history down another path. However, I can't help but think that the development of modern science would have been long delayed without Columbus.

Research on dolphins in enclosed tanks and the open sea is showing that these appealing marine mammals are highly social creatures possessing a remarkable level of intelligence.

How Smart Are Dolphins?

BY SUSAN J. WINTSCH

In a large saltwater tank under the bright Hawaiian sky, a female bottlenose dolphin named Akeakamai (*uh kay uh kuh MY*) streaks through the water and surfaces beside a trainer's platform. Flexing her powerful tail, the dolphin focuses her attention on the young male trainer and waits for the arm and hand gestures that will convey his next command. Jump over the surfboard, he signals her. With a splash, the dolphin turns and heads for the center of the pool. A quick leap over the floating board and she is back for her reward: an affectionate hug and a fish. For Akeakamai (Hawaiian for *lover of wisdom*), this is a game, but for the researchers here at the University of Hawaii's Kewalo Basin Marine Mammal Laboratory, the exercises have a serious purpose: to plumb the depths of dolphin intelligence.

The quickness and apparent eagerness with which Akeakamai fulfills the trainer's commands, and the charm of her toothy "smile," make it easy to understand why people are so fascinated by dolphins. Throughout history, in fact, seafarers and coastal dwellers in many parts of the world have had a special fondness for these friendly mammals and have believed that they think and feel much as human beings do. Greek and Roman mythology contains many stories of dolphins who aid, befriend, communicate with, and sometimes even outsmart people. Similar tales have been told innumerable times in the centuries since then. Modern accounts abound: Swimmers who nearly drowned have reported being buoyed to safety by dolphins, and many a sailor has sworn that dolphins guided a ship away from deadly reefs. Such stories—many of which are discounted by experts as exaggerations—have earned dolphins the reputation of having almost humanlike intelligence and behavior.

How humanlike they truly are remains to be seen. Nonetheless, dolphins are undeniably remarkable creatures, and many people today recognize the necessity of protecting them. Public outrage over thousands of dolphins dying each year in the nets of tuna-fishing boats led three canning companies to announce in April 1990 that they would no longer buy tuna caught in ways that harm dolphins.

But our affection for dolphins may sometimes be carried too far for the dolphins' good. Controversy grew in 1991 over programs offered at several tourist resorts in which guests paid to swim and play with dolphins in pools. Critics of the programs said the dolphins were being exploited and exposed to human diseases and that increasing numbers of dolphins were being captured to meet the demand for them. Similarly, many conservationists spoke out against marine parks that showcase performing dolphins and allow visitors to touch dolphins in "petting pools." Increasingly, animal-rights groups are saying that the place for dolphins is in their natural environment.

Some activists have demonstrated and even gone to court on behalf of dolphins. In 1989, for instance, an animal-rights organization filed a lawsuit against the United States Navy in an effort to stop a project aimed at training dolphins to guard nuclear-missile submarines. Two years later, the Navy canceled the research.

Outside military circles, most dolphin research focuses simply on learning about the animals' intelligence and behavior. At the Kewalo Basin research facility and several other institutions, scientists carry out carefully controlled experiments with dolphins in tanks. Their aim is to replace speculation about dolphin intelligence with precise data. Meanwhile, other scientists are studying dolphins in their natural habitats. What they are learning about the behavior of these animals in the wild is not only valuable in its own right but may also shed additional light on the question of dolphin intelligence.

Dolphins are a type of toothed whale. Like all whales, or *cetaceans* (*see TAY shunz*), dolphins evolved from hoofed land mammals that adapted to life in the water about 60 million years ago. Being mammals, dolphins have lungs and breathe air, which they take in through a nostril, called a *blowhole*, on the top of the head. Like other mammals, they bear live young and nurse their offspring. Most dolphins are very social animals, living together in groups.

Generally less than 3.5 meters (12 feet) long, dolphins are among the smallest of the toothed whales. However, two other toothed whales that are also considered dolphins are quite large: the pilot whale, which is up to 6 meters (20 feet) long, and the even bigger killer whale, which can attain a length of 9.5 meters (31 feet). Most

The author:
Susan J. Wintsch is a free-lance writer and editor.

kinds of dolphins, including the well-known bottlenose dolphin, live in coastal waters or the open ocean, though a few species have adapted to freshwater environments. These freshwater dolphins, much less familiar to most people than their ocean-dwelling cousins, are found in certain rivers and lakes in China, India, Pakistan, and several countries in northern South America. All dolphins are entirely carnivorous, feeding mainly on fish and squid.

The words *dolphin* and *porpoise* are often used interchangeably, but there is a difference between the two animals. Zoologists place marine dolphins, freshwater dolphins, and porpoises in three separate families. True ocean dolphins have a beaklike snout and cone-shaped teeth, whereas porpoises have a shorter, more rounded snout and teeth that are spade-shaped. Still, similarities outweigh differences, and the term *dolphin* is often applied informally to the six species of porpoise, as well as to the 37 species of ocean and freshwater dolphins. The dolphin fish, or *mahi mahi*, is a true fish with gills and thus is not related to any of the marine mammals.

Dolphins are among the most vocal of animals. Most people have heard their singsong whistles at oceanariums or on television programs, but dolphins produce several other kinds of sounds as well, including squeaks, barks, and pops. The animals apparently use these sounds to communicate with one another.

When approaching a dolphin, it is a common if somewhat eerie experience to hear still another of their sounds: the "creaky-door"

Dolphins struggle to escape from a tuna net in which they have become entrapped. The drowning of 80,000 to 100,000 dolphins each year in tuna nets sparked public protests against such treatment of an animal that human beings since ancient times have believed to be uniquely intelligent.

Facts About Dolphins

There are about 40 species of dolphins and porpoises found in the world's oceans. Dolphins are small, toothed whales that, along with other whales, belong to a group of aquatic mammals called *cetaceans,* which evolved millions of years ago from hoofed land animals.

Dolphins and porpoises are mammals, not fish. They are warm-blooded, nurse their young, and have lungs for breathing.

A few kinds of dolphins live in fresh water. They are found in lakes and rivers in China, India, Pakistan, and South American nations.

The main difference between dolphins and porpoises is that porpoises have a blunter snout and spade-shaped rather than cone-shaped teeth.

Common dolphin
Lives in all the oceans and is the most frequently encountered dolphin in the open sea; often caught in tuna nets.
Length: up to 2.5 meters (8 feet)

Killer whale
Lives in all the oceans and is the largest species of dolphin.
Length: up to 9.5 meters (31 feet)

Harbor porpoise
Lives in North Atlantic and North Pacific oceans and is the smallest of the oceanic cetaceans.
Length: up to 2 meters (6.5 feet)

Dolphins locate underwater objects by sound. They send out sound waves through the *melon,* a fatty organ atop the head, then listen for the echo when the sound waves bounce off an object.

Dolphins breathe through a *blowhole* on the top of their heads. They usually surface once or twice a minute to get air, though many dolphins can stay submerged for up to eight minutes.

Dolphins swim by moving their *fluke* (tail fin) up and down. Their fluke and side flippers help them make sharp turns and sudden stops.

Dolphin Anatomy

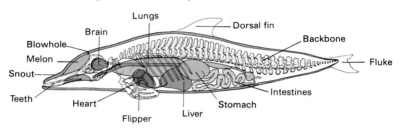

Lungs
Brain
Dorsal fin
Blowhole
Backbone
Melon
Fluke
Snout
Teeth
Heart
Intestines
Flipper
Liver
Stomach

Amazon dolphin
Lives in rivers of northern South America; one of four species of freshwater dolphins.
Length: up to 2.7 meters (9 feet)

Bottlenose dolphin
Lives in all the oceans; is the most widely studied dolphin and the species most familiar to people.
Length: up to 3.9 meters (13 feet)

Spotted dolphin
Lives in tropical oceans; those living in the eastern Pacific Ocean are the dolphins most often caught in tuna nets.
Length: up to 2.5 meters (8 feet)

clicks of the animal's *echolocation* (biological sonar) system. A dolphin echolocates by focusing pulses of clicks through a fatty bulge, called the *melon*, in its forehead and analyzing the echoes that bounce back from distant objects. In experiments conducted by the U.S. Navy, a dolphin wearing eyecups to block its vision used echolocation to easily locate a small object from a distance of 120 meters (131 yards).

Although dolphins have aroused human curiosity for centuries, scientific study of the animals did not begin in earnest until the late 1940's, when oceanariums in the United States became home to large numbers of captive bottlenose dolphins. Foremost among early researchers was John Lilly, a neuroscientist who had done pioneering research on human brain anatomy. In the mid-1950's, Lilly began studying dolphins.

Lilly became fascinated with the sounds dolphins make, and in his research he discovered that the animals also have a flair for mimicking other kinds of sounds. That mimicry, according to Lilly, can include rough, squawky imitations of human speech. Hoping to establish communication with his dolphins, he labored at teaching them to count and express themselves in English and claimed to have succeeded. After more than 10 years of research, Lilly argued that dolphins have their own complex language, legends, and histories, and an intelligence that equals or exceeds that of human beings. Today, most dolphin researchers speak well of Lilly's early contributions to the field, but they consider his later claims of philosophical, English-speaking dolphins to be an unproven theory at best.

Although "intelligence" is a slippery concept that has never been precisely defined, most scientists who have worked with dolphins believe the animals are highly intelligent. Studies of dolphin anatomy have shown that the animals are "brainy" in a literal sense—the ratio of dolphins' brain weight to the weight of their bodies is higher than that of any other animal except human beings. Moreover, dolphins learn tasks easily, and they are playful and curious. As one scientist put it, "When you look into a dolphin's eyes, you know someone's home."

In seeking to learn how that "someone" perceives the world, researchers confront several fascinating but scientifically thorny questions: Does the dolphin's large brain mean these animals possess exceptional intelligence? And if so, how is that intelligence used in their natural habitat, and what intellectual tasks might dolphins be capable of in a more controlled environment? Although answers to some of these questions remain elusive, investigators are increasingly convinced that dolphins possess, at the very least, some of the mental capacities we associate with human intelligence. Dolphins seem able to understand abstract concepts, comprehend symbols, and form mental pictures of objects and events.

These conclusions have emerged largely from controlled experiments with captive dolphins. Some of the most extensive studies of this sort, focusing on dolphin communication and thought processes, have been conducted at the Kewalo Basin research center, under the direction of University of Hawaii psychologist Louis Herman. In one line of research, Herman and his colleagues are testing the ability of Akeakamai and three other bottlenose dolphins to recognize and match objects and visual patterns; in another, they are investigating the animals' ability to understand "artificial" languages.

In the visual matching studies, the researchers have found that the dolphins possess a keen ability to distinguish between like and unlike objects. To test this ability, a researcher holds up an object for the dolphins to see, then removes it. The researcher then immediately displays the same or a different object. The dolphins report that the two objects are the same or different by touching one of two paddles at the side of the tank. One of the dolphins, a 4-year-old male named Hiapo, performs this task virtually without error.

The dolphins are also able to recognize that an object that has been shown to them, removed, and held up again in a different position is the same object. The animals apparently can mentally visualize the object in its original position just as a human subject would.

Since the early 1980's, Herman and his colleagues have learned to convey instructions to dolphins using two different artificial languages. One language uses a variety of hand and arm gestures; the other employs computer-generated whistles. Each hand signal or whistle stands for a particular object or action. If, for example, a trainer gives the gesture signifying *pipe* followed by the gesture for *over*, the dolphin responds by swimming to a plastic pipe floating in the tank and leaping over it. The dolphins can understand highly complex sequences of gestures. For example, given a sequence of five gestures—*right, water, left, Frisbee, fetch*—a dolphin retrieves a Frisbee floating to its left and carries it to a stream of water on the right. The gestures and whistles can also convey questions concerning the presence or absence of objects, which the dolphins answer by pressing the paddles attached to the side of the tank.

The dolphins have been avid learners. Early in the experiments, two of the dolphins, Akeakamai and Phoenix, became so fluent in their comprehension of the artificial languages that they immediately understood and responded to newly introduced sentences. Their ability sometimes surprised the scientists. One time, for example, Herman presented Akeakamai with an instruction he thought would not be possible for her to execute. How would she respond, he wondered, to gestures whose literal translation was the puzzling command *toss water*? To his astonishment, Akeakamai swam to the side of the tank, stopped by a streaming hose, and deftly flicked the column of water with her beak.

Another researcher whose experiments have explored dolphin intelligence is Diana Reiss, a speech and communications specialist who works with dolphins at Marine World Africa USA in Vallejo,

Dolphin Sign Language

Dolphins can learn "artificial" languages, in which sounds or gestures represent objects and actions. University of Hawaii researcher Louis Herman studies how dolphins respond to gestured commands.

Herman, *above*, signals to a bottlenose dolphin the gesture for *person.*

He follows that a moment later with the gesture for *over.*

The dolphin swims to the floating person and leaps over him.

Calif. Like Herman, Reiss has demonstrated the ability of dolphins to make associations between certain sounds and the objects or activities they represent. Since the early 1980's, she has been studying four bottlenose dolphins that have learned to use an underwater keyboard to obtain a "reward." On each of the keyboard's nine keys is a geometric form, such as a circle or a triangle, signifying a ball, hoop, belly rub, or other favored object or activity. When a dolphin hits a particular key with its beak, the animal hears a computer-generated whistle. There is a different whistle for each key and hence for each object and action represented by the symbols on the keyboard.

The dolphins quickly began to mimic the whistles and learned to associate them with the things they represented. The two male dolphins in the study, Pan and Delphi, went a step further, producing the whistles before they hit the corresponding keys. And it was not much longer before the two males were producing the whistles as they played with the objects they had learned to associate with the various sounds. They even made two whistles at once when they played with two objects simultaneously. Nor was that all. Reiss learned something about the dolphins' powers of recall after a two-year interruption of her work in the late 1980's when Marine World moved to Vallejo from Redwood City, Calif. When the research project resumed after the move, Pan and Delphi remembered how to use the keyboard and spontaneously produced two of the whistles.

Reiss and Herman do not claim that dolphins are capable of handling something as complex as the full range of English or other human languages. The two researchers, and other experts on cetaceans, have concluded, however, that dolphins most likely possess some of the mental framework upon which language ability and other capacities we call human are based. Moreover, dolphins may be mentally versatile—capable not only of learning new tasks but also of devising on-the-spot responses to unexpected situations.

While some researchers continue to investigate dolphin intelligence with captive animals, other scientists are studying dolphins in the open sea to learn more about their natural behavior and so-

Experiments with Symbols

At a marine park in Vallejo, Calif., communications expert Diana Reiss studies how bottlenose dolphins learn to use an underwater keyboard.

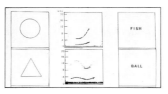

Reiss waits next to the submerged keyboard, *above,* to begin a test on dolphins in the tank. The dolphins not only associated keyboard whistles with a reward, but often made the correct sound before pressing the key.

Reiss records the whistles that dolphins make, *above.* She also incorporated whistling sounds into her keyboard, *center right.* Each key shows a symbol (first column) and produces a distinctive whistle (sound graph, center column) representing the object or other reward (third column) the dolphin receives after pressing the key.

After electronically analyzing recorded dolphin whistles and comparing them with the keyboard-generated whistles, *above,* Reiss discusses her findings with a colleague.

cial relationships. It isn't easy; wild dolphins swim at speeds up to 40 kilometers (25 miles) an hour, making it extremely difficult to track their movements or to distinguish one sleek form from another as they dart through the waves. Some scientists have tried to keep up with dolphins by using a technique called *radiotracking,* in which a radio transmitter is attached to a dolphin and monitored with an electronic receiver. Although radiotracking has yielded some insights into the movements and habits of wild dolphins, much more has been learned by directly observing dolphins from boats. Using this simple research method, scientists in two widely separated locales have become privy to the social life of the bottlenose dolphin.

One of the studies has been directed by Randall S. Wells, a behavioral ecologist affiliated with Brookfield Zoo near Chicago. Wells began observing dolphins in Florida's Sarasota Bay, on the Gulf of Mexico, in 1970 as a high school age volunteer in a dolphin

Studying Dolphins in the Open Sea
Some researchers study dolphins in the ocean to learn how they live in the wild. At Sarasota Bay in Florida and Shark Bay in Australia, scientists have learned about the life cycle and social behavior of the bottlenose dolphin.

Researchers and volunteers at Sarasota Bay corral a dolphin, *above,* so it can be given a checkup on a rubber raft, *right.*

The Florida researchers use *ultrasound* (high-frequency sound), *above,* to measure the thickness of a captured dolphin's blubber, a key to the animal's state of health.

research project. Half a world away, a group of researchers from the University of Michigan in Ann Arbor is studying dolphins in Australia's Shark Bay. The bay, an inlet of the Indian Ocean on the continent's western coast, is home to at least 300 dolphins. A few of the animals have long been used to human company and enjoy playing with swimmers.

At both Shark Bay and Sarasota Bay, the researchers have learned to recognize individual dolphins on sight by photographing them and studying their distinctive markings, mainly nicks and scars on the dorsal fin. After identifying a dolphin in this way, the scientists watch the animal closely for a set length of time and record its movements and activities.

In the course of their studies, the researchers in Florida and Australia have witnessed many aspects of dolphin life, from the daily business of finding food and rearing offspring to the drama of mating and self-defense. The researchers have seen both cooperative and aggressive behavior among the dolphins, as well as many forms

In an example of social bonding among dolphins, several male dolphins swim together in Shark Bay, *below.* The Australian researchers devote most of their time to observing dolphin behavior.

The Sarasota Bay scientists weigh a captive dolphin, *above,* before releasing it back into the ocean.

of sexual play. The Florida researchers have found that the dolphins they study stay within well-defined areas known as *home ranges.* Though this behavior seems less prevalent in Shark Bay, in both areas the animals associate in small, frequently changing groups that are all part of the larger local population. Young males swim in "bachelor" groups called *coalitions* that may change somewhat in membership from day to day. As adults, the males travel as members of stable pairs, or as individuals, moving from one group of females to another. The adult male pairs may remain stable for 15 years or more. At Shark Bay, the researchers have witnessed impressive displays of synchronized swimming by male dolphins with strong social bonds, an activity that seems to be a dolphin version of "hanging out."

After mating, male dolphins apparently do not participate in the parental care of any offspring, called *calves,* they sire. They do, however, continue to associate with their mate and calf on an intermittent basis. The bond between a mother and her calf is strong. Calves usually nurse for at least 1½ to 2 years but may remain with their mothers for up to 6 years, or even longer.

Wells and his colleagues have often observed female dolphins cooperate in caring for calves. The researchers have sometimes seen mothers forming circles, much like living playpens, around groups of

Common dolphins arc above the water in the Pacific Ocean off the California coast in a display of side-by-side swimming such as that frequently observed among pairs of male dolphins.

infants, and they have also noted females "baby-sitting" for one another's calves. But cooperative activities are not confined to females or to the rearing of offspring. The scientists at Shark Bay have on several occasions observed a coalition of males herd a female dolphin, apparently for the purpose of mating.

The scientists at Shark Bay and Sarasota Bay have compiled a wealth of information on bottlenose dolphins just by watching the animals, but the Florida researchers also employ some "hands-on" techniques. For instance, biologist Peter Tyack of the Woods Hole Oceanographic Institution in Massachusetts has been taking part in the Sarasota Bay project for several years to learn more about the whistles dolphins make. Since the mid-1960's, scientists have known that each dolphin makes a "signature whistle." Working with an associate, Laela Sayigh, Tyack studies mothers and calves to determine whether these whistles are learned and passed on.

Tyack and Sayigh attach a *hydrophone* (an instrument that detects underwater sound) with soft suction cups to the head of a temporarily captive mother or baby dolphin to record its whistles. By studying the same dolphins over several years, the scientists have learned that calves begin to produce their signature whistle in the first or second year of life. Male dolphins develop whistles that are remarkably similar to their mothers' whistles, but females develop whistles that are more uniquely their own. Tyack thinks this may be the case because a female dolphin tends to return to her mother's group after giving birth, whereas a male usually moves away. It may be critical for a daughter to clearly distinguish herself from her mother so that the daughter's calf will not become confused.

Wells and his colleagues, with the help of a veterinarian and volunteers from the environmental organization Earthwatch, capture dolphins in shallow water and hold them briefly on a rubber raft for tests and measurements. They weigh each dolphin, determine its sex, and check its health by measuring the thickness of its blubber with an *ultrasonograph*, an instrument that uses sound waves to make images of tissue. The scientists also draw a blood sample, then release the dolphin. Later, laboratory technicians analyze genetic material from the blood cells. The genetic test, called *DNA fingerprinting*, enables the researchers to tell who is related to whom in the Sarasota Bay dolphin community and how closely. These data are essential in determining the role of kinship in dolphin society.

An equally compelling question is what part intelligence plays in the social life of dolphins. Does the behavior of dolphins, including the striking degree of cooperativeness they exhibit, really demonstrate the higher form of intelligence that researchers such as Louis Herman and Diana Reiss think these animals possess? Or is their behavior mostly instinctive, actions they perform without knowing their purpose? The scientists in Florida and Australia do not yet have an answer to these questions. They say, however, that their observations suggest that dolphin behavior may be consciously purposeful, and that dolphins seem to use their large brains to consciously weave and maintain the complex social fabric of their communities.

Thus, all the evidence indicates that dolphins are capable of many complex kinds of thought, and that has led to some soul-searching among the scientists involved in dolphin research. Many investigators are asking themselves whether they have the moral right to capture these animals and hold them in captivity. Some researchers have voluntarily decided to study only wild dolphins swimming free. Others, conducting controlled experiments in enclosed tanks, have opted to use only animals that were born in captivity and so are unaware of life in the wild.

But some scientists believe that taking a few dozen dolphins from the sea each year for research purposes can be justified. It is mainly through scientists' studies of dolphins, they say, that people have become aware of these creatures' remarkable behavior and mental abilities. Without that awareness, the researchers argue, we might not have a growing outcry against the commercial exploitation of captive dolphins, much less an effort to protect those still in the ocean.

For further reading:

Booth, William. "The Social Lives of Dolphins." *Science*, June 3, 1988, pp. 1273-1274.

Ellis, Richard. *Dolphins and Porpoises*. Alfred A. Knopf, 1982.

Leatherwood, Stephen, and Reeves, Randall R. *The Sierra Club Handbook of Whales and Dolphins*. Sierra Club Books, 1983.

Reiss, Diana. *The Secrets of the Dolphins*. Avon, 1991.

Wells, Randall S. "Secrets of a High Society." *National Wildlife*, August/ September 1989, pp. 38-44.

The *Magellan* spacecraft has returned the most detailed radar images ever made of Venus' surface, revealing a world of volcanoes and other geologic activity.

Exploring the Surface of Venus

BY R. STEPHEN SAUNDERS

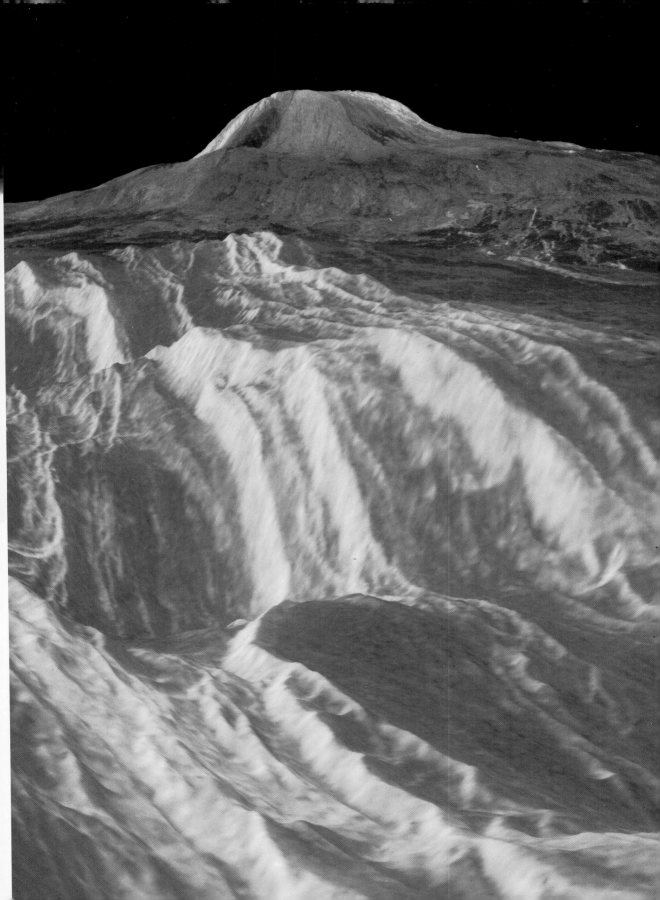

It was just after midnight on Aug. 16, 1990, when I and a group of engineers and scientists at the Jet Propulsion Laboratory (JPL) in Pasadena, Calif., gathered to view the first images of Venus returned by the *Magellan* spacecraft. Earlier that day, *Magellan* had beamed the complex radar data that would be processed into images of Venus' surface to the Goldstone radio antenna near Barstow, Calif., in the Mojave Desert. The image data were recorded on tape, and the precious tapes were then rushed to us at JPL to be "developed" in our computers.

A project of the National Aeronautics and Space Administration (NASA), *Magellan* was launched aboard the space shuttle *Atlantis* on May 4, 1989. That day, astronauts released the spacecraft from *Atlantis'* cargo bay, and it began a 15-month-long journey to Venus. Named for Portuguese explorer Ferdinand Magellan, who commanded the first expedition to circumnavigate Earth in the early 1500's, the *Magellan* spacecraft was to give us a global view of the surface of Venus.

As we saw the first images, we quickly realized that *Magellan* would perform its job of mapping Venus even better than we had hoped. The images show a planet that has been as geologically active as our own, with mountain ranges, canyons, continent-sized elevated regions, and signs of volcanic activity. *Magellan* also beamed us a number of surprises: pictures of geological features never seen before on any planet or moon in the solar system.

Venus is known as Earth's "twin" or sister planet. When these two rocky planets formed from the debris left over from the formation of the sun about 4.6 billion years ago, they were similar in size, mass, and density. Venus has a diameter of 12,100 kilometers (7,520 miles), compared with Earth's diameter of 12,756 kilometers (7,926 miles). Venus is only slightly less dense and massive than Earth. Venus is also our nearest planetary neighbor, passing within 41.4 million kilometers (25.7 million miles) of Earth at the closest point in its orbit.

Yet, despite these similarities, the two planets are very different. Earth is teeming with life on virtually every part of its surface. Scientists believe there is no life on Venus because conditions on the planet are too extreme. Venus has a thick atmosphere composed almost entirely of carbon dioxide gas, and its clouds are made of droplets of sulfuric acid. Earth has a life-nurturing atmosphere of mainly nitrogen and oxygen gas and clouds of water vapor. Because carbon dioxide gas traps *infrared* (heat) radiation and prevents it from escaping into space, a runaway greenhouse effect has occurred on Venus. The planet's atmosphere makes it an inferno, with a surface temperature of 462 °C (864 °F)—hot enough to melt lead. Venus' atmospheric pressure is almost 100 times greater than Earth's, so that standing on Venus' surface would be like standing under 900 meters (3,000 feet) of ocean water on Earth.

Why did two planets—so similar at the time the solar system formed—evolve so differently? Our desire to answer this question is one reason why scientists have sent more spacecraft to Venus than to

The author:
R. Stephen Saunders is project scientist for the *Magellan* mission at the Jet Propulsion Laboratory in Pasadena, Calif.

Venus: Earth's Twin?

Venus is often called Earth's twin because the two planets are similar in size, density, mass, and distance from the sun. Earth and Venus both have continentlike features. Earth's continents rise above ocean basins, while Venus' are elevated above vast plains. Venus' continents, however, are not as high above the plains as Earth's continents are above the ocean floor.

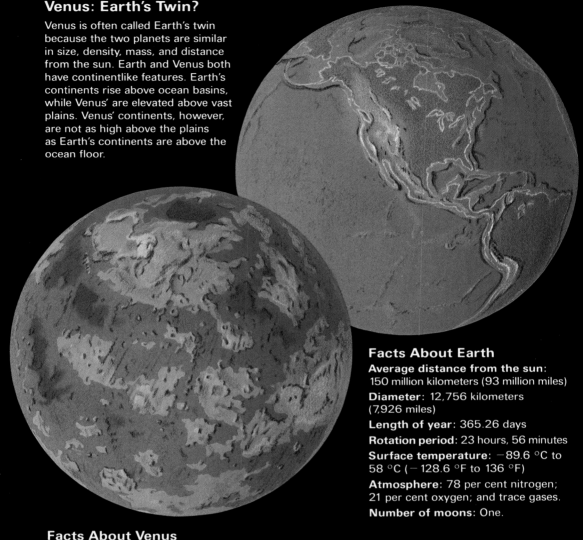

Facts About Earth

Average distance from the sun: 150 million kilometers (93 million miles)

Diameter: 12,756 kilometers (7,926 miles)

Length of year: 365.26 days

Rotation period: 23 hours, 56 minutes

Surface temperature: −89.6 °C to 58 °C (−128.6 °F to 136 °F)

Atmosphere: 78 per cent nitrogen; 21 per cent oxygen; and trace gases.

Number of moons: One.

Facts About Venus

Average distance from the sun: 108 million kilometers (67 million miles)

Diameter: 12,104 kilometers (7,521 miles)

Length of year: 225 Earth-days

Rotation period: 243 Earth-days

Surface temperature: 462 °C (864 °F)

Atmosphere: 96.5 per cent carbon dioxide; 3.5 per cent other gases

Number of moons: None.

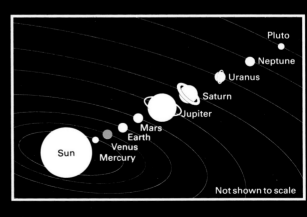

Of the nine planets in our solar system, Venus is one of four inner planets—along with Mercury, Earth, and Mars—that have rocky surfaces.

Glossary

Cold spot: An area of cold, dense material in a planet's interior.

Crust: The solid outer layer of a planet.

Downwelling: The sinking of cold, dense material in a planet's interior.

Faults: Cracks along which movement has occurred in a planet's crust.

Hot spot: An area of hot, molten rock in a planet's interior.

Mantle: The region of a planet's interior between the core and the crust, where hot and cold spots may form.

Upwelling: The rising of hot, buoyant rock.

any other planet. A total of 21 spacecraft missions have explored Venus—15 of them sent by the Soviet Union and 6 by the United States. The first planetary mission to Venus was *Mariner 2*, a U.S. spacecraft that passed within 34,760 kilometers (21,600 miles) of the planet on Dec. 14, 1962. Using infrared sensors to detect heat radiating from the surface of the planet, *Mariner 2* revealed for the first time that Venus' surface was intensely hot.

Most of the later spacecraft missions to Venus were designed to probe its atmosphere. In the late 1960's and early 1970's, the Soviet Union sent a number of spacecraft to Venus equipped with probes that measured gases as they descended through the atmosphere. Some of the probes were also designed to land on the surface. Because of Venus' intense heat, however, the landers stopped functioning after a brief time. In 1975, the Soviet *Venera 9* lander lasted for 53 minutes and radioed to Earth the first video photograph of the surface, showing sharp-edged rocks.

The search for large-scale geological features began in the early 1960's, when astronomers used radio waves sent by telescopes on Earth to explore Venus' surface. The surface is perpetually covered by dense clouds, but radio waves can penetrate them. A radio telescope on Earth sends radio waves to Venus' surface, where they reflect back and are received by the same telescope. This process is the technique known as *radar imaging*. By recording the time it takes for the signal to return, astronomers can determine the distance the radio waves traveled and, hence, the elevation of that part of Venus' surface.

The strength of the reflected signal also provides important information. With the *Magellan* radar, a weak signal corresponds to a smooth region, such as a plain. A stronger signal returns when a radio wave reflects off rough terrain, such as ridges around an impact crater. In computer-processed radar images, smooth terrain appears dark, and rough terrain appears bright. Earth-based radar images are similar, except near the point where the signal is directed straight onto the surface. There, the smooth surfaces act like mirrors and may be very bright. Using this information, scientists can gradually build up a map of the surface features.

Earth-based radio telescopes, however, provided views of only a part of Venus' surface. The first spacecraft to provide a nearly global map of the surface was *Pioneer Venus 1*, which also used radar. Launched by NASA on May 20, 1978, the spacecraft began orbiting

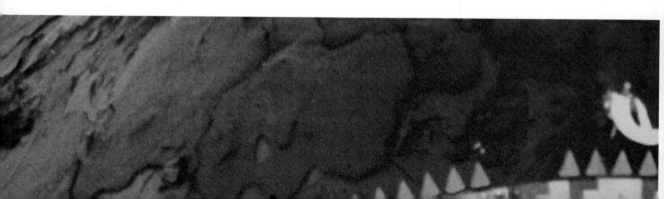

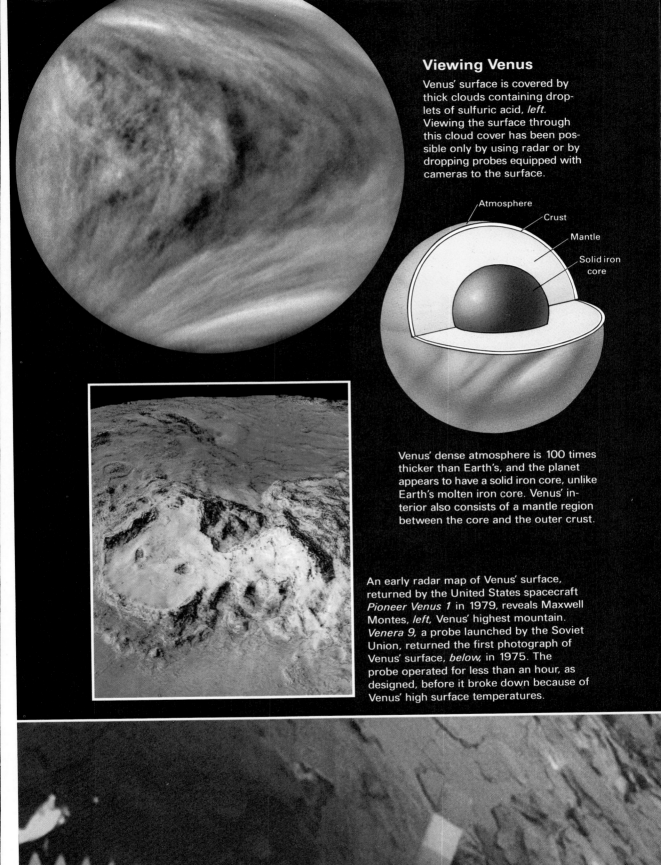

Viewing Venus

Venus' surface is covered by thick clouds containing droplets of sulfuric acid, *left*. Viewing the surface through this cloud cover has been possible only by using radar or by dropping probes equipped with cameras to the surface.

Atmosphere

Crust

Mantle

Solid iron core

Venus' dense atmosphere is 100 times thicker than Earth's, and the planet appears to have a solid iron core, unlike Earth's molten iron core. Venus' interior also consists of a mantle region between the core and the outer crust.

An early radar map of Venus' surface, returned by the United States spacecraft *Pioneer Venus 1* in 1979, reveals Maxwell Montes, *left*, Venus' highest mountain. *Venera 9,* a probe launched by the Soviet Union, returned the first photograph of Venus' surface, *below,* in 1975. The probe operated for less than an hour, as designed, before it broke down because of Venus' high surface temperatures.

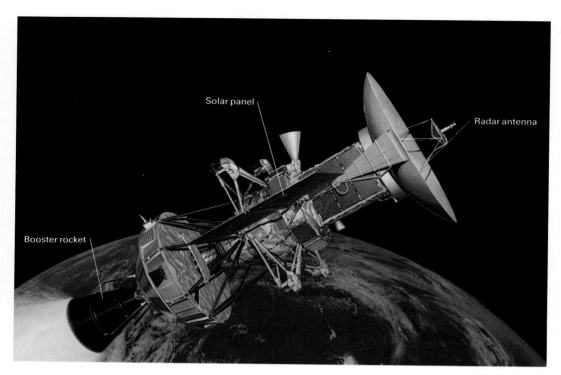

Solar panel

Radar antenna

Booster rocket

Launching *Magellan*
A booster rocket thrusts the *Magellan* spacecraft on its way to Venus in this artist's depiction. *Magellan*'s solar panels power the spacecraft's scientific instruments, including the radar system it uses to map Venus and the radios it uses to send data to Earth.

Venus on December 4 of that year. The radar map produced by *Pioneer Venus 1* revealed mountain ranges and extensive plains. The mountain ranges were found on two elevated plateaus—later named Ishtar Terra and Aphrodite Terra—which are larger than Australia and Africa on Earth.

The radar mapper on *Pioneer Venus 1*, however, could *resolve* (see the details of) only features larger than 50 kilometers (30 miles). Features smaller than 50 kilometers in diameter could not be imaged. In 1983, two Soviet spacecraft—*Venera 15* and *16*—began mapping the surface of Venus with a much sharper resolution, 1 to 2 kilometers (0.6 to 1.2 miles). The *Venera* maps showed volcanoes, impact craters, and *faults* (cracks) in the outermost layer of Venus' surface known as the *crust*. However, the path of the *Venera* spacecrafts' orbits around Venus permitted mapping of only one-fourth of the surface, near Venus' north pole.

The *Magellan* mission is the first to make a complete global map of Venus' surface, and its radar mapper has a resolution almost 10 times sharper than that of any previous spacecraft mission. When *Magellan* comes closest to the planet, its radar mapper can resolve features as small as 250 meters (820 feet) across.

With conventional radar, resolution depends on the size of the antenna. The greater the diameter of the antenna, the more detail the radar can resolve. To achieve the kind of resolution *Magellan* obtained, a conventional radar system would need an antenna more than 1 kilometer across. With *Magellan*, however, scientists used a technique called *synthetic aperture radar*. Conventional radar sends out a single radio pulse over the width, or aperture, of the antenna. *Magellan*'s radar, in effect, builds, or synthesizes, its aperture by sending out not one but several thousand radar pulses each second. As the spacecraft travels above the surface, these pulses spread out into a beam that covers an area of the planet's surface 20 kilometers (12 miles) wide.

The sheer number of reflected signals, however, requires the use of computers to sort them out and thereby produce images of the surface. The spacecraft transmits its raw data to receiving stations on Earth. The data are then processed in the Magellan Synthetic Aperture Radar Data Processing System to form images. This technique yields sharply detailed images, though *Magellan*'s radio antenna is only 3.7 meters (12 feet) in diameter.

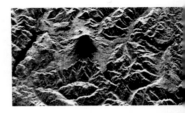

A Sharper Focus
If *Magellan*'s radar were used to image Mount St. Helens in Washington state, its image, *top,* would be 10 times sharper than that of the Soviet Union's *Venera* spacecraft, *middle.* The *Pioneer Venus 1* spacecraft could not resolve objects as small as the mountain, so its image, *bottom,* would be blank.

Magellan makes seven complete trips around Venus each day. With each orbit, the spacecraft's radar maps everything within a strip 20 kilometers wide and 17,000 kilometers (10,563 miles) long, extending from the north pole to a point near the south pole. On *Magellan*'s next orbit, it maps another strip that slightly overlaps the previous one because Venus has turned on its axis. Later, the overlapping images are put together to form a complete map.

Following the first test of the spacecraft on Aug. 16, 1990, *Magellan* began its first radar mapping orbit on September 15. Mapping proceeded successfully from September 15 to May 15, 1991, a period of 243 days—the time it took for Venus to turn once on its axis beneath the plane of the spacecraft's orbit. After May 15, *Magellan* began another 243-day cycle to fill in gaps in the map—such as the area near the south pole where mapping stopped—and to view the surface from different angles.

Viewing the previously mapped surface from different angles will give scientists more exact detail about the topography (shape) of surface features. For example, some features on Venus reflect radar signals weakly and so appear dark in radar images. The situation is comparable to the way sunlight is reflected from planets and their moons. Some areas of their surfaces reflect more light than others because they are made of material that is highly reflective. Similarly, astronomers can learn about the texture of material on Venus by studying the intensity, or strength, of reflected radar pulses. By knowing the topography, we can determine whether some areas that appear dark in a radar image are dark because they are made of smooth material or for other reasons.

Future mapping cycles may also tell astronomers whether any of Venus' volcanoes are currently active. If any volcanic eruptions occur after *Magellan*'s first mapping orbits, new images from the second mapping should show lava flows covering features that were visible in the previous images.

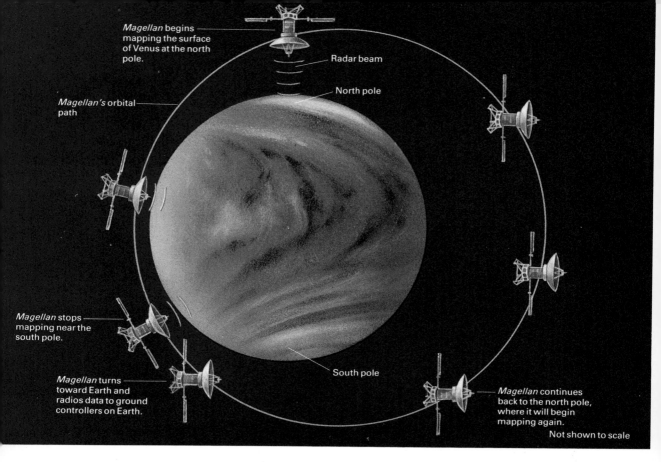

Magellan begins mapping the surface of Venus at the north pole.

Radar beam

North pole

Magellan's orbital path

Magellan stops mapping near the south pole.

Magellan turns toward Earth and radios data to ground controllers on Earth.

South pole

Magellan continues back to the north pole, where it will begin mapping again.

Not shown to scale

Mapping the Surface of Venus

Magellan uses radar to penetrate Venus' dense cloud cover and send images of the planet's surface to Earth. With each of its 1,700 orbits, *Magellan* maps an area 20 kilometers (12 miles) wide and 17,000 kilometers (10,563 miles) long from the north pole to a point near the south pole. After mapping each strip, *Magellan* turns and radios its data to Earth.

Magellan returns so much data that the computerized data-processing system cannot immediately provide full-resolution images of the entire surface. Consequently, scientists first compiled detailed images only of areas known to be of geologic interest from previous spacecraft missions. These included sites called Maxwell Montes and Sif Mons. Scientists were anxious to get a closer look at these geologic features.

Maxwell Montes is the planet's highest mountain. It towers 11,000 meters (36,000 feet) above the surrounding plains, more than 2,000 meters (6,600 feet) higher than Earth's tallest mountain, Mount Everest. The great height of Maxwell Montes intrigues scientists: When rocks on Earth are as hot as those on Venus must be, they begin to deform and crumble. Yet Maxwell Montes remains standing, though its rocks may be deformed by Venus' high surface temperatures. Scientists hope to determine what has kept Maxwell Montes' rocks from collapsing under their own weight and what forces keep this mountain range from sinking into the planet's interior because of its great weight.

Sif Mons is a volcano that resembles shield volcanoes on Earth. Shield volcanoes, such as Hawaii's Mauna Loa and Mauna Kea, have gently sloping sides built up by smooth flows of lava (in the Special Reports section, see VOLCANO WATCHING). Scientists think that Sif Mons may have been created in the same way as the Hawaiian shield volcanoes—by a *hot spot*, a plume of hot rock that originates deep in the planet's interior and melts its way through the crust to the surface. Some scientists believe that hot spots account for almost all the volcanic activity on Venus and are the primary means by which heat escapes from Venus' interior.

Although the data from the *Magellan* mission are still being compiled and evaluated, scientists agree that *Magellan* has confirmed many previous findings. For example, scientists expected *Magellan* to reveal signs of extensive tectonics. *Tectonics* (from the Greek word for *builder*) refers to the geologic processes that uplift mountains and cause quakes and faults. *Magellan*'s images confirmed that some regions of Venus have fault lines everywhere. In addition, Venus has *mountain ranges* made up of ridges and valleys like the Rocky and Appalachian mountains on Earth. Venus and Earth are the only planets in our solar system that have such mountain ranges.

Magellan also detected about as many impact craters as scientists expected to find, based on previous images from Earth-based radar and Soviet spacecraft. Meteorites create impact craters when they collide with the surface of a planet or moon. The smallest impact craters seen so far on Venus are about 3 kilometers (2 miles) in diameter. These impact craters were made by meteorites that were large enough to get through Venus' dense atmosphere without disintegrating or breaking up due to friction. Venus' atmosphere is so dense that penetrating the amount of matter in it is equivalent to going through a layer of rock more than 1 kilometer thick.

Many of the geologic observations scientists have made so far with the *Magellan* data have brought surprises. For example, Venus' mountain ranges show several unexpected troughlike valleys cutting across the mountains. The valleys may have been formed when sections of the mountains collapsed under the force of gravity.

Images from *Magellan* also show that volcanism has played a surprisingly important role in shaping Venus' surface. All of the areas mapped show widespread evidence of volcanism. At several places on Venus' plains are lava channels hundreds of kilometers long—10 times the length of similar channels on Earth, such as those found on Hawaii. Venus' lava channels were apparently cut by extremely fluid lava rapidly pouring from volcanic vents.

Features that scientists called *pancake domes* may also represent a new type of volcanism. These flattish domes on Venus are huge, up to 70 kilometers (40 miles) across and more than 1 kilometer high. Volcanologists (scientists who study volcanoes) on the *Magellan* science team believe that these structures formed due to flows of pasty, thick lava.

Most scientists did not expect to see direct evidence of winds at the surface of Venus because the atmosphere there is so slow-moving. Several areas, however, show streaks in the surface near the

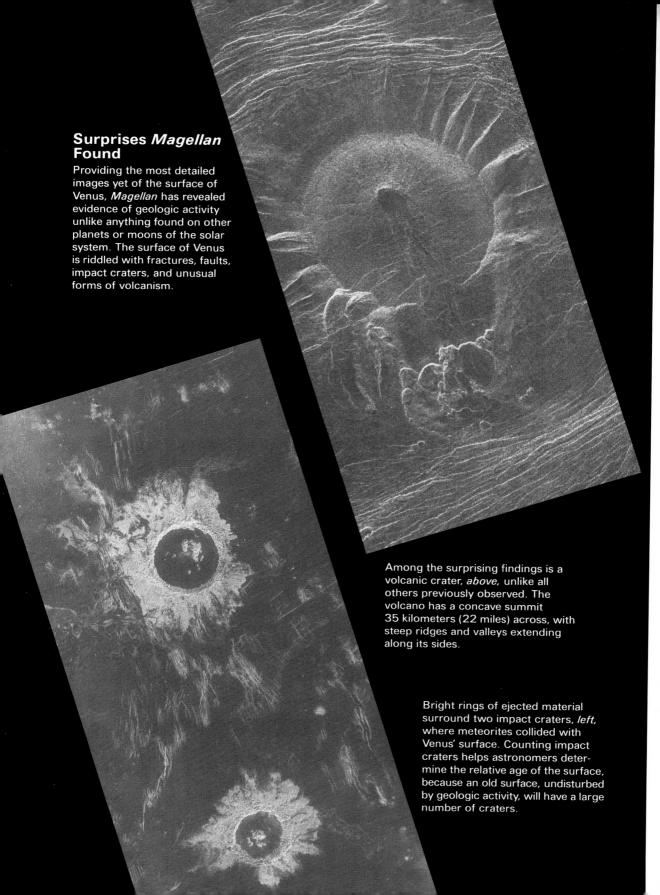

Surprises *Magellan* Found

Providing the most detailed images yet of the surface of Venus, *Magellan* has revealed evidence of geologic activity unlike anything found on other planets or moons of the solar system. The surface of Venus is riddled with fractures, faults, impact craters, and unusual forms of volcanism.

Among the surprising findings is a volcanic crater, *above,* unlike all others previously observed. The volcano has a concave summit 35 kilometers (22 miles) across, with steep ridges and valleys extending along its sides.

Bright rings of ejected material surround two impact craters, *left,* where meteorites collided with Venus' surface. Counting impact craters helps astronomers determine the relative age of the surface, because an old surface, undisturbed by geologic activity, will have a large number of craters.

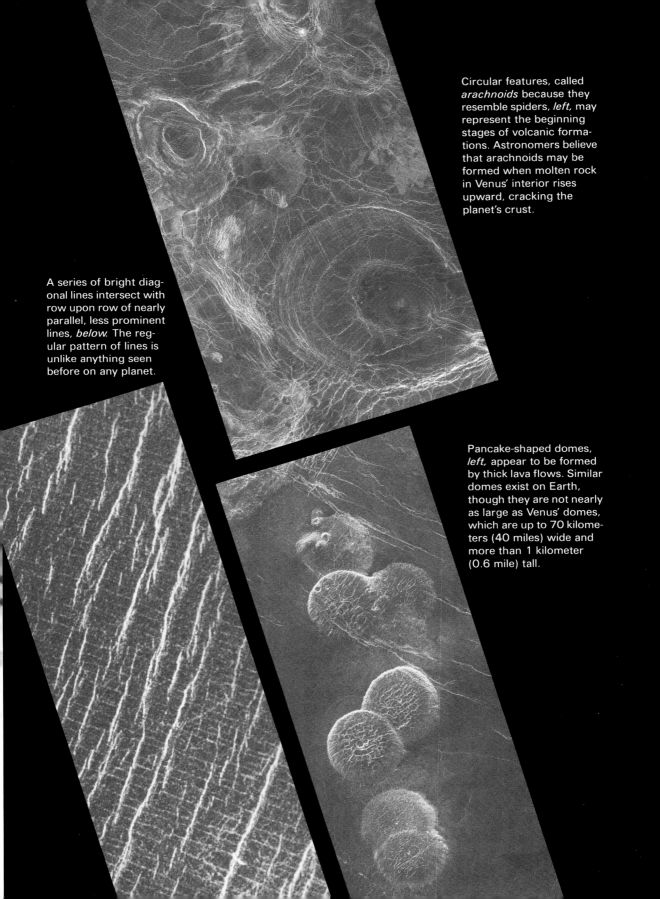

Circular features, called *arachnoids* because they resemble spiders, *left,* may represent the beginning stages of volcanic formations. Astronomers believe that arachnoids may be formed when molten rock in Venus' interior rises upward, cracking the planet's crust.

A series of bright diagonal lines intersect with row upon row of nearly parallel, less prominent lines, *below.* The regular pattern of lines is unlike anything seen before on any planet.

Pancake-shaped domes, *left,* appear to be formed by thick lava flows. Similar domes exist on Earth, though they are not nearly as large as Venus' domes, which are up to 70 kilometers (40 miles) wide and more than 1 kilometer (0.6 mile) tall.

downwind side of a hill or mountain where wind has apparently deposited dust or some other fine material. On Earth, similar streaks caused by winds are also found. When wind carries dust and sand around a hill or mountain on Earth, the elevated region disrupts the flow of the wind. Wind turbulence causes the dust and sand to drop out of the air and onto the surface on the downwind side of the hill or mountain. These deposits appear in the radar images of Venus as bright streaks. Dark streaks, indicating areas where fine surface material has been picked up and removed, also appear in the radar images. Both types of streaks show wind direction, and careful mapping of them over the entire planet may tell us much about the atmospheric circulation near the surface.

*M*agellan may also help solve one of the biggest mysteries about Venus: how continent-sized elevated regions formed. In February 1991, *Magellan* completed mapping Aphrodite Terra, the largest of Venus' highland regions. After the discovery of these regions by the *Pioneer Venus 1* spacecraft, scientists proposed at least four theories to explain their creation. The *Magellan* images of Aphrodite Terra will help test these theories.

The first theory proposes that Aphrodite Terra was formed from lightweight rock that crystallized early in Venus' history. This light, buoyant rock floated to the surface from Venus' dense *mantle*, the region of the planet's interior that lies between the outermost crust and the core. A few remnants of similar ancient crust on Earth can be found in Canada, South Africa, and Greenland, where some rocks are as old as 4 billion years.

Scientists can test this first theory by looking at the number of impact craters on Aphrodite Terra. If the surface had formed early in the planet's history, then it would have been bombarded by meteorites for a long period of time. If the theory were correct, scientists would find more impact craters on Aphrodite Terra than on nearby lowlands and other, presumably younger, regions of the planet.

A second major hypothesis is that Aphrodite was pushed up by hot spots. Because the molten rock that makes up the hot spots is less dense than surrounding rock, it tends to rise. If there were many such hot spot regions in Venus' mantle, enough rock would have risen to form Aphrodite Terra and other elevated regions.

To confirm this theory, *Magellan*'s data must show regions of different ages on Aphrodite Terra, because hot spots in different places might have welled up at different times. Volcanic features would also dominate Aphrodite's landscape, according to this theory.

A third hypothesis is that at least part of Aphrodite—the western region—was formed by a process called *mantle downwelling*. In this process, "cold spots" of dense material in the mantle *downwell* (sink) toward the core. As the material sinks, it draws in everything around it, causing rock in the crust to fold inward. As the sinking continues, and more and more rock in the crust folds inward, the crust builds up. Because more rock builds up around the sinking region than actually sinks, this thickened crust would stand higher than its surroundings and, according to this theory, account for the elevation of Aphrodite Terra and other highland regions.

The fourth theory, called the *spreading ridge model,* compares the formation of Aphrodite Terra to the formation of Earth's midocean ridges, a huge chain of mountains on the ocean floor. Along Earth's midocean ridges are central depressions called *rift valleys,* in which volcanic eruptions create new crust. This spreading ridge theory was based on images made during the *Pioneer Venus 1* mission that appeared to show a giant rift valley between mountain ridges in western Aphrodite Terra.

If Aphrodite Terra is a place where new crust is being formed, the rocks nearest the apparent rift valley should be younger than those at more distant sites. This theory also predicts that the ridges around the valley should have a pattern of faults running at right angles to the ridge. On Earth, such faults are formed as some parts of the ridges are pulled apart faster than other parts.

Scientists studying the *Magellan* data have been able to view detailed images of Aphrodite Terra. In the westernmost part, a highland area called Ovda Regio, *Magellan* revealed that the surface there is full of unexpected surprises. A preliminary assessment of the images suggests that the spreading ridge theory does not explain what we see, because none of the distinctive patterns associated with Earth's midocean ridges appear in Ovda Regio. Which of the other theories is more likely to be supported will require much more study, because both the hot spot and cold spot models appear to be consistent with the features found in Ovda Regio. The explanation might also lie in some entirely new theory.

Many other puzzles remain to be solved. Scientists want to understand the geologic processes on Venus not only because we want to know how Venus evolved but also because we want to understand similar geologic processes on Earth. Already, we have come to realize from studying Venus' atmosphere that the surface of Earth could become considerably warmer if human beings continue to add carbon dioxide to the atmosphere by such activities as burning fossil fuels. Likewise, the knowledge scientists gain from studying Venus' geology may help us understand the earthquakes, volcanic eruptions, and other geologic processes that affect the lives of billions of people here on Venus' sister planet.

For further reading:

Maran, Stephen P. "Very Volcanic Venus." *Natural History,* November 1985, pp. 35-39.

Mason, John. "The Unveiling of Venus." *New Scientist,* May 6, 1989, pp. 42-47.

Saunders, R. Stephen. "The Surface of Venus." *Scientific American,* December 1990, pp. 60-65.

Archaeologists are studying ancient artifacts, modern language patterns, teeth, and even genes in an attempt to discover when people first came to the Americas.

Who Were the First Americans?

BY DAVID J. MELTZER

In 1992, festive events will mark the 500th anniversary of the "discovery" of America by the Italian navigator Christopher Columbus. But, in truth, America was discovered long before Columbus was even born. In 1492, people were living throughout the New World, from the Arctic to the tip of South America. Since Columbus' arrival, we have learned a great deal about early Native Americans, but archaeologists still puzzle over when people actually reached the New World and where they came from.

The first clue was found in 1927. Archaeologists working near Folsom, N. Mex., found stone spearpoints embedded in the buried skeleton of a species of bison that became extinct at the end of the last Ice Age, which we now know was at least 10,000 years ago. The discovery of the ancient weapons showed that people had been living and hunting in North America at least that long ago.

Six years later, archaeologists found more ancient spearpoints—

The author:
David J. Meltzer is an archaeologist and associate professor in the Department of Anthropology at Southern Methodist University in Dallas.

this time with mammoth bones—near Clovis, N. Mex. Because scientists knew that mammoth had become extinct in North America before the species of bison found near Folsom did, the discovery pushed scientific evidence of a human presence in the New World back even further. Later, scientists dated the mammoth remains to 11,500 years ago. But there American prehistory stalled. During the next several decades, archaeologists reported finding about 50 sites thought to be older than 11,500 years. One by one, however, their claims of great age withered under the glare of scientific scrutiny.

Then in the 1970's and 1980's, archaeologists made several discoveries that may finally demonstrate that the first Americans arrived thousands—perhaps tens of thousands—of years earlier. Convincing skeptics has not been easy. At the same time, the debate over when human beings came to America spread beyond the archaeological community. Language experts, physical anthropologists, geologists, and biochemists are bringing their own special expertise and techniques to the problem. And so, even though we still do not know for certain *when* the first Americans arrived in the New World, we are learning about where they probably came from and, perhaps, their relationship to modern Native Americans.

The makers of the older spearpoints discovered in New Mexico have traditionally been called the *Clovis people*. Although archaeologists have found only a few of their bones, they believe the Clovis people looked much like modern Native Americans. These hardy people lived by gathering wild plants and by hunting game.

Because human beings did not originate in North or South America, even the first Americans must have been immigrants to this land. And because Native Americans closely resemble Asians, scientists concluded that the first Americans had come from Asia. If that were so, the crossing was probably made at the point where Asia and North America are the closest—between what are now Siberia and Alaska. Today, the continents are separated by the Bering Sea, a neck of ocean 80 kilometers (50 miles) wide. But it was once possible to walk from Siberia to Alaska.

During the last part of the most recent Ice Age, which lasted from 2 million to 10,000 years ago, the huge glaciers that covered much of the Northern Hemisphere froze up an estimated 5 per cent of the world's water, causing sea levels to fall worldwide. Geologic studies suggest that at least by 28,000 years ago, water levels in the Bering Sea had fallen enough to expose the sea floor between Siberia and Alaska, creating a land bridge called *Beringia*. By 18,000 years ago, when the Ice Age was at its height, Beringia may have been 1,500 kilometers (930 miles) wide from north to south. By about 14,400 years ago, the world's climate had warmed and the glaciers had begun to melt. The water released by the glaciers began to replenish the oceans, and the Bering Sea rose to cover Beringia. Even then, until perhaps as late as 10,000 years ago, the Bering Sea may have been shallow enough to freeze, so that it still may have been possible to walk from Siberia to Alaska in winter. Thus, people could have migrated into North America between 28,000 and 10,000 years ago.

Geologic studies suggested, however, that if the first Americans had arrived in Alaska at the height of the Ice Age, they would have been unable to move much farther south because two great glaciers may have blocked the route. The first, the Laurentide Glacier, was centered over Hudson Bay and stretched west to what is now the Canadian province of Alberta. The second, the Cordilleran Glacier, covered much of what is now the province of British Columbia. Many geologists believe that by 18,000 years ago, these glaciers had met along the northern portion of the border between British Columbia and Alberta, blocking movement southward.

When the glaciers began to melt about 16,000 years ago, a passageway about 2,000 kilometers (1,240 miles) long opened between them. When this corridor was narrow, however—less than 160 kilometers (100 miles) wide—it must have been extremely inhospitable. In fact, studies of fossilized pollen in soil samples from the corridor indicate that conditions were so severe that no plants grew there for several thousand years after it opened. And without plants, there would have been no animals. So people passing through the corridor would have been unable to gather or hunt food.

The lack of human skeletons or handmade objects older than 11,500 years, the presence of the ice barrier until 16,000 years ago, and the hostile conditions in the corridor for several thousand years after it opened led many scientists to conclude that people did not begin to move south into what are now southern Canada and the continental United States until just before 11,500 years ago. The discovery in the late 1950's and early 1960's of archaeological sites believed to be older than 11,500 years triggered a debate over whether people had arrived in the New World earlier than suspected. Although the idea of an earlier arrival tantalized archaeologists, all the sites failed to pass three deceptively simple tests.

The first test is that the site must have a human skeleton or a collection of *artifacts*, objects made, altered, or used by people. Most artifacts are easy to identify because, as they are being created, they take on shapes or patterns not found in nature. For example, no one would ever mistake a finely crafted spearpoint for a naturally occurring rock. Confusion may arise, however, if the artifact were a rock, for example, that an ancient person used as a hammer. The rock hammer would not look much different from an ordinary rock.

For example, broken stones believed to be tools were found in a huge layer of gravel just east of the Calico Mountains in the Mojave Desert in California beginning in 1964. Geologic studies indicated that the gravel layer, and thus the "tools," were 200,000 years old. In 1973, however, geologist C. Vance Haynes of the University of Arizona in Tucson calculated that in any huge natural deposit of

The Clovis People

The Clovis people were living throughout what are now lower Canada and the United States by 11,500 years ago. They were named for a site near Clovis, N. Mex., where some of the earliest known artifacts from these people were found in 1933.

Finely crafted stone points, *right,* that were used as spearpoints and knives are the most commonly known Clovis artifacts. Archaeologists believe the Clovis people entered North America from Asia across a land bridge called Beringia, *below right,* that once connected the two continents. They may have begun to move southward just before 11,500 years ago through a passageway between two glaciers that covered northern North America.

The Clovis people lived by hunting game and gathering wild plants, probably moving from place to place with the seasons. Although archaeologists have found few Clovis bones, they believe the Clovis people looked much like modern Native Americans.

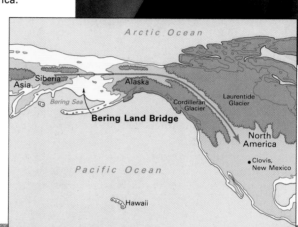

broken stones, there will always be a small number of stones whose shape makes them look like artifacts. Thus, he concluded, the Calico "artifacts" were created 200,000 years ago by nature, not people.

The second test is that the artifacts or other archaeological evidence found at a site must lie in *geologic strata* (layers of earth) that have remained undisturbed since they were originally laid down. In undisturbed strata, the deeper levels are older than the strata nearer the surface. But on occasion, newer artifacts or remains get buried in the older strata, giving the false impression they are as old as the surrounding deposit. This mixing may occur, for example, as the result of burrowing animals or erosion or because artifacts buried near the surface tumbled into a grave.

For instance, in 1961, the partial skeleton of a human infant was found in southern Alberta in strata thought to be 37,000 to as much as 60,000 years old. In 1979, archaeologist Michael C. Wilson of the University of Calgary in Alberta conducted a new analysis of the skeleton and the site where it was found. His work revealed that the skeleton and the sediment around it had washed from nearby slopes and mixed with much older Ice Age sediments. The skeleton was only about 4,100 years old.

The third test is that the site must be accurately and reliably dated. The most commonly used method to determine the age of archaeological sites—and one of the most accurate—is *radiocarbon dating*. It involves analyzing the amount of a radioactive form of carbon in wood, charcoal, bones, and other organic remains. Because radioactive carbon *decays* (changes into another form) at a known rate after the plant or animal dies, this analysis allows archaeologists to determine the age of an object to within several hundred years.

The use of other dating techniques may produce suspect dates. For example, in the early 1970's, geochemist Jeffrey Bada of the Scripps Institution of Oceanography in La Jolla, Calif., reported that nine human skeletons found in California were between 26,000 and 70,000 years old. Bada had dated the skeletons using a then-experimental technique called *amino-acid racemization*. It measures chemical changes that take place in *amino acids* after an animal dies. Amino acids are the building blocks of proteins found in bones, teeth, and other body parts. In 1985, archaeologist R. E. Taylor of the University of California at Riverside conducted a second study of the skeletons using radiocarbon dating. They found that none were more than 6,300 years old.

Many sites once thought to be more than 11,500 years old have failed one or more of these three tests. But recently, there has been a new wave of discoveries, three of which could finally prove that human beings arrived in the New World earlier than 11,500 years ago. One of the sites is in North America; the others are in South America.

Meadowcroft Rockshelter lies about 60 kilometers (37 miles)

What Is an Artifact and How Old Is It?

Along with human skeletons, evidence of early human beings can be found in *artifacts,* objects such as stone tools and weapons made by human hands, or the hearths from ancient campfires.

A finely crafted spearpoint clearly looks different from an ordinary rock, but often it is not so easy to determine what is an artifact. Other items found with a questionable object may aid in its identification. For example, animal bones, such as the bison bones found with this spearpoint, strongly suggest the object was a hunting weapon.

southwest of Pittsburgh, Pa. Rockshelters, which look like shallow caves, are areas on the side of a hill or cliff overhung by a stony ledge. A team of archaeologists under the direction of James M. Adovasio, then at the University of Pittsburgh, began digging at this large rockshelter in 1973. Over the next several years, as the archaeologists dug down 5 meters (16½ feet) through 11 strata, they found numerous artifacts, including knives and scrapers, that were all undeniably the product of human hands. The archaeologists were also delighted to find pieces of charcoal—the remains of campfires—in all of the older strata. The charcoal was radiocarbon dated to calculate the ages of the strata.

Although none of the objects found at Meadowcroft were particularly unusual, they created quite a stir. That is because radiocarbon dating indicated that the oldest geologic layer containing artifacts was about 16,770 years old.

Some criticism of Adovasio's findings focused on the animal and plant remains found in the oldest strata. From geologic studies scientists knew that 16,770 years ago, Meadowcroft Rockshelter was less than 100 kilometers (60 miles) from the southern edge of the Laurentide Glacier. But, skeptics noted, the few animal and plant remains found in the oldest strata did not represent the types of

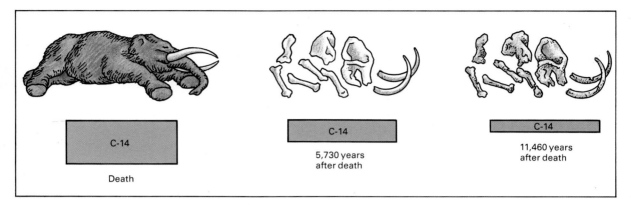

C-14

Death

C-14

5,730 years
after death

C-14

11,460 years
after death

One of the most accurate ways to determine the *absolute age* (age in years) of carbon-containing remains, such as bones, is radiocarbon dating. This involves measuring the amount of carbon 14 (C-14) in a sample of the remains. After death, C-14 changes into nitrogen 14 at a known rate. Therefore, the smaller the amount of C-14 in a sample, the older the remains.

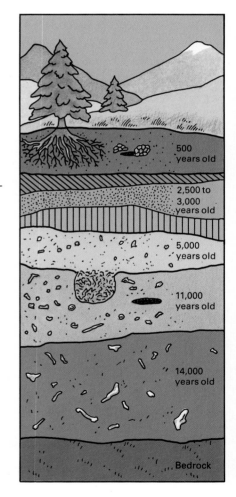

500 years old

2,500 to 3,000 years old

5,000 years old

11,000 years old

14,000 years old

Bedrock

The *relative age* of an artifact can be determined by where it is in the ground. Over the years, layers of rock and sediment called *strata* can build up at a site. Undisturbed geological strata—and, thus, artifacts—are progressively older at greater depths.

cold-weather animals and plants normally found near glaciers. Instead, they were animals and plants that lived in more temperate settings. This suggested that the remains—and, therefore, the oldest strata—actually dated from a later period when the glacier had retreated farther north and the climate had warmed. Adovasio and his colleagues countered that temperatures in and around the rockshelter may have been warmer than those in the surrounding area because of its low altitude (only 250 meters [820 feet] above sea level). In addition, the rockshelter faced south, which meant it received sun for most of the day, even in winter.

More forceful criticism concerned the radiocarbon dates for strata older than 12,000 years. Some scientists speculated that the charcoal samples may

Evidence of an Earlier Migration?

Discoveries at three archaeological sites in North and South America may provide convincing evidence that people settled in the New World before 11,500 years ago.

White tags mark layers of sediment at Meadowcroft Rockshelter, an ancient campsite near Pittsburgh, Pa. The oldest artifacts found there have been dated to 16,770 years ago.

A wishbone-shaped structure at Monte Verde, an ancient campsite in Chile, may have been used for making tools and for other community activities. Radiocarbon dating indicates the campsite was inhabited 13,000 years ago.

Painted signs and figures decorate the back wall of Pedra Furada, a rockshelter in northeastern Brazil. Radiocarbon dating indicates that people may have camped there 42,400 years ago.

have been contaminated by dissolved ancient carbon, mainly from coal deposits believed abundant in the area. In that case, the samples would appear much older than they really are.

Adovasio and his colleagues responded by pointing out that in nearly all cases, the radiocarbon dates agreed with the sequence of the strata. That is, charcoal samples identified as the oldest samples had been found in the lowest strata, and samples identified as the youngest had been found in the strata nearest the surface. In addition, Adovasio and his team found no coal deposits near the rockshelter. Finally, they noted that all the charcoal samples had been examined carefully under special microscopes for the presence of contaminating carbon particles, which, if found, were removed.

Another site that may be older than 11,500 years lies in the wild and remote plateau region of northeast Brazil. Toca do Boqueirão do Sítio da Pedra Furada is a large rockshelter that sits 19 meters (62 feet) above a valley floor. The back wall of the rockshelter is decorated with more than 1,000 painted signs and figures, including those of people, lizards, armadillos, and jaguars.

Archaeologist Nième Guidon and a team of French and Brazilian scientists began excavating at the site in 1973. Over the next 12 years, they dug more than 5 meters (16 feet) beneath the floor of the rockshelter, a depth that contained five geologic strata. In several of these strata, the archaeologists reported finding stone tools and large circular hearths containing pieces of charcoal. Guidon and her colleagues reported that radiocarbon dates for the charcoal indicated that the oldest artifacts from Pedra Furada were 42,400 years old.

Other archaeologists have challenged Guidon's findings on several points. They have questioned whether the artifacts and hearths uncovered in the oldest strata are really human artifacts. Some of the stone objects identified as tools, for example, are so crudely made that they could actually be pebbles that eroded from rock layers high above the shelter, fell, and shattered—thus resembling chipped tools. Similarly, some archaeologists argued that the oldest "hearths" actually are areas that were burned in brush fires.

Neither the claims for the great age of Pedra Furada, nor the criticisms of the claims, have won widespread support among scientists because Guidon and her team have not yet published a detailed report on their findings. Only after they do will other archaeologists be able to judge whether Pedra Furada proves that people lived in the New World at least 40,000 years ago.

Monte Verde, the remains of an ancient campsite in southern Chile, is the most remarkable of the candidates for a site older than 11,500 years. The artifacts found there are well-preserved because, shortly after the campsite was abandoned, a peat bog formed at the site. The lack of oxygen in the bog slowed decay.

Monte Verde was excavated between 1976 and 1985 by a scientific team directed by archaeologist Tom D. Dillehay of the University of

Kentucky in Lexington. The campsite consisted chiefly of 10 rectangular huts, roughly 2 by 2.5 meters (6½ by 8 feet) each. Near the huts was a wishbone-shaped structure that may have been used for such community activities as butchering meat or making tools. In and around these structures, the archaeologists found hearths, animal bones and skin, stone spearpoints, and tools made from wood, bone, and stone. Radiocarbon dates for charcoal found in the hearths indicated that the campsite had been occupied 13,000 years ago.

About 80 meters (260 feet) from the campsite, Dillehay's team also uncovered what appeared to be 26 crude stone tools and three hearths containing charcoal. Radiocarbon dating indicated that these artifacts were even more ancient—33,000 years old.

Some archaeologists have argued that the older objects are not really human artifacts. Critics have been harder pressed to find obvious flaws with the dates for the campsite. Many archaeologists who have examined Dillehay's research support his conclusions—at least for the 13,000-year old campsite—but widespread acceptance awaits final publication of his findings.

Great ages for Meadowcroft, Pedra Furada, and Monte Verde would be significant in themselves. If accurate, they would also indicate that people must have crossed the land bridge from Asia—which is 12,900 kilometers (8,000 miles) north of Monte Verde—much earlier. Although many scientists still question the evidence from Pedra Furada, the findings at Meadowcroft and Monte Verde have already convinced many archaeologists that people did, in fact, begin to move south into what are now Canada and the United States before 11,500 years ago.

Meanwhile, the search for the first Americans has expanded beyond archaeology. Linguists, physical anthropologists, and biochemists are also attempting to answer questions about exactly where the first Americans came from and how the New World was settled. Their work has focused chiefly on studies of dental patterns, language, and genetic material.

Although scientists agree that the first Americans migrated from Asia, they are still unsure of exactly where in that vast continent they originated. Studies of teeth are one way to find an answer. Teeth have distinctive features that are passed from generation to generation. As a result, similar dental patterns among groups of people indicate that they had common ancestors.

In 1977, physical anthropologist Christy G. Turner II of Arizona State University in Tempe began analyzing certain physical characteristics in thousands of teeth from prehistoric as well as modern native inhabitants of Europe, Asia, and North and South America. One of the distinctive characteristics is the number of roots in the lower first molars. Another is whether the inside surface of the incisors (front biting teeth) is flat or curved like a shovel.

According to Turner, the dental patterns of prehistoric Americans

Clues in Teeth

Studies of ancient and modern teeth suggest that Native Americans are descended from pre-historic inhabitants of northeast Asia. Differences in Native American dental patterns may represent three waves of migration to the New World, *right.*

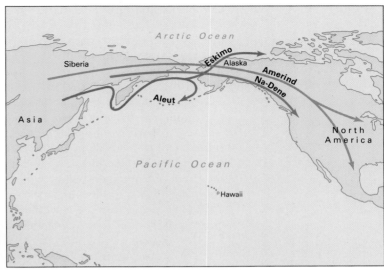

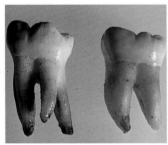

Prehistoric and modern Native Americans and northeast Asians are more likely to have three instead of two roots in the lower first molars.

The inside surface of the teeth of prehistoric and modern Native Americans and northeast Asians is also more likely to be curved like a shovel.

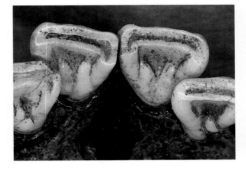

were similar to those of native peoples of a rather small area in what are now northeastern China and Mongolia. These peoples' lower first molars are likely to have three roots rather than two. In addition, the inner surface of their incisors is likely to be curved. Turner found the oldest examples of this dental pattern in ancient teeth from northeast Asia. So he concluded that all Native Americans were descended from prehistoric inhabitants of that area.

Further examination of the teeth of prehistoric and modern Native Americans revealed slight differences that led Turner to divide this group into three smaller groups. One group included Eskimo and Aleut Indians. Another included Indians living along the northwest coast of North America and in the interior of Alaska. The third included all remaining Indians in North America and all South American Indians. Turner theorized that these three groups represented three separate waves of migration to the New World.

A striking parallel to Turner's conclusions about teeth came from an unrelated field—language studies. Modern Native Americans speak a rich array of languages—some 600. Before the arrival of

Europeans in 1492, the number of languages may have exceeded 1,000. In 1984, linguist Joseph H. Greenberg of Stanford University in Palo Alto, Calif., reported that his analysis of similarities among key words in these languages had led him to conclude that all Native American languages fall into one of three language families. He named these families *Eskimo-Aleut*, *Na-Dene*, and *Amerind*.

According to Greenberg, speakers of the Eskimo-Aleut languages live along the far northern coast of North America, from the Aleutian Islands to Greenland. Na-Dene languages are spoken by Indians living chiefly along the northwestern coast of North America and in Alaska. Amerind, the most diverse of the families, includes hundreds of languages spoken by Indian groups living as far north as Hudson Bay and as far south as the southern tip of Argentina. In the early 1980's, anthropologist Stephen L. Zegura of the University of Arizona in Tucson reported a similar three-part grouping, this one based on blood groups and other inherited characteristics among modern Native Americans.

In 1986, Turner, Greenberg, and Zegura proposed that the ancestors of modern Native Americans entered the New World in three groups, which they named after Greenberg's language families. The Amerind family, they decided, is the oldest because Amerind languages are the most widespread. In addition, the languages in this family differ from the native languages of northeast Asia to a greater degree than do those in the other two families. Finally, the languages within the Amerind family differ to a greater degree among themselves. All these characteristics suggest that the Amerind family has existed—and so has been changing—longer than the other two families. Greenberg, Turner, and Zegura assumed that Clovis people were the first Americans. Therefore, they concluded that Clovis people spoke a language that evolved over the past 11,500 years into the languages that make up the Amerind family.

Greenberg, Turner, and Zegura have not won widespread scientific acceptance for their theory. Some linguists have vigorously challenged Greenberg's three-part grouping of all Native American languages. Linguist Lyle Campbell of Louisiana State University in Shreveport, for example, argues that there may be far more than three families.

Unfortunately, this debate may never be settled. Because the first Americans left no written language and because it is impossible to match modern languages with archaeological objects, we may never know what language or languages the first Americans spoke, or how those relate to Amerind.

The dental evidence is on somewhat firmer ground, because teeth provide an actual record of the past and of how changes occur over time. Still, ancient human teeth are quite rare. Although Turner has examined virtually all of the oldest specimens, his findings—like those of Greenberg—may be open to other interpretations. For example, some scientists have argued that there may have been only one migration and that changes in dental patterns occurred after the first Americans had arrived in the New World.

Some scientists hope that new studies of genes, the basic unit of heredity, may eventually help determine how many waves of immigration there were. In these studies, scientists are attempting to trace the ancient ancestry of modern people by examining similarities and differences in genetic material. Recently, they have focused on *mitochondrial DNA* (deoxyribonucleic acid). DNA is the molecule of which genes are made. Most DNA is in a cell's nucleus, but mitochondrial DNA is found in small amounts outside the nucleus of cells, where it is involved in turning food into energy. Unlike nuclear DNA, which comes from both parents, mitochondrial DNA is transmitted only by females and is unaltered by genetic mixing from generation to generation. Differences in mitochondrial DNA thus represent progressive genetic changes that have appeared over time. Scientists have recently used mitochondrial DNA to establish "family trees" among groups of people, since shared mitochondrial types indicate common ancestry.

A 1990 study by biochemist Douglas C. Wallace of Emory University in Atlanta reported that most modern American Indians were descended from ancestors with four mitochondrial DNA types. But another study reported in 1990, by biochemist Svante Pääbo of the University of Munich in Germany, found 30 mitochondrial DNA types among Native Americans.

Such apparently conflicting results should be resolved as additional studies are done. And additional research should help clarify whether the number of distinct mitochondrial DNA types present in Native Americans represents, for example, a single migration of people with different mitochondrial DNA types, as Wallace believes, or different migrations at different times.

The contributions of linguists, physical anthropologists, and biochemists may deepen our understanding of who the first people in the New World were. But it is to the archaeologists that we must look for the stone tools and other artifacts that provide firmer evidence of the time of their arrival. Such evidence will also provide new insights into how these rugged people—long before Columbus—discovered and inhabited what was then a truly new world.

For further reading:

Adovasio, James M. and R. Carlisle. "An Indian Hunter's Camp for 20,000 Years." *Scientific American*, May 1984, pp. 130-136.

Dillehay, Tom D. "A Late Ice-Age Settlement in Southern Chile." *Scientific American*, October 1984, pp. 106-117.

Fagan, Brian. *The Great Journey: The Peopling of Ancient America.* Thames and Hudson, London, 1987.

Turner, Christy G., II. "Teeth and Prehistory in Asia." *Scientific American*, February 1989, pp. 88-96.

"The First Americans." A 14-part series in *Natural History*, November 1986 to October 1987 and January and February 1988.

Studies of Hawaii's Kilauea volcano have
revealed new clues about how and why volcanoes
erupt and have helped improve geologists' ability
to forecast eruptions.

Volcano Watching

BY ROBERT AND BARBARA B. DECKER

The stream of hot lava seemed alive as it sizzled across the beach toward the sea. At times, its silvery-gray skin cracked, exposing the orange-red molten rock within. About l meter (3 feet) wide and only centimeters thick, the lava stream snaked slowly ahead of a much wider flow of lava advancing down the side of Hawaii's Kilauea (KEY lay WAY ah) volcano. As the 1100 °C (2000 °F) lava pushed slowly but relentlessly into the breaking waves, the battle of fire and water hurled huge clouds of steam into the sky.

By June 1990, Kilauea had largely completed its destruction of Kalapana, a charming rural village on the southeast coast of the island of Hawaii. Kilauea's lava had overrun parts of the area several times since 1983, when the volcano began its current period of eruption. Now the tranquil beaches, the gently waving palms, and more than 175 homes were gone. In their place was solid black lava inlaid with twisted sheets of rusty metal roofing.

The destruction of Kalapana attracted thousands of curious tourists. The most serious volcano-watchers on the scene, however, were scientists from the United States Geological Survey's Hawaiian Volcano Observatory. They tracked the direction and speed of the lava flow to warn officials about which homes were in danger and to learn more about the irregular motion of lava flows. They also collected lava samples and estimated the volume of lava being erupted.

Glossary

Active volcano: A volcano that is erupting or that has erupted during recorded history.

Explosive eruption: A violent eruption that throws up huge clouds of hot ash, gases, and rock fragments.

Effusive eruption: An eruption that consists mainly of flows of molten lava.

Hot-spot volcano: A volcano, usually within a plate, believed to be caused by an upwelling plume of especially hot rock that originates deep in the mantle.

Lava: Magma that has reached the surface.

Magma: Molten rock with dissolved gases.

Rift volcano: A huge crack created where two tectonic plates are pulling apart, through which magma wells up from Earth's interior.

Subduction volcano: A volcano that forms where two tectonic plates are colliding and one plate is overriding the other.

Tectonic plate: One of about 20 gigantic segments that make up Earth's outer shell.

Volcano: An opening in Earth's crust through which molten rock reaches the surface; also, the landform built by volcanic eruptions.

The authors:
Robert Decker is a professor of geophysics at the University of Hawaii in Hilo. Barbara B. Decker is a free-lance science writer.

Kilauea is one of the most thoroughly studied volcanoes in the world. Scientists from the Hawaiian Volcano Observatory located high above the volcano's crater, have been monitoring Kilauea's activities since 1912. Observatory scientists have pioneered or refined many of the major volcano-monitoring techniques used worldwide. Their research has also greatly advanced scientists' understanding of how and why volcanic eruptions occur. And their work has improved scientists' ability to forecast eruptions.

Volcanic eruptions of fiery lava, ash, rocks, steam, and other gases are among Earth's most powerful and spectacular events. They have played—and still play—a major role in creating our world. Steam and other volcanic gases help create Earth's atmosphere and oceans. Soils renewed by ashfalls from eruptions are among the richest in the world, and gold and silver ores are deposited from underground water heated and circulated by volcanic action.

But volcanoes are also feared because of their ability to destroy. Just since 1980, volcanic eruptions have killed 28,000 people and caused more than $2 billion in property damage. In mid-June 1991, for example, a series of eruptions of Mount Unzen in southern Japan killed more than 30 people, and eruptions of Mount Pinatubo in the Philippines killed at least 250 people. It is not surprising that to many people who live within their awesome reach, volcanoes are regarded as the homes of gods and goddesses. According to Hawaiian legend, for example, the eruption of Kilauea and other Hawaiian volcanoes is caused by a fiery goddess named Pele.

Fire from below

A volcano is an opening in Earth's crust through which *molten* (melted) rock, called *magma*, reaches the surface. Once at the surface, magma is called *lava*. The word *volcano* also describes the landform built by an eruption. These landforms may be massive, gently sloping mountains such as Kilauea, or steep, cone-shaped mountains, such as Mount Rainier in Washington state. Not all volcanoes are mountains, however. On the sea floor, they sometimes appear as huge cracks through which lava wells up from Earth's interior.

Magma forms because of the extreme heat in Earth's interior. Scientists believe this heat fuels slow currents of hot, puttylike rock that circulate in the mantle, the layer between Earth's core and crust. The extremely high pressures in the deep mantle keep the rock from melting. But as the hot rock rises, the pressure falls, lowering its melting point. Most magma forms about 80 to 160 kilometers (50 to 100 miles) below the surface, near the top of the mantle.

As the rock melts, the small amounts of water, carbon dioxide, and sulfur gases in the rock become dissolved in the magma. The liquid magma is lighter than the hot, solid rock surrounding it and so it continues to rise, breaking or partly melting the rock above it. As magma nears the surface, the gases boil out, propelling molten lava from a *vent* (opening at the surface).

Although volcanic eruptions differ in detail, most are either *explosive* or *effusive*. Explosive eruptions can blow the top off a mountain. Such violent eruptions can occur when magma is thick and sticky and contains large amounts of steam, carbon dioxide, and other volcanic gases. When magma of this type nears the surface, the escape of the dissolved gases is blocked temporarily by the thick, sticky magma. If a great avalanche, caused by an earthquake, suddenly releases the pressure of the overlying rock, a huge explosion occurs. The eruption of Mount St. Helens in 1980 was an explosive eruption of this type.

More moderate explosive eruptions usually create steep, cone-shaped mountains. The magma reaching the surface is blasted out in clouds of hot ash and rock fragments. Most of the larger fragments, which can range from cinders the size of a pea to blocks the size of a house, fall near the vent. The build-up of alternating layers of blasted fragments and thick lava flows that usually follow the explosions creates a beautifully shaped cone like that of Japan's Mount Fuji.

Effusive eruptions consist mainly of flows of molten lava. They occur when the magma's gas content is low and the magma flows easily. The lava can spew out in fiery fountains or well up into glowing ponds. This is the type of eruption for which Kilauea is famous. Effusive eruptions build *shield volcanoes*, massive but gently sloping mountains that are much wider than they are high.

How volcanoes form

For centuries, people have recognized that most volcanoes are found in long chains. The so-called *Ring of Fire* is the chain of volcanoes that encircles the Pacific Ocean along the western coasts of North and South America and the eastern edge of Asia. In the 1960's, scientists proposed the theory of plate tectonics, which helps explain what causes most volcanoes and why they form in chains.

According to this concept, Earth's solid outer shell consists of a dozen or so gigantic segments called *tectonic plates*. These plates include the continents and the ocean floor. Beneath the plates is a layer of partially melted rock upon which the plates move relative to each other. Their motion is slow, about the speed at which fingernails grow. At their edges, the plates are either colliding with, separating from, or grinding past each other.

Two types of volcanoes—*subduction* volcanoes and *rift* volcanoes—form near the edges of the plates. Subduction volcanoes form where two tectonic plates are colliding and one plate is overriding the other plate. In most cases, a plate carrying ocean floor is being *subducted* beneath (thrust under) a continental plate. As the subducting plate plunges deep into Earth's mantle, some rock above it melts and pushes up through the continental plate to form volcanoes. Mount St. Helens and other volcanoes in the Cascade Range are examples of subduction volcanoes. They have formed because of the ongoing collision of the Juan de Fuca Plate, an oceanic plate, and the North

Types of Volcanoes

Volcanoes are openings at Earth's surface that allow molten rock called *magma* to escape from below. They are classified as *subduction, rift,* or *hot-spot* volcanoes, depending on the way they form.

Subduction volcanoes form where tectonic plates collide. Earth's outer shell consists of a number of rigid plates slowly sliding on a layer of partly melted rock in the mantle. Most subduction volcanoes occur where a plate carrying oceanic crust is being *subducted* (thrust under) a plate carrying continental crust. Hot, molten rock above the subducted plate rises through the mantle and crust to create volcanoes.

Subduction volcanoes almost always produce *explosive eruptions, left,* which are sometimes powerful enough to blow the top off a mountain. Such eruptions occur when magma is thick and sticky and contains large amounts of gases.

Subduction volcanoes are usually steep, cone-shaped mountains, such as Mount St. Helens in Washington state before its 1980 eruption, *above.* They are formed of alternating layers of ash and thick flows of lava.

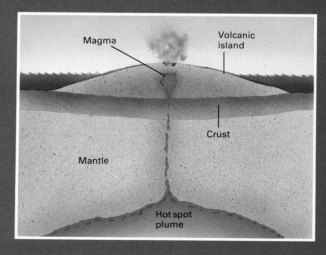

Hot-spot volcanoes form mainly within tectonic plates. Scientists believe they are caused by huge, slowly upwelling plumes of especially hot rock that originate deep in the mantle.

Rift volcanoes form where two tectonic plates are pulling apart, *below.* The separation produces huge *rifts* (cracks) between the plates. Magma wells out of the crack, creating new sea floor.

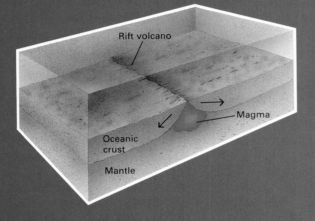

A crack cuts across a lava flow from an underwater rift volcano, *above.* Most rift volcanoes form on the crests of the mid-ocean ridges, chains of underwater mountains that encircle Earth.

Submarine rift volcanoes generally have effusive eruptions. Their lava flows often form closely packed, sacklike shapes called *pillows, right.*

Hot-spot volcanoes usually produce *effusive eruptions, below,* of molten lava that spews up in fiery fountains and flows away in molten rivers.

Hot-spot volcanoes are massive gently sloping mountains, such as Hawaii's Mauna Loa, *above,* that are much wider than they are high.

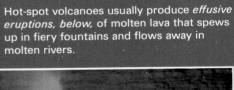

American Plate, a continental plate. Most eruptions there and at other subduction volcanoes are explosive.

Rift volcanoes form where two plates are pulling apart, because of the upwelling of magma. This separation creates huge *rifts* (cracks) between the plates through which magma reaches the surface. Most rift volcanoes are found along the crests of the midocean ridges, huge chains of undersea mountains that stretch 60,000 kilometers (37,000 miles) around Earth. Along the ridges, new sea floor is being created from the upwelling lava. These eruptions are probably effusive, but no one has ever witnessed an eruption from a deep undersea rift volcano.

A third type of volcano—a *hot-spot volcano*—usually occurs not at the edge, but within a plate. Scientists believe hot-spot volcanoes are formed by huge, slowly upwelling plumes of especially hot, partially melted rock that originate deep in the mantle. The hot-spot theory accounts for the formation of all the Hawaiian islands and the Hawaiian-Emperor Ridge, a chain of volcanic islands and undersea mountains that stretches northwestward from the Hawaiian islands.

The Hawaiian volcanoes

During the past 30 million years, the Pacific Plate has moved over a hot spot at the rate of about 10 centimeters (4 inches) a year. The rising hot-spot magma breaks and melts rock above it, forming a *conduit* (channel) in the solid rock of the plate. The lava pours out gradually, building an undersea mountain. Eventually, the mountain becomes tall enough to rise above the ocean surface as an island. As the plate moves, the conduit carrying magma up through the plate gets bent and closed off. The hot spot then forms a new conduit in the section of the plate directly above, and a new volcano is born. According to the theory, Kilauea is above the hot spot now. The older islands and undersea mountains in the Hawaiian-Emperor Ridge were formed long ago, when they were over the hot spot.

Scientists determined the ages of the rocks throughout the Hawaiian island chain using a technique called *potassium-argon dating*. With this technique, scientists measure the ratio of a radioactive form of potassium to the argon in volcanic rock. Because the potassium atoms change to argon atoms over time at a known rate, the ratio can be used to determine the age of the rock. The scientists found that the rock on Kauai, at the northwest end of the chain, is 5 million years old; by contrast, the oldest rock on the island of Hawaii—site of the currently active volcanoes—is less than 500,000 years old. Scientists believe the hot spot that fuels Kilauea has been there for at least 70 million years, because the undersea mountains at the northwest end of the Hawaiian-Emperor Ridge are that old.

Kilauea and other hot-spot volcanoes generally produce effusive eruptions. That is because hot-spot magma contains less volcanic gases than does magma beneath subduction volcanoes. In addition, hot-spot magma is, by nature, hotter than magma from subduction

Where Volcanoes Are Located

Most volcanoes exist along the edges of the tectonic plates that make up Earth's outer shell. Subduction volcanoes form where two plates are colliding. Rift volcanoes form where plates are separating. Hot-spot volcanoes, however, usually occur within plates.

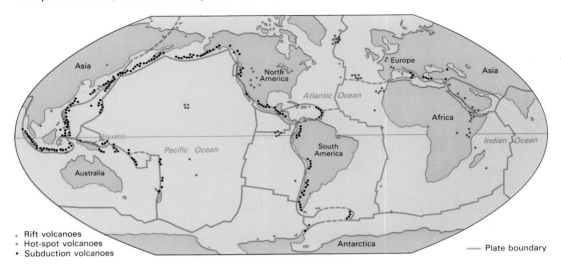

- Rift volcanoes
- Hot-spot volcanoes
- Subduction volcanoes

—— Plate boundary

volcanoes, and so it is thinner and flows more easily. (Lava erupting from subduction volcanoes is usually about 1000 °C [1800 °F]. Hot-spot lava is from 1100 °C to 1200 °C [2000 °F to 2200 °F]).

Monitoring Kilauea

Geologists at the Hawaiian Volcano Observatory rely on a number of instruments to study Kilauea. For example, they use gas analyzers to measure the chemical composition and amount of gases escaping from the volcano. Scientists believe magma that has recently entered Kilauea's *magma chamber* (main reservoir) from the mantle gives off more carbon dioxide than magma that has been in the chamber for a while. Thus, changes in the amount of carbon dioxide escaping at the surface provide clues to magma movements far below.

But the most commonly used instruments at the observatory are *seismographs*, which detect and measure the vibrations created by earthquakes, and *tiltmeters*, which detect and measure changes in the slopes of the surface of volcanoes. Scientists have learned that thousands of earthquakes occur beneath Kilauea every year as magma forces its way upward, bending the overlying and surrounding rock until it breaks. Although most of these quakes are too small to be felt, the *seismic waves* (vibrations) they produce can be measured by seismographs. By timing when seismic waves from an earthquake arrive at the 50 or so seismographs stationed on and around Kilauea, scientists can calculate the time and place the earthquake began.

In a way, the seismographs at Kilauea act as the geologists' X-ray

Studying a Volcano

Scientists study the inner workings of volcanoes, such as Kilauea, with a variety of instruments.

Geologists crouch behind a heat shield, *right,* while inserting a probe to measure temperature in a lava flow on Kilauea.

Readings from a seismograph, *left,* provide a researcher with a record of earthquake activity occurring beneath a Hawaiian volcano. Such records, made by seismographs stationed on and around a volcano, help geologists map the volcano's interior, track the underground movement of magma, and forecast eruptions.

A geologist collects gases escaping near an erupting vent on Kilauea's eastern slope. An analysis of the gas may reveal whether magma is flowing up into the magma chamber beneath the volcano.

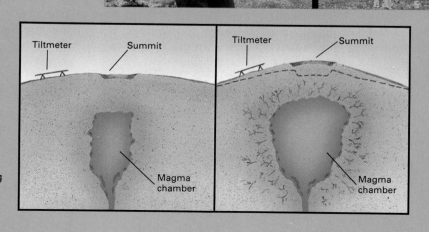

Measuring Tilt

A tiltmeter is similar to a carpenter's level placed on the slope of a volcano, *right.* It helps forecast eruptions by detecting changes in the slope. The volcano's summit bulges upward as magma rises and fills the magma chamber, *far right,* creating conditions that may lead to eruption.

Tiltmeter   Summit

Tiltmeter   Summit

Magma chamber

Magma chamber

machine, enabling them to "see" inside the volcano. That is because earthquakes do not occur in liquid magma, which moves without cracking. The earthquakes, in effect, occur in an envelope around pockets of magma. So when scientists find a region within the volcano where quakes are not taking place but that is surrounded by quakes, they can be reasonably sure that this region is a chamber that is being filled with magma or drained. Because no earthquakes occur more than 60 kilometers (37 miles) below Kilauea, scientists believe that this depth marks the top of the Hawaiian hot-spot plume.

Kilauea's "plumbing system"

Seismic studies also have helped observatory scientists map the reservoirs and channels that make up Kilauea's internal "plumbing system." They indicate that Kilauea's magma chamber is about 3 kilometers (2 miles) in diameter and extends from about 3 to about 7 kilometers (2 to 4 miles) below the surface. The chamber is not entirely filled with molten rock, however. It consists of areas of molten rock separated by more solid rock.

As magma rises, the chamber beneath Kilauea expands until the pressure exerted by the magma opens a large crack in the surrounding rock through which the magma can escape. This magma-filled crack, called a *dike*, is usually about 1 meter (3 feet) wide and can be tens of kilometers long. Sometimes, a dike breaks upward to the surface. Sometimes, it breaks to the side of the volcano, in areas called rift zones, where the rock has been weakened by many parallel cracks.

Kilauea has two rift zones, each of which is about 1 to 2 kilometers (1 mile) wide. The Southwest Rift Zone extends about 30 kilometers (20 miles) from the summit to the southwest. The East Rift Zone is the site of the current eruptions. It extends for about 50 kilometers (30 miles) from the summit to the east coast of the island and then for another 65 kilometers (40 miles) beneath the sea.

Tracking movements of magma and lava

Seismic studies enable scientists to track the movement of magma through the "plumbing system" and estimate the approximate time and place lava may break through to the surface. For example, on Jan. 2, 1983—the beginning of Kilauea's current eruption—observatory seismographs began recording *swarms* (clusters) of earthquakes. Swarms typically occur in the hours or days before an eruption begins. They indicated that magma in the volcano had started to move. Scientists studying the seismograms watched as the location of the earthquakes—and, therefore, the magma—moved beneath the rift zone. Guided by radio messages from the observatory about the location of the earthquakes, geologists were nearby when, about 24 hours later, spectacular "curtains of fire"—fountains of lava—began shooting up from a crack in the East Rift Zone.

Kilauea's "Plumbing System"

Beneath Kilauea is a huge magma chamber and a network of channels through which magma reaches the surface.

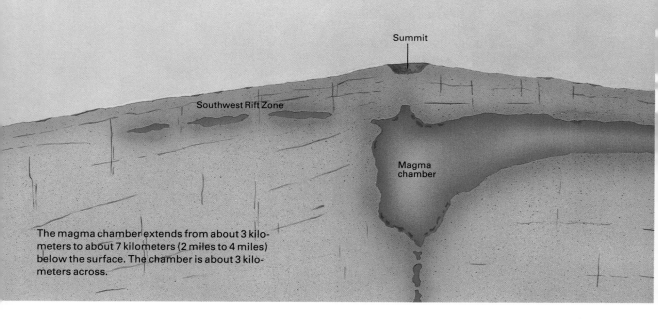

Summit

Southwest Rift Zone

Magma chamber

The magma chamber extends from about 3 kilometers to about 7 kilometers (2 miles to 4 miles) below the surface. The chamber is about 3 kilometers across.

Lava overflows the edges of a lava lake that formed over Kilauea's Kupaianaha vent in 1986. The lake grew to 100 meters (330 feet) in diameter, but by 1990, had shrunk to a pond only 10 meters (33 feet) across. It then crusted over with hardened lava.

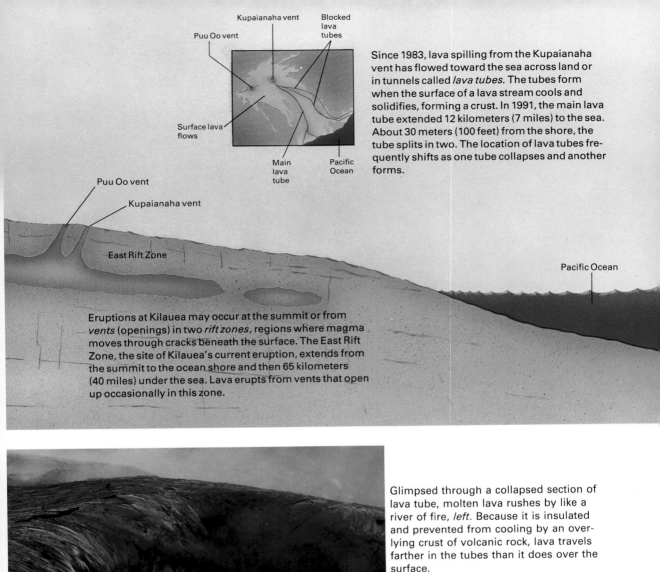

Kupaianaha vent
Puu Oo vent
Blocked lava tubes
Surface lava flows
Main lava tube
Pacific Ocean

Since 1983, lava spilling from the Kupaianaha vent has flowed toward the sea across land or in tunnels called *lava tubes.* The tubes form when the surface of a lava stream cools and solidifies, forming a crust. In 1991, the main lava tube extended 12 kilometers (7 miles) to the sea. About 30 meters (100 feet) from the shore, the tube splits in two. The location of lava tubes frequently shifts as one tube collapses and another forms.

Puu Oo vent
Kupaianaha vent
East Rift Zone
Pacific Ocean

Eruptions at Kilauea may occur at the summit or from *vents* (openings) in two *rift zones*, regions where magma moves through cracks beneath the surface. The East Rift Zone, the site of Kilauea's current eruption, extends from the summit to the ocean shore and then 65 kilometers (40 miles) under the sea. Lava erupts from vents that open up occasionally in this zone.

Glimpsed through a collapsed section of lava tube, molten lava rushes by like a river of fire, *left*. Because it is insulated and prevented from cooling by an over-lying crust of volcanic rock, lava travels farther in the tubes than it does over the surface.

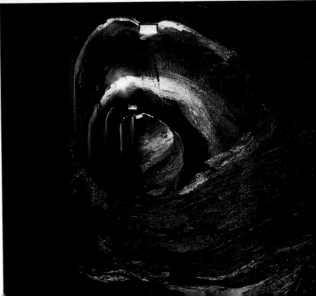

Some tubes are huge. The Thurston Lava Tube on Kilauea's eastern slope is large enough for people to walk through, *right*. It became an empty tunnel about 300 to 500 years ago, when the vent that was supplying the tube stopped erupting.

Types of Lava
Lava flows from Kilauea and other Hawaiian volcanoes take two forms. Aa (*AH ah*) flows, *above,* consist of a jumble of sharp rocks. Pahoehoe (*pah HOH ee* HOH *ee*) flows, *above right,* are smooth, billowy streams.

Not all earthquake swarms beneath Kilauea's rift zones are followed by eruptions, however. Sometimes, new dikes of magma enter the rift zones but stop before breaking through to the surface. Scientists do not understand why some dikes erupt to the surface but others do not. When volcanologists see signs of an impending eruption but no eruption occurs, it is not really a case of scientists "crying wolf." The wolf was there; for some reason, it was not hungry.

As a volcano expands before and contracts after an eruption, small changes occur in its slope. This is recorded by tiltmeters sensitive enough to detect changes in slope of only one part per million. If you built a carpenter's level 1 kilometer (⅔ mile) long, set it on a flat surface, and then slipped a dime under one end, that would be a change in tilt of one part per million. A commonly used tiltmeter at Kilauea consists of two electronic sensors connected by a horizontal tube of mercury about 3 meters (10 feet) long. Changes in the height of the mercury at the ends of the tube reflect changes in the slope of the volcano.

Scientists at the Hawaiian Volcano Observatory pioneered the use of tiltmeters in volcano research in the 1960's. Their studies at Kilauea soon revealed that even when the volcano is dormant, magma is often accumulating within the magma chamber.

Tiltmeters have also enabled observatory volcanologists to chart Kilauea's eruption cycle. This cycle consists of periods of inflation, when rising magma causes the summit to bulge slowly outward and upward like a balloon being inflated, and deflation, when an eruption causes the summit to collapse. At Kilauea, the bulge at the summit

Interesting Facts About Volcanoes

■ The word *volcano* comes from *Vulcano*, a volcanic island in the Mediterranean Sea. Ancient Romans believed that Vulcano was the chimney of the forge of Vulcan, the blacksmith of the Roman gods.

■ The most destructive eruption in U.S. history was that of Mount St. Helens in Washington state in 1980. It killed 57 people and caused more than $1 billion in damage.

■ The most powerful eruption in historic times was that of Tambora in Indonesia in 1815. It released about 10,000 times more power than all U.S. electric generating plants do in several hours. The dust cloud it produced may have caused the winterlike temperatures experienced in North America and Europe in the summer of 1816.

Krakatoa sunset

■ About 50 volcanoes erupt each year.

■ The 1883 explosion of Krakatoa in Indonesia was so loud that it was heard 4,000 kilometers (2,500 miles) away. The cloud of volcanic dust ejected by the eruption produced spectacular sunsets around the world, *above*.

■ A huge eruption on the Aegean island of Thira (also known as Santorini) in about 1600 B.C. may have given rise to the legend of the lost continent of Atlantis.

before an eruption is usually so wide—about 12 kilometers (7 miles)—and the swelling so slow—a few centimeters per week—that the changes can be detected only by tiltmeters. The slow but nearly steady rate at which Kilauea's summit expands between eruptions indicates that magma moves upward at a rate of about 100 million cubic meters (130 million cubic yards) per year.

Volcanologists also monitor changes in Kilauea's shape with electronic measuring devices that use laser beams to determine the precise distance between fixed points on the summit. An increase in the distance indicates that the summit is expanding, a sign that the magma chamber is filling. In 1987, observatory scientists became the first to use earth-orbiting satellites for this purpose. Radio signals from the satellites are picked up by receivers on Kilauea to mark the receivers' positions accurately. Repeated measurements enable the scientists at the observatory to obtain especially precise measurements of changes in the shape of the volcano.

Information from Kilauea's tiltmeters and electronic monitoring devices is used to determine how fast the volcano is inflating, a key indicator of whether an eruption is likely in the near future. Most eruptions at Kilauea occur when the bulge at the summit is highly inflated or when the rate of inflation speeds up.

Measurements of the decrease in slope during an eruption give scientists an estimate of the amount of magma moving out of the magma chamber. This may indicate how long the eruption is likely to last. When a new eruption begins at Kilauea, lava usually pours out at the rate of about 500,000 cubic meters (650,000 cubic yards) per hour. This is much faster than the rate at which magma is entering the magma chamber, so Kilauea's summit quickly deflates. For example, the current eruption along the East Rift began with the ejection of fountains of lava—sometimes 500 meters (1,500 feet) high—that occurred intermittently and lasted from several hours to a few days, separated by quiet periods of about a month.

Occasionally, however, lava comes out at a slower rate of about 500,000 cubic meters per day. This rate is similar to that at which magma enters the magma chamber, and so eruptions of this kind can last for many months or years. In mid-1986, the Kilauea eruption shifted to this slow, steady type.

This shift formed a small lava lake along the East Rift about 19 kilometers (12 miles) east of Kilauea's summit. Spillovers from the lake created several *lava tubes*. These tunnels of lava form when the surface of a lava stream cools and solidifies, forming a crust. Lava continues to flow inside the tube, however. The main tubes run for 12 kilometers (7 miles) down the flank of Kilauea to the ocean.

Because the lava in the tubes is insulated by overlying crusts of rock, the lava stays hot and travels farther than exposed lava flowing across the surface. As a result, the lava flows eventually were able to reach the sea. Normally, the sea wears away the land. But there, the lava has created new rock that is pushing back the waves. During 1990, Kilauea added areas of new land the size of several football fields to the island of Hawaii.

Sometimes, however, a lava tube becomes blocked with pieces of solid lava rock. This causes the molten lava to break through the roof of the lava tube and flow across the surface, often forming a new tube system. Such breakouts were responsible for the destruction of Kalapana in 1990.

Forecasting eruptions

Knowing a volcano's history and habits helps scientists determine how likely the volcano is to erupt again. In some ways, forecasting what a volcano will do is like estimating how well an athlete will perform. A football player who has scored in every game during the first half of the season is likely—but not certain—to score in most of the games during the second half of the season.

Forecasts of Hawaiian eruptions are regarded with interest but not panic because these eruptions are seldom life threatening. This is not the case for forecasts of possible eruptions of more dangerous volcanoes, such as Mount St. Helens.

Mount St. Helens began erupting on March 27, 1980. A week earlier, an earthquake swarm marked the volcano's awakening after more than 100 years of sleep. A bulge about 1 kilometer (⅔ mile) wide began to form high on the north side of the volcano. As the bulge grew, small eruptions blasted out a crater in the volcano's icy

The fate of volcanoes is to lose their fire and erode away like Ship Rock, an extinct volcano that rises 511 meters (1,678 feet) above the desert in New Mexico. The upper and outer layers of the volcano have worn away, leaving only spires of cooled and hardened magma.

summit. Finally, on May 18, a huge landslide and eruption occurred. The explosion killed 57 people, caused more than $1 billion in damage, and devastated more than 500 square kilometers (200 square miles) of forest.

Did geologists forecast this great eruption? The answer is yes and no. In 1978, geologists at the United States Geological Survey published a report that pointed out Mount St. Helens' dangerous past. They wrote: "In the future Mount St. Helens probably will erupt violently . . . perhaps even before the end of this century." That was a good forecast, as eruption forecasts go. But did any of the geologists monitoring the volcano on May 17, 1980, know that a deadly eruption was going to happen the next morning? The answer to that question is definitely no.

Should people be evacuated when a dangerous volcano is restless? Although evacuation may save lives, it may sometimes cause unneeded alarm and disruption. In the case of Mount St. Helens, scientists, to be on the safe side, recommended restricting travel into the area surrounding the mountain. Closing the roads, however, disrupted the lives of the people in the area and hurt local businesses. Ironically, the restrictions were being challenged in court when the great eruption occurred.

In 1985, Colombian geologists warned residents of the town of Armero that an eruption of the nearby Nevado del Ruiz volcano might cause dangerous mudflows. But only a few people had left when a small eruption melted part of the icecap on the volcano's summit. Giant floods of mud-thickened water swept down the volcano's sides, killing 25,000 people.

In 1983, a forecast in Indonesia had a more successful conclusion. When Colo Volcano on the island of Una Una was shaken by earthquakes followed by small eruptions, 7,000 people were evacuated. Five days after the eruptions began, the island was devastated by a major explosive eruption.

For volcanologists, the present challenge in forecasting eruptions lies not so much in developing new volcano-monitoring techniques as it does in applying known techniques to dangerous volcanoes. Only a few of the 1,300 potentially dangerous volcanoes in the world are being studied in detail, mostly because governments often are unable to fund such research or fail to recognize its importance. As a result, eruptions continue to take their toll in human life. Perhaps, despite our growing understanding of these violent and spectacular events, an old saying offers the best solution: "Hope for the best, but plan for the worst."

For further reading:

Bullard, Fred M. *Volcanoes of the Earth.* University of Texas Press, 1984.
Decker, Robert and Barbara. *Volcanoes.* W. H. Freeman and Company, 1989.
Tilling, Robert I.; Heliker, Christina; and Wright, Thomas L. *Eruptions of Hawaiian Volcanoes: Past, Present, and Future.* U.S. Geological Survey, U.S. Government Printing Office, 1987.

Enthusiasm for recycling is at an all-time high. But what actually happens to recyclable materials after they are separated from trash?

The Technology Behind Recycling

BY JON R. LUOMA

A plastic soft-drink bottle and a sleeping bag may not seem to have anything in common. Yet the two are linked by the technology of recycling. After serving its useful life, the bottle can be chopped up, melted down, and reborn as the sleeping bag's stuffing. Recycling technology allows yesterday's newspapers to be transformed into tomorrow's cereal boxes. Old beverage cans become new ones. Even the steel in junked cars and demolished skyscrapers and the aluminum in aging airliners can be reclaimed for new uses.

Recycling efforts have increased dramatically in the United States, chiefly because of a mounting garbage crisis. According to the U.S. Environmental Protection Agency (EPA), each American produces an average of 1.8 kilograms (4 pounds) of garbage every day. The garbage thrown away each year by households and businesses totals about 163 million metric tons (180 million short tons)—enough to fill a line of garbage trucks that encircles the Earth five times.

By the late 1980's, Americans recycled about 13 per cent of their garbage. But the greatest amount of garbage by far—about 73 per cent—went into soil-covered dumps called *landfills*. Large municipal incinerators burned the remaining 14 per cent.

Burying garbage or burning it—the two traditional methods for disposing of wastes—are not ideal solutions, according to many environmental experts. Across much of America, communities are running out of space for landfills. Even where space for new landfills is available, local residents often object to them as unsightly and environmentally unsafe. Moreover, toxic chemicals in used batteries, paints, pesticides, and other discarded items may seep from landfills that are not tightly sealed and contaminate underground water supplies. Although incinerators reduce wastes to ash, they also can pollute the air. And the ash, which may be contaminated with toxic chemicals, itself must be disposed of—usually in a landfill.

While landfills and incineration aim at getting garbage out of sight, recycling involves a different concept entirely: viewing garbage as a potential resource rather than as a waste. The tons of garbage that Americans throw out every day contain a lode of valuable materials, including aluminum, steel, copper, glass, plastics, and paper.

The benefits of recycling do not stop at stemming the tremendous flood of trash or even at extracting useful resources from it. Recycling also can bring about striking energy savings. For example, manufacturing a 12-ounce beverage can from the aluminum-bearing ore bauxite expends energy equal to 6 ounces (180 milliliters) of gasoline—half the can's volume. Industry experts calculate that a new container can be manufactured from recycled aluminum for only 5 per cent of that energy expenditure—equivalent to a thimbleful of gasoline. Thus, throwing away even one aluminum can is equivalent to wasting half a can of gas.

All these benefits have sparked efforts to improve what is actually an old technology. Glassmakers have melted and re-formed glass bottles for at least 3,000 years. Once a precious resource, paper has been recycled for hundreds of years. And manufacturers have melted down and recast scrap steel and aluminum since the late 1800's. But the recent drive to recycle huge volumes of household garbage has led to more sophisticated methods for sorting and processing. And engineers are creating new technologies to recycle such modern products as plastics and glossy papers.

Recycling consists of three key steps. The first step involves sorting reusable materials from other refuse; the second, processing the sorted materials for use as raw materials; and the third, making new products from the processed wastes.

Sorting: A crucial step

Sorting is critical because each type of recyclable material is processed differently. In most cases, recycling equipment works properly only when it receives wastes that have little "contamination" from other materials. Equipment that recycles paper, for example, can be damaged if metal or plastic is mixed with the paper.

Thirty states have passed laws that encourage people to separate recyclable materials from the stream of household trash. Some towns and cities provide drop-off centers, where residents can deliver glass

The author:
Jon R. Luoma is a freelance writer and a contributing editor to *Audubon* magazine.

Curbing the Garbage Glut

Recycling is becoming increasingly important as the amount of household and industrial waste produced in the United States grows steadily, *top right*. Most garbage ends up in landfills, even though much of it consists of recyclable materials—including paper, yard wastes, and metals, *center right*. By the late 1980's, households and businesses were recycling 13 per cent of their garbage, *bottom right*.

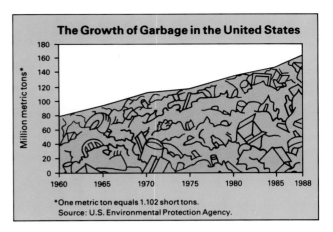

The Growth of Garbage in the United States

Million metric tons*

*One metric ton equals 1.102 short tons.
Source: U.S. Environmental Protection Agency.

and plastic bottles, newspapers, and tin and aluminum cans. And more than 1,600 U.S. communities offer curbside collection of recyclable wastes. In curbside collection, households sort recyclables before placing them at the curb for pickup by garbage trucks outfitted with separate compartments for different materials—usually glass, metals, newspapers, and plastics.

Although it's far cheaper for local governments if households separate their recyclable wastes, people cannot always be counted on to do so. Therefore, at least 40 communities have built specialized plants called *material recovery facilities* (MRF's) that accept mixed recyclables from curbside collection programs. MRF's employ a combination of people and machines to do the sorting.

One of the most highly automated MRF's in the United States opened in Johnston, R.I., in 1989. Trucks haul recyclable refuse to the plant, where newspapers are set aside and the rest is dumped onto a conveyor belt. An electromagnet then sweeps over the conveyor and picks up tin cans. Tin cans are actually made of steel plated with a thin layer of tin. The iron in the steel is attracted to the magnet.

The remaining wastes on the conveyor ride up an inclined, vibrating ramp, which uses gravity to separate heavy glass from lighter-weight aluminum and plastic. A series of "curtains"—thin metal bars suspended across the ramp—stops the aluminum and plastic containers from sliding backward down the ramp but allows glass bottles and jars to roll down. The glass items spill

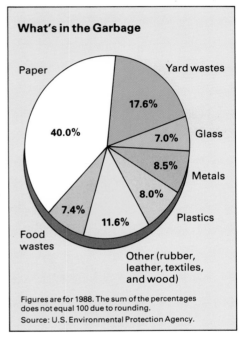

What's in the Garbage

- Paper 40.0%
- Yard wastes 17.6%
- Glass 7.0%
- Metals 8.5%
- Plastics 8.0%
- Other (rubber, leather, textiles, and wood) 11.6%
- Food wastes 7.4%

Figures are for 1988. The sum of the percentages does not equal 100 due to rounding.
Source: U.S. Environmental Protection Agency.

How Much Garbage Is Recycled

- Paper.................25.6%
- Metals................14.6%
- Glass.................12.0%
- Yard wastes...........1.6%
- Plastics..............1.1%
- Food wastes...........0.0%

Figures are for 1988.
Source: U.S. Environmental Protection Agency.

Sorting: The First Step

The recycling process begins with the separation of recyclable materials from other trash. In some communities, wastes hand sorted by residents are loaded onto trucks that have separate compartments for each recyclable material, *below.* In other communities, machines are used to separate recyclable wastes from one another, *right.*

onto another conveyor belt, where workers hand sort them by color.

The aluminum and plastic containers next move onto a steel conveyor, which carries an electric charge. This sends a current through the aluminum cans but does not affect the plastic containers. The conveyor carries the recyclables over an electromagnet. The magnet repels the current in the aluminum cans, causing them to fly off the conveyor and into a hopper. The plastics then drop onto another conveyor, where workers hand sort them by type. After sorting, the various recyclable wastes are sold to companies that process them into raw materials.

Metals: From scrap to riches

Metals fetch the highest prices of recycled materials, because recycling saves the huge costs of mining and processing ores. Recycling 1 ton of discarded aluminum, for example, eliminates the need to mine 4 tons of bauxite.

The largest single source of scrap aluminum is beverage cans. Americans recycled about 56 billion cans in 1990, just over 60 per cent of all the cans produced. Other household sources of aluminum include foil pie plates and frozen-dinner trays; lawn furniture; building siding, gutters, and frames for windows and doors.

In the first stage of recycling, aluminum cans are flattened for

Recycling Metal

Metals are the most valuable recycled materials, because recycling metals is cheaper than extracting metal from ores. In the recycling process, items are separated according to the types of metals, then melted, and re-formed. All metals can be endlessly remelted and reused.

Used aluminum beverage cans are crushed and baled for shipment to a reprocessing plant, *above.*

Chief sources of recycled metals:

Aluminum—beverage cans, foil pie plates, frozen-food trays, lawn chairs, building siding, window and door frames, gutters.
Steel—food and drink cans, automobiles, refrigerators and other appliances.

A huge electromagnet helps separate iron and steel from other materials, *left.*

Recycled aluminum is melted in an industrial furnace, *above.* The molten aluminum is then cast into rectangular blocks called *ingots, left,* which can later be formed into new products.

Items made from recycled metals:

Aluminum—any aluminum products.
Steel—any steel products.

shipment to a remelting facility, where a machine called a *hammermill* pounds the cans into shreds the size of potato chips. The shreds are next heated to burn off printed labels on the outside of the cans and the lacquer coating on the inside. The shredded aluminum is then melted in a furnace. The molten aluminum can be cast into blocks called *ingots* and, while still hot, rolled into sheets for new cans.

The recycling of other metals, such as steel, follows similar steps. Automobiles, for example, are flattened by a huge machine called a *baling crusher*. Another machine pounds or shreds the steel into fist-sized pieces for shipment. Heat burns off paint; then the metal is melted and cast into forms that manufacturers can use in making new products.

A whopping 66 per cent of all the steel discarded in the United States in 1988 was recycled. Most of that steel, however, was recovered not from the tin cans Americans dump in their household garbage but from broken-down heavy machinery, structural beams from demolished buildings, and, above all, junked automobiles.

Household recycling of discarded tin-plated steel cans occurs at a far lower rate. Only about 15 per cent of the 100 million tin cans used each day in the United States were recycled in 1988, according to the Steel Can Recycling Institute, an industry organization. Yet steel cans may offer more recycling promise than other household refuse because their magnetic properties make automatic sorting easy.

Steel became more recyclable than ever in the 1980's, when facilities called *minimills* sprang up in many parts of the United States. Minimills produce steel entirely from scrap and need lots of it to keep operating. To help satisfy the growing demand for scrap, the steel industry is setting up a nationwide collection network for steel cans.

The recycling of metals does not stop at steel and aluminum, though these are the two metals most commonly found in household wastes. Scrap copper comes from old electric wiring and telephone cables. Automobile dismantlers sell catalytic converters for the recycling value of their palladium and batteries for their lead. Gold, platinum, and other precious metals are recovered from electronic devices. All metals can be melted down for reuse again and again.

It takes huge amounts of energy to refine and smelt ores, and so recycling yields enormous energy savings: 95 per cent in the case of aluminum and 74 per cent for steel. In fact, steel recycling in the United States saves enough energy in a single year to provide the electricity needed to power the city of Los Angeles for eight years, according to the Steel Can Recycling Institute.

Paper: Beating to a pulp

Americans throw away more paper (including cardboard) than anything else. In fact, paper accounts for about 40 per cent of household and office trash by weight. At the same time, consumers collected about a fourth of the discarded paper for recycling in 1988.

The recycling of waste paper takes place in several steps, beginning

Recycling paper

Paper recycling is a fairly simple process in which the paper is turned into a watery pulp, dried, and re-formed. Although more and more paper is recycled in the United States every year, it can be reprocessed only a limited number of times. Each time paper is recycled, its fibers weaken.

Old newspapers collected for recycling, *top*, are dumped at a paper mill. There, the papers—whole or chopped—are fed into a vat of water and chemicals, *right*. A spinning blade in the vat churns the mixture, removing inks and reducing the paper to a mass of pulpy fibers. The fibers are dried on screens and formed into new paper, which is wound into rolls for shipment, *bottom*.

95

in a huge vat called a *hydropulper*, which operates much the same way as a kitchen blender. The hydropulper has a blade that agitates a mixture of paper and water, beating the paper's tightly woven woody fibers literally to a *pulp*—an oatmeallike mass of individual fibers. Detergents added to the pulp dissolve printing inks. Water then flushes the inks away. The pulp next passes through huge screens that filter out foreign material, such as staples, paper clips, or dirt.

At this point, the recycled pulp can be processed much like the paper's original wood pulp. The wet pulp is usually sprayed onto a large, flat screen. The screen permits some of the water to drain away so that the fibers begin to form a mat. The mat is pressed and dried as it travels on a conveyor belt between a series of rollers and heated cylinders. The dried paper is then wound into large rolls.

Paper mills turn recycled pulp into a number of finished products besides rolls of paper. They can recycle newspapers, for example, into a lightweight cardboard called *paperboard* for use in boxes. Most cereal boxes are now made from recycled paper, as are many other food boxes. You can identify a box made from recycled paper simply by looking inside: A gray or brown interior indicates the box is made from recycled paper. Other products made from recycled paper include toilet and facial tissue, paper towels, brown bags, cardboard egg cartons, and wallboard and insulation for construction.

Not all kinds of paper are easily recycled. The glossy papers used in magazines and catalogs present particular problems, because the clays that form the glossy coating clog the hydropulper. Moreover, while deinking detergents dissolve newspaper inks well, they are far less effective on the plastic-based inks used in magazines and, increasingly, in color images in newspapers.

But a breakthrough is at hand. Several recycling mills now under construction will pioneer a new deinking technology called *flotation*, which uses the clays in glossy papers to help remove inks. In a flotation system, air bubbles are forced upward from the bottom of the hydropulper to agitate the mixture of paper and water. Clay loosened from the glossy paper starts to sink toward the bottom of the vat but is picked up and carried along by the rising bubbles. As the clay in the bubbles rises, it acts as a kind of blotter, absorbing inks. The bubbles of inks and clay are finally skimmed from the surface. At least 20 mills plan to add flotation systems by 1992.

Glass: From bottle to bottle

Glass is also easily recycled. Glass, however, must be hand sorted by color, and this presents the chief complication in recycling it. Mixtures of clear, green, and brown glass produce a recycled container with a dark, mottled color, unacceptable to food and beverage companies, which usually use clear glass containers for their products. The 5 billion glass bottles and jars that Americans recycled in the late 1980's represented only about 12 per cent of all the glass containers produced in the United States.

Recycling Glass

Glass can be collected, crushed, melted, and reused over and over again.

Glass recyclables must be hand sorted by color, *right.* If new glass were made from a mixture of colored glass, it would have a brown color, unacceptable to food and beverage packagers.

Once separated by color, glass bottles and jars are smashed into fragments called *cullet, right.* The cullet is melted in a glass-making furnace, and the syrupy, molten glass is molded by machine into new containers, *below.*

Once glass is sorted, magnets remove any steel caps and lids. Then glass jars and bottles enter a *crusher*, a machine that grinds the glass into a gravellike material called *cullet*. Crushing also loosens any paper labels on the containers, which, being lightweight, can be removed by suction. The cullet, mixed with sand and other raw materials, is then melted into a syrupy mass in a glassmaking furnace. When the molten glass pours out of the furnace, machines mold it into new bottles and jars. Like metal, glass can be melted down over and over.

Plastics: Trouble in numbers

Plastics make up about 20 per cent of the volume of household and office trash. But only about 1 per cent was recovered for recycling by the end of the 1980's. Because the use of plastics keeps growing, several hundred U.S. communities have considered banning certain types of plastic packaging in an effort to control the garbage glut. Alarmed by the threat of bans, plastics manufacturers have begun looking for ways to recycle their products.

One of the problems facing plastics recyclers is that plastics comprise many different materials, all consisting of long chains of molecules called *polymers*. Each polymer has its own chemical structure and properties, giving us such dissimilar plastic products as a thin film of shrink wrap, squeezable mustard bottles, and hard football helmets. Altogether, there are 46 different plastics polymers in common use today. Recycling efforts so far have focused on only a few easily collected polymers, especially *high-density polyethylene* (HDPE)—used in milk and detergent jugs—and *polyethylene terephthalate* (PET)—used in soft-drink and some vegetable oil bottles.

The number of different polymers makes sorting plastics costly and time consuming. To simplify the process, 27 states have passed laws requiring plastic containers to be stamped with a code that identifies its polymer. Such coding should help as long as consumers prove willing to search for the codes and carefully sort the containers.

An automated plastics sorting process, however, may come from the Rutgers University Center for Plastics Recycling Research in Piscataway, N.J. Researchers there have developed an experimental system that identifies common polymers by means of gamma rays and infrared rays, two forms of electromagnetic radiation.

In the Rutgers system, a conveyor belt carries a variety of plastic bottles through a screening device, which resembles luggage-screening machines at airports. The device projects a weak beam of gamma rays at the bottles. Plastics polymers consist largely of carbon and hydrogen atoms, which do not reflect gamma rays. But the polymer *polyvinyl chloride* (PVC), used in some vegetable oil bottles, also contains chlorine atoms, which do reflect gamma rays. When sensors in the screening device detect reflected gamma rays, they trigger an air compressor, which expels a burst of air that knocks the PVC bottles off the conveyor. Farther along the line, a beam of infrared

Recycling Plastics

Plastics recycling is still in its infancy. Many different plastics are on the market, and they must be sorted by type for recycling. To simplify sorting, some states require manufacturers to stamp them with an identifying code. Plastics can be reprocessed a limited number of times. Only three types of plastics are being turned into new products today.

Chief sources of recycled plastics:
High-density polyethylene (HDPE)—milk jugs.
Polyethylene terephthalate (PET)—clear plastic bottles used for soda and some vegetable oils.
Polystyrene—foam coffee cups and egg cartons.

Soda bottles made of a lightweight, flexible plastic known as PET are crushed and baled before shipment to a processor, *above*. There, the bottles are shredded into flakes, *right*. PET is the most widely recycled plastic.

Most recycled PET is melted and formed into fibers. After forming, the fibers are picked up by rollers and plunged into a bath of water and chemicals, *left*. The fibers will be used to make carpeting and upholstery fabric.

Items made from recycled plastics:
HDPE—flowerpots, drainage pipes, marine piers, detergent bottles, shower stalls, recycling bins.
PET—fiberfill, carpeting, nonfood bottles, shower curtains, paintbrushes.
Polystyrene—tape holders, rulers, and other desk supplies; videocassette boxes; trays; wastebaskets.
Mixed plastic waste—plastic "lumber," park benches, picnic tables.

light strikes the bottles. More light passes through clear plastic bottles of PET than through cloudy milk jugs or opaque detergent bottles of HDPE. Sensors detect these differences in light intensity and trigger the bursts of air that separate the bottles.

A second experimental system uses a flotation tank, which sorts ground-up plastics by density: Lighter polymers, such as HDPE, tend to float, and heavier polymers, such as PVC and PET, tend to sink. In addition, a device called a *hydrocyclone*, now in use at advanced recycling facilities, also takes advantage of differences in density to sort plastics. This cone-shaped machine spins flakes of mixed plastics in water. As they spin, centrifugal force pushes the heavier plastics to the wall and gravity pulls them down the cone. The lighter plastics remain in whirling water at the center of the cone. Opening a valve at the bottom of the hydrocyclone allows heavier plastics to pour out. Another valve at the top releases lighter plastics.

At Rensselaer Polytechnic Institute in Troy, N.Y., researchers are experimenting with a system that sorts mixed plastic wastes by melting them. Each polymer melts at a different temperature, permitting workers to melt one type of plastic in the mix, draw it out of the bottom of the vat, then raise the temperature to melt another.

The nation's largest plastics recycler, Wellman Incorporated of Shrewsbury, N.J., has pioneered the recycling of clear 1-liter soft-drink bottles constructed of two different polymers. Most of the bottle—the upper, transparent portion—is made of PET. The bottom of the bottle, a more rigid cup, is HDPE. The Wellman process cuts the HDPE cup from the bottom of the bottle and shreds the PET. The shredded PET is fed into an *extruder*, a machine that melts the PET and forces the molten plastic through a narrow opening, producing threadlike fibers. Wellman sells the fibers, which are indistinguishable from brand-new plastic fibers, to carpet manu-facturers and makers of such fiber-filled items as sleeping bags and parkas. The HDPE goes into such products as detergent bottles.

At Rutgers University, scientists and engineers have turned foam coffee cups into plastic lumber. Their process converts a variety of plastics—including *polystyrene*, a polymer used in foam cups and fast-food containers—into a rigid, heavy-duty plastic. A machine first shreds the unsorted plastics into dime-sized flakes, which are washed and filtered to remove contaminants. Another machine melts the flakes into a puddinglike material, which can be molded to form boards, planks, posts, or the parts for park benches. Recycled plastics have been made into a variety of other products, including shower stalls, combs, lunch trays, videocassette holders, and flowerpots.

Leftovers again?

Although paper, metals, glass, and plastics constitute the bulk of recycled products, a wide range of other items are potentially recyclable. Americans throw away some 240 million tires each year, about one per person. About 5 per cent of those tires are recycled, chiefly by grinding them into crumbs. This *crumb rubber* can be molded into new products or mixed with asphalt for surfacing highways and athletic fields. Even yard and food wastes can be recycled as a mulch by allowing them to decay in a compost heap.

But recycling is not the magic answer to America's garbage. Even if every individual in every household were to become completely committed to it, recycling would not solve all our waste problems.

Paper and plastics, unlike metals and glass, can be turned around only a few times. Recycling processes shorten, and thereby weaken, the fibers in paper. Processors blend repulped paper with fresh pulp as a means of strengthening the finished product, but each grade of paper tends to be recycled into a slightly lower grade. Thus, high-grade office papers might get reprocessed into newsprint, newsprint into paperboard, and paperboard into tissue.

Recycling also weakens the polymers in plastics. Besides becoming less durable, plastics usually turn a muddy brown during recycling because of the colored plastics that are mixed into the process. To improve the appearance of recycled plastics products, manufacturers often dye them black.

Finding someone to buy recyclable trash poses one of the thorniest recycling problems, as many communities discovered in 1989. That year, after hundreds of communities turned to paper recycling to avoid running out of landfill space, the supply of newsprint for recycling suddenly outstripped demand. Paper mills could not process the deluge of paper or find new buyers for recycled paper and paperboard. The situation is improving, however, as newspapers begin using more recycled paper.

Just how much household trash can be recycled? Some wastes are impossible to separate and sort by current methods. For example, some food companies now package products in airtight bags that combine plastic and aluminum foil. Other food packaging becomes too contaminated with food for conventional recycling processes.

Even so, the magazine *Waste Age* estimated that, with vigorous effort, an American community could recycle half its household trash. Considering that Americans recycled only about 13 per cent of their waste in 1989, recycling efforts clearly have far to go.

Enthusiasm for recycling in 1991 was at an all-time high, however. Community support had spurred legislatures to pass laws that encourage recycling and had led industry to seek new ways of sorting and processing recyclable materials. With the backing of industry, new technology should help clean up some of America's mess. Technology, after all, made possible America's throwaway society.

For further reading

Bell, John. "Plastics: Waste Not, Want Not." *New Scientist,* Dec. 1, 1990, pp. 44-47.
Luoma, Jon R. "Trash Can Realities." *Audubon,* March 1990, pp. 86-97.
Wilcox, Charlotte. *Trash!* Carolrhoda, 1988.

An interview with Robert Bakker
conducted by Darlene R. Stille

Dinosaur Scientist

This student of dinosaur fossils tells
how he came to make the study of
prehistoric creatures his life's work
and explains how he made some of
his most important findings.

. . . why doesn't every-one maintain their first love with nature, with dinosaurs, or horses, or elephants, or whales?

The author:
Darlene R. Stille is the managing editor of *Science Year.*

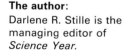

Science Year: When you were only in the fourth grade, you decided to dedicate your life to studying dinosaurs. Many fourth graders are fascinated with dinosaurs, but they grow up to be police officers, doctors, lawyers, accountants, and carpenters. What inspired you at such an early age to choose the study of dinosaurs as your life career?

Bakker: Actually, it was a magazine, the Sept. 7, 1953, issue of *Life* magazine with dinosaurs on the cover. And I still have the magazine today. At that time, I was visiting my grandfather's house in Midland Park, N.J., and this magazine was sitting on the porch table. I opened it up and found not just fantastic pictures of dinosaurs, early reptiles, and sea monsters, but an article entitled "The Pageant of Life." It was the story of how evolution works. It was wonderful. What got me was not just that dinosaurs were neat and grotesque, but that they were part of a much bigger story, a great historical pageant.

SY: What, exactly, did you learn about this bigger story from the article in *Life* magazine?

Bakker: I learned that there are wonderful things going on in nature that cause change, that cause evolution. These natural patterns of change eventually produce the spectacular natural sculpture that we call turtles or dinosaurs or horses. It produced all the wonderful prehistoric things you can see in museums. And that struck me as just about the neatest thing I could think about. So in the fourth grade, in 1954, I announced to my parents that I'd spend the rest of my life studying dinosaurs—how they evolved, how they changed, and how they were related to other things. And my parents nodded their heads and said, "That's nice, dear. It's a stage. You'll grow out of it."

SY: Why didn't you grow out of that stage?

Bakker: I'd like to turn that question around. What I would ask is why doesn't everyone maintain their first love with nature, with dinosaurs, or horses, or elephants, or whales? You take any kid to a zoo or museum and they'll be captivated by what they see. But that captivation dies away in high school. Why? I think part of it is that the adult world tells kids, "Hey, to like zoos and museums is a childish thing. You shouldn't like them. Be interested in dating and cars or making money." Maybe part of the problem we have with getting people to face our current ecological crisis is that they have lost that sense of wonder at nature. Nevertheless, you'll find a lot of adults enjoy taking their kids to the museum to look at dinosaurs.

SY: Why do you think youngsters are so totally fascinated with dinosaurs?

Bakker: I think a large part of their interest lies in the fact that dinosaurs are real monsters. They are nature's best special effects, produced by evolution. Kids like monstrous things, and they like to go to museums and see these real monsters.

SY: Did you go to the museums a lot when you were a youngster?

Bakker: Yes. We lived in New Jersey and my mom would take me to the American Museum of Natural History in New York City a couple of times a year. When I saw a brontosaur skeleton for the first time,

Robert T. Bakker

When he was 8 years old, Robert Bakker became fascinated with dinosaurs, and he has made the study of them his life's work. The results of his research have changed the way we view dinosaurs—not as sluggish, cold-blooded reptiles, but as active, warm-blooded, and highly successful animals that dominated the Earth for 165 million years. He now spends long weeks with his wife, Constance, and his team of dinosaur-fossil hunters in the rocky Badlands of Wyoming. And he also spends long hours at home piecing together not only the fragments of bone they find from Jurassic Period dinosaurs but also the larger story of what that dinosaur looked like, how it lived, and how it evolved into the form it had more than 135 million years ago.

Robert T. Bakker was born on March 24, 1945, in Teaneck, N.J., and began doing serious scientific research while still in high school. His first research project involved the study of leg movement and motion in *Anchisaurus* (also called *Yaleosaurus*), a type of dinosaur whose fossils are found in Massachusetts and Connecticut.

He attended Yale University in New Haven, Conn., where he did an elaborate series of dissections of animal legs in various species and made films showing how the front leg worked in different animals. He then began to argue that, on the basis of their leg structure, dinosaurs were fast runners and must have been able to maneuver easily. His first scientific paper was published just before he received his B.S. degree from Yale in 1968. He earned a Ph.D. from Harvard University in Cambridge, Mass., in 1976.

After graduating, he became an associate professor of geology at Johns Hopkins University in Baltimore. But, because he was the only faculty member on the undergraduate campus who thoroughly understood gross anatomy, he was given the assignment of teaching anatomy to premedical students. In addition, every summer, he taught a course in field geology and field biology, which involved six weeks of camping and digging up dinosaur fossils in Wyoming.

In 1983, Bakker moved to Boulder, Colo., where he became an associate professor at the University of Colorado and adjunct curator of paleontology at the university's museum. Bakker had long been interested in the educational aspects of museums. While at Yale, he had served as the Peabody Museum's docent in charge of special programs for children and director of the Children's Summer Program. He has also set up permanent museum exhibits at the University of Colorado Museum.

Bakker has become famous for changing our views about dinosaurs. While the traditional view of dinosaurs held that they were cold-blooded, sluggish, reptilelike creatures, Bakker argued that they were warm-blooded and fast-moving. Instead of being dull and grayish, Bakker portrayed dinosaurs as colorful creatures, perhaps even covered with feathers. On 15 expeditions in the American West to excavate at fossil beds dating from the Mesozoic and Early Tertiary periods, Bakker discovered 2 new species of Jurassic dinosaurs and 11 new species of early mammals. He has written about 40 scientific articles and a book, *The Dinosaur Heresies* (1986).

Bakker and his wife live with their dog, Prance, in the foothills of the Rocky Mountains on the edge of Boulder. His home also serves as a paleontology laboratory and an art studio. There he studies new-found fossil bones in what was once the garage area. And, in the natural sunlight that streams into the second floor, Bakker, an accomplished artist, renders on paper his action-packed visions of dinosaurs.

I thought it was great. All the bones were polished and shiny. But, again, what got me wasn't just that there were a couple of big dinosaurs. In the exhibit, there was also this wonderfully intricate story of dinosaurs: little animals and big animals, animals hatching out of eggs, and dinosaur footprints. There was a little fossil reptile with its skeleton on a mirror so you could see the underside. This was great showmanship. I'd take my drawing tablet and make drawings and sketches. My mom would sit there and read.

SY: No doubt many young people would like to spend their lives studying dinosaurs. What kind of an education does a person need for this? How should a young person wanting to study dinosaurs begin?

Digging for Dinosaur Bones

Although dinosaurs once lived all over the world, their fossils are preserved only in such areas as Como Bluff, a desolate rock formation in Wyoming, which 130 million years ago was a swamp.

Bakker and his team find tiny fossil fragments by crawling along the ground. These pieces indicate that larger bones are nearby. When the dinosaurs died, their bones were preserved in sediment layers formed by the swamp. Wind and rain erosion has exposed the bones again.

Physicist James Fila, an "unpaid professional" on Bakker's team, measures a bone from a huge whalelike dinosaur. The bone was found sticking out from an eroded rock formation at Como Bluff in 1990.

After uncovering a large fossil bone, Bakker's team members carefully clean it. Over millions of years, the buried bone has cracked and broken into many large and small fragments.

Before lifting the bone out of the ground for transport back to the laboratory in Boulder, Colo., the fossil hunters cover it with plaster. This holds all of the pieces of bone together.

At his laboratory in what was once the garage of his home, Bakker sifts through the fossil fragments in the plaster cast, sorting out the pieces he will later glue together to reassemble the limb of a now-extinct dinosaur.

Bakker: Get ahold of a chicken. It's very hard to get ahold of an entire chicken with the head and the feet. But you might find one at a farmers' market or a kosher market. And take apart the chicken; take the meat, which are the muscles, off the bones so that you can see the relationship between the muscles and the bones. And it's very important not to read any books ahead of time, because muscles have ridiculous names, difficult and confusing names. Just approach the chicken and ask, "What does this muscle do?" Then pull on the meat, and you can see how it moves the leg, for example.

SY: How would studying the bones and muscles of a chicken help a person studying dinosaurs?

Bakker: Because the chicken is built very much like the ferocious dinosaur *Tyrannosaurus rex,* and here's how you can see this firsthand: Make a few mechanical diagrams of how your chicken works, of the muscles that move the bones. Then create a chicken skeleton by taking the meat off the bones. Boil the bones gently in a 10 per cent bleach solution to get rid of the last of the meat, then let the bones dry out, and put a layer of shellac or other sealer on them. Now you have a pretty good skeleton. Put the skeleton in a shoebox and take this box of bones to a museum that has a skeleton of *Tyrannosaurus rex* on display. Look closely at *T. rex* and look closely at your chicken. You'll see that they're built pretty much the same way. Now, you can put the muscles back on the *T. rex* by making diagrams, and pretty soon, in your diagrams, you can make the *T. rex* knee move and make its tail move and its back move.

SY: Why is a chicken like a dinosaur?

Bakker: Birds are living dinosaurs. Birds are direct descendants of dinosaurs, and most of their body parts still closely resemble those of dinosaurs such as *Tyrannosaurus rex.* So you can learn a lot about extinct dinosaurs by taking apart a living species of chicken or turkey.

SY: Did you take apart a chicken?

Bakker: Sure did. Still do. And I spent a lot of time in zoos watching animals move. In order to understand dinosaurs, you've got to see the architecture of bones moving; the only way to understand a skeleton is to see it moving. You can't see a dinosaur move, but you can study how living animals move. Borrow a little handheld camcorder, go to the zoo, and make some tapes of animals moving. Watch the tapes and see how an elephant moves its knee and how that's different from the way a turkey moves. What you are seeing is the choreography of the skeleton—how these structures move.

SY: You had your formal training at Yale and Harvard universities. Other than taking apart a chicken and making observations at museums and zoos, what kind of formal education would a person need in order to study dinosaurs? What should a young person study in school?

Bakker: Well, basic science, of course, but also history. Evolution is history. You have to have a sense of the complexity of history and of the study of complex units. A good history course—English, ancient, or medieval history—is one of the most useful trainings for your

Get ahold of a chicken. . . . an entire chicken with the head and the feet. . . . And take apart the chicken—take the meat, which are the muscles, off the bones so that you can see the relationship between the muscles and the bones. . . . Just approach the chicken and ask, "What does this muscle do?"

mind. Most science is taught outside the context of time. In chemistry you learn that standard chemical reactions happen the same way every time. In biology, you learn how the heart pumps, same way every time. We do not learn about an evolving heart, an evolving cell membrane, or an evolving chemical operation. We learn nonhistorical science, and that is very misleading. You've got to train your mind to study things that change and interact and change as they interact. That's evolution.

SY: Evolution has long been a misunderstood and controversial concept. Is that because evolution is so difficult to understand?

Bakker: Evolution is the history of life. The only reason life has history is because of evolution. Evolution guarantees that life will change and it will change in both predictable and unpredictable ways. And evolution is a cruel history. Evolution works because almost all animals die soon after birth or hatching. Throughout the 3-billion-year history of life there has been this incredible natural killing-off of animals. And most plants also die after a very short time. It's very cruel. But the individual plants and animals usually differ among themselves a little bit genetically. This means that any small genetic change that by chance helps an individual animal to survive a little better can get passed along to the next generation. When I explain evolution to fourth graders they usually say, first of all, that it's really sad. Look at all the turtle kids, the crocodile kids, the ameba kids that die. But this terrible culling by death gives us evolutionary change. And that's a wondrous thing.

SY: You consider evolutionary change to be a rare event. And you believe that these changes come in short bursts. Why?

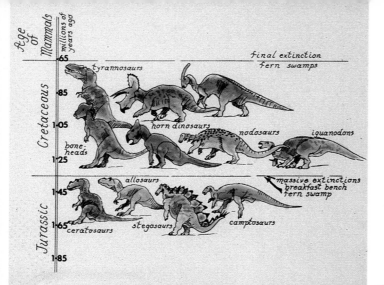

Age of Mammals | millions of years ago
Cretaceous
Jurassic

·65   final extinction
fern swamps

tyrannosaurs

·85

horn dinosaurs

·05   nodosaurs   iguanodons

bone-heads

·25

·45   allosaurs   massive extinctions
breakfast bench
fern swamp

·65   ceratosaurs   stegosaurs   camptosaurs

·85

Bakker the Artist

Not only a scientist, Bakker is also an artist, who puts his drawing ability to work in the service of dinosaur research.

Images of various species of dinosaurs that lived during the Jurassic and Cretaceous periods grace a Bakker diagram of the mass extinctions that took place at the ends of these periods.

With his drawing pad balanced on his knee, Bakker calls upon his knowledge of dinosaur anatomy to reconstruct the postures of two battling prehistoric monsters.

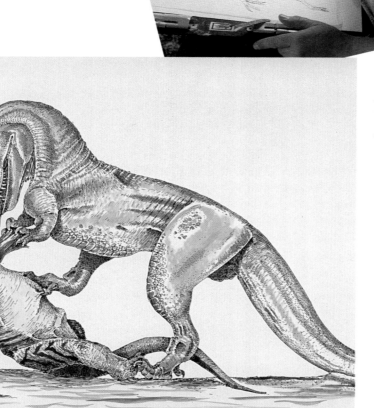

A ferocious dinosaur conquers and consumes its prey, a scene that reflects Bakker's views of dinosaurs as fast-moving, warm-blooded animals.

Bakker: I didn't come up with that idea. A man named Hugh Falconer did in 1860. Falconer was in India working as a surgeon, and he studied fossil elephants. He wrote about his studies to biologist Charles Darwin, who had just published his theory of evolution in *The Origin of Species*. Falconer told Darwin, yes, evolution occurs, but it's a rare event. I see in my fossil elephants that one species remains unchanged for a long time, despite changes in the environment. That idea was resurrected by Stephen Jay Gould in the early 1970's and called punctuated equilibrium.

SY: Why would evolution occur in these short bursts?

Bakker: A more important and interesting question is, why doesn't it occur all the time? The environment is changing, why don't the animals change all the time? Consider this scene: The ancient environment suddenly changes, so there is more grass and fewer trees. Suppose nature wants to cause evolution in the brontosaur to give it taller molars so it can eat grass. Suppose that nature could say, "All of the brontosaurs with slightly bigger teeth I will let live, and the other ones who were born with shorter teeth I am going to kill off." That's natural selection. This will make the brontosaur change its teeth. But it's not going to work, because the baby brontosaurs born with the mutations [changes in their genes] that give them better teeth might also have worse feet or foul tempers. The genes that control our shape and our physiology are not simple at all. The genes that control your front teeth are linked to other genes that control, perhaps, your hair color or your body size. So natural selection alone can't do it.

SY: What are the kinds of circumstances that you think lead to evolutionary change?

Bakker: You've got to have a very unusual event that allows you to separate some genes out to give you an improvement without some other bad thing happening. It can happen, for example, in a small population isolated and protected somewhere for a couple of dozen generations. This situation might favor the development of better teeth. And, even though that mutation causes something else bad to happen, in an isolated population there could be small, beneficial changes for a hundred generations and finally you get a new species. In order to get a new species of brontosaur, you've got to get a small population isolated from all other brontosaurs and maybe from all other predators, too, perhaps in northern Germany on a fairly big island for tens of thousands of years. That would give nature the opportunity to work on these guys and give them better teeth or better feet. Nature could also work on the side effects of these genetic changes, and, after a couple of thousand generations, produce a better brontosaur on that isolated island. Now let the water level fall and a land bridge appear, and the new species can spread from that, isolated island across Europe and Asia, giving the rest of the world a better brontosaur.

SY: Are there any other circumstances that result in a new species besides isolation?

Bakker: Probably not. Most of the time, you've got to isolate the population to get a new species. Otherwise, it's just too hard.

SY: Do you remember when you dug up your first fossil bones?

Bakker: Yes. But it wasn't a dinosaur bone, it was a fossil tortoise. It was at Scotts Bluff, at an eroded and sheer rock face in Nebraska. That was in 1964. I was on a Yale University field trip. We were going to Wyoming to dig dinosaurs, and we stopped at Scotts Bluff. I was just walking around, and I saw a little white piece of fossil bone. I still have it. It was a fossil tortoise jaw fragment that I discovered was about 30 million years old.

SY: What did you think when you uncovered this fossil?

Bakker: I wasn't thinking, I was just feeling. There was a hot wind. Out on a dig, the wind can be so hot and so dense that you can't really hear much of anything outside your own footsteps and your own breathing. When you're sitting down collecting a fossil, it's an extremely enclosed, intimate sort of experience. When you find a fossil bone, you are immediately transported back in time, and you think of the live animal that gave you these bones. In this case, it was a 40-pound tortoise living on the plains of Nebraska 30 million years ago surrounded by saber-toothed cats.

SY: And you have been digging up fossil bones ever since?

Bakker: Every summer I go out digging dinosaurs, mostly in Wyoming. We have found a lot of fossils. I used to teach a summer course in field geology and field biology through Johns Hopkins University. We spent six weeks camping in the Badlands. I always felt sad going back East from the West, and eventually, my wife, Constance, and I decided to stop going back. So we settled in Boulder, Colo., in the foothills of the Rockies.

SY: When you go out on a dig, you are part of a team. Who are the members of your team?

Bakker: Undergraduate students are often great. But the best are just interested people. Two of the best people working with me are government physicists working at the National Institute of Science and Technology. Another is a science teacher from Leadville, Colo.

SY: Is this a hobby for them?

Bakker: They take it very seriously. I call them unpaid professionals. These guys are very well trained and very well read. They do it for the real love of the science, for the love of doing it. They recognize they are making significant contributions to science.

SY: What happens after you discover a dinosaur fossil?

Bakker: You start excavating the skeleton. This is usually very difficult, because the bones are full of cracks. You can't just yank the bones out. You've got to carefully chisel out a block of rock that contains the skeleton. Then you cover that block of rock with plaster of Paris so the whole mass of rock and bones doesn't shift around and crack of its own weight. Back home, we scrape the rock off in the laboratory with needles and very small knife blades.

SY: You're not only a renowned paleontologist, but you are also a very accomplished artist. Where and how did you learn to draw?

When you find a fossil bone, you are immediately transported back in time, and you think of the live animal that gave you these bones.

Bakker: Anyone can draw. The ability to draw is not in your fingertips, it is in your eyes. If you can see structure, if you can see form, you can record it. I take people in my anatomy class to a zoo and say, "Draw that jaguar." I can't, they say. Can you see that jaguar? Yes. Is the elbow straight or bent? Well, it's bent. Is the ankle bent? Yes. Is it bent more than a dog's? Yes. Put that down. If you know how to look at structure, sort of run down a list of things in your mind, you can put it on paper.

SY: You have used this drawing ability in your research?

Bakker: Yes, you've got to. How do you read a skeleton? It looks awfully complicated. If you take the shoulder joint and make an outline drawing of the upper arm bone and the shoulder side, you'll see a bump. That bump is for the attachment of the chest muscle. That chest muscle will be pulling inward and backward. Now we've got some movement, and the drawing indicates the direction of movement. This is how you can sort of build up a movement pattern just drawing what you see.

SY: You've drawn some pretty imaginative pictures of what dinosaurs may have looked like, including some that show dinosaurs covered with feathers. Why do you think some dinosaurs may have had feathers?

Bakker: *Archaeopteryx*, an ancient bird, is a fossil with feathers. But the bones of *Archaeopteryx* are actually no more birdlike than those of *Tyrannosaurus rex*. Quite a few dinosaurs that we know from their bones were very birdlike. In fact, the structures of these dinosaurs are so birdlike that they must also have moved and acted like birds. Therefore, it is quite logical to give those kinds of dinosaurs feathers.

SY: The vision of dinosaurs that fascinated you so when you were a youth has changed greatly today, thanks in large measure to your research. You contend that dinosaurs were warm-blooded and capable of moving fast. But when you were a boy, dinosaurs were regarded as slow, stupid, lumbering, cold-blooded creatures similar to reptiles. Where did that idea come from?

Bakker: Good question. I have no idea. When dinosaurs were first dug up in the mid-1800's, paleontologists recognized right away that these extinct animals on one hand looked like crocodiles, but also looked like rhinos or elephants and also like birds. This three-way comparison was made right away. It was a weak consensus that decided they ought to be called reptiles. [*Dinosaur* means *terrible lizard.*] Nevertheless, paleontologists recognized that dinosaurs had many birdlike characteristics, and by 1860, most of the scholars all over the world accepted birds as living dinosaurs. Then, between 1920 and 1940, scholars came to view dinosaurs as being cold-blooded, gray, boring animals.

SY: Why did this change come about?

Bakker: I don't know. There was no evidence for it. There was no definitive scientific paper proving that dinosaurs were cold-blooded, gray, and stupid. It was just a shift, a drift of science. I think it was because very few scientists were studying dinosaurs at that time.

SY: How did you decide that this view was wrong?

Bakker: It was simple. One night, during my sophomore year at Yale, I was walking through the darkened museum. All those dinosaur skeletons, as they caught a little bit of light, seemed to move. I looked for a long while at those animals that were supposedly cold-blooded, stupid, gray, and bad mothers, and it occurred to me that this didn't make sense historically. Dinosaurs reigned on Earth for 165 million years. During that time, there were warm-blooded mammals alive, tiny little fur balls. Now does it make sense that cold-blooded, stupid animals would reign while intelligent warm-blooded animals would have stayed small? Does that make any historical sense? No. The dinosaurs kept on winning because they must have been fundamentally better than those little furry mammals.

SY: Exactly how did you come to the conclusion that dinosaurs were warm-blooded?

Bakker: The first thing I did was review history. I summarized the fossil history of dinosaurs and found that, for 165 million years on land, all meat eaters or plant eaters bigger than 10 pounds were dinosaurs. There was wave after wave of evolutions, extinctions, and evolutions. Every time, the big meat eaters and plant eaters that emerged were dinosaurs—different kinds of dinosaurs, but they were dinosaurs. That's incredible history, and it demands an explanation.

SY: What did you think could explain this history?

Bakker: A theory has to fit historical facts. The fact that the dinosaurs won over mammals again and again proved they were superior to mammals. Now, we've got to figure out why they were superior. In a paper I wrote in 1968 called "The Superiority of Dinosaurs," I pointed out that the limbs of dinosaurs are not like those of a lizard, frog, or crocodile. Instead, they were extremely sophisticated,

I summarized the fossil history of dinosaurs and found that, for 165 million years on land, all meat eaters or plant eaters bigger than 10 pounds were dinosaurs. . . . That's incredible history, and it demands an explanation.

adapted for moving a large animal fast for long periods of time. You can scare a lizard and it will run very fast for 10 seconds. You can scare a horse, a zebra, or wolf and they can run for 20 minutes to an hour. Big warm-blooded animals tend to have endurance. From their leg construction, you can tell when an animal is made to be an endurance runner. I studied how dinosaur legs were constructed and concluded that they were endurance runners.

SY: Did this alone prove that dinosaurs were warm-blooded animals?

Bakker: I also studied predator-prey relationships. It became very obvious to me that the maximum population of a warm-blooded predator is a 10th or 20th that of a cold-blooded predator in relation to the population size of their prey. This is because cold-blooded animals require much less meat. In Africa, on the average, there is 1 lion per 100 wildebeest, on which lions prey. If you made that lion cold-blooded, you would have 10 or 20 lions per 100 wildebeest. What happens with dinosaur fossil samples? You go out to Wyoming to dig up dinosaurs. Fossils of *Allosaurus*, a meat-eating dinosaur, are rare, while fossils of *Brontosaurus*, a plant eater, are very common. Dinosaurian meat eaters are as rare as lions and tigers and saber-toothed cats. That's exactly what they should be if dinosaurs were warm-blooded.

SY: Your ideas about dinosaurs being warm-blooded at first were not well received. Why do you think that was so?

Bakker: Well, my ideas were treated that way when I first began publishing papers in the late 1960's. The reaction of the "establishment" scientists was something like: "Who is this person, and how can we have him stoned?" The idea that dinosaurs were cold-blooded, stupid reptiles had been in place for 20 or 30 years. Everyone believed it. It was in all the books. For me to say that this central tenet of their science was wrong was very threatening. As a matter of fact,

115

Telling the Dinosaurs' Story

After finding new dinosaur fossils, Bakker communicates the excitement of discovery through interviews with the press.

During a television interview in November 1990, Bakker announces finding the first fossils of *Brontosaurus,* a Jurassic Period dinosaur, in sediments dating from the Cretaceous Period.

I was not the first to resurrect this idea at all. There was a series of papers published in 1954 concluding that dinosaurs were like warm-blooded birds and other animals. The papers were ignored. A great deal of what I did was focus attention on studies already done.

SY: One of the greatest mysteries about the dinosaurs is why they died out suddenly at the end of the Cretaceous Period 65 million years ago. A number of theories have been suggested to account for this mass extinction. What do you think killed the dinosaurs?

Bakker: Well, the most popular theory is that a comet or meteorite hit the Earth and exploded with a terrific force, throwing up a dust cloud that blocked out the sun. Suddenly, it gets cold everywhere, and everyone dies. I think this theory doesn't work.

SY: Why not?

Bakker: It completely ignores most of what is happening on land. If you want to study dinosaurs and understand them, you've got to think about frogs and turtles and salamanders and mammals, too. You can't take dinosaurs out of context. All the big animals were dinosaurs; that's true. But most animals aren't big. Go to the Amazon rain forest, or even a forest in New Jersey, and you'll find that most of the animals there are small. If you exploded a nuclear bomb right now over Brazil blocking the sunlight and chilling the Amazon rain forest, who would die first? The big deer and jaguars or the little frogs? Frogs should die first, because they are the most delicate creatures in any ecosystem; their blood is in intimate contact with the water they live in. Also, a tropical frog exposed to a chill can't hibernate, so it dies. A big animal, such as a deer or elephant, can stand a major chill and can move to another area. But have you ever heard of frog extinctions at the end of the Cretaceous Period? No. That's because no frogs died out. No turtles or salamanders died out.

In a phone interview with a magazine reporter, Bakker explains how finding *Brontosaurus* fossils in Cretaceous rock lends support to his theory that dinosaurs were wiped out by diseases, not a meteorite.

None of these delicate animals, with no defense at all against a sudden chill, died out. But dinosaurs—the biggest, most active animals that should take weeks to kill—did die. This is true of every major extinction that has ever hit the Earth. Not so long ago, there were woolly mammoths and saber-toothed cats in Chicago. There were beavers the size of Buicks all over North America. They disappeared about 10,000 years ago. Did any chipmunks or frogs or lizards go extinct 10,000 years ago? No.

SY: There have been many mass extinctions of large animals, perhaps as many as 20. What do you think caused them?

Bakker: It is very hard to come up with a theory that will kill big animals and leave little ones alone. The one thing that would do it is disease. This is a theory developed by American paleontologist Henry Osborn in 1899. He pointed out that when big animals travel, they'll spread dozens of diseases and disrupt the ecology. Whenever we humans have brought animals from one continent to another, bad things happen. Someone brought starlings from England to North America, and we have a starling problem. Introduce foreign animals and they run amuck. They do not have natural predators and also they spread disease.

SY: Why would big animals, such as the dinosaurs, start to travel?

Bakker: Whenever there was a mass extinction on land, there were land bridges connecting the continents and big animals moving across them. During most of the history of life, broad oceans have separated the continents. But, periodically, those ocean barriers get drained away and animals can move. Big animals travel very easily. Give an elephant a land bridge and the population will spread at least 1,600 kilometers (1,000 miles) in two years. Little animals don't move nearly as fast. It takes a long time for the population of a snake,

A second-grader once asked me, "What was the kindest dinosaur?" I said Brontosaurus. *I would think the kindest dinosaur would be the dinosaur with the best mother, the best family life.*

salamander, or frog to spread. Osborn pointed out that if big animals move across land bridges and start spreading, you're going to have extinctions caused by disease or disruptions to the ecosystem. There is no way to prevent it. So I like Osborn's theory. It's based in ecological reality. We know that foreign animals always cause disaster.

SY: Wouldn't some of the big dinosaurs have developed an immunity to the new diseases they encountered?

Bakker: No. If they encountered a brand-new disease, I think it would have wiped them out before they developed an immunity. And we are not talking about one disease. Every animal carries 30 or 40 diseases.

SY: There's a great deal of concern today about the problems of scientific illiteracy and shortcomings in the teaching of science.

Bakker: That's right. Most people are turned off to science and math before they reach junior high. Kids are naturally interested in science, but we turn them off because of the way most science is taught.

SY: What do you think can be done about the problem?

Bakker: Well, the schools can't do it all. A public school system could never pay enough to keep science specialists in their schools to help the classroom teachers. So you cannot expect schools alone to teach science.

SY: If our schools don't teach science, who will?

Bakker: Get the museums to do a lot more; get the zoos to do a lot more. And they want to. Especially in and near major cities, museums and zoos can help the elementary school teachers to plan curriculum. For example, lots of second-, third-, and fourth-grade teachers teach units on dinosaurs. They should sit down with staff people at the museums and the zoos ahead of time and plan ways to mix classroom exercises with studies of live animals at the zoo and fossil animals in the museum. The staff will help teachers prepare curriculum, and they can recommend books. Get all these elements working together and the kids will find this a very exciting way to learn.

SY: Do you think museums are doing a pretty good job? Is there more that they can do?

Bakker: Museums have always been at the forefront of education. But they need more support from both the private sector and the public sector. We need to pour much more money into the education part of the museums. Traditionally, grants go for the research in museums and not for educational projects. Also, curators should be chosen not only for their ability to do research, but for their ability to communicate to teachers and to the public.

SY: You are involved with many aspects of education and educational programs. You act as a consultant for dinosaur toys, books, articles, and TV programs about dinosaurs. You curated the dinosaur exhibit at the University of Colorado Museum, and you lecture to groups of students all over the country. What are some of the most memorable questions they have asked you about dinosaurs?

Bakker: A second-grader once asked me, "What was the kindest dinosaur?" I said *Brontosaurus.* I would think the kindest dinosaur would be the dinosaur with the best mother, the best family life. We know that baby brontosaurs were always protected by adults, and probably protected very well. Fossils of baby brontosaurs are extremely rare. This means the infant mortality rate was low. In that sense they were very effective parents.

SY: What are the most common questions the students ask you?

Bakker: They often ask about the Loch Ness monster in Scotland or the dinosaur alleged to be in Africa, in the Congo. They ask, "Is there any possibility of there still being a living dinosaur?" No, for the following reason: You could hide one monster in Loch Ness, it's a deep enough lake. But you could not hide a breeding population of monsters. If you want to preserve a species, you need more than one animal, you need a minimum of 500 so that they can breed every generation and can have enough diversity in their genes so that they can keep on going. You can't hide 500 or 600 monsters, because there will always be deaths. Dead animals float to the surface of lakes or swamps, they get washed up on shore, and someone is going to find them. The last big animal discovered was in 1901, the Okapi, a short-necked giraffelike thing in the Congo.

SY: You have a long list of accomplishments to your name. You've discovered and named six species of dinosaurs, and you've helped change our view about the dinosaurs, how they lived, what they looked like. Where do you see your career going now? What would you like to do next?

Bakker: Well, of course, I plan to keep on looking for dinosaur fossils in Wyoming. But beyond that, I never know. The most important things in science and in life usually come up from behind and off to the side. And they're usually not what you're focusing on. Something I dig up tomorrow could take my research off on paths I never dreamed of today. I want to be open to anything new that the future might hold. So I don't have any one great goal. I think that would be a big mistake.

Designs for safer, simpler nuclear reactors may give new life to the troubled nuclear power industry.

The New Nuclear Reactors

BY ARTHUR FISHER

The explosion that ripped apart the Chernobyl nuclear reactor in the Soviet Union in 1986 seemed to sound the death knell for an already troubled nuclear power industry. Yet circumstances since then may give new life to nuclear energy.

In August 1990, Iraq invaded Kuwait, a major oil-producing nation in the Middle East. The conflict that ensued drew attention to the perils of depending on imported energy sources. The war in the Persian Gulf did not cause the energy crunch feared by many in the United States, which today imports nearly half its oil. But most experts forecast a growing gap between the world's energy needs and its ability to meet them. The Earth contains a limited supply of fossil fuels—coal, oil, and natural gas—which is fast being depleted.

Yet even if there were enough fossil fuels to feed our energy-hungry world, consuming them could bring about an environmental disaster: global warming. When fossil fuels are burned, they release carbon dioxide and other so-called *greenhouse gases* that prevent heat from escaping through Earth's atmosphere. Coal releases more carbon dioxide than any other fossil fuel. Unless our consumption of coal and oil drops dramatically, many scientists fear that rising levels of carbon dioxide may injure the Earth's environment. Increasing carbon dioxide levels could cause crop-destroying droughts and a rising sea level that would flood coastal areas.

What are the alternatives to energy from fossil fuels? Conservation can certainly help, as it already has. So can renewable energy technologies—including solar, wind, and geothermal power—which

do not spew heat-trapping gases into the air. None of these energy sources, however, currently meets the energy needs of the United States and other industrialized nations.

The way out of this dilemma, say advocates of nuclear power, is energy from the atom, harnessed in nuclear reactors. Although nuclear energy could not replace the gasoline used in automobiles, it can replace the fossil fuels that generate more than two-thirds of the electric power in the United States.

Nuclear energy, however, has had a troubled history. At the time of its introduction in the 1950's, it was touted as a cheap, nonpolluting source of almost limitless energy. But nuclear plants soon began to suffer from a host of ills, including safety problems and rising construction and operating costs.

In the late 1980's and early 1990's, concern over global warming rekindled interest in nuclear reactors. Supporters of nuclear energy, who point out that all energy sources carry risks, now believe that new designs for nuclear reactors can help avert an energy crunch and, at the same time, avoid the cost and safety problems that have plagued the nuclear power industry in the past. How different would the advanced nuclear reactors be, and what advantages would they offer? To answer these questions, it is first necessary to discuss how present-day nuclear reactors produce energy.

The fission reaction

New or old, nuclear reactors produce energy by the same process: *nuclear fission*—splitting the *nuclei* (cores) of atoms. The atoms fissioned are those of certain very heavy and unstable elements.

Nuclear fission has a very special feature: The fragments that remain after the nucleus splits have just a tiny bit less mass than the original nucleus had. What has happened to the missing mass? It has been converted to energy. To calculate the enormous energy that fission releases, scientists use physicist Albert Einstein's famous equation $E=mc^2$, which relates mass (m) to energy (E) by means of a constant (c^2) that stands for the speed of light squared.

In 1938, two German chemists first split uranium atoms by bombarding them with *neutrons*—one of two kinds of particles that make up atomic nuclei. (The other kind are *protons*.) Soon afterward, physicist Leo Szilard calculated that a fissioned atom would release two or three more neutrons. As these neutrons bombarded and split more uranium atoms in turn, they would set up what has come to be called a *chain reaction*.

In 1942, a group of scientists led by physicist Enrico Fermi first demonstrated a nuclear chain reaction in a simple reactor built under the stands of the athletic field at the University of Chicago. The first application of nuclear fission was the atomic bomb, but even then researchers realized that nuclear energy could also be harnessed to produce electric power. The world's first large-scale nuclear power plant began to produce electricity in England in 1956.

Nuclear Power Reconsidered

Interest in nuclear power has been reawakened by concerns over dependence on oil from the Middle East and over air pollution caused by burning coal, oil, and natural gas. The supply of these fossil fuels is also limited. But fossil fuels are the chief source of electric power today.

U.S. Electric Power Sources

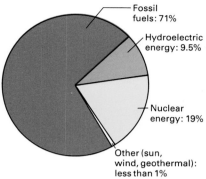

Fossil fuels: 71%
Hydroelectric energy: 9.5%
Nuclear energy: 19%
Other (sun, wind, geothermal): less than 1%

Electric Power Sources Worldwide

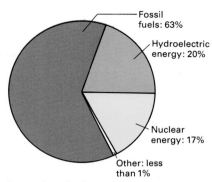

Fossil fuels: 63%
Hydroelectric energy: 20%
Nuclear energy: 17%
Other: less than 1%

Because of rounding, figures do not add up to 100 per cent.

Concentration of Carbon Dioxide in the Atmosphere

(Graph: Parts per million on the y-axis, ranging from 280 to 350; x-axis years from 1850 to 1988.)

Carbon dioxide levels in the atmosphere have risen sharply since 1900, in part due to the burning of fossil fuels. Increased levels of carbon dioxide and other greenhouse, or heat-trapping, gases may lead to a global warming trend.

Inside a nuclear power plant

There's no mystery involved in getting from the energy released by fission to electricity. A typical nuclear reactor generates electricity in much the same way as a plant that burns fossil fuel. Both use heat to boil water, make steam, and drive a turbine. The heat in a nuclear reactor, however, comes not from burning coal or oil, but from the intense energy of nuclear fission.

When a nucleus splits, its pieces—called *fission fragments*—separate at very high speeds. Their energy is eventually converted to heat when they strike the molecules of some other substance. In most reactors, this substance is water. The heated water is used to produce steam, which flows into a turbine and makes it spin. The turbine turns a generator that produces electricity. Many power plants combine the turbine and generator into a single device called a *turbogenerator.*

The reactors in nuclear power plants have four main elements in

123

Generating Electricity from Nuclear Fission

All steam-generated electricity—from fossil fuels or nuclear reactors—is produced the same way. Water is heated to produce steam, and the steam spins a turbine connected to a generator.

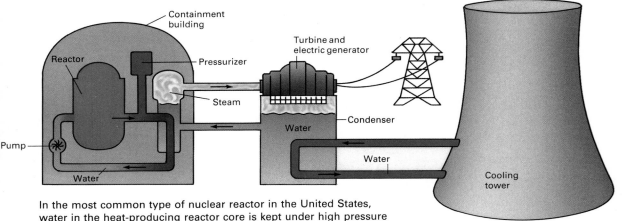

In the most common type of nuclear reactor in the United States, water in the heat-producing reactor core is kept under high pressure so it can heat past its normal boiling point without boiling. This superheated water is piped through a steam generator. The pipes act like radiators, transferring heat to water in the generator, which boils and produces steam for spinning the turbine that drives an electric generator. Steam leaving the turbine is cooled back to water by cold water piped from a cooling tower.

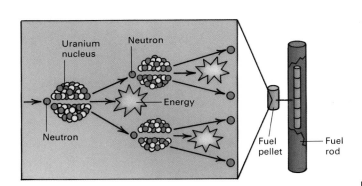

Nuclear fission, *above,* provides the energy that heats water in a reactor core. Tremendous energy is released when an atomic nucleus, which is made of particles called neutrons and protons, *fissions* (splits apart). Fission occurs when a neutron strikes a heavy nucleus, such as that of a uranium atom. Two neutrons fly out of the nucleus as it splits. These neutrons smash into two more nuclei, setting up a chain reaction.

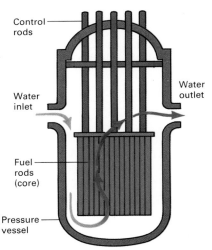

In a reactor core, fission takes place in uranium fuel pellets housed in metal rods. Neutron-absorbing control rods regulate the rate of fission. Water circulates around the fuel rods, cooling them as it carries off heat to make steam.

common. Each reactor contains nuclear fuel, control rods, a coolant, and a moderator.

■ The fuel in almost all U.S. reactors is a chemical compound of uranium called *uranium oxide*. It is formed into thimble-sized pellets that are housed in *fuel rods*—long tubes made of a metal alloy that resists extreme heat, corrosion, and radiation. A large reactor can have as many as 46,000 fuel rods assembled in up to 732 bundles. These fuel rod assemblies make up the reactor's *core*.

■ Control rods control the rate of the nuclear chain reaction inside the core. The control rods contain materials such as cadmium or boron that absorb neutrons. When lowered into the core, the control rods soak up enough neutrons to slow the reaction or even to stop it. As the control rods are lifted, the reaction speeds up.

■ The coolant carries off the intense heat generated by fission. In nearly all U.S. reactors, ordinary water serves as the coolant. More than 1.1 million liters (300,000 gallons) of water may surge through pipes in the core of a large reactor every minute. The coolant both prevents the core from melting and removes the heat energy that ultimately produces electricity.

■ The moderator is a substance that slows the speed of the neutrons emitted in fission. A slow-moving neutron has a better chance of splitting another uranium nucleus and continuing the fission process. Water acts as the moderator as well as the coolant in most reactors.

Reactors are generally classified by the type of coolant and moderator they use. The most common reactors, called *light water reactors*, use ordinary water as both coolant and moderator. The water in these reactors is kept under high pressure, which prevents it from boiling to steam until it gets hot enough to run the turbogenerator. At normal pressure, water boils to steam at 100 °C (212 °F). But this temperature is too low to give steam the energy needed to operate a turbine efficiently.

A type of reactor developed in Canada uses "heavy" water as the coolant and moderator instead of ordinary, or "light," water. Heavy water contains a form of hydrogen called *deuterium*. Unlike the nucleus of ordinary hydrogen, which has a single proton, a deuterium nucleus contains a proton and a neutron. Deuterium slows neutrons more efficiently than does the hydrogen in light water.

Hazards and safety systems

Nuclear reactors are potentially dangerous mainly because their fuel is *radioactive:* It emits radiation that can damage living cells. In high enough doses, radiation can cause radiation sickness, cancer, birth defects, and death. Because spent fuel rods remain radioactive for thousands of years, disposing of them poses a major problem. Engineers have yet to find a long-term solution for dealing with this form of radioactive waste.

To prevent radiation from entering the environment, a steel pressure vessel with walls at least 15 centimeters (6 inches) thick

Dangers of Nuclear Reactors

Nuclear reactors are potentially dangerous chiefly because their fuel is *radioactive*—that is, it emits hazardous radiation. Used fuel rods from nuclear power plants are hazardous wastes that release radiation for thousands of years. These rods are temporarily stored in pools of water on nuclear power plant grounds, *right.* No long-term storage method has yet been found.

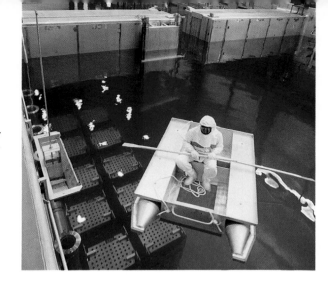

Core meltdown is another potential danger. If a reactor's core is not constantly cooled, the fuel rods may melt. This could be caused by a loss of coolant due to a leak in piping or a stuck water valve. The molten core could become hot enough to burn through the floor of the containment building, *right.* If the molten core burned down to water underground, it would set off a steam explosion that could spew radioactive gases and debris into the air, *far right.* No such accident has ever occurred.

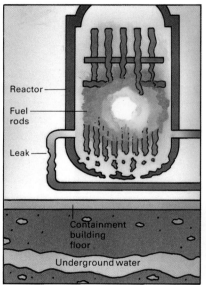

Reactor

Fuel rods

Leak

Containment building floor

Underground water

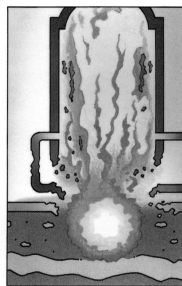

surrounds the core of most reactors. In most nuclear power plants, a domed containment building encloses the entire reactor. The containment building has walls of reinforced concrete that are at least 90 centimeters (3 feet) thick and lined with steel. Engineers have designed containment buildings sturdy enough to survive a direct hit by a jumbo jet or a tornado with winds of 480 kilometers (300 miles) per hour. No U.S. containment building has ever ruptured.

The chief danger in operating a reactor is a breakdown in the cooling system, such as a leak or pump failure. Without sufficient coolant, the intense heat in the core could damage or even melt the fuel rods. In a so-called *meltdown*, the molten core could burn through the containment building's floor and into the ground. If the core should hit the underground water supply, it would set off a steam explosion that could blow the top off the containment building, spewing radioactive gases and debris into the air. Radioactive material would also contaminate the ground water and the soil.

Engineers have designed multiple systems to prevent the core from overheating. If the core temperature rises too high, the control rods should slam down and shut off the chain reaction. If the coolant level drops dangerously low, an emergency cooling system should drench the core with water. Backup cooling systems should swing into action if the emergency system fails or proves inadequate.

These systems in today's reactors are, unfortunately, extremely complex. They rely on a maze of pipes, pumps, thousands of valves, and elaborate control mechanisms. If both the automatic emergency cooling and control-rod systems fail, technicians must intervene. Working under enormous stress, the technicians have only about 20 minutes in which to respond correctly and forestall a disaster.

The Chernobyl disaster

On April 26, 1986, an explosion and fire at the Chernobyl nuclear plant near Kiev lofted radioactive debris—including highly radioactive nuclear fuel—into the atmosphere. Fallout from Chernobyl rained down throughout Europe. The effects on people exposed to high levels of radiation from Chernobyl will not be known for years.

The disaster occurred during an ineptly run test of the reactor's power output. While trying to shut the reactor down, the plant operators violated many safety regulations, disabling automatic safety systems and pulling out far more control rods than allowed.

In U.S. reactors, fission ceases when the water coolant stops flowing, because water is no longer available to act as a moderator and slow neutrons. But the Chernobyl reactor used graphite, a flammable form of carbon, as the moderator. As the coolant level dropped, the graphite actually enabled the chain reaction to speed up. A steam explosion finally resulted, which set the graphite on fire. Unlike U.S. reactors, the Chernobyl reactor had no containment building, which might have prevented radioactive material from escaping. Reactors of the Chernobyl type are rarely used outside the Soviet Union, and even there, they are being shut down.

Nevertheless, accidents can happen in the United States, as was shown at the Three Mile Island nuclear power plant near Harrisburg, Pa., in 1979. There, a series of operator errors compounded mechanical failures, leading to a partial meltdown. Yet no one was injured and there was no major environmental contamination, though a small amount of radioactive gas escaped from the plant.

Simpler, safer designs

New designs, now under consideration by the U.S. Department of Energy (DOE), would simplify reactor systems and ease the burden on human operators. They incorporate engineering refinements

The New Nuclear Reactors

New reactor designs eliminate the complex maze of pumps and valves that are prone to failure in current reactors. By simplifying safety systems and easing the burden on human operators, they attempt to minimize the primary nuclear hazard, a loss-of-coolant accident.

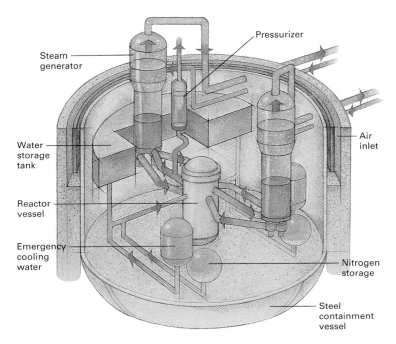

Steam generator

Pressurizer

Water storage tank

Air inlet

Reactor vessel

Emergency cooling water

Nitrogen storage

Steel containment vessel

Advanced Light Water Reactor

Hot water and steam (red arrows) travel from the core and steam generator of the Westinghouse AP600 reactor. But gravity and the pressure of nitrogen gas would force emergency cooling water (blue arrows) through the core automatically if sensors detected an abnormal rise in temperature inside the core. A large tank above the core stores additional cooling water, and air currents and evaporation would also help cool the core. This system eliminates many mechanical parts that are prone to breakdown.

Liquid Metal Reactor

Argonne Laboratory's Integral Fast Reactor submerges the core in a pool of liquid sodium (shown in blue), which can absorb large amounts of heat without much rise in temperature. This sodium is also pumped from the pool through the reactor to cool the core (arrows). Even if the pumps stopped working, the pool of sodium would continue to absorb heat from the core.

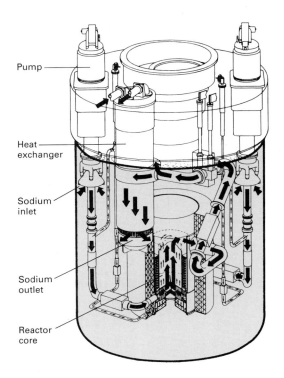

Pump

Heat exchanger

Sodium inlet

Sodium outlet

Reactor core

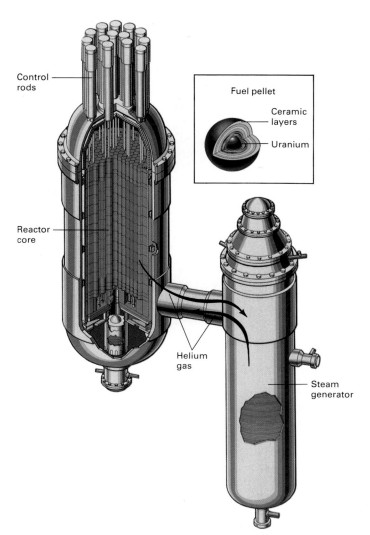

Control rods

Reactor core

Fuel pellet

Ceramic layers

Uranium

Helium gas

Steam generator

Helium-Cooled Reactor

Tiny fuel pellets (inset) are the chief safety feature of the General Atomics High-Temperature Gas-Cooled Reactor. Each pellet consists of a uranium kernel sealed in layers of heat-resistant ceramic materials. Even if the reactor lost all its helium coolant, the small amount of fissionable uranium in each pellet could not produce enough heat to rupture the pellet. Helium can be safely used at higher temperatures than water can and is a more efficient coolant.

intended to minimize the risk of a loss-of-coolant accident like that at Three Mile Island. One type of advanced reactor, described as "passively safe," relies on natural forces such as circulation by gravity and cooling by evaporation to counteract the effects of a coolant loss. Reactors with such passive safety features would give plant operators up to 72 hours to respond in an emergency, rather than 20 minutes.

Such passive safety systems stem in part from the Process Inherent Ultimate Safety (PIUS) reactor designed in Sweden in the 1970's. In the PIUS design, the core is submerged in a tank of *borated* (boron-containing) water. Under normal circumstances, the pressure of the ordinary water coolant keeps this borated water out of the core. But any disruption in the coolant's flow upsets the pressure balance, letting borated water rush into the core. Because boron atoms absorb neutrons rapidly without splitting, they would shut down the chain reaction before the core had a chance to overheat.

One passively safe design is now on the drawing board at the

The Promise of Nuclear Fusion

Nuclear fusion, the joining of atomic nuclei, offers the possibility of a safe and limitless supply of energy. The fuel for fusion is *deuterium,* a form of hydrogen found in seawater, and *tritium,* a form of hydrogen that can be manufactured. Deuterium and tritium combine to form the nucleus of a heavier element—helium—releasing a neutron and a huge amount of energy. It takes temperatures 10 times that of the sun to force hydrogen nuclei to fuse. The reaction stops when the temperature drops, making meltdown impossible. Fusion also produces little radioactive waste.

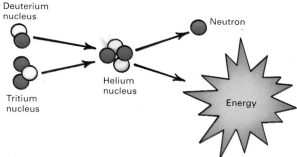

Deuterium nucleus
Neutron
Helium nucleus
Tritium nucleus
Energy

Harnessing Energy from Fusion

To produce energy from nuclear fusion, scientists must heat deuterium and tritium to at least 100,000,000 °C (180,000,000 °F). At high temperatures, the atoms lose their orbiting electrons and form a *plasma* of free electrons and hydrogen nuclei. Confining the hot plasma presents an additional problem. Thus far, experimental fusion methods use more energy than they produce.

Magnetic fields confine the plasma in a doughnut-shaped device called a *tokamak.* The magnetic fields push the superhot fuel away from the tokamak's walls and send the hydrogen nuclei speeding around the ring with enough energy to cause fusion.

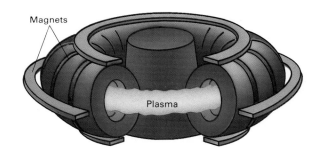

Magnets
Plasma

Intense beams of light from lasers bombard pellets containing deuterium and tritium gas in an *inertial confinement* system. The beams vaporize the surface of the pellets, setting up a counterforce that compresses the gas inside the pellet and creates temperatures high enough to cause fusion. Fusion occurs so rapidly that the plasma has no time to fly away and hit the containing walls.

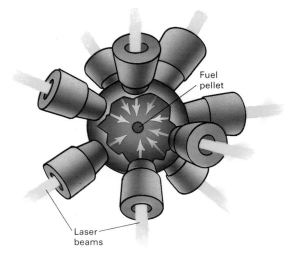

Fuel pellet
Laser beams

Westinghouse Electric Company in Pittsburgh, Pa. This advanced light water reactor relies on the force of gravity to circulate emergency cooling water. Air currents and evaporation also help cool the core. In the event of a coolant loss, these passive safety features would remove enough heat to make human intervention unnecessary for 72 hours. At that time, the operator would need only to add water to the system. Passively safe reactors could be ready for operation by the year 2000.

In the meantime, modifications in light water reactors should lessen the chance of accidents and give operators more time to respond to emergencies. The modified reactors would operate on the same principles as current light water reactors. But they would produce less power, operate at lower temperatures, and use more cooling water in proportion to fuel. A General Electric Company division in San Jose has designed such a simplified light water reactor. The design greatly reduces the number of pumps, valves, pipes, and welds—parts that can break down in the cooling system. Large nozzles would inject water from above the core and keep it submerged even if the coolant pumps failed.

Walkaway-safe reactors

Other advanced designs, described as *walkaway safe*, contain safety features that require no human intervention whatsoever. Even if all the reactor's systems failed, the staff could walk away and remain away indefinitely without risking a catastrophe. The DOE is considering two potentially walkaway-safe reactor concepts, though they will probably not be built and tested until well into the next century. Unlike the passively safe designs, these designs do not use water as the coolant. One cools with helium gas, the other uses liquid sodium.

The helium-cooled reactor is being developed by General Atomics, a firm in San Diego, and a group of utilities. Helium's advantage as a coolant is that it can safely be used at much higher temperatures than can water, and it converts heat to electricity more efficiently.

The chief safety feature of the helium-cooled reactor is its tiny fuel pellets. The pellets consist of a uranium compound sealed in onionlike layers of insulating, heat-resistant ceramic materials. Each pellet measures only about 1 millimeter (0.04 inch) across. According to the reactor's designers, this small size would keep the fissioning fuel from ever producing enough heat to rupture or melt the pellets, even if the reactor lost all its coolant.

The other walkaway-safe reactor design is a liquid metal reactor under development by General Electric and by Argonne National Laboratory, near Chicago. The reactor takes advantage of the heat-absorbing properties of liquid sodium. The reactor sits in a bath of liquid sodium, which circulates through the core and serves as the coolant. According to the reactor's designers, the sodium would continue to cool the core by convection, even if the coolant pumps stopped working.

The liquid metal reactor has another unusual feature. It belongs to a category of experimental reactors known as *breeders* because they *breed* (produce) new fuel. In a breeder, fast-moving neutrons bombard uranium 238 inside the core. The neutrons convert some of this nonfissionable form of uranium into fissionable plutonium 239, a reactor fuel. In theory, a breeder reactor could get 60 times more energy from uranium than current reactors do. The Soviet Union and France now operate liquid metal breeder reactors.

The breeder that Argonne is developing has another advantage: It recycles fuel. Engineers can extract and reprocess the most radioactive and dangerous nuclear wastes that accumulate in the reactor fuel, thus helping solve the nuclear waste disposal problem.

The fusion solution

The ultimate answer to the safety question may come from another source of nuclear energy: nuclear fusion. Fusion involves the union of two lightweight nuclei to form the nucleus of a heavier element. Less matter remains after fusion than before, and—as in fission—the missing matter translates to energy.

Nuclear fusion is most dramatically demonstrated on Earth in the explosion of a hydrogen bomb. Fusion also powers the sun and all other stars, releasing energy as heat and sunlight. In one common fusion reaction, nuclei of deuterium and tritium—two forms of hydrogen—fuse to form helium. The process releases energy and a neutron.

Since the 1950's, researchers have tried to harness the enormous energy of the stars in a controlled fusion reaction. The achievement would ensure a virtually limitless supply of energy. That is because deuterium, the form of hydrogen that would feed the fusion reaction, occurs abundantly in seawater.

Fusion has several advantages over fission as a source of power. The hydrogen fuel for fusion is plentiful and cheap, unlike the uranium that fuels fission. In addition, fusion is inherently safer because the fusion reaction is so difficult to sustain. In the event of a reactor malfunction, fusion would stop immediately and so could not cause a meltdown. Fusion reactors also produce far less radioactive waste than fission reactors do. But success has so far eluded fusion researchers because of the difficulty of designing a practical reactor.

The major problem is getting hydrogen nuclei close enough to fuse. Each deuterium and tritium nucleus carries a positive electrical charge, and so the nuclei repel each other. Most fusion researchers have attempted to overcome the repulsive forces between the nuclei by heating hydrogen to extremely high temperatures.

Heating hydrogen serves first to strip electrons from the atoms, creating a *plasma*—a gas made up of free electrons and free nuclei. At superhot temperatures, the hydrogen nuclei in the plasma collide with enormous energy, bringing them close enough to fuse. In the sun's core, where tremendous gravitational forces squeeze the nuclei together, hydrogen fusion takes place at about 10,000,000 °C (18,000,000 °F). On Earth, without this tremendous force, fusion requires temperatures about 10 times higher. Because such heat would melt any material used as walls to contain the plasma, fusion researchers have developed alternative confinement methods.

One method, called *magnetic confinement*, uses strong magnetic fields. The other main method, *inertial confinement*, uses light-amplifying devices called *lasers*. So far, neither method has yielded as much energy as it uses in heating the hydrogen.

Magnetic confinement takes place in a huge doughnut-shaped "magnetic bottle" called a *tokamak*. Magnets surround the walls of the bottle, generating strong magnetic and electric fields that both speed up the plasma—thereby heating it—and push the plasma away from the chamber walls. One fusion researcher has likened confining plasma in this way to holding Jell-O in rubber bands.

In inertial confinement, powerful beams of light from lasers bombard tiny fuel pellets containing a mixture of deuterium and tritium. The intense energy of the beams squeezes the pellets with enormous pressure for only a fraction of a second, just long enough for the fuel to become hot and dense enough to fuse. Because fusion occurs so quickly, the material has no time to fly away.

Fusion researchers face another problem besides getting hydrogen nuclei close enough to fuse. Any confinement device must keep the nuclei densely crowded over a long enough period for the fusion reaction to become *self-sustaining*—able to continue without additional heat. No experimental confinement device has yet done so.

Will fusion yield usable energy in the not-too-distant future? Pessimists joke that a successful fusion reactor is just 25 years down the road—and has been for the last 40 years. Yet concerted scientific efforts to achieve fusion continue.

In the near future, experts believe that advances in reactor technology are likely to come in improved fission reactors—passively safe and walkaway-safe designs. These experts also believe that fusion will eventually answer our long-term energy needs, but only after formidable engineering challenges have been overcome.

For further reading:

Fisher, Arthur. "Next Generation Nuclear Reactors: Dare We Build Them?" *Popular Science*, April 1990, pp. 68-76+.

Herman, Robin. *Fusion: The Search for Endless Energy.* Cambridge University Press, 1990.

Medvedev, Grigori. *The Truth About Chernobyl.* Basic Books, 1991.

Nero, Anthony V., Jr. *A Guidebook to Nuclear Reactors.* University of California Press, 1979.

While tree-planting is underway in cities
across the United States, scientists
are studying how urban environments
affect trees—and vice versa.

The "Forests" in Our Cities

BY JOSEPH WALLACE

All across the United States, people in 1991 were enthusiastically planting trees. In 1990, President George Bush had unveiled the most ambitious community tree-planting and maintenance program in the history of the United States. The President's America the Beautiful program, with public and private cooperation, called for the planting of 1 billion trees per year during the next several years. Of these, 30 million trees were to be planted in the nation's 40,000 cities and towns.

This federal initiative joined other ongoing efforts to bring more trees to urban America. TreePeople, a California group formed in the early 1970's, had spurred the planting of 2 million trees by 1990 in the Los Angeles area alone—and perhaps as many as 100 million in other cities in the United States and abroad. Tree City USA, a National Arbor Day Foundation program formed in 1976 to promote and recognize communities that create comprehensive urban forestry programs, recognized more than 1,200 cities in 1990. The American Forestry Association (AFA), a Washington, D.C., based nonprofit group, began sponsoring a program in 1988 called Global ReLeaf to oversee the planting of as many as 100 million urban and suburban trees in the United States by the year 2000.

The author:

Joseph Wallace is a free-lance writer.

Researchers studying urban trees applaud the current interest in planting more city trees. At the same time, they see the need for studying our existing city ecosystems to better understand how trees are affected by harsh city environments. Researchers are also concerned that some cities may not be prepared to meet the water and maintenance needs of millions of new trees. Nevertheless, evidence is mounting that trees benefit cities in significant ways.

The growing interest in urban reforestation reflects, in part, the increased awareness of the importance of trees to life on Earth. Every tree absorbs carbon dioxide from the air and releases oxygen during *photosynthesis*, the process by which green plants use energy from sunlight to convert carbon dioxide and water into food. This process is part of the *carbon cycle*, which keeps the amounts of oxygen and carbon dioxide in Earth's atmosphere at fairly constant levels. People and animals breathe in oxygen given off by all plants and in turn give off carbon dioxide that plants take up or that oceans absorb. But the amount of carbon dioxide in the atmosphere has begun to outstrip the amount of carbon dioxide absorbed by plants or the oceans, intensifying the *greenhouse effect*. So-called *greenhouse gases*, such as water vapor, methane, nitrogen, and carbon dioxide, naturally present in Earth's atmosphere, allow most rays of sunlight to pass through the atmosphere and warm Earth's surface. The Earth then sends the heat energy back into the atmosphere as infrared radiation. The greenhouse gases absorb much of this heat and radiate it back to Earth. This adds to the warming at the surface and makes Earth warm enough to support life.

Today, however, scientists generally agree that carbon dioxide and other greenhouse gases are increasing in the atmosphere, largely because of increased burning of fossil fuels. Another reason is the destruction of the world's rain forests to make way for agriculture and other human development.

Scientists warn that an intensified greenhouse effect could cause a steady rise in Earth's temperature. This could eventually disrupt worldwide weather patterns, turn some cropland areas into deserts, and even melt polar icecaps, flooding lowland areas.

Forests once covered about 4.68 billion hectares (12 billion acres) worldwide, but today 60 per cent of those trees are gone. In South America's Amazon rain forest and other tropical forests, at least 11 million hectares (27 million acres)—an area the size of Tennessee—is cleared each year. In the United States, nearly half the original woodland has disappeared since the first European settlers arrived in the early 1600's. The current trend in rural United States seems to be a slowing of the conversion of forestland to other uses. On the other hand, urban areas have experienced rapid deforestation over the years. In many large cities, only one tree is planted on average for every four that are removed because they died, were diseased, or were blocking construction.

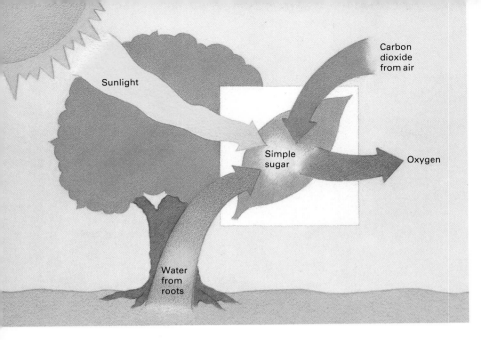

How Trees Remove Carbon Dioxide from the Air
Trees help maintain a natural balance between the carbon dioxide and oxygen in Earth's atmosphere. In *photosynthesis,* the tree's food-making process, leaves use energy from sunlight to combine carbon dioxide from the air with water drawn up from the tree's roots, forming a simple sugar. As a by-product, leaves release oxygen into the air.

The 1991 tree-planting efforts are an attempt to reverse the trend of urban tree loss. Most scientists do not believe that increasing the number of city trees will by itself prevent an intensification of the greenhouse effect. But more city trees could improve the urban environment.

The AFA estimated that, as of 1990, urban trees covered more than 28 million hectares (70 million acres) of land in the United States. Street trees represent 10 per cent of the urban "forest." Street trees include not only those that line streets in residential neighborhoods but also those planted in containers or small plots of ground within the concrete plazas or canyonlike depths of the central city. J. James Kielbaso, professor of forestry at Michigan State University in East Lansing, estimated the total number of street trees in U.S. cities in 1987 at roughly 60 million. If all the street trees were gathered together and planted 9 meters (30 feet) apart, they would form a forest the size of the Everglades.

The AFA, Michigan State University, and state forestry agencies completed surveys of 410 cities in 1989 indicating that there is room to at least double the number of street trees in U.S. cities. They say there is space available along American city streets to plant 60 million new trees. Increasing the number of city trees is not a new idea, however. But early advocates faced opposition.

The controversy dates at least to 1956, and the publication of *Man's Role in Changing the Face of Earth*, a landmark in the brief history of urban forestry according to Rowan Rowntree, a researcher at the U.S. Forest Service's Northeastern Forest Experiment Station in Syracuse, N.Y. In this book, respected city planner and philosopher Lewis Mumford stated that nature is completely eliminated from and no longer relevant to cities. But in the same book, another scientist argued that cities provide new sites for plants to colonize, and that

137

Dwindling Trees

Human development has been a major cause of declining numbers of trees throughout the world.

Tropical rain forests are being destroyed, *right,* as trees are harvested for logs or cut down to create farmland.

In the United States, forests once covered most of the land from the Atlantic Ocean to the Mississippi River. Since European settlers arrived in the early 1600's, nearly half the original forests have been cut down.

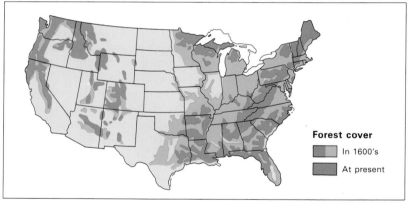

Forest cover

In 1600's

At present

How Many Trees?

City trees in the United States in 1990 covered an area about the size of Nevada.

An area the size of Tennessee is cleared each year in the world's tropical rain forests.

If planted 9 meters (30 feet) apart, the trees that line U.S. streets would fill an area the size of the Everglades.

botanists should seize the opportunity to study this new ecosystem. Then, in 1961, French geographer Jean Gottman predicted in his book, *Megalopolis*, that forests would always be part of the growing U.S. urban sprawl.

Still, researchers were slow to concentrate on the urban forest. According to Phillip Rodbell, staff urban forester of the AFA, the spur that forced scientists and the public to look at city trees in a new way came in the 1970's. Unfortunately, the spur was a disaster—Dutch elm disease. This fungal disease, spread by bark beetles, first arrived in the United States in the 1930's in infected logs from Europe. The infestation became an epidemic in the 1950's. It peaked in the 1970's, destroying huge numbers of American elm trees planted in the early 1900's. Many cities across the nation had almost no other species of tree. In a few years, these cities were virtually treeless.

There have been other destructive pests and diseases, such as a chestnut blight imported from Asia in 1904. It destroyed nearly every American chestnut tree in the Eastern United States by 1940. But the Dutch elm disease epidemic was more widespread and demonstrated that planting large numbers of a single species—creating a *monoculture*—makes that species particularly susceptible to the spread of disease. The epidemic mobilized the scientific community to begin the study of trees in urban areas.

This research has uncovered several advantages of planting trees in the city. One significant benefit is lower summer temperatures. Cities form *heat islands*, a phenomenon reported as long ago as 1833, when investigators noted that temperatures are higher in cities than in the less built-up areas surrounding them. In the mid-1980's, energy engineer Hashem Akbari and physicist Art Rosenfeld of the Lawrence Berkeley Laboratory in Berkeley, Calif., reviewed temperature changes within city centers throughout the United States. They found that since the 1940's cities have grown progressively warmer than their adjacent suburbs. By the early 1990's, summer afternoon temperatures in cities across the nation averaged as much as 5 Celsius degrees (9 Fahrenheit degrees) higher than in the nearby countryside.

Arching Dutch elm trees on the University of Illinois campus in Urbana, *top,* in the mid-1940's had died off by the mid-1960's, *bottom,* as a result of Dutch elm disease. The disease killed millions of trees and sparked urban tree research.

Using sophisticated computer models, the researchers analyzed why cities become heat islands. One important factor is the large number of dark surfaces—parking lots, buildings, asphalt roads—that very efficiently absorb and then radiate heat. But the computer models of Akbari and Rosenfeld also uncovered a less obvious reason why cities swelter all summer: not enough trees.

By providing shade, trees reduce the amount of solar heat absorbed by the ground or nearby buildings. In some regions, trees also act as evaporative coolers by releasing water vapor from their leaf surfaces. One large tree in the Midwest, for example, can give off as much as 380 liters (100 gallons) of water a day, providing the cooling power of five window air conditioners running 20 hours per day in summer heat, according to Akbari and Rosenfeld. Fewer air conditioners operating reduces the amount of coal and oil burned by local utilities, which lowers the amount of carbon dioxide released into the atmosphere. Akbari and Rosenfeld estimate that the United States could decrease its carbon dioxide emissions by 15 million metric tons (17 million short tons) annually by planting 100 million new urban trees and increasing the use of light-colored building and paving surfaces to reflect rather than absorb sunlight.

In a 1990 study of urban heat islands, Atlanta, Ga., researchers found that average temperatures in their city had risen 2 Celsius degrees (4 Fahrenheit degrees) since 1974. At the same time, Atlanta lost 20 per cent of its trees due to urban development. William L. Chameides, atmospheric chemist and director of the School of Earth and Atmospheric Sciences at Georgia Institute of Technology in Atlanta, also found that the higher average temperatures were linked to increased levels of smog. Smog forms when sunlight causes chemical reactions in hydrocarbons and nitrogen oxides in the air produced by burning petroleum products, such as gasoline in cars. High air temperatures increase this reaction. Chameides concluded

Among the benefits of planting trees in cities are the obvious ones of shade and natural beauty.

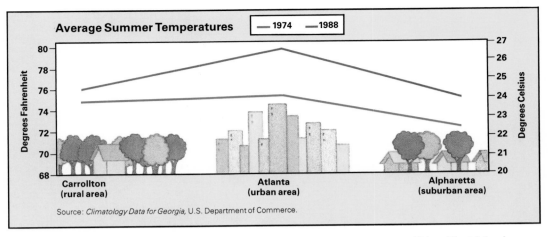

Average Summer Temperatures — 1974 —1988

Degrees Fahrenheit: 80, 78, 76, 74, 72, 70, 68

Degrees Celsius: 27, 26, 25, 24, 23, 22, 21, 20

Carrollton (rural area) Atlanta (urban area) Alpharetta (suburban area)

Source: *Climatology Data for Georgia*, U.S. Department of Commerce.

Urban Heat Islands
Few trees and abundant concrete make city temperatures higher than in surrounding areas, forming a "heat island," *above*. Average summer temperatures in Atlanta, Ga., rose 2 Celsius degrees (4 Fahrenheit degrees) from 1974 to 1988. During the same period, the city lost 20 per cent of its trees.

that city planners should consider the consequences to air quality if they fail to keep or replant trees as a city expands.

Besides helping to cool urban heat islands, city trees can help keep individual buildings warmer in winter by serving as windbreaks. The trees can also screen against noise and filter pollutants from the air, such as sulfur dioxide and airborne metals.

Research has also shown that city trees substantially reduce storm runoff because their leaves slow the rate of rainfall hitting the ground. According to Rowntree, in a storm that drops 2.5 centimeters (1 inch) of rain in 12 hours, urban greenery can reduce runoff by as much as 20 per cent, reducing erosion and the risk of flooding to homes and roads.

Thus, trees are good for cities. But are cities good for trees? No, according to the work of several research groups. Surveys by the AFA and others find that soot, car exhaust, and other pollutants can overwhelm trees. Inadequate sunlight, compacted soil, salt or chemicals spread on streets and sidewalks to melt ice, and acidic dog urine also take their toll. New York City alone lost roughly one-fourth of its trees during the 1980's because of urban stresses.

In general, researchers have discovered that the closer a tree is located to an urban center, the shorter its life span. According to AFA vice president Gary Moll, studies show that downtown street trees, such as red maple or willow oak, live an average of 7 years; in a park or the suburbs, the same trees will average 60 years; in their natural forest habitat, those trees could live 150 years.

Limited soil and planting space seems to be a major cause of premature tree death. A 1989 study of the roots of more than 1,300 street trees in downtown planting pits found that growth rates and overall health were very unstable when each tree was planted in less than 2.8 cubic meters (100 cubic feet) of soil, the size of most downtown pits according to James Urban, a landscape architect in Annapolis, Md. Root growth appeared to be stunted in trees planted

Hazards to Tree Health

Urban trees suffer many stresses usually not found in natural forestlands, such as excessive heat, inadequate light, and poor or contaminated soil.

Air pollutants, such as those from automobile exhaust, *above,* harm trees by restricting their growth. Intense air pollution can eventually kill trees. Tall buildings, *above right,* prohibit adequate sunlight from reaching trees, and small planting pits strangle root growth.

in such small areas. But growth improved as the planting area increased to 5.6 cubic meters (200 cubic feet) of soil.

Another study reported in 1989 attempted to calculate the impact of different city planting sites on urban trees. James R. Clark and Roger K. Kjelgern, urban horticulturists at the University of Washington in Seattle, chose to study the sweet gum, a tree widely planted in urban areas throughout the West and Northwest. The scientists distinguished between three types of urban forest areas, which they called *park, plaza,* and *canyon.* Park areas contain large groups of trees. Plazas, such as in parking lots and sidewalks, have more concrete than trees and are the most common urban environments. Plaza trees usually receive full sunlight, as do park trees, but they have limited soil for their roots to take up adequate water and nutrients. Canyon trees are partly shaded by tall buildings.

Clark and Kjelgern found that park and canyon sweet gums grew at an equal rate. Although canyon trees received 50 per cent less sunlight than park trees, they adjusted by producing more branches and developing larger, thinner leaves. They oriented their leaves parallel to the ground to catch as much sunlight as possible.

Plaza sweet gums were by far the least healthy. They suffered from too much light—not only direct sunlight, but light reflected from buildings, streets, and other structures. They grew at half the rate of park and canyon trees. The plaza sweet gums tended to turn their growth mechanisms on and off as summer weather conditions fluctuated because the limited soil space in which they were planted could not hold enough moisture to support steady growth. In the

Studying Urban Tree Growth

Researchers are only beginning to discover what tree species are best suited to particular urban environments and how to help those trees survive.

Canyon

Plaza

Park

A scientist measures sunlight reaching a tree, *above left,* during a 1989 study of sweet gums in Seattle. Compared with trees in parklike sites, trees in "canyons" shaded by tall buildings produced large leaves to absorb as much light as possible, *above.* Trees in heavily paved "plazas" had small leaves, damaged from too much light.

Pacific Northwest, little rain falls in the summer months. As light and heat intensified during the summer, the plaza sweet gums went into a dormant state. After several seasons, the trees died.

Clark and Kjelgern believe that in plaza environments, foresters should plant groups of large, hardy trees. Large trees can withstand heat and reduced moisture better than can small trees because their root systems are large and can draw moisture from wider areas. Groups, or islands, of trees are better protected from the sun and wind than an individual tree, mimicking the hospitable conditions of the natural forest. Temperatures in these tree islands can be noticeably lower than in the surrounding areas.

The Seattle researchers studied the health of urban trees in a naturally moist environment. But a different approach is needed in a drier environment, such as in the Southwestern desert city of Tucson, Ariz. Although Tucson could boast just three trees in 1875, in the early 1900's, city residents began widespread planting of Bermuda grass, magnolias, oaks, and other plants native to regions where nature supplies abundant water. But Tucson's water supply depends almost entirely on underground water, and after about 1950, the city began to draw more water than could be replenished from its *aquifer,* a water-laden layer of soil or porous rock below the ground's surface.

The situation reached crisis proportions in 1974, when a severe drought forced the shut-off of water to parts of the city for several days. Subsequently, city officials encouraged residents to plant as little vegetation as possible. Many homeowners responded by replacing their lawns and trees with gravel, rocks, and cactuses. From 1971 to 1983, Tucson's vegetative cover fell from 37 per cent of the city area to 28 per cent. This landscape created hot spots that increased cooling demands by as much as 30 per cent. Storm runoff increased and air pollution levels rose. Then, in the mid-1980's, landscape architects and a private organization called the Southern Arizona Water Resources Association designed a true desert city, utilizing such native desert trees as paloverdes and ocotillos.

Yet, as in so many other cities, the total amount of vegetative cover in Tucson has continued to decline, and dead or diseased trees are often inadequately replaced. To combat this trend, Global ReLeaf's local program, Trees for Tucson, seeks to plant 500,000 new paloverdes and other trees native to the Southwest by 1996.

Greg McPherson, assistant professor of landscape architecture at the University of Arizona in Tucson, helped devise a computer model that makes projections of the economic and ecological benefits of the Trees for Tucson program. The model projects that each mature tree will annually filter 18 kilograms (40 pounds) of particles from Tucson's air. Each tree will annually remove about 136 kilograms (300 pounds) of carbon dioxide from the air, directly through photosynthesis and indirectly through the reduced emissions from power plants as a result of reduced use of air conditioning. Each tree will decrease annual storm runoff by approximately 1,070 liters (280 gallons).

Another significant problem in efforts to plant city trees is measuring their demand on critical water supplies. In the Los Angeles area, there are plans to add 50 per cent more trees—a seemingly worthy objective, given the city's notorious problems with air pollution. In 1991, however, California experienced its fifth year of drought, with water supplies for agricultural and residential use sharply curtailed. Already, the struggle to supply enough water to Los Angeles diverts streams north of the city that normally drain into Mono Lake. This lake, an important breeding and resting site for migratory shore birds, has shrunk markedly as the city's water demands have grown. On the other hand, experts argue that only 4 per cent of water delivered to California's urban areas is used to maintain landscape plants, nearly all of it for lawns. Experts say that the benefit a tree provides in filtering pollutants from the air could alone outweigh the cost in terms of water to establish the tree, about 57 liters (15 gallons) per week.

Researchers also say they need to learn more about the types of trees best suited for planting in urban areas. According to the responses of 410 U.S. cities to Kielbaso's 1989 survey, 55 per cent of urban street trees belong to only six major groups: maples, oaks, pines, ashes, elms, and dogwoods. This indicates a need for more diversity to avoid another calamitous epidemic such as Dutch elm disease. Even if disease were not a problem, planting a large group of trees within a short period of time would mean that the trees will mature, age, and die at virtually the same time, creating a maintenance nightmare.

Urban environments are challenges to the hardiest of the hardy tree species. "There are no trees native to cities," says Rodbell. But researchers have learned that trees such as sycamores and pin oaks, which are native to swampy areas with poor and compacted soil, seem to do well in cities. The plane tree, golden rain tree, ginkgo, and honey locust are tolerant of urban areas' high pollution levels and high temperatures. On the other hand, poplars, silver maples, and box elders are undesirable urban trees in northern urban areas because their soft and brittle wood easily splits under heavy winter snow, creating hazards to people and property. Norway maples are fast growing and can withstand high winds and pollution, but by sending up sprouts from their roots, they invade surrounding areas.

Urban forest researchers also have found that the likelihood of creating a healthy urban forest is enhanced when a city has a formal plan for planting and maintenance. The best urban forestry programs have been able to increase the average life span of their city trees to 60 years. For example, Milwaukee, Wis., incorporated its forestry department with its public works department so that roadbuilding plans include provisions for trees, spaced according to species requirements. Chicago is hoping to develop a long-range plan for its extensive tree cover in city parks and forest preserves. But first, the city has initiated a massive survey to determine the status of existing trees. With $300,000 in federal funding allocated in 1991, the first year of the proposed three-year project, the city will map the urban forest cover using aerial photography. Then, researchers will analyze the age, size, spatial distribution, and health of the trees in selected industrial and residential zones and other areas.

Carrying out plans to expand our urban forests and to maintain our existing ones requires money and labor. The value of the volunteer labor involved in the current planting movement probably cannot be calculated. As for the ecological value of existing and expanding urban forests, researchers are still amassing evidence of benefits, while identifying potential drawbacks. Some urban forest experts acknowledge that it might be better to do more research before massive planting begins. But they also acknowledge not wanting to squelch the current tree-planting movement when it took so long to get underway.

For further information:

Lipkis, Andy and Katie. *The Simple Act of Planting a Tree*. Jeremy P. Tarcher, Inc., 1990.

Moll, Gary, and Ebenreck, Sarz. *Shading Our Cities*. Island Press, 1989.

National Arbor Day Foundation, 100 Arbor Avenue, Nebraska City, NE 68410.

Urban Forests, a free periodical published by the American Forestry Association, P.O. Box 2000, Washington, DC 20013.

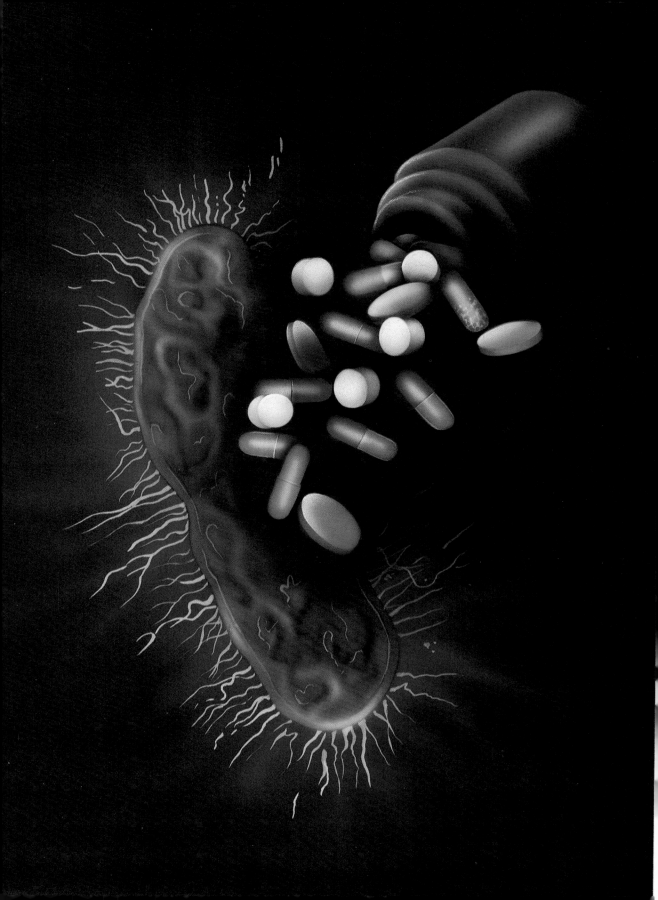

The overuse of antibiotics has intensified the battle between doctors attempting to treat bacterial infections and bacteria that have developed the ability to resist the drugs' attacks.

Drug-Bug Warfare

BY BEN PATRUSKY

Ravaged by fever and nearly delirious, the patient lay in the hospital's intensive care unit. Heavy doses of powerful bacteria-killing drugs had failed to halt the infection threatening his life. Worried doctors turned to another antibiotic, the most potent ever developed. Now they could only wait—and hope. Unfortunately, this antibiotic was no more effective than the others. The infection continued to spread. A few hours later, the patient was dead, a casualty in the continuing war between bacteria and the drugs used to destroy them.

Luckily, such bacterial victories are exceedingly rare—as they have been since penicillin, the first antibiotic medication, was introduced 50 years ago. Since then, doctors have been able to halt most life-threatening bacterial assaults with an arsenal of antibiotics that has become increasingly sophisticated. But the drug-bug war—in reality, a chemical arms race—never ceases.

Over the years, this cycle has repeated itself: A newly developed antibiotic at first proves highly effective against a disease-causing species of bacteria. But soon new *strains* (types) of the bacteria appear that are capable of resisting the drug's attack. In response, researchers must scramble to develop new chemical compounds capable of destroying the resistant bacteria.

In recent years, medical specialists have learned a great deal about

The author:
Ben Patrusky is a free-lance writer and a media consultant to several scientific institutions.

the ways in which bacteria *resist* (weaken or destroy) antibiotics, and they are putting that knowledge to use in developing new antibiotics. They have also gained a keener understanding of how the excessive use of antibiotics in people and animals is promoting the growth of resistant strains of bacteria and undermining the effectiveness of antibiotics.

Bacteria are the most ancient and most abundant form of life on Earth. There are at least 2,500 types of these one-celled microorganisms, which are neither plant nor animal. Bacteria, which first appeared at least 3.5 billion years ago, live almost everywhere. Many species are scavengers that *decompose* (break down) dead plants and animal matter. Without bacteria, the nutrients in dead organisms would not be returned to the soil and water to provide food for higher organisms. Life on Earth as we know it would soon cease.

Bacteria are also among the smallest and fastest growing of living things. One spoonful of soil may contain more than 1 billion bacteria. And, under the best conditions, a colony of bacteria may double its size in 20 minutes.

Many harmless or beneficial species of bacteria live on or in the human body. They aid in digestion or produce vitamins, for example. At times, however, other species can grow in the body. They get their nourishment by feeding on living tissue and can cause disease. These disorders range from boils, diarrhea, and ear infections to such life-threatening conditions as toxic shock syndrome and some types of pneumonia.

Bacteria often cause infection and disease by releasing *toxins* (poisons) either as they grow or when they die. These toxins destroy the membranes in healthy cells or may otherwise prevent the cells from functioning properly. Toxins released by the bacteria that cause tetanus, for example, prevent muscle cells from relaxing after contracting and interfere with the ability of nerve cells to transmit messages.

Although human beings have long been susceptible to attack by bacteria, people did not start the drug-bug war. We simply joined it. Before it was "us-against-them," it was "them-against-them." The battleground in this struggle is soil and water, where many bacteria, molds, and other microbes live. Penicillin, erythromycin, streptomycin, tetracycline, and other antibiotics exist in nature as the chemical weapons some microbes use to fight each other for food and space in their densely crowded environment. Penicillin, for example, is produced by a group of molds called *Penicillium*. Streptomycin is made by the bacteria species *Streptomyces griseus*.

As microbes evolved, certain strains acquired *genes* enabling them to produce bacteria-attacking proteins. Genes, the basic unit of heredity, *code for* (direct the production of) proteins in a cell. The bacteria-attacking proteins form antibiotics that improve the microbes' ability to survive and reproduce either by killing competitive

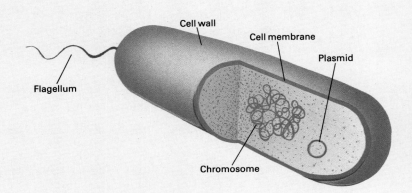

Anatomy of a Bacterium
Nearly all bacteria, one-celled organisms, have an outer protective layer called a *cell wall* and an inner layer called a *cell membrane.* The bacterium's genes are carried on a *chromosome.* Some bacteria also carry genes on ringlike structures called *plasmids.* A hairlike *flagellum* helps the bacterium move.

Cell wall

Cell membrane

Plasmid

Flagellum

Chromosome

microorganisms outright or by halting their growth. Antibiotics do this chiefly by either damaging their competitors' cell walls or disrupting their internal chemical processes.

Bacterial cells, like the cells of most other microbes, are surrounded by a protective outer layer called a *cell wall.* The wall is made up of an interlocking network of molecules—including sugars, proteins, and *lipids* (oily or fatty substances)—that serve as "bricks." Penicillin, cephalosporin, and certain other antibiotics interfere with a bacterium's ability to repair or expand its wall.

A molecule of one of these antibiotics has at its core a chemical structure called a *beta-lactam ring.* This ring is able to *bind with* (attach to) bacterial proteins that scientists named *penicillin binding proteins* (pbp's). In a bacterium, pbp's serve primarily as "bricklayers," collecting protein and sugar molecules manufactured by the bacterium and assembling them to produce new sections of the cell wall. The pbp molecules also become part of the cell wall. When the beta-lactam rings bind to the pbp molecules, however, the pbp molecules are "fooled" into accepting the rings as bricks. This creates gaps in the cell wall. As the bacterium grows, the gaps grow larger. Eventually, the contents of the cell spill out and the bacterium dies.

Other antibiotics disrupt the internal machinery of bacteria. The main targets are the *ribosomes,* structures that serve as centers for the assembly of proteins. Molecules of antibiotics such as streptomycin, erythromycin, and tetracycline bind to the ribosomes, preventing the bacterium from producing essential proteins. This halts cell growth and eventually causes the bacterium's death.

Some bacteria can defend themselves from antibiotics. These bacteria have *resistance genes,* which code for proteins that weaken or destroy antibiotic activity. Many scientists speculate that resistance first appeared in antibiotic-producing microorganisms because they

149

How Bacteria Infect Human Cells
Some bacteria invade cells, then multiply and release *toxins* (poisons) that kill the cells by destroying their membranes and internal structures, *below*.

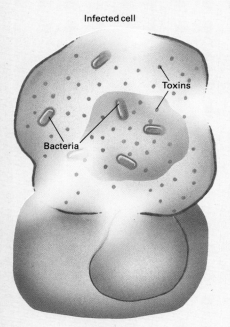

Infected cell

Toxins

Bacteria

Healthy cell

Some bacteria attach to and reproduce on the outer surface of cells, *below*. The bacteria release toxins that may enter those cells and kill them or may travel through the bloodstream and damage cells elsewhere in the body.

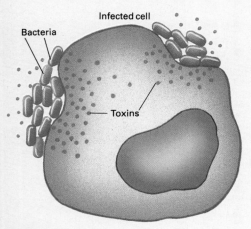

Infected cell

Bacteria

Toxins

needed a way to resist their own toxic compounds. Other scientists think that the organisms targeted by antibiotics were the first to develop resistance genes.

Resistance genes help bacteria weaken or destroy antibiotic action in a number of ways. For example, they may code for *beta-lactamase*, a chemical that chops up beta-lactam rings. In 1990, a team of researchers headed by microbiologist Alexander Tomasz of Rockefeller University in New York City discovered another, previously unknown strategy for fending off a beta-lactam attack. The researchers found that some strains of bacteria have acquired genes that code for an altered form of pbp. This form is still able to assemble cell walls, but it is different enough from the original so that beta-lactam rings are no longer able to bind to it.

Other resistant bacteria produce chemicals that inactivate attacking antibiotics by changing the antibiotic molecules' chemical structure. As a result, the altered antibiotics are no longer able to bind to ribosomes. Still other bacteria make it difficult for antibiotics to enter the cell. Another strategy is for bacteria to pump out the antibiotic if it does manage to enter. Some bacteria can do all of these things.

When the use of penicillin, the first antibiotic drug, became widespread in the mid-1940's, genes of resistance were already well established in bacteria. At first, however, antibiotic researchers did not give much thought to resistance. World War II had begun, and they were driven by the need to develop the technology for producing abundant supplies of penicillin for treating wounded soldiers. They were also thrilled by penicillin's power to fight infection.

Before this infection-fighting "wonder drug" was developed, bacterial infections and diseases had been a leading cause of death. Even minor injuries could have fatal consequences. For example, United States President Calvin Coolidge's younger son died in 1924 of blood poisoning after a blister he got while playing tennis became infected.

So it was not surprising that penicillin, streptomycin, tetracycline, and a host of other antibiotics introduced in the 1940's and 1950's seemed like miracle drugs. Because of penicillin, for example, the death rate from pneumococcal pneumonia, one of many diseases caused by *Streptococcus* bacteria, plunged from a high of between 60 and 80 per cent to from 1 to 5 per cent. Penicillin also sharply reversed the outlook for patients with other infections, such as bacterial meningitis, that almost always had been fatal.

Ironically, the widespread use of penicillin promoted the survival of penicillin-resistant bacteria. A doctor would prescribe penicillin for a patient with pneumococcal pneumonia, for example. Most of the bacteria causing the disease were vulnerable to the antibiotic. But among them might be a few bacteria that could produce beta-lactamase and so resist the drug's effect. The penicillin would kill nearly all of the nonresistant bacteria. Then, with competition eliminated, the resistant bacteria would survive and multiply.

Strains of penicillin-resistant *Staphylococcus*, another common group of bacteria, were first noticed in 1947 in a hospital in Great Britain, only six years after penicillin was introduced for general use. Some staphylococci species live harmlessly on human skin. But when they enter an opening in the skin—a surgical wound, for example—they may cause severe infection.

Within a few years, resistant strains of staphylococci had spread to hospitals around the world. At first, these strains could be contained by using higher doses of penicillin. Soon, however, even higher doses were ineffective. Doctors in the late 1940's could cure about 85 per cent of staphylococci infections with moderate doses of penicillin. By the early 1950's, the situation was reversed, with up to 80 per cent of staphylococci highly resistant to penicillin.

The resistance story was repeated with antibiotics such as tetracycline, erythromycin, and chloramphenicol that target the bacteria's ribosomes. The first versions of these drugs, introduced from the mid-1940's to the early 1950's, worked wonders with diseases caused by bacteria classified as *Gram negative*. (Penicillin is less effective against Gram-negative bacteria such as *Pseudomonas*, which causes severe infection in surgical wounds, because the microbes have an outer membrane surrounding the cell wall that blocks the antibiotics' entry.) But doctors soon detected resistance to these ribosome-targeting antibiotics as well.

Antibiotic researchers quickly fought back against resistant strains. In the late 1950's, researchers at Beacham Research Laboratories in Great Britain produced a new drug called methicillin that made penicillin-resistant staphylococci bacteria vulnerable once again—for a while at least. Like penicillin, from which it was derived, methicillin has a beta-lactam ring. But methicillin's beta-lactam ring is surrounded by a chemical structure called a *side chain* that blocks beta-lactamase molecules. The antibiotic, however, is still able to interfere with a bacterium's cell wall construction.

Just as the bacteria-antibiotic war heated up, a new and troublesome wrinkle in the resistance story came to light. Scientists

Where Antibiotics Come From
Antibiotics are natural substances made by microbes. Molds, bacteria, and other organisms in the soil may produce antibiotics that defend themselves against other microbes. Scientists have learned to use antibiotics made by molds and bacteria to make drugs for the treatment of bacterial infections.

Antibiotics Derived from Molds

- Cephalosporins
- Griseofulvin
- Penicillins

Antibiotics Derived from Bacteria

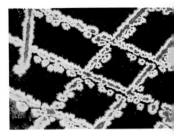

- Chloramphenicol
- Erythromycin
- Streptomycin
- Tetracyclines
- Vancomycin

Destroying Bacteria

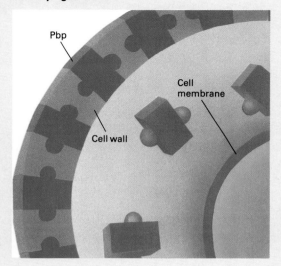

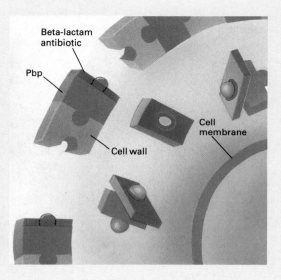

Some antibiotics contain chemical structures called *beta-lactam rings* that *bind* (attach) to bacterial proteins called *pbp's.* Pbp's help in the expansion and repair of the bacterial cell wall and also serve as "bricks" in the wall.

Once bound to beta-lactam rings, however, pbp's cannot function, and the cell wall develops gaps as the bacterium grows. Eventually, the contents of the cell spill out, and the bacterium dies.

discovered that one species of bacteria could transfer resistance genes to another. Evidence of this worrisome development first appeared in 1959 when a Japanese woman came down with a persistent case of dysentery, which may be caused by several species of *Shigella* bacteria. None of the antibiotics normally prescribed for this disease, including tetracycline and streptomycin, had any effect on the woman's infection. Soon, other cases of persistent dysentery caused by resistant *Shigella* bacteria were reported.

While studying the patients' stools for clues to this puzzle, Japanese researchers found strains of *Escherichia coli* bacteria that were also resistant to tetracycline and other antibiotics. *E. coli*, commonly found in the human intestinal tract, is normally harmless. A team of scientists led by Tomoichiro Akiba of Tokyo University discovered that the *E. coli* in the patients' intestinal tracts had developed resistance to the antibiotics and then transferred that resistance to the invading *Shigella* bacteria.

The discovery overturned the belief that resistance to antibiotics spread only in much the same way that traits are inherited among higher organisms. Genetic traits in human beings are passed only from parent to child. Bacteria also pass genes to their offspring as they reproduce. Now, scientists learned, one bacterium could transfer genes to an unrelated bacterium. This meant that disease-causing bacteria could become resistant by acquiring genes from

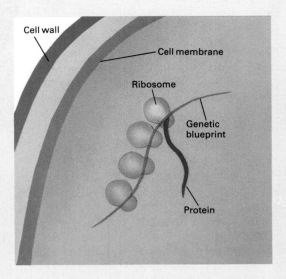

Some antibiotics target a bacterium's *ribosomes,* structures that "read" a cell's genetic blueprint and assemble new proteins needed for growth.

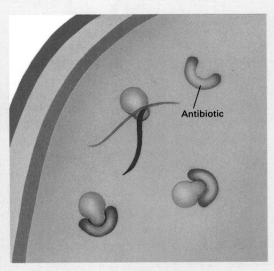

These antibiotics prevent the ribosomes from assembling proteins. Without the proteins, the bacterial cell dies.

other species, even harmless ones. It also meant that an antibiotic could become ineffective against a variety of bacterial species even faster than expected.

But how were resistance genes passed from species to species? Research in the early 1960's uncovered the key vehicle—*plasmids,* circular rings of *deoxyribonucleic acid* (DNA), the substance of which genes are made. Plasmids, which carry at least one gene, are "extra" genetic material in a bacterium. They exist apart from the bacterium's *chromosome,* a large ring of DNA that carries the microbe's essential genes.

Plasmids are able to move from one bacterium to another. Here is how the process works: In addition to resistance genes, a bacterium's plasmids may contain genes that trigger a process called *conjugation.* The genes cause the bacterium to send out a hairlike structure called a *pilus* to another bacterium. The bacteria are then pulled together. As the two bacteria are merging, the plasmid's DNA is copied and one of the copies enters the second bacterium. The bacteria then separate. The result is two bacteria with identical plasmids with resistance genes.

The next question was: How did the plasmids first acquire resistance genes? Scientists believe that resistance genes developed first in chromosomes and then moved onto plasmids.

But how did the resistance genes get from the chromosomes to the plasmids? One answer came in the early 1970's, with the identification of *transposons*, also known as "jumping genes." Transposons are pieces of DNA containing one or more genes along with genetic material that enables them to jump from one place to another on the chromosome. Transposons can also jump from chromosome to plasmid, from plasmid to plasmid, and from plasmid to chromosome. The identification of jumping genes explained how resistance genes could move from chromosome to plasmid.

Although plasmids almost certainly represent the major means by which resistance spreads, scientists have evidence suggesting that there are other ways. One may be through certain types of viruses that infect microbes. In this case, transposons carrying resistance genes jump from a bacterial plasmid or chromosome to a virus that has infected the bacterium. If the virus then invades another bacterium, the resistance genes are carried along.

Another possible avenue of transfer is by means of free DNA. Scientists had long believed that DNA quickly broke down when outside the cell. But recent studies done in water and soil suggest that such free DNA may remain stable for days, far longer than previously supposed. So although a bacterium with resistance genes may die, its DNA may remain intact long enough to be taken in by another bacterium. Once inside the second bacterium, the DNA becomes incorporated into the bacterium's chromosome.

As scientists learned more about the ways in which bacteria combat antibiotics, they put that knowledge to work creating antibiotics that were not susceptible to counterattack by resistance proteins. But the drama invariably repeats itself: Researchers discover a new antibiotic; its effectiveness leads to its widespread use; a bacterial strain with the means to thwart the drug appears and may eventually pass that resistance on to its descendants and to other species of bacteria.

In the early 1980's, however, researchers were convinced they had finally found a way to end this chemical arms race. Several drug companies had succeeded in creating powerful antibiotics that researchers believed would defeat all resistance strategies for a long time to come. These antibiotics included advanced forms of cephalosporin and penicillin that could attack Gram-negative bacteria. The drugs were also designed to break down more slowly in the body than other antibiotics do. This increases the chances that individual doses would wreak greater damage on infectious bacteria. Beyond that, researchers had surrounded the beta-lactam rings in the antibiotic molecules with side chains that they believed could keep all known beta-lactamases at bay.

The researchers' confidence was heightened further by the introduction, also in the early 1980's, of fluoroquinolones. These powerful antibiotics are not found in nature. They were designed in the laboratory. For that reason, researchers believed bacteria would have a very hard time coming up with a resistance mechanism.

In the wake of those developments, many scientists thought that the bugs were finally on the run and that there was no need for new antibiotics. As a result, many major drug manufacturers halted research programs aimed at developing new bacteria-killing molecules.

Their confidence was misplaced. Resistance to the advanced cephalosporins emerged rapidly. It was first detected in 1983 in Germany in samples of *Klebsiella pneumoniae*, a Gram-negative species that causes respiratory, intestinal, and urinary infections. Within a few years, resistant strains of *K. pneumoniae* had spread around the world.

Researchers quickly discovered the means of resistance. It did not involve a new gene but stemmed instead from *mutations* (changes) in genes coding for known beta-lactamases. These mutations allowed the bacteria to produce a new version of the beta-lactamases with an altered shape that enables it to maneuver past the side chains to get at the beta-lactam rings.

"That finding rocked everybody back on their heels," says molecular biologist and physician Stuart B. Levy of the Tufts University School of Medicine in Boston, an authority on antibiotic resistance. "Previous experience suggested that resistance required the emergence of a new gene, not a simple change in an old gene."

The advanced penicillins still seem effective. But researchers have now detected some resistance to these drugs as well in several Gram-negative bacteria, including *Pseudomonas*.

The news about the fluoroquinolones is not good either. Instead of targeting ribosomes, fluoroquinolone antibiotics home in on a protein that keeps the DNA in a bacterium's chromosome tightly coiled. If the chromosome changes its structure, it cannot function properly. In the mid-1980's, however, researchers detected fluoroquinolone resistance in *Pseudomonas* and *Staphylococcus* bacteria. But instead of altering the antibiotic, the resistant bacteria altered their own molecules so that the antibiotic is ineffective. For example, a bacterium may change the structure of the protein that keeps its chromosome tightly coiled so that the antibiotic molecule can no longer bind to this protein.

Resisting Antibiotics

Some strains of bacteria resist antibiotics by producing proteins that weaken or destroy the antibiotics.

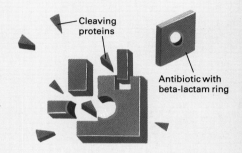

Some bacteria produce cleaving proteins, which chop up the beta-lactam ring of an antibiotic molecule.

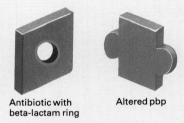

Some bacteria produce an altered form of pbp that does not bind to beta-lactam rings and so can continue to repair the cell wall.

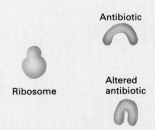

Other bacteria produce chemicals that change the shape of the antibiotic molecule, preventing it from binding to the ribosomes.

With staphylococci already resistant to penicillin and related antibiotics and resistance to cephalosporins and fluoroquinolones growing, doctors have only one antibiotic left with which to fight the most serious staphylococci infections: vancomycin. To make matters worse, in 1988, researchers in France discovered resistance to vancomycin in bacteria that can cause severe intestinal infections. Doctors worry that this resistance will spread to staphylococci.

Is there a way to stop the growing resistance threat? Scientists know what needs to be done. First, they say, we must stem the practice that got us into trouble in the first place—the overuse of antibiotics. A number of studies have shown that antibiotics are being administered inappropriately as much as 60 per cent of the time. For example,

How Antibiotic Resistance Spreads
Bacteria that resist antibiotics contain *resistance genes,* bits of *deoxyribonucleic acid* (DNA) that direct the production of antibiotic-fighting proteins. These genes can be carried on plasmids, passed from generation to generation, and transferred to other strains or species of bacteria.

Normal Reproduction

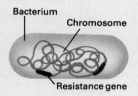
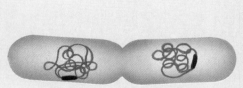
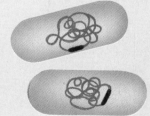

A bacterium's DNA reproduces.

The microbe divides in two.

A resistance gene in the first bacterium is now in both.

Transferring Plasmids

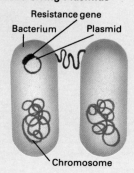
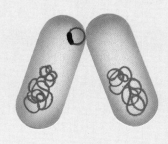
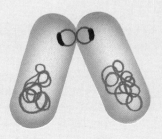

A thin structure called a pilus can cause one bacterium to connect with another.

A copy of a plasmid, including a resistance gene, is transferred to the second bacterium.

Both bacteria now contain the resistance gene.

some doctors prescribe antibiotics for patients with colds and other infections caused by viruses. The antibiotics don't affect the viruses, but they do destroy nonresistant bacteria, improving the environment for resistant bacteria. Many researchers believe that if antibiotics were administered more selectively, bacteria vulnerable to antibiotics could become dominant once again.

Resistance is a special problem in hospitals, unique environments where people with many different bacterial infections collect. Not surprisingly, antibiotic use is both common and heavy in hospitals, and these facilities are the only places the most potent antibiotics, such as vancomycin, are used.

Researchers are looking for ways to avoid the development of

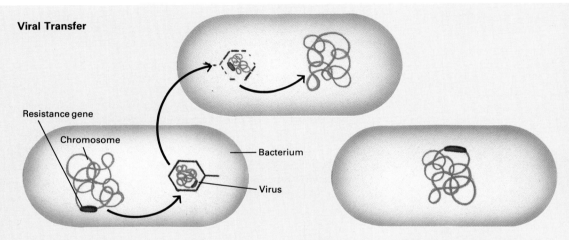

Viral Transfer

Resistance gene

Chromosome

Bacterium

Virus

Bacteria may also transfer resistance by means of *transposons,* genes that can jump onto the DNA of a plasmid or a virus that infects bacteria, *above.*

When a virus containing a transposon infects another bacterium, *center,* the resistance gene can jump into the DNA of the second bacterium, which now becomes resistant to a particular antibiotic, *above.*

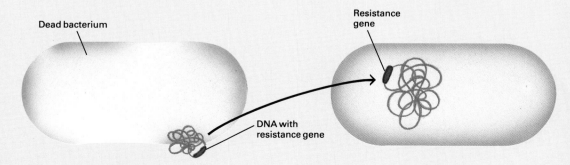

Free DNA

Resistance gene

Dead bacterium

DNA with resistance gene

Bacterial DNA containing a resistance gene may survive after a bacterium dies.

This DNA can be taken up by another nearby bacterium, making it resistant to a particular antibiotic.

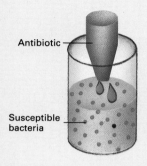

Antibiotic

Susceptible bacteria

An antibiotic added to bacteria in a test tube mimics what happens in the body.

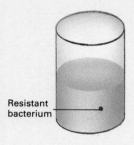

Resistant bacterium

The antibiotic kills all but the resistant bacteria.

The resistant bacteria flourish. Killing them may require a more powerful antibiotic.

resistant strains in hospital patients. George Jacoby, an infectious disease specialist at Massachusetts General Hospital in Boston, believes that one way is to avoid the common practice of continuing patients on antibiotics after surgery—sometimes for weeks—to prevent infection. But antibiotics have a protective effect that lasts only 48 hours after surgery. "After that," Jacoby says, "all you're doing is improving the environment for resistant bugs by killing off bacteria vulnerable to the antibiotic. Then if a patient develops an infection later, it will almost certainly be caused by one of the resistant strains of bacteria."

To cut antibiotic use in hospitals, some administrators have begun to require that doctors justify in writing their continued use of the drugs beyond a certain period. The use of certain antibiotics may also be restricted unless an infectious disease specialist has approved it. Medical personnel, especially those working in intensive care units where antibiotic use is heavy, are also being encouraged to wash their hands frequently and to take other hygienic precautions to avoid accidentally transmitting bacteria from patient to patient.

Another part of the resistance problem stems from antibiotic overuse in agriculture. About 50 per cent of all antibiotics produced in the United States are given to farm animals. Some of that amount is used to treat infection. Most of it, however, is added to animal feed to promote livestock growth. Although some researchers disagree, many scientists believe this practice promotes the growth of resistant bacteria strains in the animals. Livestock "are not toilet trained," microbiologist Thomas F. O'Brien of Brigham and Women's Hospital in Boston notes. "They dwell in close quarters so there's lots of cross contamination, lots of bacterial exchange and, as a consequence, lots of opportunity for plasmid transfer." In this way, resistance genes may pass among bacterial strains. Experts are especially concerned because these resistant strains can reach people who consume the meat, milk, and other products from these animals.

Among the most widely used farm antibiotics are penicillin and tetracycline. Many bacteria found in people are already resistant to these antibiotics, and so their acquiring resistance is not the big worry. Levy and others are more concerned because prolonged tetracycline use promotes the growth of bacteria that are resistant to a variety of other antibiotics as well. So extensive use of tetracycline could encourage the growth of these multidrug-resistant bacteria by killing off competing nonresistant strains.

The most worrisome development is the sudden emergence in the U.S. pig population of infections caused by bacteria resistant to nearly all commonly used animal antibiotics. So, with the approval of the U.S. government, farm veterinarians have begun to treat infected pigs with fluoroquinolones. Some microbiologists worry that bacteria in the pigs may develop resistance to these antibiotics and that the resistant bacteria may eventually be transferred to people.

Fighting Back

Scientists are using a number of strategies to develop antibiotics that kill resistant bacteria.

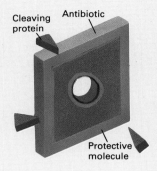

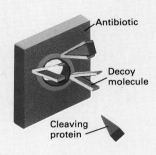

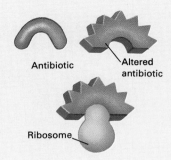

Protective molecules added to antibiotics containing beta-lactam rings prevent cleaving proteins from getting to the rings.

Decoy molecules added to beta-lactam antibiotics bind cleaving proteins, preventing them from chopping up beta-lactam rings.

Other antibiotics are redesigned so that bacteria can no longer prevent them from binding to ribosomes.

Resistance is an even more pressing problem in developing countries, according to O'Brien and other public health experts. In the United States and many other nations, only physicians can write prescriptions for antibiotics. In some developing countries, however, the drugs are available without prescription, and people may be given little guidance in their use. What often happens, O'Brien says, is that people take antibiotics in small doses for short periods. These doses are too small to completely destroy the bacteria causing the infection but are large enough to kill significant numbers of antibiotic-sensitive bacteria and give the resistant ones more growing room.

So, are bacteria winning the war? The opinion of the experts is: hardly. "Let's just say that the bacteria have simply brought us back into the fighting ring," says Levy, a founder of the Alliance for the Prudent Use of Antibiotics, a multinational educational organization. "A few years ago, some people thought the war was over and that we'd won. But then the bacteria came roaring back. Nevertheless, our arsenal remains far from empty.

"What we don't want is to have to fight the same battle with each new antibiotic. We have to reestablish the effectiveness of older antibiotics and safeguard the newer ones. For that to happen, we all have to work toward more appropriate use of antibiotics. And, we're going to have to get back to the research bench and come up with new strategies for keeping bacteria in check. But one thing we have learned is that there will never be an out-and-out victor in this battle."

BY CHRIS ELFRING

Fire and Nature

Fire is a regular, natural, and even
necessary occurrence in forests,
grasslands, and other wilderness areas.

It was dry, hot, and windy—ideal conditions for a fire. Thunder growled, and brilliant streaks of lightning flashed through the air. A lightning strike touched the ground, igniting a dry meadow. The fire scorched a wide, irregular patch in the grass but burned out quickly. The storm continued with sound and fury but little rain. Another bolt of lightning leapt from cloud to Earth, striking a tall, long-dead tree. The tree exploded into flames, and shards of burning wood flew in all directions. Smoldering embers landed on a thick layer of dead branches and dry pine needles that covered the forest floor, and the wind soon whipped them into flames.

This is a scene that repeats itself time and time again in forests and grasslands everywhere on Earth. In Yosemite National Park in 1990, Yellowstone National Park in 1988, and countless other places and times throughout the history of life, fire has shaped the landscape. Given the right conditions—the necessary blend of dry weather and plentiful fuel—such fires can be frightening. The 1988 blazes in Yellowstone park burned—to varying degrees—403,000 hectares (995,000 acres), or about 45 per cent of the park. Only favorable winds, combined with intense fire-fighting efforts, saved a historic inn and other visitor buildings near Old Faithful geyser.

Yosemite's 1990 fires also burned with startling fury. The flames blackened some 9,700 hectares (24,000 acres). The town of Foresta, within the park, lost 66 of its 86 buildings. Residents of nearby towns fled their homes. About 10,000 tourists spent a nervous night trapped in the park's central valley, escaping at 4:30 a.m. along roads flanked by blazing trees. For the first time in the park's 100-year history, Yosemite was closed.

The blazes at Yellowstone and Yosemite and the threat of still more major fires have focused new attention on the role fire plays in nature. Scientists have long known that forest fires are a normal part of the life cycle of a forest. Despite the devastation fire can cause, it is not an enemy. To forests, it is a familiar visitor. As scientists learn more about the ecological benefits brought by fire, they hope to use those lessons to improve how we manage our wildlands.

Fire is a regular natural occurrence in almost all ecosystems on land. An *ecosystem* consists of the plants, animals, and microbes living in an environment together with the nonliving components, such as soil, rocks, and water. A few land ecosystems do not burn. Polar regions, for example, are too barren of vegetation to sustain a blaze. Deserts rarely burn. Other exceptions are tropical rain forests, so damp that natural fires are rare. But rain forests do burn when people cut down the trees and set them on fire to clear land for farming.

Beyond these few exceptions, fire is a universal factor like sunshine and rain. All woodlands will burn when conditions are right. So will all grasslands. In fact, many ecosystems depend on fire.

A major role of fire in an ecosystem is to set back the "ecological clock" and begin anew the process called *succession*. Scientists use the term *succession* to describe the changes in communities of plants,

The author:
Chris Elfring is a senior staff officer at the National Academy of Sciences in Washington, D.C.

animals, and microbes that occur in an ecosystem over decades or centuries. In Western mountain regions such as the Yellowstone area, succession leads to the development of an *old-growth* (mature) forest of pine, spruce, and fir. As trees grow taller, less sunlight reaches the forest floor. Fewer plants grow beneath the trees.

The likelihood of fire increases over time. Aging trees grow steadily more combustible, and the forest floor becomes littered with dead branches and leaves that provide fuel.

Then, fire plays its critical role. Flames sweep through the forest, clearing the landscape of all but charred trunks. Suddenly, sunlight can reach the ground. The first plants to spring up are fast-growing perennial species, including many wild flowers and grasslike plants called *sedges*. In many Western areas, fireweed, a common pioneering plant with rose-pink flowers, grows from a spreading underground root system. Other plants grow from seeds that have lain dormant in the ground for years, waiting for favorable conditions. Birds, other animals, and the wind carry seeds of still other species that find a fertile seedbed in the burned area. Within a year, grasses, sedges, and wild flowers come to dominate, and the land becomes a meadow.

The return of the forest

In a few years, shrubs and tree seedlings begin to appear. Pine seedlings poking above the grasses signal the return of the forest. Lodgepole pine, a tree with a tall, straight trunk, is particularly common in Western areas that have burned. The young pines grow rapidly while the site is still open and sunny.

After several decades, the pines become so large and dense that their upper limbs block out the sun, a stage of development that scientists call *canopy closure*. The canopy of branches overhead shades the forest floor and prevents the growth of new pine seedlings, which need direct sunlight. Trees such as Engelmann spruce and subalpine fir, however, can grow in the shade of the canopy. This forest of tall pines with smaller spruce and fir might dominate for the next 150 to 300 years. Eventually, the oldest pines die, leaving a canopy of tall spruce and fir with only a few pines. This is the old-growth forest.

Just as the plant species change over time, so do the animal species. The tender young plants that sprout after a fire attract browsing animals such as mice and rabbits. Hawks, foxes, and other predators move into the area, too, because the reduced cover makes prey easier to find. In fact, certain species of hawks fly toward large plumes of smoke. Scientists believe the birds have learned to associate smoke with prey.

The abundance of grasses and other plants where once there was Western mountain forest benefits grazers such as bighorn sheep, elk, and bison. Moose, deer, and elk browse on the shrubs and small trees, such as aspen and willow, that flourish after a fire. Aspen also is a favorite food of beavers. After the forest returns, squirrels and other creatures that feed largely on tree seeds move into the area.

Glossary

Canopy: The upper branches of a forest.

Crown fire: An intense fire that burns the upper leaves and branches of a forest; also called a *canopy burn.*

Ecosystem: The group of plants, animals, and microbes living in an environment, along with nonliving features such as soil, rocks, and water.

Succession: The changes in communities of plants, animals, and microbes in an area over decades or centuries.

Surface fire, or surface burn: A fire that travels along the ground, consuming mostly undergrowth and deadwood but not killing many trees.

Wildfire: According to U.S. National Park Service guidelines, any fire that must be suppressed; not necessarily a naturally caused fire or one burning out of control.

Gradually, the aging forest lays the foundation for the next fire. As debris builds up on the forest floor, a major forest fire becomes all but inevitable. A drought often provides the trigger, but it is only a matter of time before another blaze rages through the area and the cycle begins again. These periodic fires in a large woodland region create a mixture of forested areas in various stages of succession.

Scientists have found that the plant and animal species of many regions, including much of the American West, have evolved under the influence of periodic natural fires. Many species actually need fire to flourish. Lodgepole pines, for example, grow two kinds of seed-bearing cones. One kind of cone releases its seeds regardless of fire activity. The other, called a *serotinous cone*, releases its seeds only when exposed to intense heat.

Aspen, a medium-sized tree in the poplar family with delicate leaves that tremble in the slightest breeze, also has evolved to survive periodic fires. Although aspen trees burn easily in even a moderate fire, their hardy underground roots stay alive and quickly send up thousands of small shoots called *suckers*. Scientists have counted as many as 148,000 suckers per hectare (60,000 per acre) in a burned-over aspen grove. An established root system gives aspen suckers a head start over seedlings of other tree species. Aspens grow rapidly in forest areas cleared by fire and often become the dominant tree. In fact, an aspen grove—most noticeable in the fall when its leaves turn a brilliant yellow—is often a clue that the site once burned.

Benefits of fire

Perhaps the major ecological benefit of fire is that it recycles *nutrients*, chemical elements that plants need for growth. From the soil, plants obtain nitrogen, phosphorus, potassium, calcium, and other nutrients provided by the weathering of minerals and decaying vegetation. After decades of uninterrupted growth, a forest floor is often littered with dead plant material. In cool, dry areas such as the American West, this debris decays slowly and may accumulate for centuries. Fire breaks down dead organic matter much faster than do the bacteria and fungi otherwise responsible for decay. The ashes left by a fire provide a fertilizer rich in plant nutrients.

Fire not only fertilizes the soil but also clears a space for new plants. No trees or large plants compete with new sprouts for light, moisture, or nutrients. These conditions stimulate surprisingly rapid growth, and the new growth is particularly nutritious for plant-eating animals.

Although fire creates greater diversity of habitat and stimulates plant growth, benefiting wildlife in the long term, what about the short term? Are animals killed? In most cases, surprisingly few animals die. Francis J. Singer, a research ecologist at Yellowstone National Park, made a survey of dead animals soon after the 1988 fires and collected tissue samples to determine the cause of death. He

A Natural Ecosystem Cycle

Fire is part of the natural life cycle of most ecosystems. After a severe fire kills an old stand of trees in a Western evergreen forest, the area becomes a meadow with standing dead trees. In about five years, pine seedlings appear above the grasses. The burned trees fall, and the new young pines grow rapidly in the sunny forest. Fifty to 100 years later, the trees form a dense stand that blocks the sun, a stage called *canopy closure.* As the forest ages, dead branches and other debris accumulate on the ground, providing fuel for another fire.

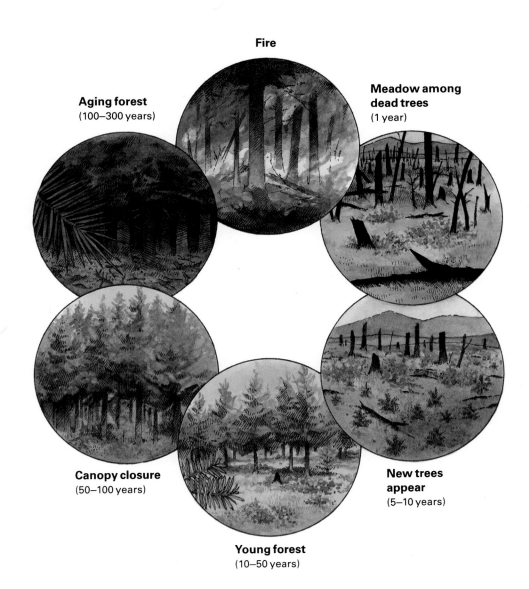

Fire

Aging forest
(100–300 years)

Meadow among dead trees
(1 year)

Canopy closure
(50–100 years)

New trees appear
(5–10 years)

Young forest
(10–50 years)

found that only 261 large mammals had died—246 elk, 9 bison, 4 mule deer, and 2 moose. Soot deposits in the *trachea* (airway) of the dead elk suggested that smoke inhalation—not flames or high temperatures—had killed most of them. These dead elk amounted to less than 1 per cent of the 31,000 elk that were living that summer in the park. Researchers who had fitted many of the park's grizzly bears with radio collars to track their movements believe two bears also died.

The reason for the low death rate is that most large mammals easily escape the flames. They simply walk or run away. Many observers of the Yellowstone fires saw elk and other wildlife grazing unconcerned a short distance from the flames.

Smaller animals also have adaptations that help them cope with fire. Burrowing animals such as gophers, snakes, and certain insects retreat underground, where the soil shields them from the heat. Quick-moving species, such as squirrels and the weasellike pine martens, outrun the flames or hide in patches of vegetation that remain unburned. Most birds are unaffected unless the fire occurs during the spring nesting season, a rare occurrence because that season is typically wet.

Most of the animals that die in fires are sick, old, or very young. More animals may die during the following winter if the fire reduces the food supply. But such deaths are natural events that help maintain a healthy population.

A burn mosaic

Another reason that so many plants and animals survive, researchers have found, is that most fires burn irregularly. The flames do not sweep uniformly across a landscape incinerating everything in their path. Instead, a fire blackens some areas but leaves many islands of untouched green. From the air, a burned forest can look like a patchwork quilt. Some patches are charred black where the blaze raged most intensely. Surrounding the black patches are brown areas of more limited damage. Even within the black patches, small green islands of vegetation remain alive. The fire might skip over a damp hollow, for instance, or a rocky outcropping might block the flames

Two Types of Forest Fires
A forest is subject to two types of fires—frequent small ones called *surface fires* or *surface burns* and occasional, more destructive ones, called *crown fires* or *canopy burns*. A surface burn, *opposite page, top,* travels along the ground, consuming mostly undergrowth and downed wood. The fire is relatively cool and kills few trees. A canopy burn, *opposite page, bottom,* rages through the upper branches of the forest with intense heat. Such blazes kill old stands of trees and clear the way for new growth. Periodic surface fires remove debris and reduce the chances of a crown fire.

A Mosaic of Destruction

Forest fires can cause great destruction in limited areas, leaving only charred trunks and ashes, *above.* But most fires create an irregular pattern of destruction, *right,* that scientists call a *burn mosaic.* The blackened patches where the fire raged most intensely are surrounded by brown belts of limited damage. Other areas remain green and unburned, providing a rich source of seeds to restore the forest.

from a patch of forest. The unburned areas provide a rich source of surviving organisms, seeds, and spores to help return the charred forest to life.

Different types of forest fires have different effects. *Surface fires*, also called *surface burns*, travel along the ground, consuming mostly undergrowth and fallen trees. These fires are relatively cool and do little damage. Unless there is a large build-up of fuel on the forest floor, surface fires do not grow large enough or hot enough to ignite the upper branches of the trees. Few trees die, and the forest typically returns to its prefire condition within three to five years.

More destructive are *crown fires*, or *canopy burns*, which result when flames spread to the upper branches of the forest. Crown fires burn with intense heat and violence. Winds drive the flames from treetop to treetop at speeds of up to 16 kilometers per hour (10 miles per hour). Hot embers and other burning debris may blow for long distances, setting fires elsewhere in the forest. Large accumulations of deadwood, which build up in the absence of surface fires, increase the chance that when a fire does start, it will leap into the canopy of the forest and cause a fierce crown fire.

Of the 403,000 hectares burned in Yellowstone in 1988, not quite two-thirds—232,000 hectares (573,000 acres)—suffered canopy burn. Some 149,000 hectares (367,000 acres) experienced surface burn, which allowed most trees in these areas to survive.

Each ecosystem has its own pattern of periodic fires—frequent small fires alternating with occasional larger, more destructive ones—depending on the area's climate and vegetation. After the 1988 Yellowstone fires, biologists William H. Romme of Fort Lewis College in Durango, Colo., and Donald G. Despain of the park's science staff reconstructed the fire history of the area. The scientists drilled into tree trunks, removing core samples from both living trees and fallen logs and checking for deposits of charcoal or partially burned wood. The researchers found that Yellowstone has a natural history of small surface burns every few years and massive canopy fires every 200 or 300 years.

Fire in other ecosystems

Forests are not the only ecosystem subject to burning. The original North American prairie offered ideal conditions for fire—periodic drought, high temperatures, and strong winds. The grasses provided abundant, continuous fuel. And there were few natural firebreaks—such as rivers or strips of land bare of vegetation—to stop a fire once it ignited. The journals of early pioneers on the Great Plains describe massive fires that blackened the sky with smoke and raced across the prairie as fast as a horse could gallop. A prairie fire could burn with surprising intensity, not stopping until a drenching rainstorm put it out or a wide river blocked its path.

Prairie or grassland ecosystems usually occur in regions that receive less rainfall than forests do. Grassland plant species have

Adapted to Fire

Many plant species have evolved traits that enable them to survive periodic fires and even flourish afterward.

The rose-pink blossoms of fireweed are often the first flowers to appear in burned areas. The plant sprouts from a spreading underground root system.

The glowing fall foliage of an aspen grove indicates that a major forest fire swept through the area several decades earlier. The hardy underground roots of an aspen tree survived the fire and sent up hundreds of small shoots called *suckers.*

The charred cone of a lodgepole pine, *left,* has been opened by the heat of a forest fire. Some lodgepole cones open at maturity, but others, called *serotinous cones,* remain closed until intense heat causes their scales to open and release their seeds, *below.*

Before fire

After fire

Seedling

After fires devastated Yellowstone National Park in 1988, park biologist Donald G. Despain uses a rectangular frame, *left,* to help him accurately count lodgepole seedlings.

adapted to survive periodic droughts, and some of the same adaptations that protect grasses from drought also help them survive fire. Many grasses have extensive underground root structures that remain alive after the aboveground growth has died. Whether the surface foliage is killed by drought, frost, overgrazing, or by a rapidly moving fire, the root system remains alive and the plant can sprout again once conditions are favorable.

In prairies, as in forests, fires enrich the soil with nutrients. Grasslands can produce a dense litter of dead and decaying material that accumulates on top of the soil. This accumulation stifles growth. Fire speeds the decay process on prairies just as it does in forests, releasing nutrients trapped in dead plant material and increasing soil fertility. The underground portions of the plants respond to the good conditions. The plants quickly grow large, lush, and green. Grazing and browsing animals such as bison and elk prefer this new prairie vegetation.

Like their woodland counterparts, prairie animals typically show little fear of fires. Bison and other large mammals often simply outrun the flames. Small grassland species such as mice and prairie dogs hide underground.

Large prairie fires rarely occur today because little is left of the prairie. As settlements spread West in the 1800's, farms, ranches, and towns broke up the once-vast expanses of grassland into smaller and smaller pieces. The breakup of the prairie limited the ability of fire to spread. To protect homes and property, fire fighters quickly put out any wildfires that did start.

Conservationists trying to restore and preserve prairie remnants recognize the importance of fires. Periodic burning promotes the vigorous growth of native prairie plants and suppresses competing nonnative species. In fact, fires are so vital to a prairie ecosystem that if they do not occur naturally, they must be started deliberately. Trained fire crews set controlled burns, carefully managed to minimize danger to nearby property.

Early policies of fire management

Until recently, the idea of deliberately burning a forested area would have seemed unthinkable. Fire management meant fire suppression, especially in the national parks. Yellowstone became the first national park in the United States in 1872. In 1886, Congress assigned the U.S. Cavalry to guard the park against illegal hunting and to fight forest fires. That was the beginning of a policy of fire suppression that applied to all the nation's parklands and wilderness areas and lasted almost a century.

Early attempts to fight forest fires were not very effective, but the ability to combat fire increased dramatically after the end of World War II in 1945. The Forest Service and other federal agencies converted military airplanes for use in fire fighting. Aircraft could reach even distant back country quickly, moving equipment and personnel to hot spots or dropping large loads of water or fire-retardant chemicals.

Through the 1950's and 1960's, forest managers and the public focused on preventing and fighting fires. The Forest Service conducted a famous advertising campaign starring Smokey Bear, who proclaimed, "Remember: Only YOU can prevent forest fires." Indeed, despite the benefits fire can bring, it can be terribly destructive. Fire destroys trees that may have taken centuries to grow. When flames strip the vegetation from hilly land, soil erosion increases. An intense blaze can bake or burn the soil, reducing its ability to absorb water and sometimes destroying beneficial soil organisms. And the aftermath of a fire is not pretty. A blackened landscape can hurt tourism.

Changes in fire policy

Gradually, however, attitudes toward fires began to change. In the early 1960's, scientists and conservationists began to acknowledge the essential role fire played in natural ecosystems. Wilderness managers began to seek strategies to handle fire as a natural process while still protecting people and property.

For the National Park Service, the turning point came in 1963. That year, a committee of scientists headed by ecologist A. Starker Leopold, son of the famous naturalist Aldo Leopold, prepared a landmark report at the request of the secretary of the interior. The so-called Leopold report proposed that the highest goal of the national parks was to maintain the "biotic associations"—that is, the relationships of living things—present when the first Europeans arrived in North America. Park managers were to strive to maintain or re-create a "reasonable illusion of primitive America." The report

An elk grazes on the tender new shoots growing in Yellowstone after widespread forest fires there in 1988. Such new growth is a favorite food of many grazing and browsing animals because it is high in nutrition.

Fires are so important to wilderness areas that if they do not occur naturally, managers must set them. A member of a fire crew helps manage a controlled burn on a restored prairie, *right*. Periodic burning promotes the growth of native prairie plants and suppresses unwanted species.

called for a more ecologically sound approach to park management, including an end to total fire suppression.

The recommendations in the Leopold report became official park policy in 1968. Since then, the National Park Service has used the Leopold report as a guide to fire management. When deciding how to manage fires, policymakers take into account the causes of the fires. About 10 per cent of all fires have natural causes, almost always lightning. On rare occasions, a blaze may start when a falling rock strikes a spark from another rock or an erupting volcano spews red-hot lava. The remaining 90 per cent of all forest fires are caused by people—most often careless smokers, campers, or workers using machinery in the woods. Park officials decided that lightning-caused fires in certain parks should be allowed to burn as long as they did not threaten lives, buildings, or rare resources.

The prescribed-fire plan

Managers drafted fire management plans for each park that spelled out in advance the conditions under which fires would be permitted to burn. These *prescribed fires* are any blazes—whether started by lightning or set by fire crews—that meet certain conditions, including posing no foreseeable danger to human lives or buildings. All other fires, including all fires accidentally started by people, are referred to as *wildfires*. Park policy calls for all wildfires to be fought quickly and aggressively.

In 1972, Yellowstone was one of a number of parks that adopted plans allowing natural fires to run their course. Between 1972 and

1987, park rangers allowed some 235 prescribed fires to burn in Yellowstone. Of those, 205 fizzled out after burning less than half a hectare. Park managers felt that the new policy was a success.

The massive Yellowstone fires of 1988 put the prescribed-fire policy to a real test. Unusually hot, dry conditions had left the forests as dry as tinderboxes. Also, much of Yellowstone had a 100-year accumulation of dead wood and other litter. And a large proportion of the park's trees were aging lodgepole pines, 200 years old or more, which were highly combustible. Under those conditions, a huge fire was almost inevitable.

Lightning sparked some of the Yellowstone fires; careless people started others. At first, park managers followed their plans to let the prescribed fires burn. When they realized the extraordinary intensity of the blazes, they mounted an all-out fire-fighting effort. But the fires became huge and roared across the landscape.

The destruction caused by the 1988 Yellowstone fires sparked furious protests over the Park Service policy for prescribed fires. Were the park managers wrong? Did allowing natural fires to burn worsen the devastation?

After the Yellowstone fires were quelled, two independent teams of experts tried to answer those questions. Not just Yellowstone, but all the nation's remaining wildlands stood to be affected by the answers. The 10-member Fire Management Policy Review Team, made up of foresters and wilderness managers, released its report in December 1988. The Greater Yellowstone Ecological Assessment Panel, a team of 13 scientists headed by botanist Norman L. Christensen of Duke University in Durham, N.C., issued its report in April 1989. Both reports called for more study of the ecological role of fire, followed by careful revision of fire-management plans for parks and wilderness areas. But both groups of experts affirmed that the park managers had been right to allow fire to play its natural role.

A forest without fire is like prey without predators. A fire roaring from treetop to treetop, consuming the forest, is certainly frightening. But nature is ever changing, and fire is—in the long run—as important to the ecosystem as sunshine or rain. The long-term benefits outweigh the short-term destruction. The challenge for the people who manage our forests, parks, and other wilderness areas is to find a balance that allows fire to play its natural role in the environment without endangering lives or property.

For further reading:

Chandler, Craig C., and others. *Fire in Forestry: Forest Fire Behavior and Effects.* Wiley, 1983.
De Golia, Jack. *Fire: The Story Behind a Force of Nature.* KC Publications, 1989.
Patent, Dorothy H. *Yellowstone Fires: Flames and Rebirth.* Holiday House, 1990.
Wuerthner, George. *Yellowstone and the Fires of Change.* Haggis House Publications, 1988.

The creation of machine parts no bigger than
a dust speck could lead to the development
of devices that we cannot even imagine today.

Microscopic Machines

BY IVAN AMATO

The surgeon picks up a syringe and approaches the man on the operating table. The patient's coronary arteries are dangerously clogged with fatty deposits, which must be removed to prevent him from suffering a heart attack. The doctor injects a cloudy solution into the vein in the man's arm. The solution contains thousands of microscopic "robot surgeons," each equipped with a tiny motor to propel it through the bloodstream, chemical detectors for locating the life-threatening blockages, and miniature scalpels for cutting them away. Within half an hour, the swarms of tiny robots have navigated through the patient's blood vessels to his heart, located the trouble spots, and sliced the lumpy, yellowish deposits off the artery walls. Normal blood flow has been restored.

For the time being, such medical scenarios will have to remain on the technological dream list—and they may never become reality. No one has built anything remotely like these fictional microrobots. But scientists and engineers in the United States and elsewhere have already made a variety of gears, levers, rotors, and other mechanical parts the size of specks of dust. Such components—made of the element silicon or of metals or other materials—may someday be assembled into tiny robots and various other kinds of microscopic

Glossary

Actuator: A machine part that exerts a force and accomplishes work.

Etch: To create patterns by wearing away a material with chemicals or reactive gases.

Mask: A glass plate containing the pattern for making a computer chip circuit or a micromachine part.

Photoresist: A material that is chemically altered when exposed to light.

Sensor: An electronic component that serves as a detector or a measuring device or both.

Silicon: A hard, nonmetallic element that is used to make electronic microchips and micromachine parts.

The author:
Ivan Amato is a staff writer at *Science* magazine.

machines designed to perform specific functions. These micromachines would be so small that dozens could easily fit inside a sesame seed.

The recent advances in the miniaturization of machine parts represent the beginnings of a new branch of engineering whose practitioners think small—*extremely* small. Micromachine technology is still so new that it doesn't yet have a widely accepted name. Some researchers call it *microengineering*, while others refer to it as *microdynamics* or *micromechanics*. Whatever they call their new discipline, these engineers work in a realm where objects are measured in fractions of a millimeter. (One millimeter is about 0.04 inch.) At that scale, a grain of sand looks like a boulder and mechanical principles such as friction, wear, and lubrication take on new, poorly understood meanings.

Such factors may present problems that cannot be overcome. If they can be surmounted, however, microengineering may usher in a revolutionary new machine age. We may see the creation of all kinds of teensy devices combining electronic detectors called *sensors* with mechanical parts called *actuators* that do work. In addition to performing microscopic surgery, such micromachines might pump minute amounts of chemicals, focus laser beams in optical computers, and power tiny tools whose uses can only be guessed at for now.

A handful of relatively simple microdevices have already made it to the marketplace. Some computer printers, for example, form letters by spraying tiny amounts of ink onto the paper through microscopic nozzles developed by engineers at the International Business Machines (IBM) Research Laboratory in San Jose, Calif. But most currently available microdevices are sensors, which react to changes in their environment, for example, by bending under pressure. Engineers at the Honeywell Corporation's Physical Sciences Center in Bloomington, Minn., have developed microsensors that measure airflow in the ventilation systems of buildings or in the instruments that hospitals use to monitor patients' breathing. Other companies have developed tiny sensors for measuring pressure in automobile engines or in the human heart.

Meanwhile, researchers are working on various kinds of microscopic actuators that may be perfected in the 1990's. Some of these will perhaps work like minuscule hands or tweezers for manipulating tiny objects, such as individual cells under a microscope. Miniature pumps and valves are also a possibility and would have a variety of applications. Medical researchers envision an artificial pancreas for treating diabetes that would pump tiny amounts of insulin as needed into the bloodstream.

Microengineering came to national attention in June 1988 when electrical engineer Richard S. Muller and his colleagues at the University of California's Berkeley Sensor & Actuator Center announced that they had made a tiny silicon motor, the first

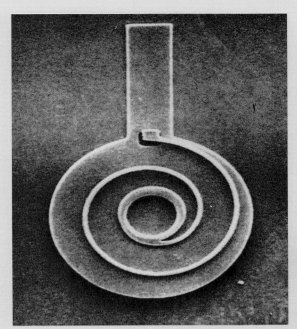

Engineers have made a variety of silicon microdevices, some of them experimental and others already in use. Experimental microdevices include a coiled spring, *left;* a sliding mechanism, *below left;* and a motor with an eight-pronged rotor, *below.* Tiny silicon sensors, *bottom,* are in wide use.

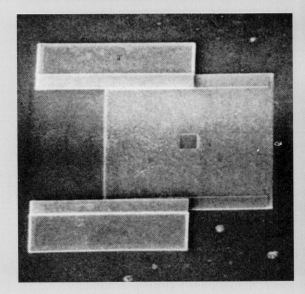

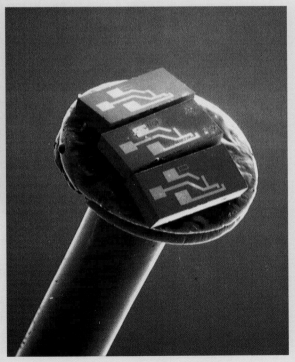

Three silicon sensors shown on the head of a pin, *right,* can be fed through blood vessels on a thin filament to measure blood pressure in the heart.

How Micromachine Parts Are Made

Using techniques pioneered by computer chip makers, scientists create microparts by first drawing a large-scale image of the part, then photographically reducing it. The image of the part, called a *mask,* is projected onto a wafer of silicon. Chemicals are used to *etch* (dissolve) away all but the tiny parts. The steps are repeated to build a micromachine.

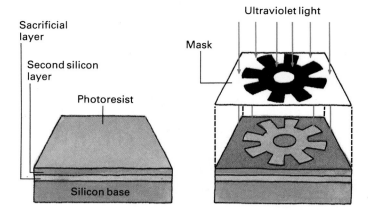

The manufacture of a micropart begins with a silicon "sandwich" consisting of a silicon base and an upper layer of silicon separated by a sacrificial layer of another material that will later be etched away. A coating of a light-sensitive material called a *photoresist* is added to the surface of the top layer.

The silicon sandwich is covered with a mask that consists of an image on a glass plate. Ultraviolet light is shined through the mask. The ultraviolet rays pass through only the clear portions of the mask. The rays penetrate the exposed areas of the resist layer, weakening them.

electrically powered microdevice containing a rotating part. The device's rotor, the part that spins, was smaller than the width of a human hair. (A human hair is about 0.05 millimeter in diameter.) The cogs of the rotor were the size of red blood cells. When the researchers used static electricity to activate electrodes surrounding the rotor, the rotor began to spin haltingly. Although the movement was crude, and the rotor later jammed, the experiment showed that engineers' visions of microscopic machines could become reality.

The achievement at Berkeley came almost 30 years after researchers first began to think small. In 1959, Nobel Prize-winning physicist Richard P. Feynman predicted that scientists would someday build machines and tools as tiny as dust specks and then use them to manufacture even smaller things. Feynman had no idea how that feat would be accomplished, however, and to many ears his speculations were the wildest kind of blue-sky fantasy. But with the coming of the microelectronics revolution in the computer industry in the 1970's, what had been fantasy suddenly seemed like a distinct possibility.

The history of the computer industry is a story of constant miniaturization, as engineers learned to cram more and more electronic components into a smaller and smaller amount of space. In the 1960's, electronics manufacturers began building complex circuits on fingernail-sized pieces of silicon. By the 1970's, these tiny circuits, which had become known as *microchips,* contained thousands of elements. Today, a single microchip can hold millions of components.

The production of silicon microchips begins with a procedure

An etching chemical is applied to dissolve the weakened areas of the resist layer, except where the mask has made the image.

Another etching chemical is used to dissolve the silicon and sacrificial layers around the tiny part. This leaves the rotor, still attached to the underlying sacrificial layer.

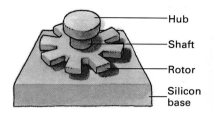

Hub
Shaft
Rotor
Silicon base

The steps are repeated to etch other parts, such as a shaft and hub, out of new layers of silicon. Eventually, all the sacrificial layers are dissolved, allowing the rotor to spin freely.

called *microlithography*, which involves several steps. First, a large, detailed drawing of the chip is made, and the drawing is photographed. The photographic image is then greatly reduced and imprinted—usually as a stencillike pattern of metallic lines—on a glass plate. The finished plate is known as a *mask*. Next, a palm-sized silicon wafer gets a coat of a *photoresist*, a plastic material that, when exposed to ultraviolet light, is chemically weakened. When the mask is placed over the coated wafer and exposed to ultraviolet light, the ultraviolet rays that are not blocked by the mask transmit the image of the chip to the wafer. The regions of the photoresist that are weakened by the process are then *etched*, or eaten away, by solvents or gases. The etching exposes the underlying layer of silicon in a pattern that corresponds to the mask pattern.

Once this process has been completed, the engineers usually deposit additional thin films of silicon, metal, or insulating materials onto the exposed silicon pattern and repeat the etching process several more times. In this way, they can build up extremely complicated patterns and structures on the wafer, all no more than a few thousandths of a millimeter thick. Each patterned layer is connected to the next, becoming part of the final device or part of the formation of the next layer.

Silicon is an excellent *semiconductor*, a material that conducts electricity better than insulators such as glass but not as well as conductors such as copper. Silicon is an ideal material for electronic microchips because it can be processed together with an insulating material such as silicon dioxide. But silicon also possesses unusual mechanical properties. Although it is brittle and fragile when it is in the form of wafers, at microscopic dimensions silicon's crystal structure makes it highly resistant to stress. At that scale, it is in fact stronger than steel. Thus, by 1980, some engineers were suggesting the possibility of crafting mechanical devices as well as electronic components from silicon. That idea received a major boost in 1982 from Kurt Petersen, an IBM researcher and now a chief scientist at Lucas/NovaSensor, a microengineering company in Fremont, Calif. Petersen argued that by adopting and modifying the miniaturization techniques pioneered by the electronics industry, it would be possible to create a variety of microdevices from silicon and to mass-produce them. Moreover, he said, silicon's mechanical and electronic properties made it an ideal material for the production of integrated devices consisting of actuators combined with sensors and other electronic devices.

Today, a growing number of researchers in the United States, Europe, and Japan are forging a new area of science and technology. These microengineering pioneers are showing ever-increasing skill at making miniature parts out of silicon as well as other materials.

To make microparts out of silicon, engineers use standard microlithography along with a variety of chemicals that etch into silicon wafers at different rates and in different directions. By controlling the etching times of these chemicals, or by using a chip on which has been deposited an underlying layer of a chemical-resistant material, engineers can dig out extremely precise microscopic pits or holes and form tiny walls and other structures.

Using these etching techniques, researchers have learned to chemically "chisel" around and underneath prepatterned gears and rotors to separate them from their base and allow them to move freely. This procedure involves depositing a "sacrificial layer" of a material such as silicon dioxide on the original blank chip and then overlaying it with another silicon layer from which the moving part is to be fashioned. After this "sandwich" is exposed to ultraviolet light projected through the microlithography mask and the silicon layers are etched, chemicals are used to dissolve the sacrificial layer. As that layer dissolves, the rotor, lever, or other part in the upper layer of silicon is liberated. This technique has enabled engineers to create a variety of gears, rotors, sliding mechanisms, and other microscopic devices with moving parts. And because 1,000 or more copies of a device can be etched onto a single silicon wafer, researchers say that it may one day be possible to manufacture micromachines by the tens of thousands at a cost of only a few cents apiece.

Although silicon seems likely to remain the primary microengineering material for some years, some metals also show promise. Several researchers, including electrical engineer Henry Guckel of the University of Wisconsin in Madison, have been scoring successes in using metals such as tungsten and nickel to create micromachine

Engineering Challenges in the Microworld

The design and building of practical micromachines confronts engineers with many challenges. Physical phenomena such as friction and the behavior of fluids may affect these tiny devices differently than they do ordinary machines. Overcoming these problems may require engineers to develop new materials for creating the tiny parts and new types of lubricants to help prevent malfunctions.

Friction

Micromachine parts that slide against each other often stick together. The surfaces of tiny parts usually have areas of roughness that cause friction. Even static electricity and the forces that bind molecules together can contribute to friction problems at these microscopic scales. One solution may be the development of new kinds of lubricants.

Warping

Thin silicon parts often warp. This occurs because silicon layers must be produced at a high temperature, and cooling causes stresses within the material that may make it change shape. When that happens, parts can no longer be correctly positioned with one another. One solution may be thicker silicon parts.

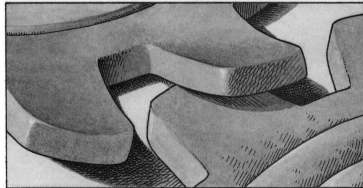

Wear and Tear

After many hours of operation, the hole at the center of a spinning rotor can become enlarged, causing the rotor to wobble. Engineers are also making tests to see whether cracks could develop in microparts. They want to know which kinds of parts are most affected by wear and tear and how this will limit the working lifetime of micromachines.

Air and Fluid Resistance

Air and fluid molecules (shown here not to scale) seem huge in the world of micromachines. These molecules can slow the motion of some microparts far more than they would the parts of normal-sized machines, especially such parts as rapidly spinning rotors.

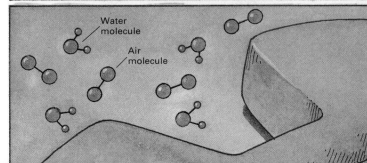

Water molecule

Air molecule

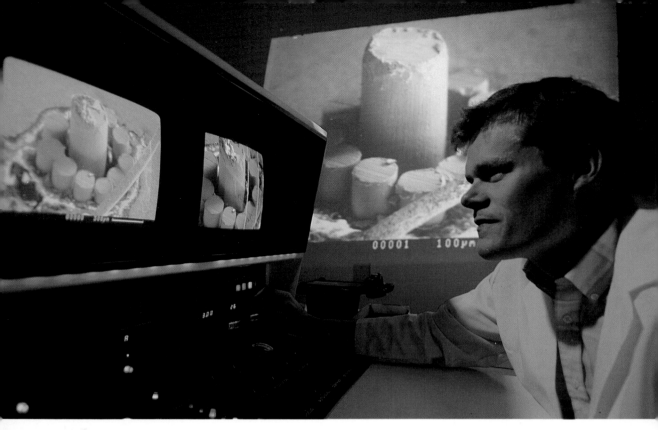

Creating Stronger Microparts
A University of Utah researcher, *top,* examines a magnified "wobble motor." The motor is a bit larger and produces more rotational force than silicon micromotors, but it cannot yet be mass-produced. Metal gears, *above,* made at the University of Wisconsin are thicker and stronger than silicon gears.

parts. Metal seems to have one big advantage over silicon for many micromachine parts—structural rigidity. Although silicon is extremely strong at microscopic dimensions, the silicon etching techniques developed so far work well only for thin structures. Most silicon micromachine parts are so thin that they tend to warp from internal stresses. Researchers hope to find ways of making silicon parts thicker, but for now only metal can be made into thick parts.

Guckel and his colleagues have made all-metal microgears that are slightly larger than the silicon gears made in some laboratories. But at a diameter of 0.1 to 0.2 millimeter—2 to 4 times the width of a human hair—they are still smaller than grains of salt. The researchers made the gears using a technique called *electroplating*. In this procedure, an electric current is used to draw dissolved *ions* (electrically charged atoms) of nickel or chromium into tiny molds. The molds have been etched into a layer of *plexiglass* (a type of hard plastic) on a metal plate. After the metal ions have filled the molds and solidified, a sacrificial layer underneath the plexiglass is dissolved to free the part.

Instead of ultraviolet light, the Guckel team used X rays generated by an atomic-particle accelerator. These exceptionally powerful and short-wavelength X rays, directed through a mask, enabled the researchers to etch deep molds with perfectly vertical sides, essential for the production of thick parts. Guckel thinks gears and other microparts made of metal, because they are thicker and stronger, may be better suited for powering drills and other tiny tools than similar parts made of silicon. So far, X rays have not been widely used in the making of silicon parts because the rays tend to damage the silicon. And there is another reason as well: cost. The use of X rays, especially those generated by a particle accelerator, to make microparts is an expensive proposition that may not be commercially practical. Due to these drawbacks, most micromachine engineers are sticking with methods employing ultraviolet light and chemical etching agents.

Although microengineering may indeed herald the beginning of a new machine age, researchers must first solve several fundamental problems. Besides the warping that can make silicon parts curl up like potato chips, there are other difficulties involved with operating in the microworld. In that hidden realm, a fine grain of flour could bring a rotor grinding to a halt—perhaps with a screech that a nearby flea could hear—in just a few seconds. In addition, familiar phenomena such as friction, air resistance, electrical charge, wear, and the behavior of fluids must be redefined because their effects are different at microscopic dimensions than in the everyday world. At tiny scales, where the spaces between parts are vanishingly small, standard lubricants can work instead like adhesives. Blood, which to a human surgeon flows freely, might seem like molasses to a robot surgeon that is no bigger than a red blood cell.

Overcoming such obstacles will undoubtedly keep engineers busy for years to come, but there is already cause for optimism. Even now, engineers are solving some of the warping and sticking problems that doomed their earliest micromotors to short lives. For example, Muller and his colleagues have learned to deposit silicon layers in a way that lessens the stresses that lead to warping. Through refinements in the microlithography process, they have also crafted sets of gears so precise that they mesh with absolutely no slippage.

The sheer tininess of micromotors, however, may present another, altogether different problem: They may be too small to do much of anything requiring the application of force. Think of trying to move a stone with a whisker and you will see the difficulty facing researchers. "Little machines don't produce big forces," says engineer Stephen Senturia of the Massachusetts Institute of Technology (MIT) in Cambridge. "So scaling machines down may make them so weak they can't do any useful mechanical work." Part of the answer to that concern may lie in making parts thicker.

Another possibility is to build somewhat bigger micromachines,

Microtechnology at Work Today

A sensor barely visible on a person's palm activates an automobile airbag in a collision. The automotive industry is one of the biggest users of microsensors, which can monitor and regulate many vehicle systems such as antilock brakes and engine pressure.

ones that are perhaps 20 times the width of a human hair. At the University of Utah in Salt Lake City, engineer Stephen Jacobsen has been doing just that. Jacobsen and his co-workers have been using conventional machine tools to painstakingly assemble small metal and plastic components into what they call "wobble motors," since the devices' rotors wobble as they spin. This form of motion can reduce the effects of friction and thus produce more *torque,* or rotational force. Jacobsen thinks wobble motors would be better suited than other kinds of micromotors for controlling the movements of the tiny robotic machines foreseen by many engineers. Wobble motors and other larger-sized micromachines being developed have one big disadvantage of their own, however: As yet, they cannot be mass-produced. Unless a way can be found to manufacture them by the thousands, such devices will almost certainly be too expensive to be widely used.

For all varieties of microdevices, the list of challenges goes on. In developing micromachines that would have to withstand harsh environments, such as those of outer space or the interior of jet engines, engineers must find ways of protecting delicate parts against damage. Researchers must also learn how to connect micromachines requiring human guidance to control systems large enough for people to operate.

Because of the many obstacles that must be overcome, the Micromachine Age—assuming there will be one—is unlikely to arrive until sometime after the year 2000. In the meantime, however,

many kinds of microsensors are being perfected and are coming into widespread use. So far, most of these are pressure sensors for automotive and medical uses. Most such sensors consist of an ultrathin disk called a *diaphragm* built on a tiny silicon chip. The diaphragm, which is also usually made of silicon, is created by etching away an intermediate layer of material. The diaphragm is engineered so that the slightest bending caused by a pressure change alters the electrical resistance of a pattern of *resistors* (components that control voltage) in a precise way. Circuitry on the chip, or attached to it, detects the change and translates it into an electrical signal, which in turn is translated into a pressure measurement.

Most of the pressure sensors used in automobiles go under the hood to monitor engine pressure for the on-board computers that help control the car's combustion and exhaust emissions. Other kinds of sensors are also being used in many new cars, measuring everything from engine coolant temperature to the moment-by-moment position of the crankshaft. Cars built in coming years will most likely include microsensors that keep track of all of a vehicle's temperatures, pressures, airflows, mechanical motions, and other operating factors.

Medical microsensors are often used to measure blood pressure inside patients' hearts. The sensor is attached to the end of a plastic filament, which the physician snakes through the blood vessels to the heart. But other kinds of medical sensors may soon be available to doctors. For example, engineer Kensall Wise and his associates at the

Micromachines of the Future

Scientists envision many future uses for micromachines. A microscopic "surgeon," for example, might someday clean fatty deposits from inside human arteries. Sensors in the device would enable it to home in on deposits, and miniature sawlike blades would chop the obstructions into fragments small enough to be flushed away by the bloodstream.

Center for Integrated Sensors and Circuits at the University of Michigan in Ann Arbor are working on a new kind of brain probe. This silicon probe is thinner than a sewing needle and has 32 microsensors that can eavesdrop on the electrical activity in small groups of *neurons* (nerve cells). Wise thinks the technology used in the probe might eventually be used to make tiny medical devices that can be inserted into the brain to detect and control epileptic seizures and other neurological disorders.

Wise foresees a dazzling future for microsensors. He envisions sensors that "see," "hear," "feel," "taste," and "smell" the world with a precision and sensitivity exceeding that of the human senses. Used in the manufacturing industries in the not-so-distant future, hundreds of widely distributed sensors could continuously gather data about the temperatures of vats, the flow of fluids through pipes, the pressure in tanks, and the progress of chemical reactions. Computers and technicians would instantly receive and analyze these data to make adjustments in the factory's processing equipment.

Microsensors should also be of great value in space exploration, especially aboard satellites and unmanned spacecraft, in which compactness and light weight have always been high priorities. Besides taking up less space than conventional sensors, microsensors weigh less and use less power. Also, they usually respond faster to changes in their environment.

While many of the applications of microsensors are already with us, or easily foreseen, the uses of true micromachines—sensors plus actuators—are far less certain. "We're in the process of discovering what is possible," says MIT's Stephen Senturia. But he predicts "some very good applications coming down the road." Senturia is betting, for one thing, that micromachines will play an important role in the coming *photonics* technologies in computers and telecommunications. Instead of shunting electrons through circuits as electronic equipment does, photonic devices will manipulate light signals. Other likely developments Senturia foresees include microrefrigeration systems for cooling electronic circuits and miniature gyroscopes that could be used in compact guidance systems for missiles and space probes.

Other researchers predict a number of far-out possibilities that may or may not come to pass. They envision tiny exploration robots that could easily be packed into a space probe, then set loose to range over the surface of another planet gathering and analyzing soil samples; speck-sized "inspectors" designed to crawl through pipes in atomic reactors and other hazardous environments looking for tiny structural defects; and perhaps even little airborne "soldiers" that could descend on an enemy camp like a cloud of angry gnats to destroy weapons and equipment.

Even the most optimistic engineers say that those and other futuristic predictions will probably remain just intriguing ideas for a long time to come. Nevertheless, some scientists have already started to think even smaller. Pursuing what would be the ultimate in miniaturization, these researchers are learning to manipulate matter on a scale thousands of times smaller than that of today's most minuscule gears and levers. Their territory is the realm of individual atoms and molecules, where distances are measured in *nanometers* (millionths of a millimeter) or in even smaller units called *angstroms* (10-millionths of a millimeter). This infant discipline is known as *nanotechnology*.

In early 1990, nanotechnology researchers at IBM used a device called the scanning tunneling microscope (STM) to arrange individual xenon atoms in the form of their company's logo. The STM emits an electric current from the tip of a superfine needle, and with that current the researchers prodded the atoms into the desired alignment. Other investigators have used STM's to dig nanometerwide trenches or punch equally minute holes in various materials. And with a technique called *electron-beam lithography*—similar to ultraviolet microlithography but substituting high-energy electrons for light—scientists have etched materials with some of the smallest patterns ever made.

Some visionaries, looking decades or more ahead, see a technological future that boggles the mind. Perhaps most prominent among them is K. Eric Drexler, a former MIT researcher who now heads the Foresight Institute, a "think tank" in Palo Alto, Calif. Drexler predicts a Nanomachine Age in which trillions upon trillions of molecule-sized robot "assemblers" will do humanity's bidding. Using molecular raw materials, the assemblers would "build" foods and fuels or construct full-sized homes and buildings. The ultratiny robots might also arrange molecular components into computers the size of sugar cubes; fabricate virus-sized surgeons that can enter the nuclei of cells to repair faulty genes; and, of course, build more robot assemblers.

Although such scenarios may be unbridled flights of fancy, the molecular parts inside cells, bacteria, and viruses show that today's microengineers have not begun to approach the limits of miniaturization. Nobody knows what developments the future might bring. But many microengineers at this point believe that almost any little thing seems possible.

For further reading:

Amato, Ivan. "Small Things Considered." *Science News*, July 1, 1989, pp. 8-10.
Pool, Robert. "Microscopic Motor Is a First Step." *Science*, Oct. 21, 1988, pp. 379-380.
Scientific American Editors. *Microelectronics: A Scientific American Book.* W. H. Freeman & Co., 1977.
Stewart, Doug. "New Machines Are Smaller Than a Hair, and Do Real Work." *Smithsonian*, November 1990, pp. 85-95.

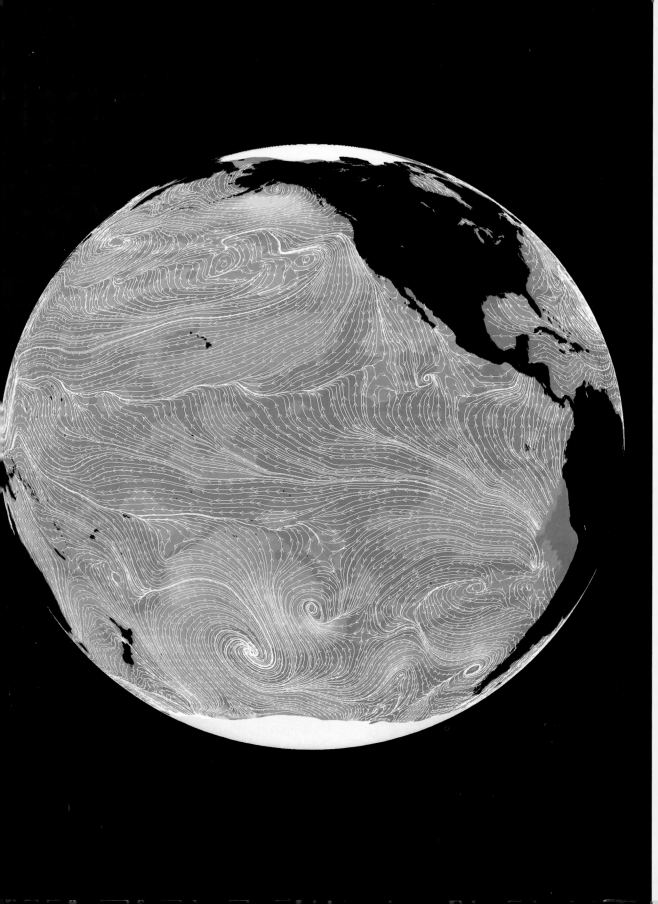

Using research ships, satellites, and a wide array of instruments in the sea, oceanographers have begun a worldwide study of the ocean's circulation and how it affects Earth's climate.

Currents and Climate

BY ARNOLD L. GORDON

In my many years as a seagoing oceanographer, I have participated in a number of expeditions aboard research ships to study various parts of the world's vast ocean. Each expedition took me to a different region of the ocean, where I gathered data about the properties of the water, such as its temperature and chemical makeup, and examined how the water circulated. But such properties differ throughout the ocean, and my observations gave me only tiny pieces of a gigantic puzzle. I often wished that I could look at all regions of the global ocean at the same time to get the big picture. But, while sitting on a small ship in the middle of a huge sea, this seemed like a dream. Today, however, with satellites that can scan the entire global ocean in a single day and with cooperation among oceanographers from many countries, this dream is coming true.

A big part of that realization is the World Ocean Circulation Experiment (WOCE), a seven-year-long study begun in 1990 and involving hundreds of oceanographers. A total of 42 nations, including Australia, Japan, the Soviet Union, the United States, and most of the countries of Europe, are participating in WOCE.

The study aims to learn how ocean water circulates and how that circulation influences, and is influenced by, the atmosphere. Understanding this is crucial to predicting whether and how much Earth's climate may be changing. It should help us determine if the world is

Satellite data reveal wind patterns that create surface currents on the ocean, *opposite page.*

191

overheating, a possibly catastrophic phenomenon known as *global warming*.

Scientists link global warming to human activities—such as burning fossil fuels and destroying forests—that release carbon dioxide and other gases into the atmosphere. These gases, called *greenhouse gases*, trap heat energy from the sun as it radiates from Earth's surface. Scientists warn that the continued release of excess greenhouse gases could raise global temperatures, altering climate and melting glacial ice. One result would be an increase in sea levels, causing flooding of low-lying coastal areas worldwide. Shifting patterns of rainfall and heat could also bring destructive flooding to some regions and extensive droughts to other areas.

But the ocean may play a significant role in slowing the rate of global warming. Covering 70.8 per cent of Earth's surface and accounting for 97 per cent of all the liquid water on the planet, the ocean removes and stores heat and a large percentage of the greenhouse gases that would otherwise remain in the atmosphere.

Scientists estimate that as much as 50 per cent of the carbon dioxide put into the atmosphere as a result of burning fossil fuels has been absorbed by the ocean. Marine organisms take up carbon dioxide, and ocean plants use carbon dioxide to produce food by the process called *photosynthesis*. Some marine animals also use carbon to make sea shells. When marine plants and animals die, they transfer carbon into the deep ocean because some of their remains fall to the ocean floor. Heat and pressure eventually harden these sediments into carbon-containing rock, such as limestone.

The ocean also has a large capacity to absorb heat from the atmosphere. As the atmosphere warms by the greenhouse process, the surface water takes in much of this heat, slowing the rate of climate warming. Ocean currents and other processes carry this heat to cooler regions and into the colder, deeper layers of the ocean.

Much is unknown, however, about the ocean's capacity to store and move heat and greenhouse gases. As greenhouse gases build up in the atmosphere, will the ocean continue to retard warming and moderate Earth's climate to the same extent? Will the ocean absorb the excess greenhouse gases rapidly or slowly? And how will the rate of absorption change over time? Until we can answer these questions, we will not be able to predict how the global climate may change. The oceanographers participating in WOCE believe that achieving a better understanding of ocean circulation will help provide some of the answers.

Until recently, no one would have attempted such a large and complicated study because the technical equipment necessary was not available. The development of modern instruments for monitoring the ocean—particularly Earth-orbiting satellites—has for the first time enabled oceanographers to view the ocean in its entirety. And with the cooperative efforts of oceanographers in many countries,

Glossary

Global warming: The heating of Earth's atmosphere, due to increased levels of heat-trapping gases.

Greenhouse gas: An atmospheric gas, such as carbon dioxide, that traps heat radiating from Earth's surface.

Gyre: The circular path of a wind-driven current.

Mixing: The transfer of heat from the ocean surface to lower depths due to turbulent wave motion.

Phytoplankton: Tiny marine plants.

Thermohaline circulation: A vertical current started by the sinking of cold, dense water.

Wind-driven circulation: Currents set in motion by the force of the wind.

The author:
Arnold L. Gordon is professor of oceanography at Columbia University in New York City and is a member of the senior research staff at the university's Lamont-Doherty Geological Observatory.

A Worldwide Experiment

From 1990 to 1997, hundreds of oceanographers and technicians will participate in the World Ocean Circulation Experiment (WOCE), using research ships, merchant ships, and thousands of circulation-monitoring instruments.

Oceanographers and technicians prepare to place a current-monitoring instrument in the ocean as part of WOCE.

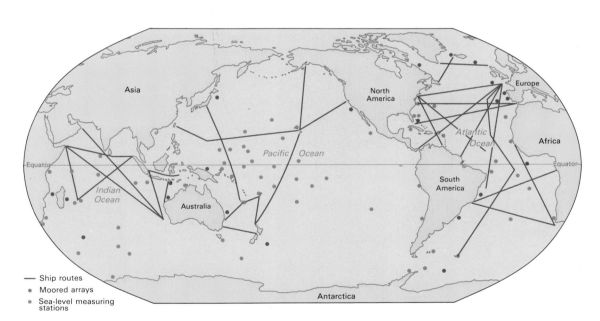

WOCE will monitor the ocean more extensively than has ever been done before. Oceanographers will measure sea levels at oceanographic stations on about 66 island locations, while merchant ships will record water temperatures along 21 major shipping lanes. Scientists will also deploy dozens of groups of underwater meters that measure the speed of currents at various depths.

the WOCE program will be able to pool a vast array of scientific instruments.

As the project got underway, our knowledge of how the ocean circulates was still relatively elementary. In the late 1940's and early 1950's, Norwegian oceanographer Harald U. Sverdrup and U.S. oceanographer Walter Munk used mathematical calculations and measurements of ocean currents taken since the early 1900's to describe the basic motions of the ocean currents that are driven by the wind. This *wind-driven circulation* moves surface water in horizontal currents—that is, parallel to Earth's surface. Wind-driven circulation often takes the form of large circular paths called *gyres*. The gyres are shaped by the wind pattern, the confining continental boundaries, and by the influence of Earth's rotation.

United States oceanographers Henry M. Stommel and Arnold Arons created a theory of another type of circulation in 1958. This *thermohaline circulation* involves vertical movements of water—from the surface to the sea floor. Surface water becomes cold and dense in Earth's colder polar regions. This cold, dense water sinks until it reaches the ocean floor, where it spreads horizontally, forcing the water already on the bottom upward, establishing a kind of conveyor-belt movement.

Both types of ocean circulation move vast amounts of water and in so doing, moderate Earth's climate. For example, the Gulf Stream, a wind-driven current flowing along the western edge of the North Atlantic Ocean, carries an estimated 100 million cubic meters (3.5 billion cubic feet) of seawater each second toward higher latitudes. Some of this water reaches the Greenland, Labrador, and Norwegian seas. The amount of water carried by the Gulf Stream is 500 times greater than the amount carried to the sea by Earth's largest river, the Amazon, in South America. As the Gulf Stream moves heated water from the tropics and subtropics toward the North Atlantic, surface water evaporates, transferring heat and moisture into the atmosphere over the North Atlantic and surrounding land masses. The climate of northwestern Europe and the eastern region of North America is significantly warmer and wetter as a result.

As some of the water driven northward by the Gulf Stream releases heat into the atmosphere, the surface water gradually cools. The colder the water, the greater its density. Eventually, in the region within the Greenland, Labrador, and Norwegian seas, this cold, dense water begins to sink and becomes what oceanographers call *North Atlantic Deep Water*, initiating a global-scale thermohaline circulation pattern.

This deep ocean current is slower than the Gulf Stream but still moves an estimated 15 million to 20 million cubic meters (530 million to 700 million cubic feet) of water per second to the deep ocean floor. It then flows southward along the ocean bottom toward the equator and the South Atlantic Ocean and eventually into the Indian and

Pacific oceans. As it moves, it pushes the water in its path upward toward the surface. This water warms at the surface and eventually flows back to the North Atlantic to close the circulation loop. Scientists estimate that if it were not for this conveyor-belt type of circulation bringing warmer deep ocean water to the North Atlantic, the northern North Atlantic region would be up to 6 degrees Celsius (11 degrees Fahrenheit) cooler.

Thus, thermohaline circulation influences climate by redistributing heat throughout the ocean. This circulation also affects the storage of carbon within the deep ocean. The remains of dead marine organisms on the ocean floor represent the principal "storehouse" of carbon in the ocean. However, slight variations in the thermohaline circulation are expected to alter the ocean's ability to store heat and carbon. If the thermohaline circulation is rapid, a greater injection of cold polar surface water would result in less carbon dioxide and heat being removed from the atmosphere. If the circulation flows slowly, however, more heat would accumulate in the deep ocean. Additionally, more carbon would be stored in the deep ocean due to the accumulated remains of sinking marine organisms. Both of these effects may help forestall a global warming.

We know that atmospheric activity influences the rate at which these deepwater currents form. For example, the amount of fresh water entering the North Atlantic, either by precipitation or river runoff, reduces the salt content of ocean water and thus lowers the amount of dense water that would otherwise form and sink. At the end of the last Ice Age, about 10,000 years ago, the North Atlantic Deep Water formed at a slow rate due to the melting of glaciers, which added vast amounts of lighter fresh water to the North Atlantic Ocean. Could global warming cause changes—such as melting polar ice—that would similarly disrupt how quickly the currents form? This is one of the many questions that scientists participating in WOCE hope to answer.

The scientists involved in WOCE are using an array of ocean-monitoring instruments. These include remote-sensing instruments on satellites, research ships equipped with scientific instruments, volunteer merchant ships that carry water-temperature probes, and drifters and meters that measure currents. Data from these instruments will be entered into powerful computers to be stored in their vast memory banks. Theoretical models of ocean circulation, developed with computers, can then be tested by comparing their predictions with observations.

A major element of WOCE will be global measurements of surface currents, temperatures, and winds by using remote-sensing devices on satellites. Satellite sensors monitor vast areas of the ocean on a daily basis, obtaining data far more rapidly than slow-moving research vessels can. Several satellites were scheduled to be launched by the United States, the European Space Agency, and Japan during

Ocean Circulation and Climate

Wind-driven ocean currents play a major role in moderating Earth's climate by moving warm water at the equator to cooler regions.

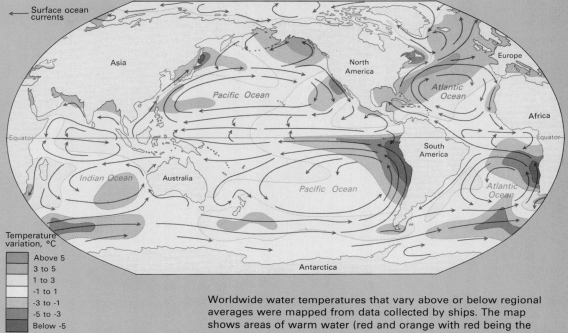

← Surface ocean currents

Temperature variation, °C

- Above 5
- 3 to 5
- 1 to 3
- -1 to 1
- -3 to -1
- -5 to -3
- Below -5

Worldwide water temperatures that vary above or below regional averages were mapped from data collected by ships. The map shows areas of warm water (red and orange with red being the warmest) and cool water (blue areas with dark blue being the coldest) as they typically appear during winter in the Northern Hemisphere and summer in the Southern Hemisphere. Wind-driven currents (arrows) in the Atlantic Ocean move warm water from the tropics to cooler regions in the North Atlantic. As surface water cools, heat and water vapor are transferred to the atmosphere, causing these northern regions to be warmer and wetter.

An infrared satellite image, *right,* helps oceanographers monitor wind-driven currents such as the Gulf Stream, which is visible as a bright red stream near the coast of North America. The false-color image reveals surface water temperatures in parts of the Gulf of Mexico and the Atlantic Ocean. (Red and yellow areas represent the warmest regions; blue and purple indicate the coldest.)

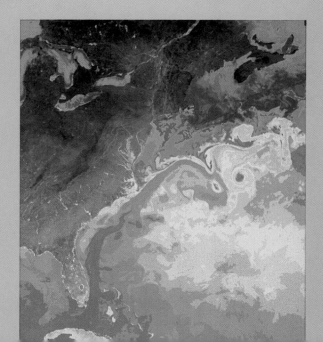

How the Ocean Traps Carbon Dioxide

A major goal of the Joint Global Ocean Flux Study is to understand how much excess carbon dioxide the ocean can remove from the atmosphere. Scientists fear that increasing levels of this gas may lead to global climate warming.

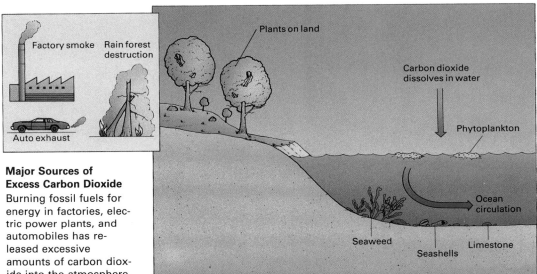

Major Sources of Excess Carbon Dioxide

Burning fossil fuels for energy in factories, electric power plants, and automobiles has released excessive amounts of carbon dioxide into the atmosphere. The destruction of rain forests has also led to increased levels of the gas, because trees and other plants take carbon dioxide out of the air to make food in the process of photosynthesis.

Where Does the Carbon Dioxide Go?

Marine plants, such as phytoplankton and seaweed, absorb carbon dioxide during photosynthesis, just as plants on land do. Some carbon dioxide dissolves in surface water. When water containing carbon dioxide becomes cold and dense, it sinks and circulates along the ocean floor. Shellfish combine carbon with calcium to form their shells. The remains of shellfish and marine plants settle on the ocean floor as sediments, which eventually harden into calcium carbonate rock, or limestone.

The ocean contains the vast majority of Earth's carbon, compared with the amount found in soil, animals, and plants on land; in fossil fuels; or in the atmosphere.

the WOCE's seven years of observations. The European Space Agency was to launch the first of these satellites—named *ERS-1*—in mid-1991. Two more will be sent into orbit in 1992. One will be operated by Japan, and the other will be operated jointly by the United States and France.

The satellites will carry *infrared sensors*, heat-sensing devices that measure the warmth of surface waters. Scientists will gather satellite data on sea-surface temperature to create temperature maps showing how warm and cool surface waters are being distributed throughout the global ocean. Scientists also collect data on the speed and direction of ocean currents by using a satellite instrument known as an *altimeter*, which gives off a radio signal. By recording how long it

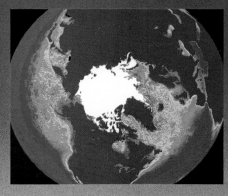

Monitoring the Ocean

Oceanographic studies use instruments under, on, and above the sea surface to study the ocean's role in moderating Earth's climate. Some studies focus on the ocean's circulation, and others monitor the growth of phytoplankton.

Phytoplankton blooms (red and yellow areas) are greatest in the North Atlantic Ocean during the spring. By monitoring satellite images of these blooms, scientists can calculate how much carbon dioxide is being removed from the atmosphere each season.

A satellite monitors the growth of phytoplankton, which float in the upper layers of the ocean and take in carbon dioxide during photosynthesis.

Phytoplankton

Buoy

Drogue

Surface drifters, consisting of a buoy carried along by an underwater drogue, move with wind-driven currents. The buoy radios its position to a satellite. By monitoring the drifter's changing position, oceanographers can determine the speed and direction of the current.

A water sampler suspended from a research ship uses electronic sensors to check the water's temperature, saltiness, and oxygen content. Small bottles attached to the sampler collect water from different depths so that researchers can analyze the water's chemistry.

Probe

Freighters and other commercial ships voluntarily carry probes that measure the temperature of water at depths as great as 400 meters (1,300 feet). Some ships are equipped to radio their data instantly to a communications satellite.

Subsurface floats give off sound waves that are received by devices called *hydrophones* anchored to the sea floor. As the floats drift within range, the hydrophones record their movement. When oceanographers later retrieve the hydrophones, the recordings of float movements tell oceanographers the speed and direction of subsurface currents.

Current meters, placed at various depths along a cable anchored to the sea floor, measure current speeds at that particular site.

Hydrophones

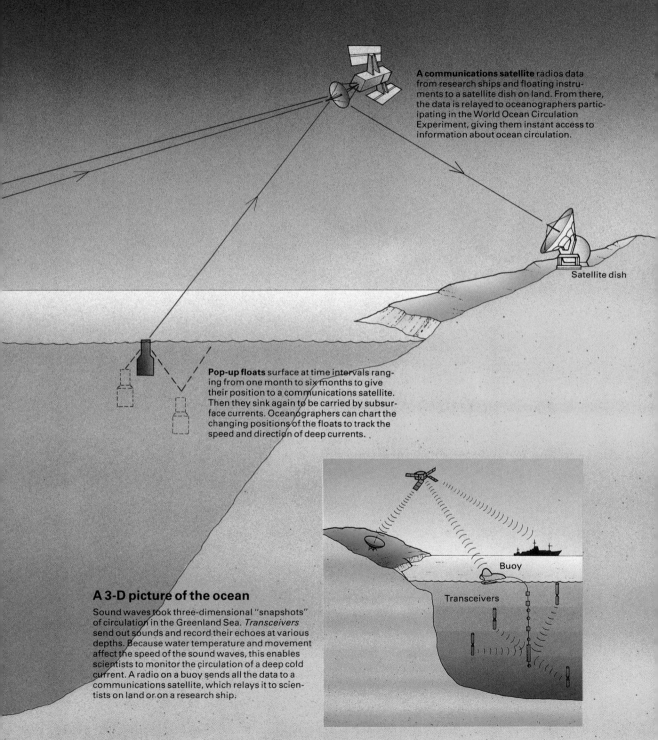

A communications satellite radios data from research ships and floating instruments to a satellite dish on land. From there, the data is relayed to oceanographers participating in the World Ocean Circulation Experiment, giving them instant access to information about ocean circulation.

Satellite dish

Pop-up floats surface at time intervals ranging from one month to six months to give their position to a communications satellite. Then they sink again to be carried by subsurface currents. Oceanographers can chart the changing positions of the floats to track the speed and direction of deep currents.

Buoy

Transceivers

A 3-D picture of the ocean

Sound waves took three-dimensional "snapshots" of circulation in the Greenland Sea. *Transceivers* send out sounds and record their echoes at various depths. Because water temperature and movement affect the speed of the sound waves, this enables scientists to monitor the circulation of a deep cold current. A radio on a buoy sends all the data to a communications satellite, which relays it to scientists on land or on a research ship.

takes for the signal to be reflected from the surface of the ocean back to the satellite, scientists can calculate the general *topography* (shape) of the sea surface to an accuracy of a few centimeters. Because a wind-driven current alters the shape of the surface in a pattern that corresponds with the current's direction, oceanographers can use altimeter data to monitor the path and the speed of the current.

Another instrument, called a *scatterometer*, measures the strength of surface winds. Wind blowing on the ocean surface creates little waves called *capillary waves*. Each capillary wave has a measurable *amplitude*, the distance between the valley of the wave and its crest, which is determined by the force of the wind. The scatterometer can be used to measure this amplitude—and thus the force of the wind.

Almost 20 research ships will also be major factors in the WOCE study. The German research ship *Meteor* began the first of many data-gathering expeditions in early 1990. Following prearranged routes that divide the ocean into various research sections, the WOCE research ships will stop every 50 kilometers (30 miles) for scientists and technicians to lower electronic sensors into the water. The sensors measure the water's temperature and *salinity* (salt content) at various depths. The sensors also measure the concentration of oxygen dissolved in the water. This oxygen is derived from the atmosphere and marine plants.

These measurements give oceanographers a way to trace the patterns of ocean circulation. Scientists assume that samples of water with similar characteristics, such as temperature, salinity, and oxygen content, are part of the same current. Measuring water properties at various sites can help them deduce the direction and speed of currents at various depths.

During these expeditions, scientists will also use chemical tracers to learn more details about ocean circulation and a process called *mixing*. Ocean turbulence due to waves forces some warm surface water downward, where it mixes with colder subsurface water. Like ocean currents, mixing distributes heat within the ocean and so is an important process for oceanographers to study.

Some chemical tracers provide information about the time scales of ocean circulation and mixing processes. For example, we know that chlorofluorocarbons (CFC's) first entered the atmosphere in the 1930's as a result of their use in such products as air conditioners, foamed plastics, and cleaning solvents. The first type of CFC, known as *CFC-12*, was gradually replaced by another type, *CFC-11*. Thus, each year, the ratio of CFC-12 to CFC-11 in the atmosphere changes. When the CFC's dissolve into surface waters, they keep the same ratio they had in the atmosphere. By measuring the CFC ratio in ocean water at various depths, oceanographers can determine when that water was last at the surface.

Merchant ships will also take part in WOCE. Freight-carrying ships passing frequently along 21 major shipping lanes will be equipped

An oceanographer uses a computer to analyze data on ocean circulation. Oceanographers participating in WOCE will also use computers to construct mathematical models of the ocean's circulation patterns that may help them better predict weather and climate changes. They will test these theoretical models against observations made during WOCE.

with probes that record water temperatures from the surface to a depth of 500 meters (1,600 feet). Temperature data will be transmitted along thin wires that connect the probes to the ship. The data can be stored on the ship and then collected when the ship reaches port.

WOCE researchers will leave other instruments in the ocean. *Surface drifters*, as the name implies, measure surface circulation. Each drifter consists of a floating buoy connected to a *drogue*, an object that moves freely with the water at a depth of a few meters. The buoy is equipped with an antenna and power supply to transmit the drifter's position to a satellite which, in turn, radios this information to oceanographers at land stations. Oceanographers can then track the movement of currents by following the changing position of the surface drifter.

Air temperature sensors on the buoys may provide additional information on global warming. Weather data show that average air temperatures over land have steadily increased since the early 1960's, but the average temperature of the atmosphere over the ocean does not appear to be warming as rapidly. This indicates that the ocean has been absorbing excess heat and perhaps slowing global warming. Air temperature data collected by surface drifters will help investigate this possibility. Scientists will deploy about 1,100 surface drifters in the Pacific Ocean in 1991, spaced about 500 kilometers (300 miles) apart. In 1992 and 1993, a similar number will be placed in the Atlantic Ocean. Plans for the Indian Ocean and the ocean around Antarctica will be developed in 1992.

Subsurface drifters are weighted so that when they are released from a ship they descend to a predetermined depth and drift freely with the currents at that level. These drifters are unaffected by surface waves and wind and hence provide an accurate depiction of deeper ocean currents. The WOCE plan calls for 1,000 subsurface drifters to be placed 1,500 meters (4,900 feet) below the surface at an average spacing of 500 kilometers.

Three types of subsurface drifters will be used in the WOCE program. Two types of subsurface drifters will be tracked by sound waves, which travel easily through ocean water. The first type uses *hydrophones* (instruments that record sound) anchored to the ocean floor. Scientists release drifters that give off sound signals, which the anchored hydrophones detect and electronically store. After several hydrophones receive signals from a drifter, scientists can track the drifter's movements.

The second type uses hydrophones that drift, recording the signals they pick up from moored sound sources. The hydrophones pop to the surface after several months to transmit data to a satellite.

A third type of subsurface drifter, which does not rely on sound, pops up to the sea surface every few months and radios its position to a satellite. Then, it sinks again to a predetermined depth and drifts with a subsurface current until it is time for it to pop up again.

Current meters will be used to measure the speeds of ocean currents at specific sites. Research ships set out current meters attached to anchored cables. Placed on the cable at various depths, the meters electronically record the speed of currents at those depths. The meters will remain in position for up to three years, until scientists send a signal to a release mechanism that separates the cable from its anchor. The cable and current meters then float to the surface for a ship to retrieve.

Finally, oceanographic stations located on some 66 islands around the world will monitor changes in sea levels. Because warmer global temperatures would melt the polar icecaps, raising sea levels, scientists predict that a steadily rising sea level would be one sign of the onset of global warming. The sea-level changes recorded during the WOCE study can be compared with data from as long ago as the early 1800's, when sea levels were first monitored.

Two other oceanographic studies, though not part of WOCE, also aim to improve our understanding of the ocean's role in moderating climate. The Joint Global Ocean Flux Study focuses on how marine plant life absorbs carbon dioxide during photosynthesis. In particular, scientists are looking at *phytoplankton*, tiny plants that dwell in the upper layers of the ocean. When they take in a great deal of carbon dioxide, phytoplankton reproduce and grow rapidly, forming what are called *blooms*. Remote sensors on satellites can detect *chlorophyll*, a green pigment in plants that absorbs energy from the sun for use in photosynthesis. By monitoring as much of the blooms as the sensors can detect, scientists can calculate a lower limit for how much carbon dioxide the phytoplankton remove from the atmosphere.

The other study, called the Greenland Sea Tomography experiment, used a method called *ocean acoustic tomography* for monitoring the interior of the ocean. The method was developed jointly by oceanographers Carl Wunsch of Massachusetts Institute of Technology in Cambridge and Walter Munk of Scripps Institution of Oceanography in San Diego. This method uses sound waves to create a series of cross-sections of the temperature and currents in the ocean. The cross-sections can be combined by a computer to create a three-dimensional view of the ocean, much as a physician's computerized tomography (CT) scanner uses X rays to create three-dimensional views of the human body.

In ocean acoustic tomography, scientists monitor the time it takes a pulse of sound to travel from a source to a receiver that may be several hundred kilometers away. This gives scientists information about the water's temperature, because sound waves travel more quickly through warm water than cold water. Scientists can also use this technique to measure currents, because sound travels faster when moving with currents than against them. To get a three-dimensional view of a body of water, scientists place *transceivers* (instruments that send and receive sound signals) at various depths and later combine the data from each layer of the water.

Oceanographers in 1991 were studying data gathered during the Greenland Sea Tomography experiment, which was conducted in 1988 and 1989. They are particularly interested in measurements of a deepwater current in the Greenland Sea, which is the largest component of the North Atlantic Deep Water. As scientists continue to study the results from this experiment, they should learn much more about how deepwater currents move.

By the time WOCE is completed in 1997, scientists will have analyzed vast amounts of data from it and other oceanographic studies. Using this data, scientists will be able to improve the various computer models they have devised to describe the ocean's circulation. In turn, this will enable scientists to better understand how the ocean circulates and interacts with the atmosphere today and to predict how this interaction may change in the future. When the data are in, oceanographers may know whether the thermohaline circulation will continue at its present rate or at an altered rate that would influence the onset of global warming. Their research may also explain in more detail how environmental changes can alter thermohaline circulation and the ocean's ability to store heat and greenhouse gases. Armed with this knowledge, we may be able to say whether the changes human beings have made in Earth's environment will lead unrelentingly to global warming.

For further reading:

Bramwell, Martyn. *Oceans.* Watts, 1984.
Cook, William J. "Secrets of the Sea." *U.S. News & World Report*, Aug. 21, 1989, pp. 48-55.
MacLeish, William H. *The Stream.* Houghton, 1989.
Washington, Warren M. "Where's the Heat?" *Natural History*, March 1990, pp. 67-72.

Astronomers have learned a great deal about the
Galaxy we inhabit, but many mysteries remain,
especially about what lies at the galactic center.

Mysteries of
the Milky Way

BY THEODORE P. SNOW

The author:
Theodore P. Snow is professor of astrophysics at the University of Colorado in Boulder and author of *The Dynamic Universe*.

On a clear, moonless night, the sight of the Milky Way stretching across the sky rarely fails to inspire thoughts of the mysteries of the cosmos. To the ancient philosophers, this hazy band of light was simply a faraway rain cloud. Today, we know that the Milky Way is a galaxy, a vast collection of stars, about 100 billion in number. One of those stars, our sun, is a typical, though minor, member of this celestial club, and the Milky Way, in turn, is only one among hundreds of billions of other galaxies.

Although we have learned a great deal about the Milky Way, astronomers continue to make new findings. Since the early 1970's, astronomers have found that most of the Galaxy's matter may actually be invisible. Evidence reported in the late 1980's has also shown that the Milky Way may have formed as a result of the merger of several smaller galaxies. And astronomers are still puzzling over evidence of extremely energetic activity detected in the late 1980's in the very center of the Galaxy. To some, this activity suggests that at the Milky Way's heart lies an extremely massive *black hole*, an object so dense and so massive that nothing, not even light, can escape the pull of its gravity.

Even astronomers' measurements of the size of the Milky Way have changed. And in January 1990, astronomers reported evidence that the shape of our Galaxy's central region may be significantly different from what was believed for many years.

Because Earth is inside the Galaxy, it is impossible to see directly the Galaxy's overall form and size. Instead, astronomers have deduced the structure of the Milky Way by rather ingenious methods, borrowing from what is known about other galaxies and making observations of the Milky Way through telescopes on the ground and in space.

Their methods have produced a detailed notion of what the Milky Way would look like if we could somehow travel to a position far outside it. If we could view the Galaxy from one side, or edge-on, we would see a huge, thin disk of stars and glowing clouds of gas and dust, with a bulge in the center. Above and below the central bulge of the Galaxy are several large, spherical clusters of stars. These groupings, called *globular clusters*, contain perhaps 100,000 stars each.

If we viewed the Galaxy from above, or face-on, we would see that the disk has a spiral structure, a bit like a pinwheel, though not as regular. Unlike some spiral galaxies that have elegant, gently curving arms emerging from the center, our Galaxy is made of bits and pieces of spiral arms, forming segments that are not part of a simple overall pattern. All the stars in the disk and the globular clusters orbit the center, giving the Galaxy an overall spin, much like a record on a turntable.

Of course, astronomers cannot actually view the Galaxy from afar. The tale of how they arrived at this picture of our Galaxy resembles a detective story in which scientists used telescopic observations and the laws of physics to assemble various clues. With each new discovery, another piece of the galactic puzzle fell into place.

The Shape and Makeup of the Milky Way

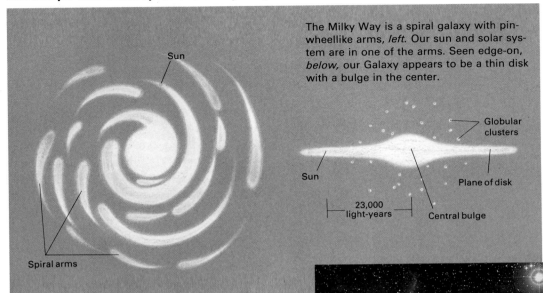

Sun

The Milky Way is a spiral galaxy with pin-wheellike arms, *left.* Our sun and solar system are in one of the arms. Seen edge-on, *below,* our Galaxy appears to be a thin disk with a bulge in the center.

Globular clusters

Sun

Plane of disk

23,000 light-years

Central bulge

Spiral arms

During the early 1900's, the size and shape of the Milky Way were almost completely unknown, as was the location of its center. In the first decade of the 1900's, Dutch astronomer J. C. Kapteyn of the University of Groningen surveyed the sky to determine the concentration of stars in space around the sun. He found that the numbers of stars appeared to decline in all directions from the sun. Kapteyn reasoned that the sun was therefore in the center of the Galaxy because the concentration of stars there was likely to be higher than at the Galaxy's outskirts.

By about 1917, however, evidence was building that the sun is far from the center of the Milky Way. American astronomer Harlow Shapley, then at Mount Wilson Observatory near Pasadena, Calif., observed that the Galaxy's globular clusters are concentrated around a point in space tens of thousands of *light-years* from the sun. (A light-year is the distance that light travels in a year, about 9.5 trillion kilometers [5.9 trillion miles].) Shapley reasoned that the globular clusters were orbiting the center of the Galaxy—which he concluded was some 50,000 light-years from our solar system, in the direction of the constellation Sagittarius.

The next major step in revealing the structure of

Stars surround the Horsehead Nebula, one of the Milky Way's clouds of gas and dust. Stars, gas, and dust make up the visible matter of the Galaxy.

the Galaxy came from studies of the motions of stars near the sun. In the early 1920's, Swedish astronomer Bertil Lindblad analyzed the motions of many stars. He was able to detect these motions due to small shifts in the wavelengths of the stars' light. These shifts are caused by a phenomenon called the *Doppler effect*. The Doppler effect is familiar to most people as a change in the pitch of sound when an object, such as a train or automobile, approaches and recedes. As a train approaches an observer, for example, the sound of its whistle is relatively high-pitched, but as the train passes and recedes, the whistle has a lower-pitched sound.

The Doppler effect also causes an apparent change in the frequency, or wavelength, of light due to the motion of a light-emitting object toward or away from an observer. Astronomers can observe this change in frequency by attaching a device called a *spectrograph* to a telescope. Light collected by the telescope passes through the spectrograph and is broken down into the *spectrum*, the colors of the rainbow. The shortest wavelengths correspond to the color blue and the longest to the color red.

If a star is moving toward Earth, astronomers will observe that all the wavelengths of its light are slightly shifted toward the shorter-wavelength, or blue, portion of the spectrum. Conversely, if a star is moving away from Earth, astronomers will observe that the wave-length of its light is shifted slightly toward the longer-wavelength, or red, portion of the spectrum. The greater the shift, the faster the speed of the object. By measuring these small shifts, astronomers can deduce the relative motions and speeds of stars. Lindblad found that the stars near the sun and the sun itself were moving in circular paths around a distant point. He deduced the direction to this center of circular motion, finding it almost exactly the same as Shapley had—toward the constellation Sagittarius.

In 1927, a more extensive analysis of star motions by Dutch astronomer Jan Oort confirmed the picture developed by Shapley and Lindblad. Oort noted that some stars appear to be gaining on the sun as they orbit the galactic center, while others fall behind. Oort realized that these velocity differences were due to the different distances of the stars from the center. The situation was comparable to that of cars on a race track: Those in the inside lanes pull ahead of those farther out. By measuring the Doppler shifts of stars at different distances from the galactic center, Oort estimated both the size of the race track—that is, the size of the Galaxy—and the direction toward its center. Oort's work firmly established that the Galaxy is a great disk, with the sun orbiting near one edge. Lindblad and Oort also estimated that the sun was 30,000 light-years from the center, as opposed to Shapley's estimate of 50,000 light-years.

In 1930, American astronomer Robert Trumpler offered an explanation for the different measurements. He reasoned that the space between stars—the *interstellar medium*—is filled with dust particles that dim the light of these stars. When the existence of interstellar dust was taken into account, Shapley's estimated distances to the globular clusters could be reduced. Astronomers then agreed that the sun was about 30,000 light-years from the center of the Galaxy and that the entire Galaxy was about 60,000 light-years across. Trumpler's findings also explained why Kapteyn mistakenly thought that the concentrations of stars thinned out in all directions from the sun. Their numbers only appeared to diminish because dust obscured distant starlight.

Although astronomers had discovered the size and overall shape of the Galaxy by 1930, they were uncertain about the arrangement of its stars and clouds of gas and dust. By the 1950's, astronomers had used telescopes to observe thousands of other galaxies and had found that many, including the nearby Andromeda galaxy, are pinwheel-shaped, with hot, bright stars concentrated in bands that spiraled from the center. This led to the general suspicion that our own great disk might be spiral-shaped. In 1951, astronomer William W. Morgan of the University of Chicago measured the distance to many of the Milky Way's hot, bright stars and found them concentrated in bands, rather than spread uniformly through the Galaxy. This pattern of star concentration indicated that our Galaxy, too, probably had spiral arms.

But the same interstellar dust that made star clusters appear dim also obscured all but a small portion of the Galaxy's disk. This made it impossible for astronomers using optical telescopes to see most of the stars in the Galaxy. Fortunately, visible light is only a narrow band of the *electromagnetic spectrum*, the range of radiant energies that includes the short-wavelength gamma rays and X rays and the long-wavelength radio waves. Radio waves can penetrate the interstellar dust. Astronomers first used radio telescopes in the 1940's to "see" the Galaxy at these longer wavelengths.

In the early 1950's, Dutch physicist Hendrik C. van de Hulst predicted that atoms of hydrogen—the most abundant element in the universe—should give off radio waves at a particular wavelength. The notion was significant, because hydrogen is the principal element making up giant clouds that tend to be concentrated in spiral arms. In 1951, using a radio telescope, American scientists Harold I. Ewen and Edward M. Purcell first detected the emission from interstellar hydrogen. By applying their knowledge of the Doppler shift to analyze the radio wavelengths, astronomers were able to measure the relative motions of hydrogen clouds in the Galaxy. From the motions, scientists deduced the overall structure of the galactic disk. Their observations led to accurate and complete maps of the spiral structure of the Milky Way.

Thus, by the end of the 1950's, astronomers had learned that our Galaxy consists of a great disk with spiral arm segments. Since then, this basic picture has not changed much, though the distance of the

The Milky Way We Cannot See

Astronomers have explored the Milky Way at wavelengths of radiation that are not visible to the human eye. Telescopes that detect radio waves, X rays, and infrared radiation have given us new insights about our Galaxy.

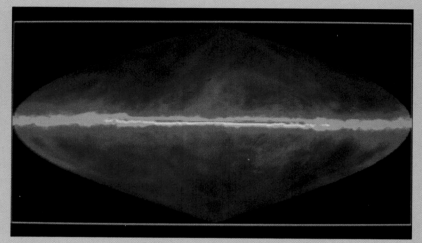

Radio telescopes, *above,* showed that hydrogen gas is concentrated in the disk of the Galaxy, *right.*

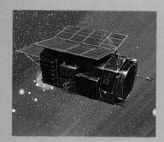

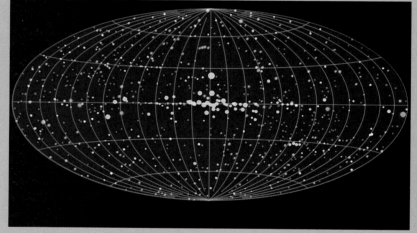

An orbiting X-ray tele- scope, *above,* revealed that most of the Galaxy's high-energy sources of X rays are in the disk and central bulge, *right.*

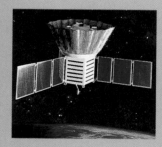

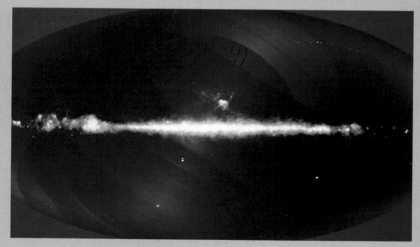

An orbiting far-infrared telescope, *above,* showed that nearly all the Gal- axy's dust is concentrated in the disk, *right.*

sun from the center, long thought to be about 30,000 light-years, is now believed to be about 23,000 light-years.

The shape of the Galaxy's central region, however, came into question in 1990, based on findings by American astronomers Leo Blitz of the University of Maryland at College Park and David Spergel of Princeton University in New Jersey. The astronomers reexamined data that described the motions of hydrogen gas in the outer regions of the Galaxy. They found that this gas had a somewhat *elliptical* (oval-shaped) orbit, rather than a roughly circular orbit, as previously thought. This suggested that the central bulge of the Galaxy is elliptical rather than spherical. Astronomers have observed other galaxies with oval-shaped central regions. These are known as *barred spiral galaxies*, and it now appears that the Milky Way may be one of them.

If this is what the Milky Way looks like, of what does it consist? First, and most obviously, it is made of stars of many types. A census of stars in the Milky Way shows that small, dim stars are far more common than large, hot, bright ones. Our sun is a star that is a bit above average in mass and *luminosity* (the amount of energy given off per second) compared with the much greater number of small, dim stars in the Galaxy. These low-mass stars are more plentiful because more of them form when the force of gravity causes interstellar clouds to collapse.

A star shines because of nuclear reactions that take place in its core, where nuclei of the simple, or light, atomic elements fuse together to form heavier ones, releasing energy in the process. First, hydrogen nuclei fuse to form helium. Then, helium nuclei fuse to form carbon. Stars form all the elements heavier than helium, and they expel these elements into the interstellar medium when they run out of nuclear fuel. Stars the size of the sun can last for 10 billion years. Smaller stars may burn for hundreds of billions or even trillions of years. But the most massive stars in our Galaxy—and elsewhere—live only about 10 million years. They burn up their nuclear fuel relatively quickly and die.

Astronomers believe that our Galaxy formed about 10 billion or more years ago, so some of its original low-mass stars are still in the prime of their lives. But all the original massive stars have long since run out of fuel. For stars of this size, the end comes violently as the core of the star collapses. The core forms a tiny dense remnant called a *neutron star*, while the star's outer layers explode in a *supernova*, sending chemical elements out into the interstellar medium. If the star is massive enough, its core may continue collapsing forever and become a black hole. Stars of moderate to small mass expel their outer layers of gas but do not collapse so violently when they run out of fuel. These stars end as *white dwarfs*.

Knowing how stars evolve and die has helped astronomers understand the composition of the interstellar gas and dust, which

Discovering the Galaxy's Spiral Arms

Because we are located inside the Milky Way Galaxy, astronomers had to deduce the spiral arm structure of our Galaxy by observing the motions of distant stars and gas clouds. These motions can be detected due to the Doppler shift—the apparent change in the wavelength of light as a light-emitting object moves toward or away from an observer.

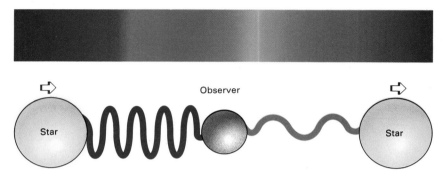

The spectrum of visible light is made up of the colors of the rainbow, *top.* If an object is moving toward an observer, *above,* its light will be shifted toward the blue, or short wavelength, part of the spectrum. If an object is moving away, its light will be shifted toward the red, or long wavelength, part of the spectrum.

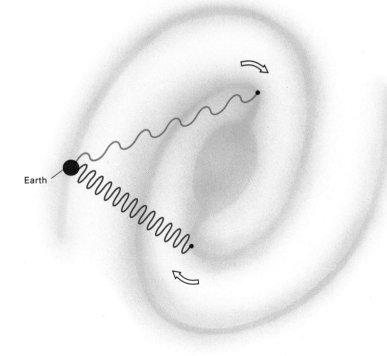

Using radio telescopes in the 1950's to detect gas clouds that could not be seen with optical telescopes, astronomers found that some clouds were moving away from us and some toward us, *left.* This was due to the Galaxy's rotation. Because of that rotation, each spiral arm had a distinct velocity. By calculating the velocity from the Doppler shift, astronomers could pinpoint the location of each spiral arm.

Refining Our View

Until 1990, astronomers thought the Milky Way was a normal spiral galaxy with a round central bulge, *top left,* around which our sun travels in a circular path, *top.* But studies reported in January 1990 indicate that our Galaxy is a barred spiral with an oval-shaped central bulge, *above left,* and that our sun travels in an elliptical orbit, *above.*

constitutes some 10 to 15 per cent of the mass of the galactic disk. Astronomers have come to think of matter in the interstellar medium as part of a stellar recycling process. The Galaxy evolves, or changes over time, because the material that stars return to the interstellar medium is enriched in more and heavier chemical elements that formed through nuclear reactions. If our Galaxy had little or no interstellar gas and dust clouds, as some galaxies do, then eventually no new stars could form, and the Milky Way would probably not continue to evolve. Without the chemical enrichment that has already occurred in our own Galaxy, none of us would be here today to observe it and write about it. Our solar system and life on Earth could not have evolved without the heavy elements, such as carbon, oxygen, and iron, formed by the stars that came before us.

Astronomers study the composition of the Galaxy's interstellar matter by using telescopes that detect radiation at ultraviolet and infrared as well as radio wavelengths. The elements in interstellar gas clouds give off or absorb radiation at characteristic wavelengths. By comparing these wavelengths with the known wavelengths of elements and compounds in our laboratories on Earth, astronomers can identify the makeup of the interstellar matter. By measuring the abundance of the material's elements and the amount of energy it radiates, astronomers can also infer its temperature and density.

They have found that the interstellar medium contains regions of hot and cold gas. Some parts of the Galaxy contain gas clouds that are relatively dense and incredibly cold, with temperatures of around 15 to 20 degrees above *absolute zero* (the lowest possible temperature, which is equal to -273.15 °C [-459.67 °F]). At the other extreme are low-density gases heated by supernova shock waves and other stellar explosions to temperatures as high as 1,000,000 °C (1,800,000 °F).

Astronomers have observed that the overall structure of the interstellar medium is patchy. The cold, dense gas clouds tend to congregate along the spiral arms of the galaxy. Between these clouds are regions of hot gas. Astronomers have likened the interstellar medium in the Milky Way to Swiss cheese because it consists of tunnels and channels of hot, low-density gas filling the voids between regions of denser, colder clouds.

The greatest component of the Galaxy may be something very mysterious. The Milky Way once appeared to consist almost entirely of stars and interstellar gas and dust, but astronomers began to gather evidence in the 1970's that the region surrounding the disk may contain much more matter than previously thought. Furthermore, we now find indications that there may be a lot more matter present even in the disk than we can see in the form of stars or gas.

Many astronomers are certain that more than 90 per cent of the Galaxy's matter may be invisible—that is, it gives off no detectable radiation. They call this invisible mass *dark matter*. Astronomers deduced the existence of dark matter from observations of the orbital speeds of stars and gas clouds far from the galactic center, beyond the orbit of the sun. If the mass of the Galaxy were concentrated in the central region, as originally thought, then the orbital speeds of stars in the outer regions should decrease with increasing distance from the center. But beyond our sun, toward the outlying regions of the Galaxy, the orbital speeds of stars and gas clouds do not decline but remain nearly the same. The fact that the orbital speeds of objects far from the center do not drop off rapidly can be explained only if there is a great deal of mass outside the disk exerting a gravitational force on these outlying gas clouds and stars. Scientists now believe that a spherical halo of dark matter extends far beyond the visible parts of the Galaxy, though its exact dimensions are still unknown.

Astronomers have proposed a number of candidates for what the dark matter might be—ranging from a previously unsuspected but vast population of very dim stars, to black holes, to hypothetical elementary particles smaller than an atom, to planet-sized objects known as *brown dwarfs*. So far, no one knows what the dark matter is.

Extremely energetic activity at the core of the Galaxy is equally puzzling. Using radio, infrared, X-ray, and gamma-ray telescopes, we can penetrate the interstellar clouds of gas and dust to view this activity at the center of the Milky Way.

The first indication that something unusual was occurring at the galactic center came in the 1950's, when radio astronomers detected gas clouds swirling around the core at speeds up to hundreds of kilometers per second. (Normally, interstellar clouds move much slower, at speeds of only a few kilometers per second.) In the 1980's, the Very Large Array—a collection of 27 radio telescopes near Socorro, N. Mex., that can be combined to focus sharply on a particular region of the sky—revealed a tiny area where gas clouds move at even higher speeds.

Since then, radio telescopes also have revealed intricate structures of gas near the galactic center, including two gigantic plumes of gas that are roughly perpendicular to the plane of the Galaxy. Located between the two plumes is a smaller spur of gas that is also perpendicular to the galactic plane. Because the Galaxy's rotation should pull the gas in the plumes and the spur toward the plane of the disk, these unusual structures indicate that some force other than rotation is controlling the motions of the gas near the core. Some astronomers have suggested that the gas was originally ejected from the center of the Galaxy in an enormous explosion and that a magnetic field then confined the plumes and spur and kept them perpendicular to the plane of the Galaxy.

Perhaps even more surprising than the presence of these structures is the existence of a brilliant but tiny source of intense radio, infrared, X-ray, and gamma-ray emission at the center of a large cluster of stars in the heart of the Galaxy. Radio astronomers were the first to recognize this source and gave it the name *Sagittarius A* (indicating that it is the brightest radio source in the constellation Sagittarius). Using improved techniques for mapping the details of such distant objects, astronomers in the 1980's showed that the source actually consists of a few smaller bright points. Astronomers think that one of these bright spots is the true center of the Milky Way—the single point about which the entire pinwheel rotates. But it has proven difficult to tell which point holds this distinction.

The total luminosity given off from the Sagittarius A region is about 10 million times that of the sun, and interstellar gas in the area is extremely hot. Infrared and radio waves emerge from a very small region, comparable to the size of the solar system. Energetic X rays come from a similarly small region, but not necessarily the same one: There is a slight difference in position between the points emitting infrared radiation and X rays.

So how do astronomers explain all this mysterious, energetic

Did Our Galaxy Form from a Cloud of Dust and Gas?

One theory of how the Milky Way formed is based in part on observations that old stars are in clusters outside the central bulge.

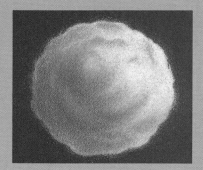

According to this long-standing theory, gravity caused a huge cloud of gas and dust to collapse.

Stars made from the gas and dust formed in clusters just outside the collapsing cloud, which began to flatten due to its rotation.

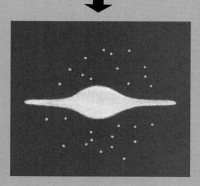

The cloud eventually became a thin disk where new stars formed. But the oldest stars remained in the outer clusters.

activity? There are two competing ideas. One group of astronomers believes that a combination of a compact cluster of hot stars, a recent supernova explosion, and a modest black hole with the mass of about 100 suns account for the activity observed. Another group of astronomers believes that the presence of a supermassive black hole with the mass of about 1 million suns could explain all the complicated phenomena at the galactic core.

Both groups believe that some type of black hole must be present at the center of the Galaxy. Although black holes cannot be detected directly because they are invisible, calculations show the black hole's gravitational force would cause nearby gas particles to collide rapidly, heating the gas to high temperatures. The high temperatures, in turn, would cause the gas to give off most of its energy in the form of X rays. The strong source of X rays in the Milky Way's center, therefore, indicates the presence of a black hole.

Supporters of the idea that there are several high-energy objects in the galactic core point out that the strong X-ray source and the brightest infrared-emitting spot are in different locations. These two forms of radiation should come from exactly the same place if they were created by a single object such as a supermassive black hole. These astronomers point out that a compact cluster of hot stars would produce the high-temperature gas detected by radio telescopes, and this hot gas would, in turn, heat the interstellar dust detected by infrared telescopes. Only a modest black hole is needed, this group argues, in order to produce the energetic X rays. Finally, they say that a supernova occurring sometime in the last 100,000 years could have ejected gas from the center, creating the spur observed by radio telescopes.

Astronomers who believe the center contains a supermassive black hole point out that only a very massive central object—too massive to be a cluster of ordinary stars—could cause the extremely rapid motions of gas clouds around the galactic center. These astronomers also argue that many other galaxies have central hot spots, which are almost certainly supermassive black holes. The many similarities between those galactic centers and our own support their theory that the Milky Way also has a supermassive black hole at its core.

How these conflicting notions will be resolved is unclear. Astronomers continue to make infrared and X-ray observations, and these will help further pinpoint the exact positions of the bright spots. Eventually, the discrepancies will be sorted out, and gradually, astronomers will come to agree on the most likely explanation.

Astronomers are also concerned with how the Milky Way came into being. A long-standing theory held that the Galaxy began as an enormous cloud of gas. Gravity caused the gas to condense into the Galaxy's first stars—those in the globular clusters. But then the cloud collapsed inward and within a relatively brief time—about 1 billion years or less—formed the flattened disk that surrounds the central bulge. Gravity pulled the interstellar matter into the disk, and this explains why the disk is the only region of star formation observed today.

Studies of stars in the globular clusters and in the disk show that the oldest stars—and, therefore, the ones that formed first—are in the globular clusters. The youngest stars—those that formed most recently—are found in the disk. Astronomers can determine the relative ages of stars by studying their chemical composition. Stars in the halo, such as those in globular clusters, contain only small quantities of the heavier elements. On the other hand, the sun and other stars that orbit within the galactic disk contain much greater quantities of the heavy elements. Because the heavier elements had to be created by an earlier generation of stars, this is just what would be expected if the stars in the halo formed first and those in the disk formed later.

One problem with this theory is that it seems to require that the ages of the globular clusters should be about the same. If all of the interstellar matter—the stuff of star-making—collapsed into the disk within 1 billion years, then the star-making process in the clusters would have begun and ended within that time. Since the late 1980's, however, astronomers have shown that the clusters range in age from 11 billion to 16 billion years. If these ages are correct, how could star-making have

Did Our Galaxy Form from Merging Smaller Galaxies?

A new theory of the Milky Way's formation is based on findings that the ages of the outer star clusters differ widely.

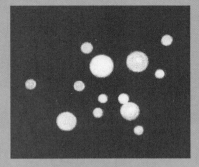

This new theory holds that the Galaxy formed from many smaller galaxies, containing stars of different ages.

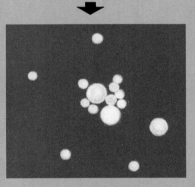

The force of gravity pulled some of these smaller galaxies together and eventually some of them merged.

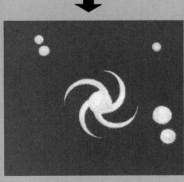

One group of merging galaxies formed the Milky Way, and some small galaxies became its satellite galaxies.

Mysteries at the Center of the Galaxy

Astronomers observe extremely energetic activity in the central region of our Galaxy, *below*. The source of this energy is a mystery, but some astronomers believe it may be due to the presence of an incredibly massive black hole.

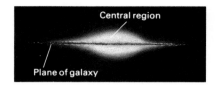

Central region

Plane of galaxy

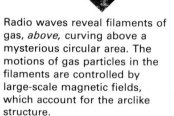

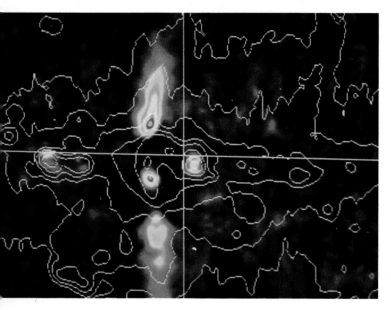

Radio waves reveal filaments of gas, *above,* curving above a mysterious circular area. The motions of gas particles in the filaments are controlled by large-scale magnetic fields, which account for the arclike structure.

A radio image shows two bright plumes of gas hundreds of light-years long, *above,* that extend above and below the plane of the Galaxy at the Milky Way's center. The plumes may be confined by a magnetic field that is perpendicular to the plane of the Galaxy.

continued within the clusters for several billion years after the Galaxy's interstellar matter had collapsed into the disk?

Another theory holds that the Galaxy did not form from a single, gigantic cloud but instead by the merger of several smaller galaxies, which were themselves created from individual clouds. These smaller galaxies were not all the same age. As they merged, some of their material became dispersed throughout the new system and formed a disk, while other parts, particularly the globular clusters, remained separate entities as we see them today.

This new theory of galaxy formation through mergers appears to apply to other galaxies as well. By observing extremely distant galaxies, astronomers are able to study those galaxies soon after their formation. Because of the great distances to these galaxies, their light has taken a long time to reach us and, therefore, we are seeing them as they were when they were forming about 10 billion to 20 billion

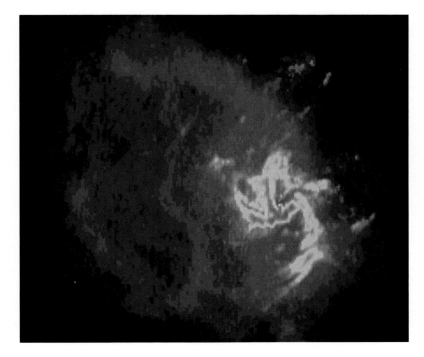

Gas clouds (blue, orange, and yellow) appear to be spiraling around a central, invisible object in this false-color map of radio waves in the Galaxy's core.

years ago. Studies of those young, distant galaxies suggest that all large galaxies may be the result of mergers of smaller ones.

It is fitting, then, that in upsetting our traditional view of how our own Galaxy formed, we have found evidence that the system of stars we call home is actually very much like some of the most spectacular objects in the known universe. Perhaps somewhere else, very far away, the light from the formation of our Milky Way is just now reaching alien astronomers who are marveling at the wondrous power and brilliance of its birth throes. Maybe these extragalactic colleagues will learn as much about their own galaxy from observing ours as we have learned about ours by observing theirs.

For further reading:

Bok, Bart J. and Priscilla F. *The Milky Way*. Harvard University Press, 1981.
Ferris, Timothy. *Galaxies*. Sierra Club, 1980.
Hodge, Paul. *Galaxies*. Harvard University Press, 1986.
Townes, Charles H., and Genzel, Reinhard. "What Is Happening at the Center of Our Galaxy?" *Scientific American*, April 1990, pp. 46-55.
Whitney, Charles A. *The Discovery of Our Galaxy*. Iowa State University Press, 1988.

From ancient times to the present,
scientists have been trying to
understand the nature of
this still mysterious force.

Questions of Gravity

BY LARRY ARBEITER

Everyone knows what gravity does. On Earth, it's the force that keeps our feet on the ground, whether we live in Indiana or Indonesia. Gravity makes a barbell heavy and pulls rivers downhill to the sea. Without it, we couldn't pour milk into a glass or keep food on our plates. Gravity gives everything its weight, from the lightest snowflake to the heaviest mountain. It defines *up* and *down*.

In space, gravity holds the moon in orbit around the Earth and holds Earth and the other planets in orbit around the sun. Gravity keeps our sun and hundreds of billions of other stars together in our Galaxy and binds great clusters of galaxies throughout the universe.

Although we see its effects everywhere, gravity's exact nature remains somewhat mysterious. Completely understanding the nature of gravity is one of the greatest challenges of modern physics.

The study of gravity has intrigued the most brilliant scientists throughout history and spawned some of the most important scientific theories ever proposed. For nearly 2,000 years, scholars thought of gravity as it was described by the Greek philosopher Aristotle in the 300's B.C. According to Aristotle, objects fall to Earth simply because they are trying to return to their natural places. Aristotle and those who followed him observed that feathers fall more slowly than lead balls and, therefore, believed that heavy objects fall faster than lighter ones.

What Gravity Does

The effects of gravity are everywhere around us. On Earth, *above left,* gravity defines *up* and *down,* holding our feet on the ground and the oceans in their basins. In space, *above right,* gravity keeps the moon in orbit around Earth and keeps the Earth and other planets in orbit around the sun.

The author:
Larry Arbeiter is director of the University of Chicago's news office and a free-lance science writer.

In the A.D. 1600's, the Italian scientist Galileo provided a more accurate way to measure the rate of falling objects. Galileo rolled balls of different weights down slightly inclined planes and found that it took each ball the same amount of time to reach the bottom. This experiment proved that all objects would fall to Earth at the same rate were it not for air resistance.

Galileo made observations of the way objects behave in space as well as on Earth. He reasoned that a moving object will travel in a straight path unless some force diverts it. Therefore, because the planets of our solar system are moving in curved orbits around the sun, he proposed, they must be acted upon by some force. Today, we know that force is the gravitational attraction of the sun.

A few decades later, the British astronomer and mathematician Sir Isaac Newton combined the work of Galileo and other scientists into the first scientific theory of gravity. According to Newton, the force that causes a ripe apple to fall from a tree is the same force that holds the moon in orbit around the Earth. Newton developed mathematical formulas that accurately predicted gravity's effects and published them in a massive work called *Principia Mathematica* in 1687.

Newton's theory describes gravity as an attractive force between all objects. Newton found that the strength of the gravitational force between two objects is directly proportional to their *masses,* the amount of matter of which they are made. If the mass of one of the objects could double, so would the force of gravity. (The pull of Earth's gravity on an object's mass gives the object what we call its *weight.*) Newton also related the strength of gravity to the distance between the centers of two objects. If the distance doubles, the force of gravity drops to one-fourth its former strength.

Soon after Newton published his theory, scientists of that time used it to explain that ocean tides are caused by the gravitational pull of the sun and the moon. Astronomers used Newton's formulas to plot the orbital paths of comets and planets based on the gravitational force of the sun. Even today, scientists use Newton's theory to plot the courses of satellites and spacecraft.

Newton's theory explains that gravity varies slightly from one place to another on Earth. The pull of Earth's gravity increases as an object moves closer to the planet's center. So a person weighs slightly—very slightly—more when standing at sea level than when standing on the peak of a mountain. Even at Earth's surface, our planet's gravity varies from place to place because of differences in the density of the rocks and minerals that lie directly below ground. Geologists using extremely sensitive devices called *gravimeters* will detect a stronger than normal force of gravity above ore deposits, which are relatively dense, and weaker than normal gravity above deposits of petroleum, which is less dense.

According to Newton's theory, gravity is a force that acts through empty space. Newton himself was unhappy with this idea of "action at a distance" but could come up with no alternative. Newton's theory also could not explain Galileo's finding that all objects, no matter what their mass, fall to Earth at the same rate. Newton treated as coincidence this exact correlation between gravity's pull on an object and that object's *inertial mass*, its resistance to a change in motion.

In 1915, the German-born physicist and Nobel Prize winner Albert Einstein announced a new explanation of gravity that accounted for these phenomena. Gravity, as Einstein explained it, was not a force at all. Instead, it was the curvature of the "fabric" of the universe, which he called *space-time*. Space-time is a combination of the three dimensions of space—height, width, and depth—with a fourth dimension: time.

Einstein's theory is difficult to grasp because we perceive space in only three dimensions. The notion of a four-dimensional universe arises from mathematics, not everyday experience. Nonetheless, we can imagine curved space-time. Picture a sheet of tightly stretched canvas supporting several large rocks. The depressions the rocks create in the canvas correspond to the curves in space-time. If you were to roll a ball across the canvas, it would veer toward the rocks as if pulled by them. The most massive rocks would indent the sheet the most and create the most powerful "gravitational fields."

As strange as the idea of curved space-time might be, in some ways, Einstein's theory appeals to common sense. Einstein reasoned that because gravity affects all objects the same way, it must be a property not of the objects, but of what they have in common—space-time. Gravity as curved space-time neatly explains why the gravity of a body such as Earth pulls all objects at the same rate, no matter what their masses.

But it was difficult to prove that Einstein's theory was superior to Newton's. To be considered so, Einstein's theory would have to match the mathematical accuracy of Newton's theory in every way and account for some things that Newton's could not. Unfortunately for scientists trying to test the theories, the predictions of the two were different only in describing objects far more massive or moving

Glossary

Black hole: An object in space that is so massive and so dense that nothing, not even light, can escape the gravity at its surface.

Gravimeter: A device that measures Earth's gravity at a specific location.

Gravitational lens: A galaxy or other extremely massive body whose gravitational field distorts light traveling toward Earth.

Gravitational waves: Ripples in space-time caused by the movement, collapse, or explosion of very massive objects in space.

Graviton: According to theory, a subatomic particle that transmits the force of gravity.

Inertia: Resistance to a change in motion.

Mass: The amount of matter in an object.

Space-time: The three dimensions of space (depth, width, and height) plus one other dimension, time.

Newton's Mysterious Force

In the late 1600's, English astronomer and mathematician Sir Isaac Newton described gravity as an attractive force that reaches across empty space to pull objects toward each other. Newton developed extremely accurate mathematical formulas—still valid in most circumstances today—to describe the effects of gravity on Earth and in the solar system.

Earth

Moon

Gravity and distance

Newton discovered that the gravitational force between two objects is inversely proportional to the distance between their centers.

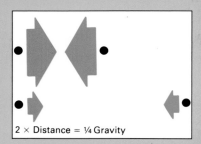

2 × Distance = ¼ Gravity

As the distance between two objects doubles, the force of gravity drops to one-fourth its former strength, *above*.

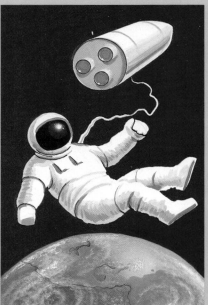

The force of gravity on an astronaut 26,000 kilometers (16,000 miles) from the center of Earth is one-sixteenth that on Earth's surface.

Gravity, mass, and weight

Newton found that the amount of matter in an object—its *mass*—is directly proportional to the force its gravity exerts. If the mass of an object could double, so would the pull of its gravity.

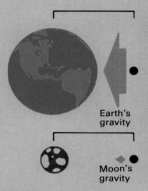

Earth's gravity

Moon's gravity

The moon is one-fourth the size of Earth but has 81 times less mass. Thus, the moon's pull of gravity is 81 times weaker than Earth's.

An object's *weight* is the gravitational force on it. A person who weighs 120 pounds (54 kilograms) on Earth would weigh only 20 pounds (9 kilograms) on the moon. The person would weigh even less if the surface of the moon were as far from the moon's center as the surface of Earth is from its center.

Gravity, hammers, and feathers

Newton calculated that gravity accelerates all objects—no matter how massive—at the same rate because gravity's force on an object is related to its mass, which in turn determines the object's resistance to a change in motion.

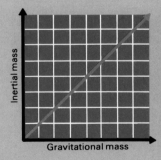

Inertial mass

Gravitational mass

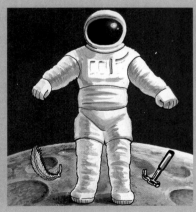

The more massive something is, the more resistance it has to being moved. This is called *inertial mass*. The strength of gravity's pull on an object—its gravitational mass—is exactly equal to the object's inertial mass.

A feather and a hammer dropped on Earth will fall at different rates. This is because air resistance has a greater effect on the fall of the feather.

A feather and a hammer dropped on the moon will fall at the same rate. This is because the moon has little or no atmosphere, and thus air resistance does not affect the fall of the feather.

far more rapidly than anything on Earth. Both Newton and Einstein, for example, had predicted that gravity could bend the path of a ray of light. But Einstein's theory predicted a bend twice as sharp. According to Einstein, the path of a ray of light should bend near a massive object such as a star because light must follow the curve in space-time made by the star.

In 1919, hoping to test the two theories, British astronomer Sir Arthur Eddington set out to measure this deflection of a distant star's light as it passes our sun. He led an expedition of scientists to a tiny island off the west coast of Africa, where they could clearly observe a total eclipse of the sun. During the eclipse, while the sun's light was momentarily blocked by the moon, the astronomers made very precise measurements of light coming from a star far beyond the sun but, at that moment, so closely aligned with it that the star's light just skimmed along the surface of the sun on its way to Earth. From these measurements, they calculated the apparent position of the star during the eclipse. Eddington compared this position to the position of the star when the sun was not aligned with it. By examining the distance between the true and the apparent position of the star, he found that the starlight was bent by precisely the amount Einstein had predicted.

The theory also accounted for an unusual feature of the orbit of the planet Mercury. Mercury follows an oval-shaped path around the sun. This oval—Mercury's orbit—is not fixed in space but slowly rotates in the same direction as Mercury itself. Newton's theory could not account for this *precession* of Mercury's orbit. Einstein's theory, which states that the curvature of space-time can pull bodies slightly sideways as well as together, precisely explained it.

Einstein's theory has been tested in other ways. In 1979, gravity's ability to bend light was confirmed more dramatically, when astronomers discovered a mirage created when light rays from a distant source curved and spread out as if distorted by an enormous lens in space. This *gravitational lens* is actually a galaxy or other extremely massive body between the Earth and the distant source of light. The gravitational field around the massive body can create double and triple images of distant objects or even arcs. If a distant object is aligned precisely with the gravitational lens, the light may be bent into a complete circle, which astronomers call an *Einstein Ring*.

Gravity not only bends light, according to Einstein, but can also slightly weaken it. Einstein predicted that light would lose some of its energy when it climbs "uphill" in space-time—that is, out of a gravitational field. The energy of light is related to its color or wavelength, with weaker light being redder than more energetic light. Einstein called this change in the energy and wavelength of light the *gravitational redshift*. Scientists have detected the redshift in light radiating from the sun and stars and even from Earth's surface.

The curved space-time around an object can also lead to time delays for light and other forms of radiant energy passing near the object. This is because a curved path between two points is longer than a straight path. In the late 1970's, scientists detected such a time delay in the transmission of radio signals to and from the *Viking* space probes on Mars. The scientists measured the time it took for signals to travel from Earth to the space probes and back again when Earth and Mars were at different positions in their orbits. The scientists found that the transmission was delayed when the signals traveled very near the sun and the strongest part of its gravitational field.

Einstein's theory has allowed scientists to predict the dramatic gravitational effects of stars much more massive than the sun. For example, in 1938, physicists proposed that the gravity of a star six to eight times as massive as our sun will eventually cause the star's core to collapse. The star will shrink to about 10 kilometers (6 miles) across, only one-thousandth of one-trillionth of its former volume. In 1967, astronomers found evidence that such objects, called *neutron stars*, actually exist. Neutron stars are incredibly dense. One thimbleful of such a star, if it could be brought to Earth, would weigh 200 million metric tons (220 million short tons). Astronomers predict that the core of a star even more massive than a neutron star will eventually collapse in upon itself forever. Such a star becomes an infinitely small and infinitely massive *black hole*. The extreme density of a black hole curves space-time so steeply that nothing, not even light rays, can escape the immense pull of its gravitational field.

An especially exciting prediction of Einstein's theory is the *gravitational wave*. According to the theory, when very massive objects move suddenly, explode, or collapse, they produce ripples in the fabric of space-time, much as a stone dropped into a pond sends waves across the pond's surface. Moving at the speed of light, these waves carry energy, but their effects are extremely weak: If a star near our solar system collapsed to form a neutron star, the violent implosion would create gravitational waves that jostled objects on Earth by far less than the diameter of an atom.

Gravity waves have never been directly measured, but most scientists believe they have indirect evidence that the waves do exist. It comes from a pair of neutron stars discovered in 1974 that orbit each other in less than eight hours. According to Einstein's theory, these orbiting stars are emitting gravity waves, and so they are losing energy. Accordingly, they should be slowly moving closer and thus orbiting each other more rapidly. During the last fifteen years, astronomers have measured the stars' orbits very accurately and found that they have indeed speeded up. This is strong evidence that the stars are emitting gravity waves.

The twin stars, a "smoking gun" that seems to prove the existence of gravity waves, increased scientists' enthusiasm to directly detect waves on Earth. Scientists in the United States and Europe are eagerly searching for the waves, using extremely sensitive instru-

Einstein's Curved Space-Time

Physicist Albert Einstein in the early 1900's proposed that gravity was not a force at all—but a curvature in what he called *space-time,* the three dimensions of space plus one dimension of time. According to Einstein, a massive object such as the sun "dents" space-time just as a bowling ball would depress a soft mattress. The Earth orbits the sun as if it were rolling around the edge of this depression.

Einstein predicted that the gravitational effect of the sun and other stars could deflect even light, because light would have to move in a curved space-time made by a massive object. Astronomers proved Einstein's theory in 1919, when they showed that light from a distant star was deflected as it passed near the sun, *below.*

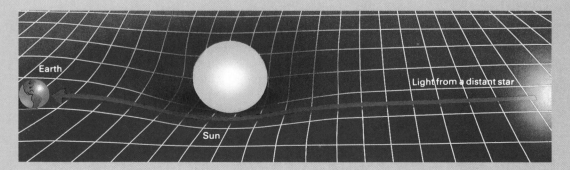

Gravity waves and black holes

Einstein's theory predicted that the gravity of some objects in the universe would cause tremendous distortions of space-time, creating effects so bizarre they are difficult even to imagine.

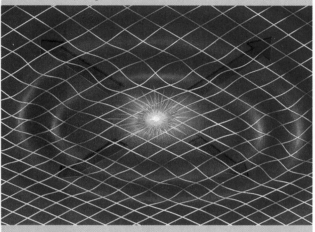

Gravity waves, ripples that move outward through the fabric of space-time, are created by such violent events as the explosion of a huge star, according to Einstein's theory, *above.*

A black hole is created by the collapse of a very massive star. Matter in a black hole is so incredibly dense and distorts space-time so greatly that nothing, not even light, can escape its gravity.

ments. If such experiments detect gravity waves emitted by colliding black holes, exploding stars, or other violent events, the finding will be another confirmation of Einstein's theory and will provide a new way to view the universe.

After all its experimental successes, Einstein's theory of gravity might seem perfectly complete. Compared with it, Newton's theory is only an approximation—a very good one, but valid only for objects in weak gravitational fields or that move slowly compared with the speed of light. But could Einstein's theory also be only an approximation? Perhaps, in circumstances extreme enough, Einstein's theory could also fail to predict every action of gravity.

Scientists have important reasons for believing that Einstein's theory may not completely describe gravity. The source of their doubt stems from what they know about the other forces in the universe. Aside from gravity, physicists have discovered three other fundamental forces: *electromagnetism, the strong force,* and *the weak force.* These three forces rule the realm of atoms and smaller particles. Atoms consist of a nucleus, typically made up of protons and neutrons, surrounded by one or more electrons. Electromagnetism holds electrons in orbit around the nucleus and its residual effects hold some atoms together in molecules. Electromagnetism is responsible for light, electricity, and magnetism. The strong force binds tiny particles called *quarks* to form protons and neutrons. Its residual effects hold protons and neutrons together in the nucleus. The weak force is responsible for some types of radioactive decay.

Physicists believe that these three forces and gravity were joined into a single force at the beginning of time. This "master force" was present at the *big bang,* the moment when the universe exploded into being at temperatures 10 trillion trillion times greater than at the center of the sun. A fraction of a second later, as the universe expanded and cooled, gravity and the other three forces separated from each other.

Many scientists believe that if the forces were once united, they should still have a great deal in common, and one mathematical theory should describe them all. But gravity seems to be an oddball. According to modern theories, the other three forces are all transmitted by tiny particles far

Gravity and the "Master Force"

Gravity is one of the four fundamental forces of nature. Physicists believe that all four forces were once part of one master force. Determining how this could be so is one of the great problems of modern physics.

Atoms and fundamental forces

An atom consists of a nucleus orbited by one or more electrons. Nuclei are made up of protons and neutrons, which, in turn, are made up of quarks. Among these fundamental building blocks of matter operate the electromagnetic, strong, and weak forces, transmitted by tiny particles of energy. But scientists have not found a way to describe gravity in these terms.

Unifying the forces

Experimental physicists have found evidence of photons, gluons, and W and Z particles, which transmit three of the fundamental forces, by smashing atoms together in powerful particle accelerators. But so far they have not found a particle that transmits the force of gravity.

Force	Responsible for	Transmitted by
Electromagnetic	Electricity, magnetism, and light	Photons
Strong	Binding particles in the atomic nucleus	Gluons
Weak	Some types of radioactive decay	W and Z particles
Gravity	Attraction between objects	Gravitons?

How the forces came to be

According to the big bang theory, at the moment the universe exploded into being with an unimaginably hot temperature, all four forces were united as one master force. Within a tiny fraction of a second, the universe began to cool, and the forces split off to become the four fundamental forces known today, *below.* Theoretical physicists have found mathematical ways to explain how the electromagnetic, strong, and weak forces were once unified. But no one agrees on how to include gravity.

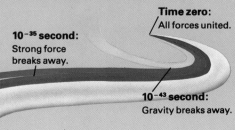

Time zero:
All forces united.

10^{-35} second:
Strong force breaks away.

10^{-43} second:
Gravity breaks away.

10^{-12} second:
Weak and electromagnetic forces break away.

Matter

smaller than the atom. Physicists have observed evidence of these particles in the reactions that take place inside powerful atom-smashers called *particle accelerators*. The electromagnetic force is transmitted by packets of energy called *photons*, which are given off and absorbed by electrons and other charged particles. The strong force is transmitted between quarks by particles called gluons, and the weak force is transmitted by particles that physicists call W and Z. But according to Einstein's theory, gravity, unlike the other forces, arises from the curvature of space-time.

Gravity doesn't fit in for other reasons. The strong, weak, and electromagnetic forces affect only certain subatomic particles, while gravity affects everything in the universe. And gravity is barely felt inside the atom. The strong force between neutrons and protons in the nucleus is 100 million trillion trillion trillion times stronger than gravity. Yet gravity becomes stronger as the amount of matter increases. Inside the atom, gravity is virtually powerless; from planet-sized objects to stars and galaxies, gravity rules the universe.

Scientists are hard at work trying to create a unified theory that shows how gravity and the other three forces are derived from the "master force." Many physicists believe the best hope for unifying the forces is through tiny particles that can be described geometrically. The *superstring theory* states that all particles are made of unimaginably tiny "strings" of pure energy. Even more surprisingly, these strings would exist in 10 dimensions—the 4 of space-time plus 6 more that we cannot observe. By vibrating and interacting in complex ways, the strings could produce all the known particles of matter as well as the fundamental forces. Proponents of this theory say that a tiny loop-shaped particle of energy called the *graviton* would transmit the force of gravity.

Some scientists imagine even stranger things. They think that the strength of gravity may weaken as the universe expands. Others believe that we may one day find a negative force that reverses gravity, or that the universe is filled with mysterious *shadow matter* worlds that coexist with the world of normal matter but interact with it only by exerting gravity.

These notions suggest that the nature of gravity is still one of the most important questions in physics. During the last 300 years, scientists have thought of gravity as a mysterious force acting at a distance, as curved space-time, and now as unimaginably tiny vibrating strings. Each of the theories has come steadily closer to describing gravity. But, so far, the powerful force we feel every time we take a step has proved too strange to be understood completely.

For further reading:

Narlikar, Jayant V. *The Lighter Side of Gravity*. W. H. Freeman, 1982.
Nicolson, Iain. *Gravity, Black Holes, and the Universe*. David & Charles, 1981.
Wheeler, John A. *A Journey into Gravity and Spacetime*. W. H. Freeman, 1990.
Will, Clifford M. *Was Einstein Right? Putting General Relativity to the Test*. Basic Books, 1986.

Science News Update

See page 240

See page 264

Science Year contributors report on the year's major developments in their respective fields. The articles in this section are arranged alphabetically.

See page 268

See page 305

See page 346

Agriculture

A new variety of rice that can be harvested twice in one season in Texas was planted on 24,000 hectares (60,000 acres) of Texas farmland in spring 1991. The variety, called Texmont, is also the first commercially available grain in the United States produced from only one parent by a culturing technique that uses anthers, the male part of the flower, and the chemical colchicine.

Researchers at the Texas A&M University research center in Beaumont selected a parent plant for its trait to ripen early. They placed pollen-covered anthers from this plant in a laboratory dish with a solution of salts, sugars, vitamins, and hormones. The dish remained in darkness for two weeks. Then the scientists placed it under light to cause the pollen to grow. The resulting callus (a thickened, unstructured mass of cells) formed plantlets, small immature plants.

At this point, the plants could continue to develop, but they would be sterile, having only one set of chromosomes from the male parent. A plant must have two sets of chromosomes in order to produce fertile seeds through which the plant is reproduced. Therefore, the scientists treated the plantlets with colchicine, which causes the number of chromosomes in each plant cell to double.

This technique enabled the scientists to develop Texmont rice in just one year, instead of the two to five years that are normally required for developing new rice varieties. Normally, botanists breed new plant varieties by fertilizing seeds from a female plant with pollen from a male plant. Each parent contributes one set of chromosomes and, therefore, traits to the new plants. Undesirable traits must be bred out in successive generations until the desired trait—rapid maturity, in the case of Texmont rice—appears in the offspring. The Texas botanists, using only one parent, worked with fewer traits and thus achieved success rapidly.

Farming in space. In summer 1990, Purdue University received a grant from the National Aeronautics and Space Administration (NASA) to de-

A U.S. agricultural researcher at Temple, Tex., checks moisture in a "time tunnel" designed to mimic atmospheric carbon dioxide levels from the present to more than 100 years ago. At the tunnel entrance, where air contains 1991 levels of carbon dioxide, plants grew 30 to 50 per cent larger than plants in tunnel areas with 1860 levels of carbon dioxide.

Agriculture

sign a self-sustaining agriculture system for use in space. The Purdue project, headed by horticulturist Cary Mitchell, brings together researchers specializing in plant physiology, waste processing, food processing, food composition analysis, nutrition, and systems engineering.

Scientists are in a race to develop methods to farm in space, not to send food back to Earth, but to supply food to astronauts and future space colonists. If space explorers were not dependent upon food from Earth, they could travel for longer periods and greater distances. Also, producing food in space should be less expensive than producing it on Earth and sending it into space, which can cost as much as $5,000 a pound, reported Mitchell. Providing that the technology is successful, NASA says that farming on the moon may be possible by the year 2010, and on Mars by the year 2020.

Embryos communicate early. Without a chemical message from a protein called *interferon*, a sheep embryo will die, reported researchers with the University of Missouri at Columbia at the summer 1990 meeting of the American Society of Animal Science. A sheep embryo secretes interferon to tell the mother's body she is pregnant, encouraging it to produce hormones necessary to maintain her pregnancy. The researchers reported that their discovery of the role of this protein is a major breakthrough for livestock producers, who now annually lose millions of livestock offspring because fetuses are not carried to term.

Interferons protect cells from viruses and stimulate the immune system. Zoologist and research leader R. Michael Roberts said that a successful pregnancy in sheep seems to require very early involvement of the mother's immune system. He also reported that injecting interferon into ewes at the time the embryos normally produce interferon increased lamb production by at least 10 per cent. The scientists reported less success with beef and dairy cattle, but they say they are optimistic that they can eventually overcome problems with these animals. The discovery of interferon's role in pregnancy might have applications in human medicine as well, according to

Roberts, especially among women who have reproduction problems.

Edible food coatings. Food scientist Antonio Torres of Oregon State University in Corvallis devised a way of putting a thin, moisture-proof layer between the cone and the ice cream in prepackaged ice cream novelties, according to a December 1990 report. The layer is made of edible cellulose, a substance in plant cell walls.

The layer maintains the crispness of cones with scoops of ice cream perched atop them. Companies that process food constantly look for solutions to a range of storage problems their products face, such as preventing pizza crusts from becoming soggy under the tomato sauce and keeping mold off salami.

Torres is experimenting with two other coatings, one made from corn protein, and another made from *chitin*, the substance that makes up the hard outer covering on such creatures as lobsters and crabs. The chitin-based coating might be useful to preserve poultry, eliminating the need for the chemical injections currently used.

Stronger, cheaper rayon. If commercially feasible, a new process to make rayon using cornstalks, straw, and waste from paper manufacturing could within the next five years replace the longer present method that uses high-quality wood pulp. The process, announced by Purdue University scientists in early 1991, can extract fiber from straw, cornstalks, and paper to produce a low-cost rayon almost instantly. The current manufacturing method takes 18 hours.

The new method, developed by Purdue professor of food science Lifu Chen, uses zinc and chlorine to produce rayon. Both elements were used in rayon production at least 100 years ago, but the techniques used then did not produce fibers with sufficient strength to make fabric.

In Chen's method, the plant material's cellulose is dissolved in zinc chloride. The cellulose molecules stick together, forming fibers that can be extracted from the mixture. These fibers are several times stronger than those in rayon currently produced. Also, the zinc chloride in Chen's process is recyclable, unlike the toxic chem-

"Killer" Bee Alert
Scientists continued to watch for highly aggressive Africanized honey bees in the southern United States in 1990 and 1991. A technician, *right,* vacuums a sample of bees from a colony near Tucson, Ariz. Another researcher, *below,* measures photographically enlarged bee wings, looking for the minutely shorter wings of Africanized bees, which look very similar to European honey bees.

Agriculture

Continued

icals now used in the most common manufacturing method.

Plant peptides kill microbes. In June 1990, biochemist Jesse Jaynes of Louisiana State University at Baton Rouge reported that he had produced artificial *lytic peptides* that kill virtually all types of disease-causing bacteria and fungi in plants. Protein compounds known as lytic peptides, found naturally in plants, help plants resist disease. Jaynes' discovery could benefit crop production worldwide.

He reported that the peptides may benefit animals, too. He found that these peptides attack microorganisms and tumors in laboratory animals. The compounds seem to enhance animal immune systems and speed up the healing of wounds.

Animal and veterinary scientists have joined Jaynes to investigate further the compounds' spectrum of biological effects. A Swedish pharmaceutical conglomerate announced in February 1991 that it is interested in testing the lytic peptides for the treatment of human ills, including cancer.

Fuel from garbage. A new technology to produce *ethanol* (ethyl alcohol), a clean-burning substitute for gasoline, from certain plant sugars could help reduce garbage piling up in landfills. The process received the 5 millionth U.S. patent in March 1991.

Microbiologist Lonnie Ingram of the University of Florida's Institute of Food and Agricultural Sciences at Gainesville developed the technology, the first to convert the sugars in the plant substance hemicellulose into ethanol. Plant material is made up of 25 to 40 per cent hemicellulose.

Ingram's process is based on genetic engineering. He combined the genetic traits of two types of bacteria to create a new strain that can convert organic matter—including agricultural waste, yard waste, and newspapers—into ethanol. The university noted that, prior to Ingram's discovery, no known fermenting agent, including yeast, could cause such a conversion of hemicellulose. [Steve Cain and Victor L. Lechtenberg]

In WORLD BOOK, see AGRICULTURE.

Anthropology

A reexamination of two fossilized thumb bones from South Africa, reported in December 1990, challenged previous findings that *Australopithecus robustus* was capable of making tools. *A. robustus*, a ruggedly built hominid, became extinct between 1.5 million and 1 million years ago. Hominids include human beings and our closest human and prehuman ancestors.

The fossilized thumb bones, estimated to be from 1.5 million to 2 million years old, had been found in a cave at Swartkrans, near Pretoria. In a 1989 report, physical anthropologist Fred Grine and anatomist Randall L. Susman of the State University of New York at Stony Brook argued that the two thumb fossils were different enough from each other to support the conclusion that the bones had belonged to two extinct species—*A. robustus* and the more modern *Homo erectus*. Fossils of both hominid species had been found at Swartkrans. But the scientists also concluded that the fossils were similar enough to the thumbs of modern human beings to indicate that both

H. erectus and *A. robustus* might have been able to make the simple stone tools found at the site. Previously, anthropologists had believed *A. robustus* was not capable of making tools.

Anthropologists Erik Trinkaus and Jeffrey Long of the University of New Mexico in Albuquerque, however, questioned those conclusions in their 1990 study. They argued, based on their analysis of the size and structure of the fossils, that the thumb bones might have come from just one hominid species. In addition, they suggested that the fossils are similar to the thumb bone from a *H. erectus* skeleton found in Kenya in 1984. Although Susman strongly defended his findings, the ability of *A. robustus* to make tools remained unconfirmed.

Oldest African primate. The discovery in Morocco of the oldest known primate fossils ever found in Africa was reported in September 1990 by a team led by paleontologist Bernard Sigé of the University of Montpellier in France. The fossils, which include only teeth, are about 58 million years old.

Clues to Ancient Diet

Minute, stony plant remains called *phytoliths* stuck to the teeth of extinct animals can be used to identify the plants the animals ate, according to research reported in October 1990. Microscopic examination of a tooth from *Gigantopithecus, right,* a giant Asian ape that became extinct about 300,000 years ago, shows phytoliths common in grasses (blue) and bamboo (red), *below.*

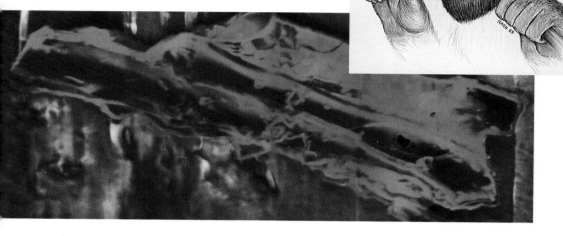

Anthropology

Continued

The scientists speculate that the primate, named *Altiatlasius*, belonged to the group of primates that includes tarsiers, one of the smallest living primates. The researchers also suggested that *Altiatlasius* may have been an ancestor of the *anthropoids*. One of the two main types of primates, anthropoids include monkeys, apes, and human beings.

Identifying ancient diets. Microscopic plant remains stuck to the teeth of extinct animals may provide information about their diets, according to a study published in October 1990 by a team of scientists led by paleontologist Russell L. Ciochon of the University of Iowa in Iowa City. The scientists found *phytoliths* attached to the teeth of *Gigantopithecus blacki*, an extinct giant ape that lived in China and Southeast Asia between 1.5 million and 300,000 years ago. Phytoliths are stony particles that form in and between the cells of some plants from dissolved silica in water taken up by the plants' roots. Because phytoliths differ from one plant species to another, they can be used to identify the plants an animal has eaten.

Scientists previously had assumed that *Gigantopithecus* mainly ate bamboo, which is plentiful in that region. But Ciochon and his colleagues found that *Gigantopithecus*, like modern gorillas, also ate grasses and fruits.

Neanderthals in the Near East. A March 1991 study of mammal teeth found with Neanderthal fossils in Israel suggests that Neanderthals lived in the Near East earlier than previously believed. The research was reported by a team of scientists led by geochronologist Rainer Grün of Cambridge University in England.

Grün and his colleagues dated the mammal teeth using *electron spin resonance* (ESR). ESR is a technique that measures the amount of naturally occurring radiation absorbed by buried objects, such as bone, that contain the mineral calcite. The older the object is, the higher the level of radiation.

Grün and his team found that the teeth—and, therefore, the fossilized remains of two Neanderthals found

Anthropology

with them—were between 125,000 and 80,000 years old. These dates are at least 20,000 years older than the age of the oldest known Neanderthal fossils previously found in the Near East.

Grün's findings support earlier discoveries indicating that Neanderthals and early modern human beings either coexisted at or alternately occupied certain sites in the Near East over a long period. Fossils of people more anatomically similar to—and perhaps ancestors of—modern Eurasians have been found in Israel and dated to 80,000 to 90,000 years ago. Because fossils of both groups have now been dated to similar ages, Grün's study also provides more evidence for the theory that neither hominid descended from the other.

No cannibalism. Contrary to common belief, European Neanderthals may not have engaged in ritual cannibalism, according to research reported in April 1991 by anthropologist Tim D. White of the University of California at Berkeley and archaeologist Nicholas Toth of the University of Indiana in Bloomington. Ritual cannibalism involves eating human tissue as a symbolic act.

The scientists studied a damaged Neanderthal skull found in 1939 at Monte Circeo, about 100 kilometers (60 miles) south of Rome. Previous studies of the skull suggested that it had been deliberately cracked open, perhaps in order to eat the brain.

White and Toth compared the Italian fossil skull to skulls from Melanesia whose bases were broken to make them fit onto trophy poles. They concluded that almost none of the damage to the Italian skull was caused by hominids, because the pattern of damage was so different from that seen in the Melanesian skulls—which were known to have been broken by people. Instead, the scientists argued that the damage may have resulted from gnawing by a carnivore or from changes occurring as the skull became fossilized. [Eric Delson]

In the Special Reports section, see Who Were the First Americans? In World Book, see Anthropology; Neanderthals; Prehistoric people.

Archaeology, New World

A new chemical process that for the first time enables scientists to date prehistoric rock paintings directly should provide much more precise ages for such artwork. The results of the first test of the process, developed by scientists at Texas A&M University in College Station, were reported in December 1990.

Rock paintings, called *pictographs*, have been found throughout the Western United States as well as in many other areas of the world. The art is important to archaeologists because it is often the only surviving record of the beliefs, rituals, and other nonmaterial aspects of prehistoric cultures.

Previously, however, there was no way of assigning an *absolute*, or calendar, date to a pictograph. Archaeologists could obtain only an approximate age based on an analysis of images in the painting or on the age of objects found near the pictograph. For example, a pictograph showing a spear thrower would be judged older than a pictograph showing a bow and arrow, because spear throwers were used by ancient hunters before the invention of the bow and arrow.

Scientists also dated pictographs by obtaining radiocarbon dates for *organic deposits* found near the rock art. Organic deposits contain carbon from once-living things. Theoretically, archaeologists should have been able to radiocarbon date the pictographs as well because ancient artists often used organic materials such as animal blood, grease, or fat to mix the paint or help it stick to the rock wall. But there was no way to separate the organic matter in the painting from the inorganic material in the underlying rock.

In addition, the amount of material needed for analysis using traditional radiocarbon dating is relatively large—several grams, or about 1 tablespoon. Removing a sample that size from a pictograph could badly damage it.

New separation technique. The Texas scientists appear to have solved this problem by developing a chemical technique to separate the organic from the inorganic material. Their process also involves the use of acceleration

The age of a prehistoric *pictograph* (rock painting) in southwestern Texas was determined to be between 3,000 and 4,000 years by a new chemical process reported in December 1990. The process has for the first time enabled scientists to date pictographs directly by analyzing the carbon content of a tiny sample of the painting.

Archaeology, New World

Continued

mass spectrometry (AMS), an advanced form of radiocarbon dating for which only tiny amounts of organic substances are required.

For their study, the scientists obtained samples from a pictograph in a vandalized rockshelter in southwestern Texas, one of many in that area. Archaeologists had previously estimated that ancient Indian artists began creating these pictographs about 3,000 to 4,000 years ago.

The Texas scientists bathed the samples in oxygen kept under low temperature and low pressure. The oxygen converted the carbon in the sample to water and carbon dioxide. After the water was removed, the carbon was separated from the carbon dioxide and reduced to graphite, which was analyzed using AMS. Results indicated that the pictograph is 3,865 years old, plus or minus 100 years.

The Texas scientists believe that archaeologists should be able to use the new technique to date pictographs from other prehistoric cultures. These findings could help archaeologists expand their knowledge of the cultural life and history of the people who created such paintings.

Ancient shrimp fishery. A 5,000-year-old archaeological site on the Pacific coast of southern Mexico, thought to have been merely a mound of discarded clamshells, was actually a sophisticated shrimp fishery. That conclusion was reported in March 1991 by a team of scientists headed by archaeologist Barbara Voorhies of the University of California in Santa Barbara.

The site, called Tlacuachero, is one of five coastal sites once inhabited by the Chantuto Indians, a group of hunters and gatherers who lived in the region between 3000 and 2000 B.C. Previous excavations at the sites had revealed mounds of clamshells. Archaeologists had concluded that the shells had been discarded after the Chantuto had removed the meat from the clams.

Voorhies and her team, however, discovered that most of the clams in the Tlacuachero mound had never been opened. In addition, the clams were

Archaeology, New World

Continued

smaller than those that would normally be collected for food.

The scientists also discovered a flat, clay-lined floor at the site with postholes, holes in which wooden posts once stood. They concluded that the postholes represent the remains of a *ramada*, a structure with a thatched roof and open walls. Other postholes in the floor may have held the legs of drying racks. Finally, they found what appear to be the remains of shrimp.

Today, the area around Tlacuachero is known for its abundant harvests of shrimp, which the local inhabitants preserve by drying in the sun. Voorhies and her colleagues concluded that the mounds at Tlacuachero and the other sites were platforms on which ancient shrimp harvests were sun-dried. If the archaeologists' theory is correct, the Chantuto people attained a level of sophistication in economic specialization, food preservation, and architecture seldom found in prehistoric hunting and gathering societies.

Ancient trade. For more than 100 years, archaeologists have reported finding artifacts made of *obsidian* (volcanic glass) at archaeological sites of the Hopewell Indian culture in southern Ohio. The sites have been dated to between 200 B.C. and A.D. 400. Obsidian, a black, shiny material, was a prized item in the extensive trading network that existed among Hopewell groups. It was used to make spearpoints, knives, and ceremonial blades. In addition, obsidian flakes were often placed in Hopewell tombs.

The origin of the obsidian was a mystery, however, because there are no obsidian deposits in the Midwestern United States. Some archaeologists had speculated that the obsidian came from Mexico or volcanic areas in the Western United States. This mystery was partially solved in 1969, when chemical analysis linked a few Hopewell artifacts to obsidian outcrops in Wyoming.

In July 1990, archaeologists from Pennsylvania State University in University Park announced new findings on the geological sources of Hopewell obsidian. They also reported that they had pinpointed the time period during

Alaskan Burial Cave
Archaeologists explore the entrance of a 1,000-year-old burial cave in the Aleutian Islands, *below,* where the mummified remains of more than 30 Aleut Indians were found in June 1990. Among the artifacts discovered in the cave was a carved wooden model of a kayak with a paddler, *right.*

which the obsidian trade took place.

For their study, the scientists analyzed 31 Hopewell obsidian artifacts using two techniques—neutron activation analysis and atomic absorption spectroscopy. These techniques enabled the scientists to establish the pattern of rare trace minerals in the obsidian.

The scientists compared the pattern of minerals in the Hopewell obsidian with that of obsidian samples from deposits in the Western United States. They confirmed the 1969 finding that some of the Hopewell artifacts came from Obsidian Cliff in Yellowstone National Park. But they also found that some of the obsidian had come from deposits in eastern Idaho. In addition, they noted that some specimens did not come from either place.

Next, the scientists used a dating technique called *obsidian hydration analysis* to determine the age of the Hopewell obsidian. When obsidian is freshly chipped—as archaeologists assume it was when it was being traded in ancient times—its surfaces begin to absorb water. By measuring the thickness of the layer containing water, scientists can calculate the age of the obsidian. The Pennsylvania scientists calculated that the Hopewell obsidian had been quarried and had entered the Hopewell trading network between 78 B.C. and A.D. 347.

On this basis, the archaeologists theorized that the Hopewell traded obsidian for a much longer time than archaeologists had previously believed. In addition, the obsidian was apparently brought into the Midwest a number of times over the 400-year period. Archaeologists had believed that the Hopewell had obtained the obsidian in a single trading episode or collecting trip. These new findings should enable archaeologists studying Hopewell archaeological sites to obtain more precise dates for artifacts found there and learn more about the use of obsidian in Hopewell society. [Thomas R. Hester]

In the Special Reports section, see SCIENCE AND THE VOYAGE OF COLUMBUS; WHO WERE THE FIRST AMERICANS? In WORLD BOOK, see ARCHAEOLOGY.

Archaeology,
Old World

The discovery of a vast network of underground vaults reportedly containing tens of thousands of terra-cotta figurines was reported in August 1990 by Chinese archaeologists. The vaults were found near the ancient city of Xi'an in central China.

The complex is believed to be part of the burial site of Emperor Jingdi, who ruled from 157 B.C. to 141 B.C. and consolidated the Han Empire. The Han dynasty, which lasted from 202 B.C. to A.D. 220, was one of the most important periods in Chinese history. During that era, the Chinese invented paper and spread their culture to Korea and Vietnam.

Investigations of the burial complex so far have revealed 24 vaults. Each is about 4 meters (13 feet) wide and from 25 to 290 meters (82 to 950 feet) long. The terra-cotta figurines represent men, boys, and horses, most of which are about 60 centimeters (2 feet) tall. The human figures, which reportedly have individualized features, are naked, which suggests that they may once have been dressed in costumes.

Although many of the vaults contain row after row of human sculptures, others have only figures of horses with terra-cotta carts. In addition, some of the vaults were apparently emptied by grave robbers in ancient times.

Neanderthal hunters. Stone tools and animal bones found in a cave in Italy suggest that Neanderthals, an early form of *Homo sapiens*, became sophisticated big-game hunters sometime between 55,000 and 40,000 years ago. In a report published in summer 1990, anthropologists Steven L. Kuhn and Mary Stiner of the University of New Mexico in Albuquerque argue that the findings contradict the widely held belief that, throughout their history, Neanderthals were simple foragers. Hunting large animals by ambush had previously been associated only with *Homo sapiens sapiens*—modern-looking human beings.

Neanderthals lived in Europe and Asia from about 150,000 to 35,000 years ago. Anthropologists have long believed that Neanderthals lived mainly by gathering wild plants, while

A 3,500-year-old calf figurine, found in Israel in June 1990, is the first known example of a "golden calf" whose worship by the ancient Canaanites was condemned by the early Israelites. The calf, which was made of bronze and other metals, may have once been highly burnished so that it resembled gold. The figurine stands about 11 centimeters (4⅓ inches) tall.

Archaeology, Old World

Continued

occasionally hunting small game and scavenging meat from the carcasses of animals killed by large predators.

Findings at Neanderthal sites dating from 120,000 to 50,000 years ago have consisted mainly of partial skeletons of animals that were old at the time of death. Archaeologists have interpreted these findings as evidence that Neanderthals obtained the bones by scavenging the kills of other animals.

Grotta Breuil, the cave excavated by Kuhn and Stiner, lies on the west coast of Italy, southeast of Rome. In layers of earth dated to between 34,000 and 40,000 years old, the archaeologists found sharpened stone blades, flakes of stone, and spearpoints among the bones of many animals killed while relatively young and healthy. The bones included nearly all parts of the animals' skeletons. Kuhn and Stiner contend this suggests that Neanderthals killed the animals by ambush hunting and then carried their carcasses to the cave for butchering and eating.

"Golden" calf. Archaeologists exca-

vating an ancient Canaanite temple in Israel reported in June 1990 that they had found a calf figurine that is the only known example of the religious images whose worship was denounced by the ancient Israelites. The figurine, which is about 3,500 years old, was found near the ancient city of Ashkelon by archaeologists from Harvard University in Cambridge, Mass.

The figurine is about 11.4 centimeters (4½ inches) long and 11 centimeters (4⅓ inches) tall. It was made of bronze, copper, and probably silver, and was highly burnished so that it resembled gold. The figurine was found lying on its side near a broken pottery shrine, in which it was probably housed.

Many early Hebrew documents, including Old Testament accounts, refer to the Canaanite practice of worshiping golden calves, a practice the Israelites tried to eliminate. Scholars believe that the Canaanites did not worship the calves themselves. But because these ancient people believed that the gods rode on calves, these animals came to

A Temple Dedicated to Healing

The discovery of the ruins of a 4,000-year-old temple, *bottom,* apparently dedicated to Gula, the Babylonian goddess of healing, was reported in June 1990. The temple was found at the ancient religious center of Nippur in modern Iraq, *below.* Archaeologists believe that clay figurines found at the site, such as one of a man holding his stomach, *below right,* may have been used to show the goddess the source of a worshiper's illness.

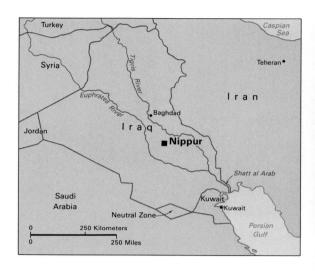

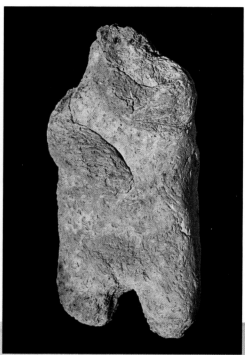

Archaeology, Old World

Continued

represent the gods, and worshipers made sacrificial offerings to statues of calves.

The Sphinx's face. The first computer reconstruction of the face of the Great Sphinx at Giza, Egypt, was published in April 1991 by a team of scientists and computer experts directed by archaeologist Mark Lehner of the University of Chicago. The Great Sphinx, which has a human head and a lion's body, was built in about 2500 B.C. for the ancient Egyptian King Khafre. Over the centuries, the Sphinx's face has been badly eroded. In addition, part of the head is missing.

To produce the reconstruction, Lehner and his team first created intricately detailed maps of the front and sides of the Sphinx using a series of stereoscopic photographs. The maps were then used to create a three-dimensional computerized outline of the facial area. Finally, the archaeologists "fleshed out" the features on the computer outline.

Babylonian temple. The discovery of the ruins of a 4,000-year-old temple dedicated to Gula, the Babylonian goddess of healing, may shed new light on the early practice of medicine. The temple was found at Nippur, an ancient Babylonian religious center about 96 kilometers (60 miles) southeast of Baghdad, Iraq. The excavations at the site were being conducted by scientists from the University of Chicago under the direction of archaeologist McGuire Gibson, who announced the finding in June 1990.

Gibson reported that the temple, which dates from 1600 B.C. to 1200 B.C., may cover an area as large as a football field. At the site, the archaeologists found a number of small clay figurines that were apparently left as offerings to Gula by sick people hoping to be cured. One figurine shows a man clutching his throat; another, a man holding his stomach. According to Gibson, the figurines were meant to show Gula where the sick people hurt.

The Chicago archaeologists also found a number of figurines of dogs, which were considered sacred to Gula and were believed to have healing powers. Dogs may have been used to lick people's wounds.

The ancient Babylonians had a complex system of health care that included physicians, herbal doctors, magicians, and priests. The Chicago archaeologists hope that the study of the temple will provide new information on medical care in Babylonia.

Lost Greek monument. The discovery in Greece of a long-lost marble monument marking the site of a battle fought in 86 B.C. was reported in December 1990 by archaeologist John Camp of the American School of Classical Studies in Athens, Greece. In the battle, the ancient Roman army then occupying Greece defeated invaders from the Black Sea area. Previously, the monument was known only through an account written by the ancient Greek historian Plutarch several decades after the battle.

Camp and four graduate students from the University of California at Berkeley found the monument on a hilltop near the ancient town of Chaironeia. The monument, which is 90 centimeters (3 feet) wide and 30 centimeters (1 foot) high, was inscribed with the names of two Greek men who showed the Roman soldiers a back route up the hill, which was held by the invaders.

First Cypriots. People may have inhabited Cyprus as long as 10,000 years ago, 2,000 years earlier than scholars previously thought. That conclusion was reported in November 1990 by archaeologist Alan H. Simmons of the University of Nevada-Reno.

At a collapsed rockshelter, Simmons found more than 1,000 stone tools and beads mixed with the bones of animals known to have become extinct by about 8000 B.C. Sediments found with the stone artifacts were radiocarbon dated to about 10,000 years ago.

According to Simmons, the findings also suggest that hunting by early Cypriots may have played a major role in the extinction of a number of animal species that once lived on the island. Most other scientists believe that the animals died out before people colonized Cyprus. [Robert J. Wenke]

In the Special Reports section, see SCIENCE AND THE VOYAGE OF COLUMBUS; WHO WERE THE FIRST AMERICANS? In WORLD BOOK, see ARCHAEOLOGY; BABYLONIA; CANAANITES; PREHISTORIC PEOPLE; SPHINX.

Astronomy, Extragalactic

Between June 1990 and June 1991, astronomers reported several new discoveries concerning the most distant objects in the universe. Because light from these objects has taken billions of years to reach Earth, astronomers are viewing these objects as they appeared not long after the big bang—the explosion that began the expansion of the universe about 10 billion to 20 billion years ago. As a result, the discoveries are also revealing new information about the early universe, particularly the period when galaxies (vast collections of stars bound together by gravity) and huge clusters of galaxies began to form. See also Close-Up.

X rays from afar. Data from a satellite launched in 1990 gave clear indications that galaxies and clusters of galaxies formed within a few billion years after the big bang, according to a January 1991 report by German astronomers Joachim Truemper and Guenther Hasinger of the Max Planck Institute for Extraterrestrial Physics in Heidelberg, Germany.

The two astronomers announced that the German *Rosat* satellite, an orbiting X-ray observatory, had revealed clusters of objects that gave off much of their radiation at X-ray wavelengths. Follow-up studies of some of these objects using optical telescopes revealed that the objects were *quasars*. Quasars are extremely powerful and distant sources of electromagnetic radiation, such as X rays and visible light. Astronomers think quasars are located at the cores of newly formed galaxies.

Data from the optical telescopes indicated that the light from these distant quasars was shifted toward the longer, or red, wavelengths of their spectra. This *red shift* occurs when a light source is moving away from an observer. The greater the red shift, the faster the object is receding, and more distant objects recede faster than those closer to Earth. Measuring red shifts enables astronomers to calculate how far the objects are from Earth.

The astronomers determined that the quasars were some 8 billion to 10 billion *light-years* from Earth. (A light-year is the distance light travels in one year, about 9.5 trillion kilometers [5.9 trillion miles].) This meant that these quasars were clustered when the universe was still relatively young—between 2 billion and 7 billion years after the big bang.

The *Rosat* findings also indicated that there are far more quasars than had previously been suspected. In one small area of the sky, *Rosat* detected more than 100, indicating that there are about 4 million quasars in the known universe.

Previous X-ray satellites, which were not able to resolve sources of X rays in as much detail as *Rosat*, had detected faint X rays coming from all regions of the universe. Until *Rosat* made these findings, the source of this background radiation was a mystery. Now it seems that much of it comes from quasars.

How far the galaxies? In February 1991, astronomer Nino Panagia of the Space Telescope Science Institute in Baltimore announced that he and his colleagues, using the *Hubble Space Telescope*, had more precisely determined the distance from Earth to the Large Magellanic Cloud, the nearest galaxy to our own Milky Way. Even the closest galaxies are so far away that measuring their distances is extremely difficult. Previous estimates of the distance to the Large Magellanic Cloud had ranged from 150,000 to 180,000 light-years. The Hubble astronomers found the distance to be 169,000, plus or minus 9,000 light-years.

The astronomers measured the distance by observing the remains of Supernova 1987A, a star that exploded in the Large Magellanic Cloud in February 1987. In a picture taken by the *Hubble Space Telescope* in 1990, a faint ring of light around the remains of the star is visible (see SPACE TECHNOLOGY [Close-Up]). The ring was a puff of debris blown off the star long before it exploded. That debris is now glowing because it is illuminated by the flash of light from the 1987 supernova.

By measuring the size of the ring on the picture, and knowing how long it took for the flash of the supernova, traveling at the speed of light, to reach the ring and make it glow, astronomers were able to calculate the dimensions of the ring. Knowing the dimensions of the ring and the size it appears when viewed from Earth, they could then calculate the distance from Earth to the

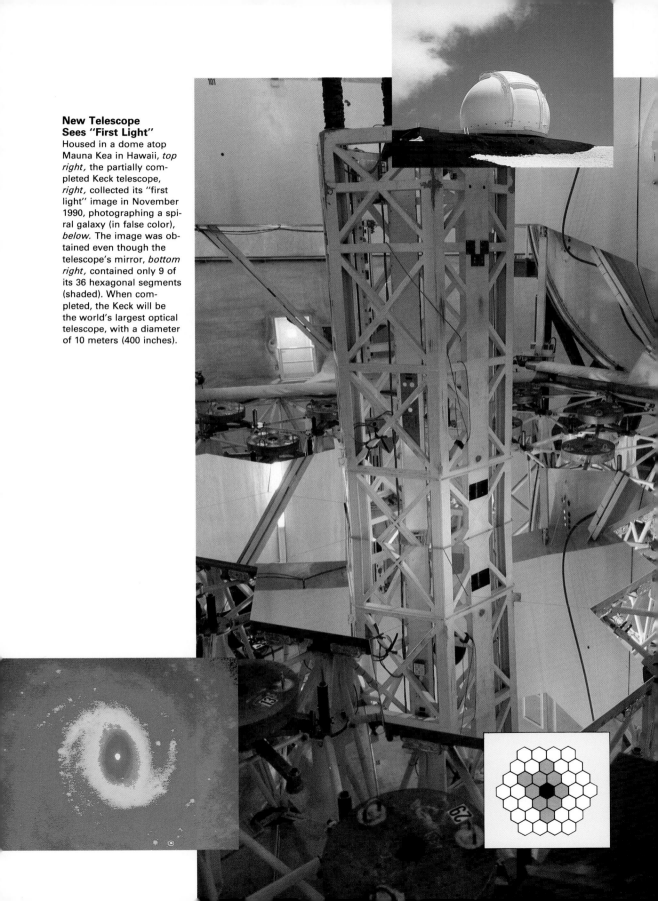

New Telescope Sees "First Light"

Housed in a dome atop Mauna Kea in Hawaii, *top right,* the partially completed Keck telescope, *right,* collected its "first light" image in November 1990, photographing a spiral galaxy (in false color), *below.* The image was obtained even though the telescope's mirror, *bottom right,* contained only 9 of its 36 hexagonal segments (shaded). When completed, the Keck will be the world's largest optical telescope, with a diameter of 10 meters (400 inches).

A Universe of Clumps and Voids

Headlines in newspapers and magazines early in 1991 announced the death of the big bang theory, the notion that the universe began when a hot, dense mixture of matter and energy exploded into existence sometime between 10 billion and 20 billion years ago. Yet the rumors of the big bang's death were "greatly exaggerated" (as the American writer Mark Twain once said about rumors of his own death).

The headlines were based on a new three-dimensional map of the universe published in January 1991. The map showed galaxies clumped together into superclusters hundreds of millions of *light-years* across. (A light-year is the distance light travels in one year, about 9.5 trillion kilometers [5.9 trillion miles].) But the map, rather than disproving the big bang theory as many news accounts reported, actually cast doubt on another theory known as *cold dark matter*. Since 1984, many astronomers have accepted this theory as the best explanation for how galaxies formed in the early universe.

Galaxies are collections of hundreds of billions of stars bound together by gravity. Gravitational forces also bind galaxies together in clusters, and clusters, in turn, appear to be part of even larger structures called *superclusters*. What scientists are having trouble understanding is how these large structures could have formed in the time that has elapsed since the big bang.

Because astronomers cannot easily determine the distances to objects seen in the sky, it is difficult to produce three-dimensional maps of the universe. But by measuring the motion of the galaxies—which astronomers attribute to the expansion of the universe following the big bang—we can gauge the distance of a galaxy by its speed. The faster a galaxy is receding, the farther away it is. Astronomers measure a galaxy's speed using devices called *spectrometers*, which split up the light from a galaxy into a *spectrum* (a rainbow of colors whose wavelengths and intensities can be determined). Light from objects that are moving away is shifted toward redder (longer) wavelengths. Thus, astronomers can use the measured red shift of a galaxy as an indication of its distance from Earth.

To map the universe, astronomers record and analyze the spectra of hundreds or thousands of galaxies, a task that requires large telescopes and a great deal of time. In fact, only small portions of the sky have been mapped to any great extent. Since the early 1980's, astronomers Margaret Geller and John Huchra of the Harvard-Smithsonian Center for Astrophysics in Cambridge, Mass., have been leading a project that has so far mapped four thin wedges of the sky to distances of 300 million light-years. Their maps show that

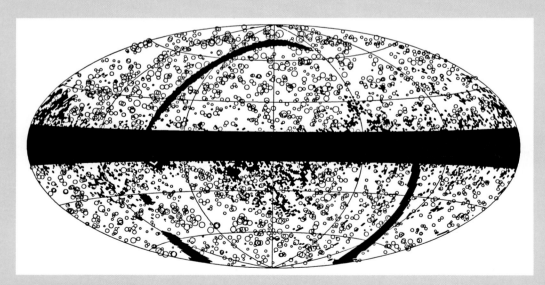

Galaxies (circles) are clumped together in vast superclusters separated by large voids, according to astronomers who published this map of the universe in January 1991. Black bands represent unmapped areas.

the galaxies are distributed in large superclusters, which can span distances of several hundred million light-years, separated by equally large empty spaces, or voids. In 1989, Geller and Huchra announced the discovery of the largest known concentration of galaxies, called the *Great Wall*, a sheetlike structure at least 500 million light-years across.

Astronomers were not sure what conclusions to draw from the existence of such structures, because only a small fraction of the universe had been mapped. The task is akin to trying to deduce the appearance of Earth from a map that includes only the Rocky Mountains.

Yet several recent studies indicate that the huge superclusters and voids are common features of the universe. In early 1990, British astronomer Thomas J. Broadhurst of the University of Durham in England and his collaborators announced the results of four surveys that mapped narrow portions of the sky to distances as great as 7 billion light-years. The researchers found regular concentrations of galaxies separated by gaps of 300 million to 400 million light-years.

The study that led to the misleading media reports about the big bang was published in *Nature* magazine in January 1991 by British astronomer Will Saunders of Oxford University in England and nine collaborators from Britain and Canada. This study received significant attention among astronomers because its results were damaging to the cold dark matter theory and because some of the researchers had themselves been proponents of the theory.

Using optical telescopes at various observatories around the world, Saunders' group obtained red shifts for 2,163 galaxies. Their survey covered a larger volume of space than any previous survey, out to distances of about 500 million light-years, and thus gave a more representative view of the universe. Their maps also show that galaxies are clumped together, forming large superclusters hundreds of millions of light-years long separated by large voids, confirming that such large structures are commonplace.

Astronomers believe that the galaxies formed as the result of tiny variations in the density of matter soon after the big bang. A region of space in which matter is more tightly bunched serves as a "seed" for larger structures. The bunched matter will exert a stronger gravitational force on surrounding matter, pulling in material and growing in size. But there does not seem to be enough visible material in the universe to have formed the large structures—the clusters and superclusters—in the time that has elapsed since the big bang.

Evidence about the nature of the early universe as revealed by the cosmic background radiation shows that the early universe was free of concentrations of matter dense enough to eventually produce superclusters. The cosmic background radiation was given off by the opaque gas that filled the universe until about 100,000 years after the big bang. At that early time, the universe was at a temperature of several thousand degrees, but as the universe expanded, it cooled. The background radiation was measured by the *Cosmic Background Explorer* (*COBE*), a United States spacecraft, from late 1989 until Nov. 19, 1990. The radiation that *COBE* measured corresponds to a temperature of 3 degrees above absolute zero, as predicted by the big bang theory.

Data from *COBE* indicated that there was almost exactly the same amount of microwave background radiation in every direction in the sky. Any lumpiness in the opaque gas should have produced bright, or hot, spots evident today in this radiation. Because no such bright spots were seen, astronomers concluded that the early universe must have been extremely smooth and uniform just after the big bang.

For galaxies and superclusters to have evolved from such a smooth early universe, theorists have previously proposed the existence of large numbers of invisible particles called cold dark matter, which could provide the added gravitational force to shape the clusters and superclusters. According to this cold dark matter theory, much of the mass of the universe, perhaps up to 99 per cent, is made up of cold dark matter. Gravity would have forced the cold dark matter together and ordinary matter would have been pulled along to form the galaxies. But cold dark matter cannot form large structures fast enough if the original "seeds" are too small or the structures too large.

The new galaxy maps, along with the precise new measurements of the smoothness of the cosmic background, are squeezing the cold dark matter theory from both directions. The universe seems too clumpy today and too smooth in the past for cold dark matter to account for the formation of galaxies. Although theorists are not quite ready to give up entirely on the cold dark matter theory, they are considering other types of dark matter that could contribute the tremendous gravitational force needed to explain the existence of vast superclusters.

As for the big bang theory itself, *COBE*'s precise measurement of the cosmic background radiation actually strengthens the case for a universe that originated in a big bang. While the cold dark matter theory may be having difficulties staying alive, the big bang theory is in robust health.   [Laurence A. Marshall]

ring and, therefore, to the Magellanic Cloud.

This type of mathematical calculation is a far more precise way to determine distance to an object than calculations based on the object's brightness. When using brightness to determine distances, astronomers must first find a *standard candle*—an object whose intrinsic brightness is known. (*Intrinsic brightness* is the rate at which the object gives off energy.) Astronomers can then compare the intrinsic brightness of the object with its *apparent brightness*—that is, how bright the object appears as viewed from Earth. The fainter the object appears, the farther away it is.

More distant galaxies. Most galaxies lie millions or billions of light-years beyond the Large Magellanic Cloud, and their exact distances from Earth are even more uncertain. Astronomers in 1990 announced two new and more precise methods to measure distance.

In June, astronomers George H. Jacoby and Robin Ciardullo of the National Optical Astronomy Observatories in Tucson, Ariz., and Holland C. Ford of Johns Hopkins University in Baltimore reported on one new type of standard candle—*planetary nebulae* (clouds of gas ejected by aging stars) in galaxies in the Virgo cluster. This is one of the nearest clusters of galaxies to the Milky Way.

The intrinsic brightness of planetary nebulae is known from previous studies of planetary nebulae in our Galaxy. By comparing this known intrinsic brightness with the apparent brightness of the Virgo cluster nebulae, astronomers could calculate the nebulae's distance. Using this method, Jacoby and his colleagues calculated that the Virgo cluster was 48 million light-years from Earth. Previous estimates ranged from 39 million to 78 million light-years.

In December, astronomer John Tonry of the Massachusetts Institute of Technology (M.I.T.) in Cambridge announced a different technique, which promises to field even more precise measurements for galaxies even farther away. Tonry's method involved analyzing the images of distant galaxies taken with optical telescopes that have large light-gathering mirrors.

Tonry noted that, when viewed through a large optical telescope, distant galaxies appear more uniformly bright than nearby galaxies, just as a beach appears to have a more uniform color when one is too far away to see the individual grains of sand. Large telescopes resolve nearby galaxies clearly and can detect their variations in brightness. A more distant galaxy, however, would appear smoother because its brightness would not appear to vary.

Tonry measured the "smoothness" of the image of a galaxy by using a *charge-coupled device* (CCD), an electronic camera attached to a telescope. CCD's consist of light-sensitive silicon chips that can record between 70 and 100 per cent of the *photons* (particles of light) that strike a telescope mirror. A CCD image consists of many tiny dots called *pixels* (picture elements). By measuring the brightness of each pixel within an image of a galaxy, Tonry determined how smooth the galaxy was and, therefore, how distant. His value for the distance of galaxies in the Virgo cluster is just slightly greater than 48 million light-years.

These distance measurements not only help astronomers map the universe but also give them an indication of its age. When astronomers know the distance to the galaxies, along with the rate at which they are moving apart, they can calculate the time the expansion of the universe began. Both Jacoby's and Tonry's measurements indicate that the big bang occurred about 12 billion years ago. This is more recent than the 15-billion- to 18-billion-year range most astronomers have previously accepted.

The largest galaxy. The discovery of the largest known galaxy was reported in October 1990 by astronomers Juan M. Uson of the National Radio Astronomy Observatory in Socorro, N. Mex.; Stephen P. Boughn of Haverford College in Pennsylvania; and Jeffrey R. Kuhn of Michigan State University in East Lansing. The three astronomers announced that the central galaxy in a cluster of galaxies known as Abell 2029 was 8 million light-years across. The galaxy gives off the light of 2 trillion stars like our sun. For comparison, the Milky Way is about 100,000 light-years

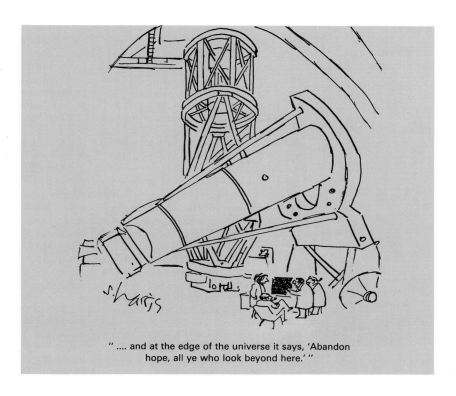

" .... and at the edge of the universe it says, 'Abandon hope, all ye who look beyond here.' "

Astronomy, Extragalactic

Continued

in diameter and has hundreds of billions of stars.

Astronomers believe that galaxies like the giant in Abell 2029 have grown to enormous size by colliding and merging with neighboring galaxies—a process some have called *galactic cannibalism*. The details of this process, however, remain unclear.

Uson and his collaborators found that the galaxy in Abell 2029 appears surprisingly uniform in shape. They had expected that if the galaxy formed as a result of merging with its neighbors, its appearance would be more lumpy and irregular. How the galaxy got so large, then, remains a problem to be solved by further research.

Quasar explosion. After examining data recorded by a Japanese X-ray satellite called *Ginga*, astronomers Ronald A. Remillard and Bruce Grossan of M.I.T. announced in January 1991 that the satellite had observed a remarkably violent explosion of a distant quasar. The satellite recorded the explosion on Nov. 13, 1989, when it observed the quasar almost doubling in

brightness, giving off in three minutes almost as much energy as our sun gives off in 1 million years.

Even when they don't explode, quasars are extremely energetic. Astronomers believe that a quasar generates so much energy because its core is actually a *black hole* located in the center of a very young galaxy. (A black hole is a region of space so densely packed with matter that neither light nor anything else can escape the force of gravity at its surface.) As gas from the surrounding galaxy is pulled toward the black hole, the gas heats up to millions of degrees and emits powerful electromagnetic radiation into space.

The energy from a quasar is often given off in a narrow jet, like the beam of a flashlight. Remillard and Grossan suggested that this was the case with the quasar that *Ginga* observed, and that the brightening of the quasar occurred when a massive cloud of gas fell into the black hole. [Laurence A. Marschall]

In the Special Reports section, see MYSTERIES OF THE MILKY WAY. In WORLD BOOK, see ASTRONOMY.

Astronomy, Galactic

The Milky Way galaxy is more complex than astronomers had previously suspected, according to a number of findings reported between June 1990 and June 1991. Major attention was focused on the age of the Galaxy and how it formed.

Dating globular clusters. Globular clusters (spherical groupings of stars in the outer portions of our Galaxy) are not all the same age and may have formed over a period of several billion years, according to several studies reported in 1990 and 1991. Astronomers previously believed that all the clusters, which contain the oldest stars in the Galaxy, formed at about the same time. As a result, astronomers drew conclusions about how our Galaxy formed, and those conclusions may now have to be discarded.

Canadian astronomers at Dominion Astrophysical Observatory in Victoria, B.C., reported in August 1990 that they had found relative ages for several globular clusters and that the ages differed from each other by some 2-billion years. In April 1991, Australian astronomers at the Australian National University reported an age difference of 3 billion years between a pair of globular clusters.

Astronomers can determine the *relative age* of a globular cluster—its age in comparison with other clusters—by determining its abundance of heavy elements, such as oxygen and carbon. These elements are formed in stars during nuclear reactions, are dispersed into space, and then become part of new stars that form out of clouds of gas and dust. The first stars to form had the fewest heavy elements, and these are the types of stars found in the oldest clusters. Astronomers previously had estimated that the globular clusters formed over a period of about 1 billion years. This was based on the standard view that our Galaxy started as a round ball of gas. Some stars formed within the cloud, and then the cloud collapsed under its own weight. The rotating cloud flattened into a disklike shape. Stars that formed after the collapse lie in the disk, while the stars that formed before the collapse remained in globular clusters outside the disk. The standard theory held that the collapse of the cloud took place within about 1-

billion years, but this could not be the case if the globular clusters differ in age by 2 billion or 3 billion years.

The results of both the Australian and Canadian studies indicate that the globular clusters formed over a longer period than 1 billion years.

Milky Way formation. Astronomers Michael Feast, P. A. Whitelock, and B. S. Carter of the South African Astronomical Observatory announced in November 1990 their discovery of relatively young stars above and below the plane of the galactic disk. This also posed problems for the standard theory of galaxy formation, because no recent star formation should have taken place in these regions, according to the theory.

Astronomers had predicted that there would be an orderly progression of stellar ages in the Milky Way—from the oldest in the globular clusters, to somewhat younger stars just above and below the plane of the disk, to the Galaxy's youngest stars, in the plane of the disk. But other astronomers reported in October 1990 that the thin plane of the disk may be older than the region just above and below this thin section, the exact opposite of what the standard theory predicts.

Millisecond pulsars. The number of millisecond pulsars in globular clusters appears to be far greater than astronomers previously thought, according to a June 1990 report by astronomers at the California Institute of Technology (Caltech) in Pasadena, the University of Arizona in Tucson, and the University of California at Berkeley. A pulsar is an extremely compact, dense star that gives off a beam of radiation that sweeps the sky as the star rotates. A millisecond pulsar rotates on its axis hundreds of times per second. On Earth, millisecond pulsars may be detectable with radio telescopes as regular pulses of radiation.

The team of astronomers, led by Shrinivas Kulkarni of Caltech, reported that there may be as many as 10,000 millisecond pulsars in all of the Galaxy's globular clusters. The astronomers based this estimate in part on the number of millisecond pulsars found during several searches using radio telescopes. But they also estimated the number of pulsars that might go unno-

A Jet of Gas in the Great Nebula in Orion

In November 1990, astronomers aimed the *Hubble Space Telescope* at the Great Nebula in Orion, a cloud of gas and dust where new stars are forming, *right*. They obtained the most detailed photograph ever of a section of the nebula (boxed area), revealing regions of ionized gas, *below*, such as sulfur (red) and hydrogen (green). A close-up image of this region, *bottom*, clearly shows for the first time a jet of gas (arrow) coming from a recently formed star (bright dot). Astronomers believe that shock fronts from such jets strip electrons from atoms, causing gases to become ionized.

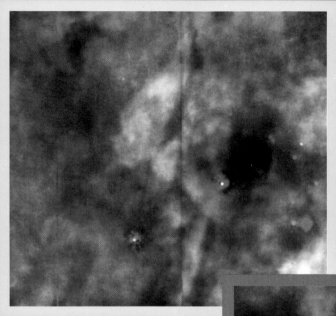

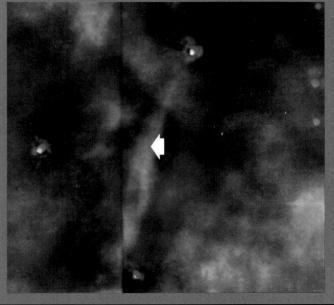

ticed because their beams of radiation do not happen to sweep across Earth, or because their emissions are too faint to be detected, or because their orbital motions cause their observed rate of pulsation to vary. The latter might not be detected because radio telescope searches are designed to detect only sources with perfectly regular pulses.

In a separate study, astronomers at the Carnegie Institution of Washington in Washington, D.C., and the National Radio Astronomy Observatory in Socorro, N. Mex., in June 1990 measured the radio emission from several globular clusters without trying to detect individual pulsars. They then estimated the number of millisecond pulsars necessary to produce the observed radio emission. Because millisecond pulsars are more energetic than normal pulsars, the astronomers concluded that there are at least 1,000 millisecond pulsars in the Galaxy's globular clusters. This is fewer than the estimate by Kulkarni and his colleagues but still much more than astronomers previously suspected.

A pulsar will normally have a very rapid spin when it forms, but over time its spin slows as it loses energy to its surroundings. So astronomers expect that as a pulsar ages, its rate of pulsing will slow. The discovery of a millisecond pulsar in a globular cluster, where all stars are thought to be very old, came as quite a surprise when the first one was found in the late 1980's. Astronomers determined, however, that an aging pulsar would rotate faster if matter were added to it. Thus, pulsars that acquire new material—such as gas from a companion star in a *binary* (double-star) system—may become millisecond pulsars despite their age.

Astronomers now think that this accounts for the millisecond pulsars in the globular clusters. The millisecond pulsars are thought to be part of binary systems in which a pulsar and a normal star orbit one another. The normal star enters a phase in which it ejects gas in a stellar wind, or it begins to expand. The pulsar's gravitational field then captures this ejected or expanding gas in a process called *mass transfer*.

The right binary systems. The difficulty with having so many millisecond pulsars is that the globular clusters do not seem to have enough binary systems of the proper type.

In January 1991, however, Kulkarni and his colleagues suggested one possible explanation. They reason that there are many more mass-transfer binary systems than previously thought, but that most of them are undetectable.

The binary systems should be detectable as sources of X rays when mass transfer gets underway. During this phase of mass transfer, gas from the normal star is compressed into a disk surrounding the pulsar and heated to such high temperatures that it glows strongly at X-ray wavelengths. Astronomers have found several X-ray-emitting binary systems in the globular clusters but not nearly enough to account for the observed number of millisecond pulsars.

According to Kulkarni, the phase when mass transfer causes strong X-ray emission may be much briefer than previously expected. If this is so, a much smaller number of mass-transfer systems will be detectable from Earth.

A supermassive black hole? Further evidence supporting the theory that a supermassive black hole lies at the very center of our Galaxy was reported in November 1990 by radio astronomers Farhad Yusef-Zadeh of Northwestern University in Evanston, Ill.; Mark Morris of the University of California at Los Angeles; and Ronald Ekers of the Australia Telescope National Facility. A black hole is a region of space where a large amount of matter has collapsed under its own gravity, creating such an intense gravitational field at its surface that nothing, not even light, can escape. Astrophysicists think a supermassive black hole can form at the core of a young galaxy as many stars fall together and merge.

The three astronomers made very detailed radio maps of the galactic center showing tiny blobs of gas whose shapes appear to have been distorted by a rapid outflow of gas from the center of the galaxy. These blobs not only represent the action of a very energetic object such as a supermassive black hole but also help pinpoint the galactic center. [Theodore P. Snow]

In the Special Reports section, see MYSTERIES OF THE MILKY WAY. In WORLD BOOK, see ASTRONOMY.

Astronomy, Solar System

The United States spacecraft *Magellan* completed its first radar mapping cycle of Venus in May 1991. It returned the most detailed images to date of this planet's surface, revealing a world of complex and intriguing geologic processes. (In the Special Reports section, see Exploring the Surface of Venus.)

Dust devils on Triton. Two scientists at the California Institute of Technology in Pasadena proposed in October 1990 that plumes seen on Neptune's moon Triton may be similar to whirling wind columns on Earth called *dust devils*. Meteorologists Andrew Ingersoll and Kimberly Tryka based their theory on images returned by the *Voyager 2* spacecraft as it flew past Triton in August 1989. They noticed numerous dark patches on Triton's surface, which is mostly covered with bright areas of nitrogen frost.

The two scientists noted that the dark patches would absorb more sunlight than the surrounding white patches of frost and therefore would be heated to a higher temperature. If the heating were intense enough, they pro-

posed, air above the hot spots would rise, carrying dust from the surface with it and forming the plumes photographed by *Voyager 2*. Dust devils on Earth form in desert regions where sunlight heating the ground creates upward, twisting winds that carry dust hundreds of meters into the air.

Ingersoll and Tryka's theory also attempted to account for temperature variations in Triton's atmosphere. Planetary scientist Leonard Tyler of Stanford University in California and his colleagues at Stanford and the Jet Propulsion Laboratory (JPL) in Pasadena reported the variations in 1989. During the *Voyager* fly-by of Triton, Tyler's group used radio waves from *Voyager*'s radio antenna to determine the density and temperature of the gas comprising Triton's atmosphere. Astronomers can determine the density of gases by observing how radio waves are *refracted* (bent) by gas molecules as they pass through the atmosphere. Knowing the gases' density, scientists can derive their temperature.

Tyler reported that Triton's atmos-

The swirling white clouds of a huge storm system spreading across the equator of Saturn were revealed in an image taken in November 1990 by the *Hubble Space Telescope.* The storm lasted several weeks and covered an area about 24,000 kilometers (15,000 miles) wide.

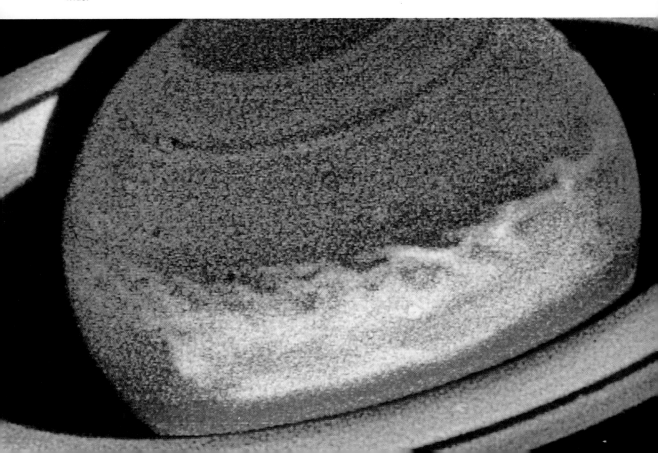

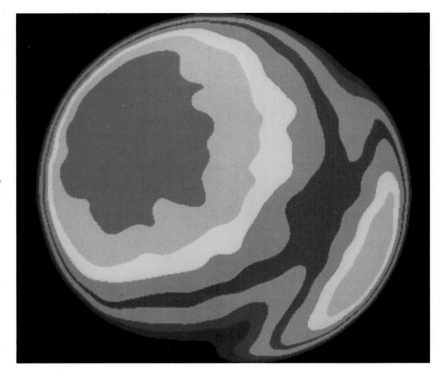

A temperature map of Mercury reveals one of two hot spots (red area) with subsurface temperatures as high as 669 °C (1263 °F), according to a June 1990 report by radio astronomers. The hot spots, centered on the planet's equator and created by the sun's radiation, indicate that Mercury is heated entirely by the sun and does not have a hot molten core.

Astronomy, Solar System

Continued

phere is warmer than the moon's surface and that the atmosphere's temperature near the surface increases with altitude—rather than decreasing. Ingersoll and Tryka theorized that the temperature increases could be caused by rising hot air in the dust devils.

The dust-devil hypothesis has some difficulties, however, according to other scientists. *Voyager*'s cameras revealed indirect evidence for perhaps 6 to 12 plumes and directly observed 2 plumes that lofted material 8 to 10 kilometers (5 to 6 miles) above the surface. Scientists argue that so much wind activity requires a tremendous amount of energy, and solar heating of the dark patches may not supply enough to power all the plumes.

Ingersoll and Tryka themselves pointed out that it may be difficult to loft dust particles in the very thin atmosphere of Triton, which has a pressure $1/100,000$ of the atmospheric pressure at Earth's surface. Winds in such an extremely thin atmosphere must move at speeds of about 1 to 10 meters (3 to 30 feet) per second to pick

up dust particles from the surface and carry them aloft.

Finally, some scientists challenged the interpretation of the radio experiments conducted by Tyler and his group. These scientists argued that data indicate the temperature in Triton's atmosphere decreases immediately above the surface. Such an interpretation lends support to the view that the plumes observed on Triton are caused by geysers like those on Earth.

Stormy Saturn. A major storm broke out on Saturn in late September 1990. Amateur astronomer Stuart Wilber of Las Cruces, N. Mex., was the first to discover the atmospheric disturbance, which appeared as a spot on Saturn's surface. The storm spread in October to become a turbulent white band encircling the planet and covering about one-sixth of the surface.

Astronomers Reta Beebe of New Mexico State University in Las Cruces and Christopher Barnet of the National Aeronautics and Space Administration's Goddard Space Flight Center in Greenbelt, Md., used ground-based telescopes to track the movement of the white clouds marking the storm over a period of weeks. The two astronomers found that the spreading of the clouds generally followed the wind patterns in Saturn's atmosphere, which had been mapped in 1980 and 1981 by the *Voyager 1* and *2* spacecraft. Thus, the storm's cloud material, once formed, was carried through the atmosphere much as cloud systems in Earth's atmosphere are moved about by winds.

The most interesting question facing astronomers concerned the origin of the storm. Saturn is composed mostly of hydrogen and helium gases with a small mixture of other gases such as ammonia. Saturn is so large that its internal heat rivals or exceeds the amount of warmth it gets from the sun. Most of Saturn's internal heat was generated when the planet formed about 4.6 billion years ago and is still rising slowly from the deep interior to the surface.

The cause of the observed storm on Saturn may be an especially vigorous rising column of hot gas that pushed high into the atmosphere. As the gas rose into the cooler upper atmosphere, ammonia vapor in the column would condense to form clouds. These clouds then would move across the planet due to winds.

Radar bounced off Titan. Radio astronomer Duane O. Muhleman and colleagues at Caltech and JPL have been successfully bouncing radio waves off Titan, Saturn's largest moon.

Muhleman and his colleagues have conducted two sets of experiments. The first was performed in June 1989 and reported in May 1990. The second was performed in July 1990 and reported in October.

The scientists were seeking to obtain radar images of Titan's surface, which is obscured by a thick haze that blocks visible light but can be penetrated by radio waves. The scientists beamed the radio signals from the Goldstone radio telescope in Owens Valley, Calif., and listened for their return on the world's largest radio telescope, the Very Large Array near Socorro, N. Mex.

Titan's surface has been a puzzle. The cameras of *Voyagers 1* and *2* could not penetrate the haze that shrouds the moon. However, other instruments on those spacecraft revealed that Titan has a thick nitrogen atmosphere containing large amounts of methane and other hydrocarbon gases. The methane gas in Titan's atmosphere may be an indication of a surface ocean of liquid methane, which may also contain other hydrocarbon molecules. These other molecules, such as ethane, would be produced from the breakdown of methane gas by sunlight in the upper atmosphere. As they are formed, they condense and fall to the surface to dissolve in the ocean. Below this liquid layer might be sediment made of other organic compounds.

The scientists performed their radio-wave experiment on three successive nights in June 1989 when Saturn and Titan were high in the sky above each telescope. In May 1990, they reported that they had received a strong radar return on one night and little or no radar signals on the other two nights. The strength of the returned signal provides important information about the properties of the surface. For example, a strong signal is returned when a radio wave reflects off rough terrain. A weak signal, or none at all, may indicate the presence of hydrocarbon liquids.

Astronomers think that Titan, like Earth's moon, always keeps the same side toward its planet in what is called *synchronous rotation*. If Titan does orbit Saturn this way, then during the three nights of observation, the portion of Titan visible from Earth rotated only slightly. Because radar results were so different on one of the three nights, Titan's surface features may vary significantly from region to region, rather than being uniform throughout.

The very strong radar return from Titan was similar to what scientists encountered during previous experiments in which radar signals were bounced off the icy satellites of Jupiter. Muhleman and his colleagues therefore concluded that the strong radar return on Titan was caused by a region of frozen water. The very weak, or absent, radar signals encountered on two nights suggest regions that could be liquid such as the proposed methane ocean.   [Jonathan I. Lunine]

In WORLD BOOK, see NEPTUNE; SATURN; SOLAR SYSTEM.

Books
of Science

Here are 25 outstanding new science books suitable for the general reader. They have been selected from books published in 1990 and 1991.

Anthropology. *The Anasazi: Ancient Indian People of the American Southwest* by J. J. Brody combines text and beautiful photographs to document the culture and art of the Anasazi, a people who developed an advanced civilization by the A.D. 700's in what is now New Mexico, Arizona, and parts of Utah and Colorado. (Rizzoli, 1990. 239 pp. illus. $75)

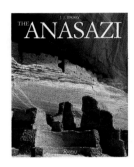

Astronomy. *The Shadows of Creation: Dark Matter and the Structure of the Universe* by Michael Riordan and David N. Schramm examines the possibility that most matter in the universe is invisible and the implications this has for the ultimate fate of the universe. (W. H. Freeman, 1991. 277 pp. illus. $18.95)

Touring the Universe Through Binoculars by Philip S. Harrington suggests that the best way to observe some stellar objects is with binoculars of low power and wide field. Harrington takes the reader on a tour, using only binoculars, from the moon through the solar system and beyond. (Wiley, 1990. 294 pp. illus. $24.95)

Biology. *The Ants* by Bert Hölldobler and Edward O. Wilson is a richly illustrated, encyclopedic survey of the approximately 8,800 species of ants, the communities they form, and their social behavior. (Harvard Univ. Press, 1990. 736 pp. illus. $65)

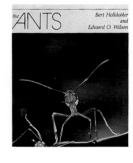

Genome: The Story of the Most Astonishing Scientific Adventure of Our Time—The Attempt to Map All the Genes in the Human Body by Jerry E. Bishop and Michael Waldholz describes efforts to determine the location and function of the 50,000 to 100,000 human genes, the basic units of heredity, an effort that will revolutionize the treatment and prevention of disease. (Simon & Schuster, 1990. 352 pp. $22.95)

Engineering. *The Pencil: A History of Design and Circumstance* by Henry Petroski describes the science of engineering as reflected in the history of the common pencil, comparing modern pencils with those made 200 years ago. (Knopf, 1990. 434 pp. illus. $25)

The Truth About Chernobyl by Grigori Medvedev, translated by Evelyn Rossiter, is an absorbing account of the 1986 explosion of a reactor at the nuclear power plant in Chernobyl in the Soviet Union. Medvedev is the engineer who headed the official investigation of the disaster. (Basic Bks., 1991. 274 pp. $22.95)

Environment. *One Earth, One Future: Our Changing Global Environment* by Cheryl Simon Silver describes the basic science involved in the analysis of environmental problems. The text explores the effects of human activity on the environment, including global warming, rising sea levels, destruction of forests, and depletion of the protective ozone layer in the upper atmosphere. (National Acad. Press, 1990. 196 pp. $14.95)

General science. *Models of My Life* by Herbert A. Simon is the autobiography of the economist who won the 1978 Nobel Prize in economics for his research on the decision-making process in business. This book records his accomplishments in psychology, artificial intelligence, computer science, and other fields of science. (Basic Bks., 1991. 415 pp. illus. $26.95)

Frontiers of Science, edited by Andrew Scott, contains 14 chapters written by prominent scientists engaged in research on new drugs, computing, particle physics, and alternative energy sources. (Blackwell, 1990. 201 pp. illus. $24.95)

Theories of Everything: The Quest for Ultimate Explanation by John D. Barrow explains the challenge to scientists of finding a mathematical theory that will explain the origin, structure, and development of our universe. Barrow names eight essential components for such a theory. (Clarendon Press, 1991. 223 pp. illus. $22.95)

The Threat and the Glory: Reflections on Science and Scientists by Peter B. Medawar contains 23 essays, book reviews, and radio talks by the author, a British zoologist who shared the 1960 Nobel Prize for physiology or medicine with Australian physician Sir Macfarlane Burnet for his work in immunology. The general theme is to inform the reader about what is possible in science. (HarperCollins, 1990. 291 pp. $22.50)

Mathematics. *Islands of Truth: A Mathematical Mystery Cruise* by Ivars

Books
of Science
Continued

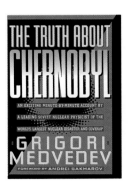

Peterson, a continuation of the author's earlier book *The Mathematical Tourist* (1988), shares some of the mathematical mysteries at the frontiers of research. The book also examines why mathematics is the ideal system for describing and explaining natural phenomena. (W. H. Freeman, 1990. 325 pp. illus. $19.95)

Envisioning Information by Edward R. Tufte provides several hundred superb designs for the visual display of complex data. The illustrations originated in 17 countries over a period of seven centuries. (Graphics Press, 1990. 126 pp. illus. $48)

Medicine. *Medieval and Early Renaissance Medicine: An Introduction to Knowledge and Practice* by Nancy G. Siraisi describes how the scientific and medical knowledge of the Middle Ages drew on learning acquired from antiquity and the Islamic world, and how over time such knowledge became increasingly organized and systematic. (University of Chicago Press, 1990. 250 pp. illus. $10.95 paper)

Patenting the Sun: Polio and the Salk Vaccine by Jane S. Smith records the story of the testing and development of the first successful poliomyelitis vaccine in 1954, of the team effort that made it possible, and how the vaccine stopped a major childhood crippler. (Morrow, 1990. 413 pp. illus. $22.95)

Natural history. *Burning Bush: A Fire History of Australia* by Stephen J. Pyne describes the influence of fire on the evolving plant life of Australia and shows that fire is the most powerful environmental determinant on the continent. (Henry Holt, 1991. 520 pp. illus. $27.95)

A Parrot Without a Name: The Search for the Last Unknown Birds on Earth by Don Stap is an account of the author's two expeditions in the Amazon region of Peru to collect and identify exotic birds, culminating in the discovery of a previously unknown species. (Knopf, 1990. 224 pp. illus. $19.95)

Wild Ice: Antarctic Journeys by Ron Naveen and others describes the array of wildlife inhabiting the Antarctic region and the urgency of protecting the fragile environment of Antarctica, home to penguins, petrels, seals, whales, and fish. (Smithsonian Institution Press, 1990. 224 pp. illus. $29.95)

Physics. *Fusion: The Search for Endless Energy* by Robin Herman is a popular account of efforts to sustain controlled nuclear fusion, a process that promises to produce a cheap, inexhaustible source of energy by fusing two atomic nuclei. The author traces the theoretical, technical, and political obstacles that have prevented achievement of this goal and speculates about the prospects for success. (Cambridge Univ. Press, 1990. 267 pp. $19.95)

Psychology. *Intelligence: The Psychometric View* by Paul Kline is a clear analysis of the arguments in favor of intelligence testing and why testing is a valid method for measuring certain kinds of human ability. (Routledge, 1991. 166 pp. $15.95)

Space exploration. *Mission to Mars* by Michael Collins, an *Apollo 11* astronaut who went to the moon, argues that sending astronauts to explore Mars should be the next great project of the United States National Aeronautics and Space Administration. Collins lays out the physical, technical, and psychological challenges that must be met before human beings walk on Mars. (Grove Weidenfeld, 1990. 307 pp. illus. $22.50)

Technology. *Levitating Trains and Kamikaze Genes: Technological Literacy for the 1990s* by Richard P. Brennan introduces readers to the new technology that will affect their lives, including advances in space travel, biotechnology and genetic engineering, computer science, superconductivity, medicine, and arms control. (Wiley, 1990. 262 pp. illus. $18.95)

Technology in World Civilization: A Thousand-Year History by Arnold Pacey is a global view of the development of technology between the years 700 and 1970 in which the author theorizes about why the same inventions were created in different places at the same time. (MIT Press, 1990. 238 pp. illus. $19.95)

Zoology. *The Pinnipeds: Seals, Sea Lions, and Walruses* by Marianne Riedman describes 33 species of seals and their fascinating ways of adapting to life in the water. Among the topics covered are seals' diet, breeding behavior, and social organization. (University of Calif. Press, 1990. 439 pp. illus. $34.95)　　　[William Goodrich Jones]

Botany

An important gene has been present in magnolia leaf cells in a form virtually unchanged for at least 17 to 20 million years. This discovery, widely reported during summer 1990, was the work of seven scientists from the University of California in Riverside, the University of Georgia in Athens, the University of Idaho in Moscow, and DNAX Research Institute in Palo Alto, Calif.

The gene *codes* for (directs the production of) a protein called *rubisco*. Rubisco is an enzyme that captures carbon dioxide from the atmosphere during photosynthesis, the food-making process of plants. Because rubisco is the most abundant protein in leaves, and because plant leaves account for most of the mass of living things on Earth, rubisco is Earth's most abundant protein.

The researchers analyzed preserved magnolia leaves taken from the Clarkia fossil beds, the site of an ancient lake in northern Idaho. Many of the leaves retained their colors—bright green, red, and yellow—when first broken out of the rocks. But after exposure to the air and sunlight, they soon dried and turned brown.

The scientists scraped the leaves off the rocks onto a sterile card and placed the card into a solution that protected the leaves' genetic material from disintegration. These specimens were stored on dry ice until they were analyzed. The scientists speculated that the leaves had remained well preserved and moist for as long as 20 million years, probably because there was little or no oxygen in the cold, deep waters of the ancient lake into which the leaves fell and sank.

Using a technique called *polymerase chain reaction* (PCR), the researchers multiplied part of the leaf's gene that controls production of a part of the rubisco molecule. Then they determined the exact makeup of the gene.

When the researchers compared the ancient gene with that of modern magnolia leaves, they found that the molecules were nearly identical, yet different enough to show that the ancient magnolia was a separate species.

The scientists say they hope to use

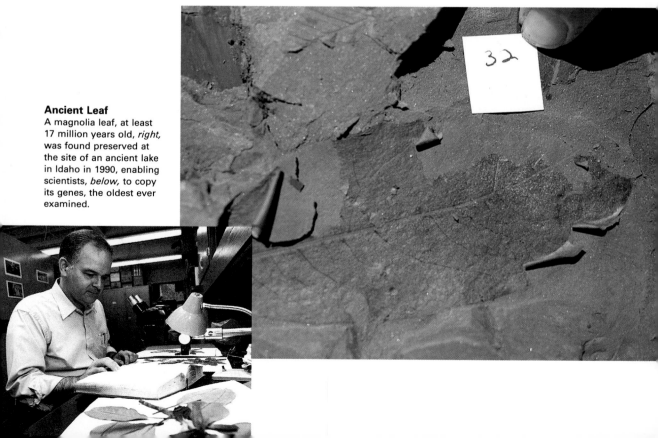

Ancient Leaf
A magnolia leaf, at least 17 million years old, *right,* was found preserved at the site of an ancient lake in Idaho in 1990, enabling scientists, *below,* to copy its genes, the oldest ever examined.

A technician rearranges plastic trees in a model forest "planted" in a wind tunnel at Oxford University in England in 1990. The experiment is designed to show whether altering planting patterns will reduce damage caused by high winds, which annually destroy millions of valuable trees in England. Sensors wired to the model trees record wind stresses and feed the data to a computer for analysis.

Botany

Continued

PCR to investigate plant material from other sites in the United States, some of which are 40 or 50 million years old. See Genetics (Close-Up).

Living "fossil." A dogwood tree known only from fossils found in Europe and Asia and thought to be extinct for 4 million years is alive and well in eastern China, according to a report published in June 1990. Paleobotanists (scientists who study ancient plants) from Washington State University in Pullman made the discovery.

The scientists compared fruit from the living Chinese dogwood with 15-million-year-old fossilized fruit of the extinct dogwood. They found that both belonged to the same species. The Chinese tree had been discovered in 1928 but was misclassified.

Plant "aspirin" fights infection. Botanists have long known that plants manufacture their own salicylic acid, the basic component of aspirin, acetylsalicylic acid. But until recently, no one knew how plants used the substance. Researchers from Rutgers The State University of New Jersey in Piscataway

and New Brunswick reported in November 1990 that salicylic acid causes tobacco plants to produce a protein that fights infection by the tobacco mosaic virus (TMV).

The scientists inoculated tobacco plants with TMV. After 24 hours, salicylic acid levels began to rise until, 48 hours after inoculation, the leaves produced as much as 20 times the normal amount of salicylic acid. At this point, the infection-fighting protein increased rapidly. Even without inoculation with TMV, applying salicylic acid to the leaves caused the protein to increase.

Similar results were reported in November 1990 in experiments with cucumber plants conducted by a team of 10 researchers working at the Ciba-Geigy Corporation in Basel, Switzerland, and Research Triangle Park, N.C. These researchers believe that salicylic acid also causes the plants to begin resisting attack by fungi and bacteria as well as viruses.

Altering chloroplasts. Success in introducing foreign genes into the chloroplasts of tobacco seedlings was re-

Botany

Continued

ported in November 1990 by other scientists at Rutgers. Molecular biologists have been able to insert genes into the nuclei of plants, but they have previously had problems inserting genes into chloroplasts, structures outside the cell nucleus that contain chlorophyll, the green pigment that absorbs energy from sunlight.

The genes the researchers chose to insert make the chloroplasts resistant to certain herbicides. Without these genes, seedlings grown in the presence of those herbicides appear nearly white because the chloroplasts cannot produce chlorophyll. When the chloroplasts have the appropriate gene, the seedlings turn green, even after exposure to the herbicides.

The researchers coated microscopic pellets of tungsten with multiple copies of the gene and then used a special "gene" gun to fire these pellets into seedlings treated with herbicides. Only one gene was incorporated into a seedling for every 50 blasts of the gun, but some plants were successfully altered and passed the chlorophyll-producing trait on to succeeding generations.

Calcium channels in plant cells. Plant physiologists Barbara Pickard and Jiu Ping Ding at Washington University in St. Louis, Mo., reported in August 1990 the presence of calcium channels in plant cell membranes. Calcium channels, which allow electrically charged calcium ions to move in and out of cells, are important features of animal cells, and there is mounting evidence that they might play a role in plant cells. The researchers believe that these channels are responsible for detecting gravity and redirecting plant growth in response to physical signals, such as wind and rain.

Pickard and Ding demonstrated the existence of the channels by sealing a tiny pipette tip against a plant cell membrane. They applied suction to the pipette, which opened calcium channels. The flow of calcium ions through the open channels produced a mild electric current. [Frank B. Salisbury]

In the Special Reports section, see THE "FORESTS" IN OUR CITIES. In WORLD BOOK, see BOTANY.

Chemistry

Chemists in the United States and Germany reported in September 1990 that they had found a way to *synthesize* (create in the laboratory) large amounts of a bizarre, ball-shaped molecule made up entirely of carbon atoms. The molecule consists of 60 interlinked carbon atoms. It had been dubbed *buckminsterfullerene* when its existence was first suspected in 1985 because it resembles the geodesic domes popularized by the late architect R. Buckminster Fuller. The scientists said carbon can also be coaxed into larger spherical molecules with up to several hundred carbon atoms. Buckminsterfullerene and these other so-called *fullerenes* may have applications as lubricants or other useful materials. See MATERIALS SCIENCE.

Speeding drug research. A way to synthesize as many as 10,000 molecules of experimental drugs on a square piece of glass smaller than a thumbnail was announced in February 1991 by investigators at the Affymax Research Institute in Palo Alto, Calif. The technique could greatly reduce the time required for developing new drugs.

The conventional approach to drug development can be quite laborious. Researchers looking for new compounds of medical value often prepare molecules called *peptides*, which are short chains of *amino acids* (the building blocks of proteins). They then evaluate how well each peptide molecule binds with biological molecules such as *enzymes* and *antibodies*. Enzymes are proteins that make many body processes possible; antibodies are disease-fighting proteins produced by the immune system. Strong binding between a peptide and enzyme or antibody is evidence that the peptide may be useful as a drug.

This screening test is effective but slow. The peptides and biological molecules are mixed in plastic trays that allow only 96 peptides to be evaluated at a time. By contrast, the Affymax method makes it possible to test thousands of compounds at once.

The Affymax scientists first use amino acid solutions to synthesize thousands of different peptides at pre-

Fullerenes: Carbon in the Shape of a Soccer Ball

Magnified nearly 10 million times, 60- and 70-atom *fullerene* molecules are packed together like eggs in a crate, *bottom.* Scientists in 1990 and 1991 discovered how to make large quantities of these carbon molecules, one of only three known forms of carbon. The others are graphite and diamond. When graphite is heated in a vacuum chamber, carbon atoms begin linking together, *below, left to right,* their bonds forming pentagons and hexagons that join to form a sphere much like a soccer ball.

From the Lab: Synthetic Diamond

Diamond received a rare honor in 1990. *Science* magazine, one of the world's most prestigious journals of original scientific research, named diamond the "Molecule of the Year." Although diamond occurs naturally, scientists can "grow" it in the laboratory. And new techniques to create the molecule in the laboratory may lead to an inexpensive protective diamond coating that can be applied to anything from eyeglass lenses to turbine blades. Many researchers believe that the technology could make diamond films nearly as common as paint and asphalt.

Long cherished as a symbol of love, wealth, purity, and natural elegance, diamond is a crystalline material made nearly entirely of carbon atoms, each one linked to four neighbors in a three-dimensional network. The symmetrical arrangement of these atoms and the strong bonds between them are responsible for diamond's unsurpassed transparency and hardness. Diamond is also unmatched for its heat conducting and electrical insulating ability.

Scientists since the 1950's have been able to grow extremely thin diamond sheets on natural diamonds and the surfaces of other materials using a family of techniques called *chemical vapor deposition* (CVD). Since the late 1980's, materials scientists have been rapidly sharpening their skills at creating these synthetic diamonds. Unlike such substances as *cubic zirconia*, *spinel*, and *strontium titantate*, which jewelers sell as imitation "diamonds," synthetic diamond is real diamond, though not naturally created.

CVD diamond-making processes usually begin with inexpensive but carbon-rich gases such as methane, which contain carbon and hydrogen atoms bonded together. Scientists inject the gas into a sealed chamber kept at a low pressure and add energy to the gas molecules, often in the form of heat or microwaves. When the gas molecules absorb enough energy, the carbon-hydrogen bond begins to break down.

The resulting molecular fragments travel over a heated sample in the chamber. Here, carbon atoms deposit, link to one another, and slowly thicken into a continuous sheet of synthetic diamond on the sample's surface. Materials scientists have grown diamond films on metals, minerals, and other materials.

In 1952, William G. Eversole of Union Carbide Corporation first grew diamond films this

Several times stronger than natural diamond, a synthetic diamond is undamaged by a powerful laser beam.

way. Unfortunately, his diamond films grew so slowly that it would have taken many months to get a layer as thick as this page. The project fizzled because no one thought it had much commercial potential.

In 1955, a team of researchers at the General Electric Company (GE) in Schenectady, N.Y., reported making tiny diamond grains with a different process. Their method mimicked the conditions deep within the Earth, where high temperatures and pressures create natural diamonds. The researchers used a 907-metric-ton (1,000-short-ton) press and temperatures in the thousands of degrees to transform nuggets of graphite—the form of carbon used for pencil "lead"—into little diamond grains. The tremendous pressure and heat created by the process rearrange the carbon bonds that form graphite into diamond's stronger and more symmetrical network of carbon atoms.

Since 1957, when GE commercialized the process, this high-pressure diamond-making technique has grown into a half-billion-dollar industry. Many toolmakers now increase the cutting ability and durability of saws, drill bits, and other cutting implements by coating them with synthetic diamond films.

Until the 1960's, the high-temperature and high-pressure method seemed the only practical way of making synthetic diamond. But a series of advances, mostly by researchers in the Soviet Union during the 1970's and in Japan during the early 1980's, advanced the prospect of growing diamond films under the much milder, low-pressure conditions used in CVD diamond making. To promote more rapid diamond growth, the researchers experimented with different mixtures of gases. They also varied temperatures and pressures to come up with the best growth conditions. Eventually, these researchers reported growth rates hundreds of times faster than Eversole's, and by 1984, research showed that CVD might be a practical way of growing diamond.

Now CVD researchers routinely produce diamond films as well as similar materials called *diamondlike coatings*, which have the same hardness as diamond but with slight imperfections in molecular structure. Although diamondlike coatings lack diamond's perfection, they have fewer sharp crystal *facets* (faces) than genuine diamond films. For this reason, diamondlike coatings are smoother and hence may be more appropriate for coating items such as telescope mirrors and ball bearings.

Scientists still do not entirely understand the chemical and physical processes that make CVD diamond growing possible. Many questions remain about how diamond films form on different surfaces. No one yet clearly understands how different types of carbon-containing gas, and the types of molecular fragments that break from them, help or hinder the process. Despite these and other questions, researchers have used a mix of trial and error and scientific intuition to discover reliable techniques to produce synthetic diamond. [Ivan Amato]

cise locations on a glass chip. To screen the peptides for their biological activity, the researchers expose the chip to enzymes, antibodies, or other kinds of biological molecules to which *fluorescent* (light-emitting) molecules have been chemically attached. A laser is then beamed at the chip. The laser causes the fluorescent molecular tags to light up wherever a biological molecule has bound with a peptide. The peptides so identified can later be investigated to learn whether they might be useful as drugs.

Glass-plastic hybrids. Glass and plastic are normally incompatible; a mixture of molten glass and plastic hardens into an unusable mass. But chemist Bruce M. Novak of the University of California at Berkeley reported in August 1990 that he had succeeded in blending the two materials.

Novak's glass-plastic hybrids consist of an interlocking network of *silicates* (materials found in glass) and *organic polymers* (long chains of carbon compounds typically found in plastics). To make these networks, Novak dissolves in water a number of raw materials used in making glass and plastic. He then adds a *catalyst* (a substance that speeds up a chemical reaction without itself being changed). The catalyst causes the materials to form tiny silicate and polymer regions that link with each other in a stable formation.

Because the silicate and polymer regions of the networks are microscopic in scale, the blends are completely uniform and display properties of both glass and plastic. Like the strongest plastics, the blends can be struck with a hammer without shattering. They also have the light weight and elasticity typical of plastics. And, like fine optical-grade glass, they are highly transparent and free of distortion. Novak said the hybrid materials might make effective safety glass for windshields and lightweight lenses for optical instruments and eyeglasses.

Antifreeze molecule. The laboratory synthesis of a chemical that protects an Atlantic Ocean fish in subfreezing temperatures was reported in April 1991 by researchers at Virginia Polytechnic Institute in Blacksburg. The compound, known as *antifreeze peptide* (AFP), is derived from the winter

265

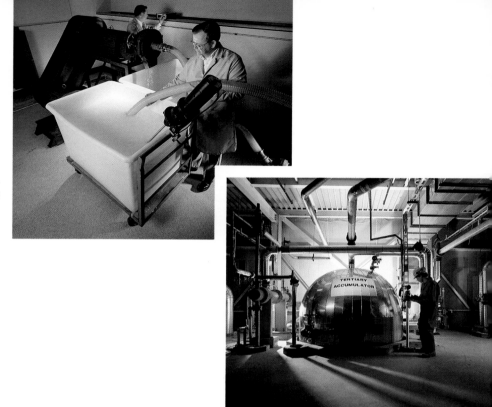

Safer Paper Products
Technicians at Repap Technologies in Valley Forge, Pa., test wood pulp made in an experimental process that produces fewer pollutants, *right.* A pulp cooker called a *tertiary accumulator, far right,* yields pulp that can be bleached without forming poisonous by-products called *dioxins.*

Chemistry

Continued

flounder, a fish that lives in cold waters off the east coast of the United States. AFP is much more effective than salt in preventing ice formation.

The scientists analyzed the flounder gene that directs the production of the peptide and constructed an artificial, lengthened version of the gene. They then inserted copies of the synthetic gene into bacteria, which produced the peptide according to the "blueprint" in the genetically engineered gene.

Both the natural and artificial compounds seem to prevent freezing by binding with water molecules in such a way that the molecules cannot get close enough to one another to form ice crystals. Although the natural chemical protects the flounder from freezing at temperatures as low as −3 °C (27 °F), the researchers think their version may prevent ice formation at slightly lower temperatures because it is twice as large as the natural peptide.

The synthetic chemical appears to be safe for the environment. It thus might prove ideal for preventing ice formation on roadways, replacing corrosive rock salt. It might also be used to protect citrus groves from freezing temperatures and as a deicing agent on airplane wings.

Chemical data storage. The development of a novel system for storing computer data in the molecular structures of chemical compounds was announced in October 1990 by researchers at the University of Tokyo in Japan. The new process could lead to the production of ultrahigh-density optical storage disks that store up to 100 million bits of information in an area the size of a fingernail.

The system records information converted to *digital* form (as a series of 1's and 0's) with a pulsed beam of ultraviolet light. The beam is projected onto a layer of molecules called *trans-azobenzenes* on a transparent disk. The ultraviolet light converts these molecules into patterns of *isomers* (compounds with the same chemical formula but different structures) called *cis-azobenzenes.* An electric current then changes those molecules into other isomers called *hydrazobenzenes.*

The chemically encoded information is read by shining visible light through the molecular patterns. The patterns alter the light, and those variations are converted into electrical signals that can be read as digital data.

The main drawback with chemical data storage, which has been under study throughout the world, has been that the compounds used are unstable: The light beam used to read the chemically encoded information often destroys it. The Tokyo team solved that problem when it converted the unstable cis-azobenzenes to hydrazobenzenes. The hydrazobenzene molecules can be penetrated by light beams without being altered.

Artificial nose. An "electronic nose" was unveiled in March 1991 by researchers at the University of Warwick in England. The artificial nose is modeled after the human nose, which contains millions of nerve cells. Different groups of these nerve cells are sensitive to particular chemical compounds. The molecules producing a certain odor stimulate these cells and cause them to transmit a characteristic signal to the brain. The brain interprets the signal as a distinct smell.

Compared to the complexity of the human nose, the artificial nose is extremely simple, containing just 12 smell sensors. The tube-shaped sensors, made of a ceramic material and covered with a catalyst, are heated to about 349 °C (660 °F).

Odor molecules that hit the sensors break down, altering the electrical conductivity of the sensors. A computer detects the pattern of electrical changes on the group of sensors and interprets it as a particular smell.

Each sensor is able to detect just one chemical compound at a time, but the sensor can be adjusted to "smell" different compounds by varying the type or amount of catalyst applied to it. Thus, the nose can be "fine-tuned" to distinguish any number of odors. The instrument may someday be used in factories to monitor the quality of food, liquor, or perfumes, or to detect gas leaks. [Gordon Graff]

In WORLD BOOK, see CHEMISTRY.

Computer Hardware

Home computers staged a comeback in 1990 and 1991, as three major computer manufacturers in the United States brought out new, low-priced models designed for home and home-office use. The three were International Business Machines Corporation (IBM), headquartered in Armonk, N.Y.; Apple Computer, Incorporated, of Cupertino, Calif.; and Tandy Corporation of Fort Worth, Tex. About 15 per cent of the households in the United States and Canada had home computers by 1990.

IBM's PS/1, introduced in June 1990, is the company's first computer aimed specifically at the home user since an earlier IBM personal computer, the PCjr, failed to find a large market and was withdrawn in 1985. The PS/1 is run by the Intel Corporation's 80286 microprocessor, which makes it far more powerful than the PCjr. At the same time, the PS/1 is easier to use. Instead of typing keyboard characters to issue commands, the user selects symbols called *icons* that represent file folders and other office items.

The PS/1 comes with a *modem*—a device for transmitting computer data over telephone lines—and software for communicating with other computers and with electronic information services. Software for word processing and accounting is also included.

The most popular version of the PS/1, which sells for $1,999, includes a color monitor and a 30 megabyte (MB) hard-disk drive for storing data. (Computer memory is measured in units called *bytes*. One byte is the amount of data needed to make a letter, number, or symbol. A computer with 1 MB—1 million bytes—of memory can hold the equivalent of about 500 double-spaced typed pages.) A basic model, with a black-and-white monitor and no hard-disk drive, sells for $999.

Tandy's 1000 RL, introduced in July 1990, was intended for people who have had little or no experience with personal computers. It offers a version of Tandy's DeskMate interface, which employs icons to represent common commands and programs. The RL includes software for such household

267

Visitors to Boston's Computer Museum can see how a computer works by touring a computer mock-up that stands 50 feet (15 meters) high. These teen-agers are resting on a *video board*—the part of the computer that transmits the electronic signals that produce images on the computer monitor. The walk-through computer exhibit opened on June 23, 1990.

Computer
Hardware
Continued

tasks as balancing a checkbook, itemizing expenses, and planning meals. The 1000 RL sells for $1,299 with a hard-disk drive and color monitor. The basic model sells for about $750.

Three new Macs. Apple unveiled three lower-priced models of its Macintosh personal computer in October 1990. The Classic, with a black-and-white monitor, is the least expensive of the new Macs. Although not targeted specifically at home users, the machine found wide acceptance in that market.

The Classic sells for about $1,500 with a 40 MB hard-disk drive and 2 MB of *random access memory* (RAM)—the computer's working memory into which programs and data are loaded from disks. A Macintosh Classic without a hard-disk drive and with a single megabyte of RAM is priced at $999.

Two other Macintosh models also found many purchasers. The Macintosh LC, Apple's first low-cost color computer, is designed primarily for the school market. It sells for about $3,000.

The IIsi is the speediest and most powerful of the new Macs. It incorpo-

rates Motorola Incorporated's 68030 processor, capable of 20 million cycles per second, or 20 megahertz (MHz). (The higher the number of cycles, the faster the computer can work. The Macintosh Classic, by comparison, runs at 10 MHz, as do the IBM PS/1 and Tandy 1000 RL.) The basic IIsi, priced around $3,700, includes 2 MB of RAM and a 40 MB hard-disk drive. The price does not include a monitor.

Anticipating increased interest in voice-based computing, Apple provided the LC and IIsi models with microphones and the capacity to incorporate sound into text. The new Macs also include software and hardware for *networking*, the linking of computers to share data. Networking is particularly important in business applications.

Portable computers became more powerful and more portable than ever in 1990 and 1991. Much of this market was captured by *notebook computers*—portable computers no larger and barely heavier than a standard three-ring notebook.

Even smaller than a notebook computer was the checkbook-sized computer introduced by the Hewlett-Packard Company of Palo Alto, Calif., in April 1991. The 95LX weighs only 312 grams (11 ounces), yet it includes a calculator, 512 kilobytes of RAM, and a built-in spreadsheet program. Two AA batteries can power the computer for up to two months. The 95LX is priced at $699.

New NeXT. In September 1990, NeXT, Incorporated, of Redwood City, Calif., introduced a new version of its NeXTstation, a powerful computer aimed at the workstation market. Workstations bridge the gap between personal computers and minicomputers, providing tremendous speed and power for producing graphics. NeXT's new computer makes it easier to process full-color images and use those images in desktop publishing. It runs at 25 MHz and includes 8 MB of RAM and a 105 MB hard disk. The computer is priced at $4,995.

CDTV. In April 1991, Commodore Business Machines Incorporated of West Chester, Pa., introduced CDTV, a compact disc player that uses a standard television set as a monitor. CDTV takes advantage of CD-ROM (*compact disc, read-only memory*) technology, which stores the equivalent of tens of thousands of printed pages on a single disc. (Read-only memory contains data that cannot be altered or erased.) The player, which sells for about $900, is operated by a handheld remote control device. It can also be connected to a computer keyboard. See also COMPUTER SOFTWARE.

Computer phones. In April 1991, American Telephone & Telegraph Company announced plans to combine a computer with a telephone. The so-called Smart Phone will interact with other computers, thus allowing users to pay bills, carry out routine banking transactions, and shop for products. To place a call or perform other tasks, the user presses symbols on the phone's small display screen. The Smart Phone was scheduled to be available by spring 1992 and to cost between $150 and $200.   [Keith Ferrell]

In WORLD BOOK, see COMPUTER.

New Macintosh Line
A new line of lower-priced products was introduced in 1990 by Apple Computer of Cupertino, Calif. It included three Macintosh computers: the Classic, IIsi, and LC, *below* (left to right). Prices started at $999 for the least expensive version of the Classic. Working with the Macs were inexpensive new laser printers *right*— the StyleWriter (left) and Personal LaserWriter (right).

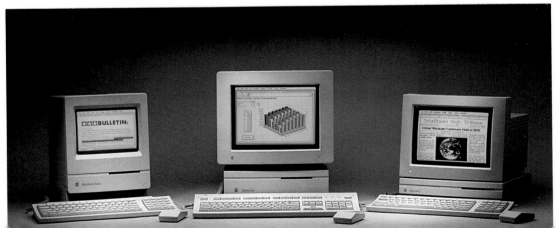

Computer Software

Computer programs capable of responding to handwritten commands were introduced in 1990 and 1991. *Pen-based computing*, as this technology is called, was expected to add another dimension to computer use.

At present, computer commands are usually issued by typing on a keyboard or by pointing an electronic mouse. But in pen-based computing, the user "writes" on a sensitive computer screen with an electronic pen. Manufacturers expect pen-based computing to be used initially by people who work away from their desks or who fill out many forms—salespeople, for example.

PenPoint, software for operating a pen-based system, was introduced by Go Corporation of Foster City, Calif., in January 1991. Commands are issued by specific preprogrammed movements of the pen: For example, a word can be changed by circling it and a phrase deleted by crossing it out. Pen-Point can also identify handwritten letters and numbers and turn them into type, though users must adjust their handwriting somewhat to suit the software's capabilities.

PenPoint requires a *notepad computer*, a special kind of computer that is operated by handwritten commands. Go has licensed PenPoint to several computer manufacturers as a means of establishing it as the standard system for pen-based computing. These manufacturers were expected to bring out notepad computers, priced from $3,000 to $6,000, by the end of 1991.

Graphical user interfaces (GUI's) continued to gain popularity during 1990 and 1991. A GUI enables the user to activate programs and functions by pointing a cursor at symbols called *icons*, rather than by typing characters on a screen. Many people find GUI's simpler to use than typed commands. GUI's were pioneered in the Macintosh computers made by Apple Computer, Incorporated, of Cupertino, Calif.

Windows 3.0 —a GUI released by Microsoft Corporation of Redmond, Wash., in mid-1990—became one of the best-selling personal computer programs of all time. More than 2 million copies, priced at about $100, were sold in the first year of its release. Microsoft supplies software to the International Business Machines Corporation (IBM).

Many industry analysts felt that the popularity of Windows indicated a loss of prestige for OS/2, a competing operating system also made by Microsoft. (An operating system acts as a "traffic director," enabling computers to process information and run software.) OS/2 was intended to operate IBM's powerful PS/2 personal computer but failed to attract a large number of buyers. Windows works in the PS/2 and in less sophisticated machines.

Early in 1991, Microsoft released a Windows version of Excel, its popular spreadsheet program. A spreadsheet is a software tool for manipulating numbers and making mathematical projections, such as business forecasts. Many other software companies announced plans to bring out Windows-compatible versions of their programs.

Simpler GUI. An even simpler, and in some ways more powerful, GUI than Windows was introduced in November 1990 by GeoWorks, Incorporated, of Berkeley, Calif. GeoWorks Ensemble, which sold for $199.95, provides word processing, database management, telecommunications software, and other programs. Ensemble's commands and functions can be adapted to individual skill levels. And where Windows requires sophisticated computers with large amounts of memory and fast microprocessors, Ensemble is designed to operate in less sophisticated models of IBM personal computers.

New operating systems. In May 1991, Apple introduced a long-awaited upgrade of the operating system for its popular Macintosh personal computers. Macintosh System 7.0 extends the Mac's desktop publishing capabilities by providing sharply defined type faces in all type sizes. System 7.0 also makes it easy for files to be shared in computer networks. Moreover, a user can enter a change in one program—word processing, for example—and have it show up in another program, such as spreadsheets.

In June 1991, Microsoft upgraded its widely sold DOS (*d*isk *o*perating *s*ystem) program, which operates IBM personal computers. The new version, MS-DOS 5.0, enables programs that require a lot of memory to run faster. And instead of typing commands, the user selects commands from "menus."

A couple deflect swirling computer chips as they journey through a tunnel into the heart of a computer by means of a virtual reality video game from Vivid Effects, in Toronto, Canada. The game allows people to step into and interact with animated computer graphics. A video camera captures users' movements, and computer software creates images of them for display on a screen.

Computer Software
Continued

Interactive multimedia continued to receive a great deal of attention from the computer software industry in 1991. Multimedia products can combine text, sound, still images, motion pictures, and animation. By means of a computer, users can interact with the information, not only choosing to read about a topic but also selecting films or pictures of it, and—where appropriate—a spoken presentation or music. Multimedia products are generally distributed on compact discs (CD's), which are capable of storing enormous amounts of data.

One such interactive multimedia product is the Timeline of History, Science, and Invention, a CD released by Xiphias, Incorporated, a Los Angeles company, in April 1991. Users can identify a particular year or era on a timeline and see and hear information about the leading scientific discoveries and inventions in that period. Or, a specific invention or discovery can be selected, and the program guides the user to the correct time period. The CD, which sells for around $100, was made for use with CDTV, a new product from Commodore Business Machines International (see COMPUTER HARDWARE).

Many publishers in 1990 and 1991 viewed multimedia and CD-ROM (compact disc, read-only memory) as attractive formats for electronic magazines and books. Read-only memory contains data that cannot be altered or erased. In April 1991, Time Warner Incorporated of New York City brought out a CD-ROM version of *Time* magazine's coverage of the war in the Persian Gulf.

Planetary simulation. Educational software that offers an opportunity to manage the ecology of an entire planet was introduced in October 1990 by Maxis, Incorporated, of Orinda, Calif. SimEarth provides "tools" for altering environmental and geological conditions and for witnessing the likely effects of these changes on evolutionary processes over millions of years. SimEarth sells for $69.95 and is available for both Macintosh and IBM personal computers.   [Keith Ferrell]

Deaths
of Scientists

Notable scientists and engineers who died between June 1, 1990, and June 1, 1991, are listed below. Those listed were Americans unless otherwise indicated in the biographical sketch.

Anderson, Carl D. (1905-Jan. 11, 1991), physicist who discovered a subatomic particle called the *positron*. The positron has a mass equal to that of the negatively charged electron but carries a positive electrical charge. For his discovery, Anderson shared the 1936 Nobel Prize in physics with Austrian cosmic-ray researcher Victor F. Hess.

Bardeen, John (1908-Jan. 30, 1991), physicist who twice won the Nobel Prize in physics. He shared it in 1956 with Walter H. Brattain and William Shockley for the invention of the transistor, a tiny device used to control the flow of electric current. Bardeen shared the physics prize again in 1972, with Leon N. Cooper and John R. Schrieffer for their theory of *superconductivity*, the ability of some substances to conduct electricity without resistance at extremely low temperatures.

Baumgartner, Leona (1902-Jan. 15, 1991), immunologist and pediatrician who was New York City's commissioner of health from 1954 to 1962. She fought successfully to fluoridate the city's water supply.

Bernstein, Richard B. (1923-July 8, 1990), chemist who pioneered in *femtochemistry*, the study of ultrafast chemical processes that occur in fuel combustion, explosions, and other rapid events. Bernstein was awarded the National Medal of Science in 1989.

Castle, William B. (1897-Aug. 9, 1990), hematologist who discovered the cause of pernicious anemia, a previously fatal disease caused by the body's failure to utilize vitamin B_{12}.

Frank, Ilya M. (1908-June 22, 1990), Soviet physicist who shared the 1958 Nobel Prize in physics with Pavel A. Cherenkov and Igor Y. Tamm for discovering and interpreting the Cherenkov effect, a principle that enables scientists to detect high-energy particles and measure their velocity.

Friedman, Maurice H. (1903-March 8, 1991), physician and physiologist who developed the rabbit test to determine pregnancy in the 1930's.

Harker, David (1906-Feb. 27, 1991), biophysicist and crystallographer who led a group at the Roswell Park Memorial Institute in Buffalo, N.Y., that in 1967 determined the complex structure of the protein *ribonuclease*.

Head, Howard (1914-March 3, 1991), aircraft engineer who became a designer and manufacturer of sporting goods. He invented the lightweight aluminum ski and the oversized Prince tennis racket.

Hill, Sir Austin Bradford (1897-April 18, 1991), British epidemiologist who led one of the first research teams to establish a link between cigarette smoking and cancer, in 1952.

Hofstadter, Robert (1915-Nov. 17, 1990), physicist who won the Nobel Prize in physics in 1961 for research that led to the precise determination of the size and shape of the proton and neutron, the two types of particles that make up the nucleus of an atom.

Hunt, J. McVicker (1906-Jan. 9, 1991), psychologist whose book *Intelligence and Experience* (1961) showed how early experiences affected children's development. His research inspired the United States government's Project Head Start preschool program.

Hutchinson, George E. (1903-May 17, 1991), British-born zoologist considered one of the fathers of the science of ecology. Hutchinson was one of the first to warn of the effect of burning forests on global warming.

Johnson, Clarence L. (Kelly Johnson) (1910-Dec. 21, 1990), aeronautical engineer for Lockheed Corporation who helped develop more than 40 airplanes and spacecraft.

Klopsteg, Paul E. (1889-April 28, 1991), physicist and inventor who held more than 50 patents for scientific instruments and other devices and who helped organize the National Science Foundation.

Land, Edwin H. (1909-March 1, 1991), inventor of instant photography and founder of the Polaroid Corporation. Land held 537 patents, second only to Thomas Edison. One of Land's patents was for polarized light filters, which allow only light waves vibrating in one direction to pass through, eliminating glare and reflections.

Levinthal, Cyrus (1922-Nov. 4, 1990), biophysicist whose work in the 1960's directly linked genes with the proteins for which they *code* (provide genetic

Carl D. Anderson

John Bardeen

Leona Baumgartner

Deaths
of Scientists
Continued

Robert Hofstadter

Karl A. Menninger

B. F. Skinner

instructions), a major advance in molecular genetics.

Luria, Salvador E. (1912-Feb. 6, 1991), Italian-born biologist and physician who shared the 1969 Nobel Prize for physiology or medicine with Max Delbrück and Alfred D. Hershey for their discoveries about the reproduction and genetic structure of viruses.

Maguire, Bassett (1904-Feb. 6, 1991), botanist who led many expeditions to South America. He discovered Cerro de la Neblina (Mountain of the Clouds), an isolated, botanically rich mountain on the border of Brazil and Venezuela.

Masursky, Harold (1923-Aug. 24, 1990), astrogeologist who played a major role in planning missions of the *Explorer* and *Magellan* space probes.

Menninger, Karl A. (1893-July 18, 1990), psychiatrist who helped his father and brother found the Menninger Clinic in Topeka, Kans., one of the world's leading clinics devoted to treating emotional disorders.

Mitchell, J. Murray, Jr. (1928-Oct. 5, 1990), meteorologist who was one of the first scientists to warn of increasing evidence of global climate warming.

Noyce, Robert N. (1927-June 3, 1990), physicist who invented *integrated circuitry* (a system of putting an entire electronic circuit on a single chip). Noyce helped found Fairchild Semiconductor and Intel Corporation, two leading manufacturers of semiconductors, the electronic chips used in computers and telephones. He was awarded the National Medal of Science in 1979 and the National Medal of Technology in 1987.

Penney of East Hendred, Lord (William G. Penney) (1909-March 3, 1991), British mathematician and nuclear physicist who directed the development of Great Britain's first atomic bomb in 1952. He was made a life peer in 1967.

Perls, Laura (1905-July 13, 1990), German-born psychoanalyst who founded the Gestalt school of psychotherapy with her husband, psychiatrist Frederick S. (Fritz) Perls.

Piotrovsky, Boris B. (1908-Oct. 15, 1990), Soviet archaeologist who in 1939 discovered the Urartu civilization, which flourished from the 800's to the 500's B.C. in what is now Armenia.

Rose, Albert (1910-July 26, 1990), physicist whose work in converting optical images to electrical signals led to the development of the modern television picture tube. He also invented the *image orthicon*, a vacuum tube used in TV cameras from the 1940's to the mid-1960's.

Sears, Ernest R. (1910-Feb. 15, 1991), plant geneticist who transferred genetic material from wild grasses into cultivated wheat, breeding strains resistant to various diseases and insects.

Shorb, Mary S. (1907?-Aug. 18, 1990), microbiologist whose research led to the discovery in 1947 of vitamin B_{12}.

Skinner, B. F. (Burrhus Frederic Skinner) (1904-Aug. 18, 1990), psychologist best known for his research into the learning process. He invented the Skinner box, an apparatus used to demonstrate his theory that rewarded behavior is repeated.

Slichter, William P. (1922-Oct. 25, 1990), physical chemist whose research contributed to the development of semiconductors.

Smith, Lyman (1912-April 10, 1991), orthopedic surgeon who developed a number of new medical procedures, including use of the enzyme chymopapain to treat ruptured spinal disks without surgery.

Sperti, George S. (1900-April 29, 1991), biophysicist and inventor who developed the hemorrhoid treatment Preparation H. He also cofounded the basic science laboratory at the University of Cincinnati, where he taught from 1924 to 1987.

Spurr, Stephen H. (1918-June 20, 1990), forest ecologist who was a cofounder and former president of the Organization for Tropical Studies, a consortium of universities and scientific institutions offering research facilities and study programs in the tropics.

Weeks, Dorothy W. (1893-June 4, 1990), physicist who specialized in *spectroscopy*, the study of the bands of colors formed when radiant energy is broken up into individual wavelengths.

Wyeth, Nathaniel C. (1912?-July 4, 1990), engineer who invented the polyethylene terephthalate (PET) plastic soda bottle and some 25 other products and processes. His brother was painter Andrew Wyeth.　　　　[Sara Dreyfuss]

Dentistry

The possible dangers posed by mercury used in dental fillings prompted widespread concern and debate among dentists and the public alike in 1990 and 1991. A report released in August 1990 by dentist Murray Vimy and physiologist Fritz Lorscheider, both at the University of Calgary in Alberta, Canada, indicated that vapors from amalgam fillings containing mercury caused a dramatic decline in the kidney function of six sheep that were each given 12 fillings.

More than 100 million people in the United States have received dental amalgam fillings, which contain 50 per cent mercury and a 50 per cent mixture of silver, copper, tin, and zinc. Although mercury vapor is released from these fillings during chewing or tooth brushing, the American Dental Association (ADA) maintains that these releases are too small to produce any harmful effects. High levels of mercury can cause a wide range of symptoms and harm the kidneys, nervous system, and immune system.

Mercury amalgam fillings have been used widely for about 150 years and currently make up about 80 per cent of all fillings found in the U.S. population. Other fillings made of ceramic, plastic, or gold are not as widely used because they are less durable and more costly than amalgam.

As a result of the Canadian study and others, the U.S. Food and Drug Administration (FDA) requested a panel of dental professionals, patients, and researchers to investigate in March 1991 the possible risks associated with mercury fillings and to determine the need for further studies. Although the panel concluded that none of the research showed mercury amalgam to be a direct hazard to human health, they agreed that additional studies were needed to resolve questions about amalgam safety.

Patch may replace needles. A product that enables dentists to administer local anesthetics without using needles was introduced in November 1990. The new item—a waferlike, adhesive patch that delivers a numbing substance to the gums—gained approval

"Actually, I'm not the Tooth Fairy. I'm the Plaque Fairy—and I'm here to remind you to floss."

Dentistry
Continued

from the FDA to be tested on patients in early 1991.

According to the maker, Noven Pharmaceuticals, Inc., in Miami, Fla., when the patch is placed on the gums, it provides adequate anesthesia for such dental procedures as light drilling, cleaning, injections, and minor gum surgery. Several sizes will be offered for use with different types of dental work.

The ADA estimates that 10 million to 12 million people never visit a dentist, primarily because of fears about pain related to dental procedures. Another 35 million individuals put off dental appointments because of "dental anxiety." Presumably, much of this anxiety arises from a fear of needles and the pain associated with injections of local anesthesia.

Improving dental implants. A new method may create a bond that would give a dental implant the mobility and shock-absorbency of a natural tooth. Daniel Buser, an oral surgeon at the University of Berne in Switzerland and the Harvard School of Dental Medicine in Boston, reported this finding with his colleagues in November 1990.

Dental implants, which are typically a hollow cylinder made of titanium, have been used for about 30 years to replace missing teeth. The implants are traditionally fixed to the jawbone, making them rigid and liable to fracture.

In the experimental procedure, which was performed on monkeys, the oral surgeons left part of the original tooth root at the base of the tooth socket. They then placed the implant over the root. One year later, they checked the implants with a microscope and found that the type of surface that forms on a natural tooth root also developed on the implant. Ligaments from the gum tissue surrounding the implant had attached themselves to this surface and to the bone that forms the tooth socket. Because such ligaments attach natural teeth to their sockets, the surgeons concluded that this bonding method would improve the durability of implants. [T. Howard Howell]

In WORLD BOOK, see DENTISTRY.

Drugs

Medical researchers have learned that certain drugs that dissolve blood clots can reduce the severity of heart attacks if patients receive treatment within six hours of the attack. But opinions differ about which drug is the best. In 1990 and 1991, two studies compared the effectiveness of three clot-dissolving drugs—tissue plasminogen activator (TPA), streptokinase, and an altered form of streptokinase called APSAC. United States doctors typically prefer TPA, and European doctors generally use streptokinase. TPA therapy costs more than $2,700 for a single treatment, while streptokinase costs $200 for the same treatment. APSAC costs about $1,700.

Comparing clot-busters. In July 1990, Italian researchers reported the results of an international trial comparing streptokinase and TPA. This trial showed that the drugs appeared equally effective and had a similar number of side effects. The Italian researchers concluded that there was no difference in safety or effectiveness between the drugs.

In March 1991, the preliminary results of the *International Studies of Infarct Survival* were announced. About 46,000 patients in the United States and Europe were randomly chosen to receive one of the three clot-dissolving drugs. The head statistician for the study, Richard Peto of Oxford University in England, announced that the three drugs appeared to work equally well. The death rates were the same for each of the three groups of patients.

Physicians have also been concerned about the possibility of strokes caused by these drug treatments. Although many physicians believed TPA was the safest drug, the results from the internatonal study suggested that streptokinase may be safer. Only 0.3 per cent of the patients who received streptokinase suffered a stroke. Twice as many patients taking APSAC or TPA suffered strokes. Final analysis of the international trial was pending in mid-1991.

Reducing cholesterol. Three studies suggesting that lowering cholesterol in the bloodstream with drug treatment can lead to a reduction in the amount of cholesterol deposited in blood vessel walls were completed in 1990. Researchers from the University of California at Los Angeles reported in December 1990 their study of 103 men who had undergone surgery for *atherosclerosis* of the arteries to the heart. Atherosclerosis is a condition in which the arteries become narrowed by a build-up of fatty deposits, calcium, and scar tissue.

Half the men were advised to modify their diet to lower cholesterol levels and received no drugs. The other half did not modify their diet but received drugs to lower their cholesterol levels. After four years, 18 per cent of the patients given drugs had a decrease in the severity of their atherosclerosis, and 52 per cent had no change. Just 6 per cent of the patients who received only dietary counseling showed some improvement, and almost 80 per cent showed worsening of their disease. The authors concluded that drug therapy to lower cholesterol levels could stop or reverse the build-up of cholesterol-laden deposits.

Cardiologists at the University of California at San Francisco also reported in December 1990 a similar study of 72 patients with severely elevated cholesterol levels. Some patients were advised about modifying their diets to lower cholesterol levels, while others also received drug treatment. When the patients' coronary arteries were reevaluated after two years of treatment, there was improvement in the drug-treated patients but worsening in the patients treated only by dietary change.

A third study, published in November 1990 by cardiologist Greg Brown and colleagues at the University of Washington in Seattle also found that some atherosclerosis patients who received drug therapy had a partial reversal of their disease. In addition, the researchers presented evidence that the changes led to fewer heart attacks and fewer deaths.

Combating asthma. The number of asthma cases in the United States rose 39 per cent between 1980 and 1987, according to a July 1990 report by the Centers for Disease Control (CDC) in Atlanta, Ga. Asthma is a chronic respiratory disorder causing breathing difficulty, coughing, wheezing, and shortness of breath. Although asthma is only rarely fatal, the CDC noted that the number of deaths from this disease had also increased.

Researchers from McMaster University in Ontario, Canada, reported in October 1990 that a cortisone derivative called *budesonide* given as an inhaled spray produced an improvement in patients with mild asthma. Although physicians have long known that cortisonelike drugs such as budesonide can relieve asthma symptoms, only patients with severe cases received the drugs because cortisone and its derivatives can have serious side effects. Juniper reported that budesonide administered as a spray produced only mild side effects.

The effectiveness of a new class of asthma drugs called *leukotriene antagonists* was reported in December 1990. These drugs can stop the inflammation of lung airways during asthma attacks. Scientists from McMaster University studied 12 asthma patients who exercised vigorously to bring on an asthma attack. If the patients received a leukotriene antagonist before they exercised, the severity of their attack was reduced by almost two-thirds.

Another group of researchers at Beth Israel Hospital and Harvard Medical School, both in Boston, reported similar results. They induced asthma attacks in 13 patients and found that a leukotriene antagonist produced a 50 per cent reduction in the severity of the attacks.

Analgesic hazard. Women who regularly used *phenacetin*, a drug chemically related to acetaminophen, were more than 16 times more likely to die from diseases of the kidney or bladder than women who did not use the drug. This finding was reported in January 1991 by Swiss scientists who studied more than 1,200 women. The women who used phenacetin also had an increased likelihood of developing cancer, heart disease, and high blood pressure.

The study had closely monitored the women's health since 1968. Half of the women regularly used phenacetin; the other half did not. [B. Robert Meyer]

In the Special Reports section, see DRUG-BUG WARFARE. In WORLD BOOK, see DRUG.

Ecology

Much interest during 1990 and 1991 focused on the ecological consequences of the warming of Earth's atmosphere due to increases in what are known as greenhouse gases in the atmosphere. These gases, primarily carbon dioxide (CO_2), are increasing as a result of human activities, such as the burning of fossil fuels and the destruction of large tracts of tropical rain forests.

Greenhouse gases trap heat from the sun in Earth's atmosphere by a process known as the *greenhouse effect*. The greenhouse effect is beneficial because it makes the planet warm enough to support life. But scientists fear that recent droughts and worldwide temperature increases are the result of too much carbon dioxide and other greenhouse gases in the atmosphere. See METEOROLOGY.

CO_2 levels and plant growth. Botanists and researchers have much to learn about how ecosystems will respond to increases in CO_2, botanist Fakhri A. Bazzaz of Harvard University in Cambridge, Mass., reported in November 1990. Bazzaz compiled a summary of research on the subject that showed that different species of plants respond in different ways to changes in CO_2 levels in their environment. Changing CO_2 levels not only can affect *photosynthesis* (the process by which plants convert CO_2 and water to sugar), but also can affect plant respiration. During respiration, plants give off CO_2.

Bazzaz reported that photosynthesis at first increases when plants are exposed to higher than normal levels of CO_2 but that this effect may not be permanent in all species. Some species adjust to increased CO_2 levels with a decline in photosynthesis. The differences can occur among plant species within the same community, making it hard to predict overall changes in an ecosystem's growth, Bazzaz reported.

Predator-prey cycles. Findings that cast doubt on the previous understanding of predator-prey cycles were reported in August 1990 by Shahid Naeem, an ecologist at the University of Michigan in Ann Arbor. Traditionally, biologists believed that predator

ADAPTING TO THE ENVIRONMENT

Zebra mussel trouble
Populations of zebra mussels, *below,* in the Great Lakes were exploding in 1991. A worker at an electric power plant on Lake Erie uses high-pressure water to remove zebra mussels from the plant's water intake area, *right.* A diver in Lake Erie brings up freshwater clams, which are threatened by the tiny mussels' rapid population growth, *bottom.*

Ecology

Continued

populations increase or decrease in response to increases or decreases in the populations of their prey. For example, the Arctic hare and lynx go through 10-year population cycles in which the size of the lynx population (the predator) lags that of the hare population (the lynx's prey).

In the traditional view, an increase in the population of the hares should provide more food for the lynxes, who would then increase their numbers. Then, presumably, as the population of lynxes increases, they cause a decline in the hare population. With few hares left, the lynx population should decline, and the cycle should start again.

Naeem analyzed 25 groups of predators and their prey and came to the conclusion that only 6 groups followed the traditional cause-and-effect model. The other 19 groups did not affect each other's population changes, he determined. Naeem's work supports the idea that numbers of prey decline for reasons such as stress and aggression within their own population, and that predators influence their population growth less than previously thought.

How ecosystems change. In February 1991, Keith Van Cleve, head of the Division of Forest Services at the University of Alaska in Fairbanks, and four other scientists reported a study of Alaskan forests called *taiga*. Taiga are needleleaf evergreen forests found in subarctic regions of Alaska, Canada, and the Soviet Union. The scientists recorded the effect of ecological conditions, referred to as *state factors*, on the taiga. The five state factors are (1) the climate of a region, (2) the organisms living in the region, (3) the surface features or *topography* of a region, (4) the type of soil in a region, and (5) time.

Among the team's findings are that differences in topography have major effects on the Alaskan taiga. According to the study, time's effects are limited because fires occur regularly in the forest. When a fire destroys mature trees and other plants, the ecosystem returns to an earlier condition, when seedlings and young plants predominated.

Understanding how state factors affect ecosystems can help scientists better understand what causes change in ecosystems, Van Cleve believes. According to ecologists, studying the growth of the world's taiga is especially important because these vast forests contain 20 per cent of the Earth's carbon and produce large amounts of CO_2. Thus, environmental factors that may alter the development of the taiga may affect the global environment.

Zebra mussels. In December 1990, ecologists and marine biologists gathered in Columbus, Ohio, to share research on the zebra mussel and discuss possible solutions to problems caused by the creature's growing population in the Great Lakes. The zebra mussel is a small, freshwater mollusk that resembles a clam. Native to the Caspian Sea region of the Soviet Union and to western Europe, zebra mussels first appeared in the Great Lakes in the mid-1980's. Scientists believe a European cargo ship had released some of the organisms into the lakes.

Because zebra mussels have no known predators in the Great Lakes, their population has grown so much that they are damaging water treatment and industrial plants in some areas by blocking intake pipes. Large numbers of zebra mussels also harm marine life by removing nutrients from the water, according to ecologists.

Although some scientists fear the zebra mussel will continue to spread, others disagree. William P. Kovalak, a biologist with the Detroit Edison Electric Company of Detroit, Mich., who participated in a study on the zebra mussels, reported in December that the zebra mussel population decreased in western Lake Erie in 1990. It is uncertain whether this trend will continue, however, he said.

At the Columbus conference, Susan W. Fisher, an entomologist at The Ohio State University in Columbus, reported that potassium, if used in the proper amounts, will kill the zebra mussel but not harm other aquatic life. Potassium is most commonly found in salts such as potassium chloride. Researchers in late 1990 were studying ways of applying potassium to zebra mussels. These include piping potassium-salt solutions into infested areas or painting a potassium-based paint on affected surfaces.[Robert H. Tamarin]

In WORLD BOOK, see ECOLOGY.

Electronics

The consumer electronics market was in transition during 1990 and 1991. The growth in sales of home entertainment equipment continued to slow in the United States, while no popular new products took up the slack.

VCR programmer. In late 1990, Gemstar Development Corporation of Pasadena, Calif., introduced VCR Plus, a remote control device that instantly programs videocassette recorders (VCR's). Although more than 70 per cent of U.S. households have a VCR, many people still have difficulty programming their machines to record television shows. To simplify the process, Gemstar assigned a number code to each television program and encouraged leading U.S. newspapers to publish the codes along with their television listings—which they began to do in 1990. To record a specific program, a viewer enters the code into VCR Plus by pressing the numbers on a keypad. The code instructs VCR Plus to program the VCR for the time and channel of the broadcast. The new programmer sells for about $60.

Digital compact cassettes. A tape product that could have a very bright future, the digital compact cassette (DCC), was announced in January 1991 by N. V. Philips, the giant electronics firm headquartered in the Netherlands. Like the compact disc (CD) and digital audiotape (DAT), the DCC stores sounds as a numerical code. These recordings reproduce sound more precisely than analog records or tapes, which store sound in the form of a wave pattern. DCC and DAT players, unlike CD players, can record as well as play music.

DCC approaches digital recording technology in an interesting way. Philips engineers studied the human ear and decided it was unnecessary to record sounds that people cannot actually hear. DAT, on the other hand, holds tones that are too similar for the human ear to distinguish. Although DCC contains less information than DAT—making the tapes easier to manufacture and duplicate—the apparent sound quality remains the same.

The audio industry has been looking

New Electronic Products

A handheld device introduced by Gemstar in 1990, *right* (atop the videocassette recorder), enables viewers to tape programs simply by entering a code number printed in TV listings. A Kodak system that stores photos on compact discs for viewing on a computer screen, *below right,* was scheduled for release in early 1992.

Electronics

Continued

for a device that allows consumers to record music digitally ever since the CD was introduced in 1983. DAT machines were once thought to be the sought-after product. But DAT encountered problems on its way to market.

DAT was developed primarily by the Sony Corporation and other Japanese manufacturers, and machines were not shipped to the United States until 1990 because of problems over music copyrights. The copyright holders feared that consumers would make illegal recordings without paying royalties. The issue still has not been resolved, even though the machines sold in the United States can make only a single copy from an original DAT or CD.

During the long wait for DAT, enthusiasm for it waned, and many observers expect the rival DCC format to become the consumer favorite. DCC players, unlike DAT players, will also play standard analog tapes. Moreover, DCC tapes and players should cost less than their DAT counterparts. DAT machines cost about $800 in early 1991, while DCC players were expected to sell for around $600 in 1992, when they should reach the market.

Finally, Philips owns its own record company, the London-based Polygram, and believes it can resolve the copyright issue. Several other recording companies reportedly support DCC because DCC machines play analog tapes, a lucrative part of their business.

Photo CD's. Another intriguing new product scheduled to reach the market in 1992 is a photo CD system announced by the Eastman Kodak Company of Rochester, N.Y., in autumn 1990. With this system, consumers can digitally store their 35-millimeter photographs on a compact disc and display them on a computer screen or TV set. Viewing requires a special player, which will also play standard CD's. Kodak will transfer a customer's roll of exposed film to CD and send back a disc along with prints. Kodak expects the cost of storing a roll of film on CD to be under $20, while the players are expected to cost less than $500.　　[Elliot King]

In WORLD BOOK, see ELECTRONICS; TAPE RECORDER; VIDEO CAMERA.

Energy

In November 1990, 36 solar-powered cars from around the world participated in the 1990 World Solar Challenge Race in Australia. A car made at the Engineering University of Biel, Switzerland, won the 3,000-kilometer (1,870-mile) race with an average speed of 65.5 kilometers (40.7 miles) per hour. Arriving 24 hours later, a car made by Japan's Honda Motor Company finished second with an average speed of 55 kilometers (34.2 miles) per hour. *Sunrunner*, a solar-powered racer made at the University of Michigan in Ann Arbor, finished third with an average speed of 52.8 kilometers (32.8 miles) per hour.

The Biel car used highly efficient solar collectors in which the electrical contacts are below the solar cells' surface. Usually, the contacts are placed on top of the cells. The contacts carry the electricity formed from the sunlight captured by the collectors. By placing the electrical contacts below the collectors' surface, greater area is available for the collection of sunlight. The Biel team also achieved greater efficiency by arranging the surfaces of the solar collectors in pyramid shapes to reduce losses of sunlight due to reflections that result from a flat cell surface.

The University of Michigan's *Sunrunner* had won the General Motors Corporation's Sunrayce USA in July 1990. Thirty-two university teams from the United States and Canada competed in the 2,615-kilometer (1,625-mile) race from Lake Buena Vista, Fla., to Warren, Mich.

A solar-powered plane called the *Sun Seeker* flew from Desert Center, Calif., to Spot, N.C., between Aug. 4 and Sept. 3, 1990. The plane used 700 silicon solar cells attached to a flexible plastic that allowed them to be fitted to the curved surface of the wings. The solar cells supplied electricity to batteries, which operated a propeller to get the plane off the ground. For most of the flight, the *Sun Seeker* rode air currents like a glider and did not use the propeller.

Eric Raymond, a professional hang glider from Lake Elsinore, Calif., designed and built *Sun Seeker* with mate-

A cleanup worker stands inside the Chernobyl nuclear power plant in the Soviet Union in 1991, five years after a 1986 accident destroyed one of the plant's reactors. Scientists reported that radiation levels are still dangerously high at the plant.

Energy

Continued

rial donated by Sanyo Electric Company, a Japanese firm. Raymond wanted to end the flight at Kitty Hawk, N.C., the site of history's first airplane flight in 1903, but bad weather forced him to end the flight in nearby Spot.

Solar energy storage. A way to store solar energy in the soil of areas with dry, warm climates to be used months later for heating water or buildings was announced in November 1990 by researchers at Lawrence Berkeley Laboratory in Berkeley, Calif. The researchers designed and built their new solar heating system with Israeli scientists in the Negev desert in Israel. There, the researchers used a solar collector during the summer to heat water to about 70 °C (150 °F). They pumped the water underground through tubing arranged in a *helix* (spiral) shape.

It took several months for the ground around the helix to heat to about 65 °C (149 °F). Then, as the weather cooled, cold water was passed through the helix to be heated by the warmth gradually collected in the ground. The warmed water could then

be piped into a building to be used for heating, according to Christine Doughty, staff scientist at Lawrence Berkeley Laboratory.

Oil recovery. A new method of flooding abandoned oil wells with special chemicals called *lignins* could cheaply recover as much as 150 billion barrels of oil in the United States. Douglas G. Naae, a research scientist with Texaco Incorporated's Exploration and Production Division in Houston, made this announcement in August 1990. The amount of oil that could be recovered is roughly equal to 50 years of the nation's annual oil production, according to the Department of Energy (DOE).

With traditional drilling methods, only about 33 per cent of the oil in an oil field can be collected. Flooding the well with water can remove additional oil, but this still leaves as much as half of the original volume of oil in the ground. Additional oil can be extracted by flooding the well with chemicals called *surfactants*, which act in a manner similar to detergents to loosen oil from rock and soil so that it can be flushed

Energy

Continued

out with water. Surfactants are expensive and hard to obtain, however, which has limited their use, according to Naae. Because current extraction methods cannot remove all the oil in deposits, about 300 billion barrels of oil remain in old oil wells in the United States, said Naae.

Lignins are found in the wood of trees. They can be used to flush out oil in a manner similar to surfactants, but lignins are cheaper and more plentiful. In the United States, according to Naae, paper and pulp mills produce approximately 18 billion kilograms (40 billion pounds) of lignins each year as a by-product.

The United States currently uses about 16 million barrels of oil per day, according to the DOE. Approximately 55 per cent of that is produced in the United States. At the current rate of usage, the DOE estimates that the supply of oil found in the United States will last only about eight or nine years. Better oil recovery methods would make that supply last longer, Naae reported.

Nuclear waste disposal. On Nov. 27, 1990, the Department of Energy dedicated the $1.3-billion center, called the Defense Waste Processing Facility (DWPF), at the Savannah River site, a production plant for nuclear weapons near Aiken, S.C. The processing facility can reportedly convert highly radioactive waste from nuclear bomb and energy production into a form of glass for safe and permanent disposal.

Workers will mix the highly radioactive waste with fine particles of glass. The glass and waste mixture will then be heated to approximately 2100 °F (1149 °C), which will melt the glass. The melted glass will then be poured into stainless steel canisters, which will be welded shut.

Safety of an "electric" road. A possible solution to a potential health problem from powerful electromagnetic fields generated during the operation of a test road for electric cars was devised in early 1991 by researchers at the Southern California Edison Company in Rosemead, Calif., and the Los Angeles Department of Water and Power. The test road is designed to transfer electric power to specially modified, battery-powered vehicles. If

The world's first offshore windmill for electric power generation was installed off Sweden. A Swedish power company announced in early 1991 that it will test the windmill for five years and may add as many as 97 more windmills.

Energy

Continued

successful, the technology could greatly increase the range of electric vehicles by charging their batteries as they pass over the road.

The test road works by conducting electricity through a metal cable buried in the roadbed. The cable creates an electromagnetic field at the surface of the road, which a metal plate on the bottom of the vehicle converts to electric current.

According to a researcher with the Los Angeles Department of Water and Power, some scientific studies have suggested that strong electromagnetic fields such as those that would be created in the powered roadway could be implicated in the development of cancer.

Researchers at the utilities developed a method in January and February 1991 to reduce the electromagnetic field around the cable by reducing the current through the cable. To compensate for the reduced current, they lowered the plate on the bottom of the car.

Methanol power. General Motors received permission in October 1990 from the U.S. Environmental Protection Agency to start manufacturing a methanol-powered model of the Chevrolet Lumina. Methanol is a type of alcohol that can be made from corn or by heating carbon monoxide and hydrogen under pressure in the presence of a catalyst (a substance that causes or speeds up a chemical reaction but remains unchanged).

Methanol produces fewer pollutants such as hydrocarbons and nitrogen oxides when burned than does gasoline. Because the energy content of methanol is approximately half that of gasoline, a methanol-powered car can travel only half as far on a tank of fuel as a gasoline-powered car can, however. General Motors plans to begin selling the methanol car in California in the early 1990's. The first methanol cars will be *flexible fuel vehicles* designed to run on either methanol or gasoline. [Marian Visich, Jr.]

In the Special Reports section, see THE NEW NUCLEAR REACTORS. In WORLD BOOK, see ENERGY SUPPLY; SOLAR ENERGY.

Environment

United States President George Bush in November 1990 signed the 1990 Clean Air Act, the most far-reaching environmental legislation in the United States since the 1970's. The new legislation will help reduce the amount of smog, *acid rain* (rain containing sulfuric acid and nitric acid resulting from air pollution), and levels of airborne toxic chemicals. It calls for the reduction of air pollutants from many sources, including automobiles, electric power plants, and factories.

The Clean Air Act requires automobile manufacturers to reduce emissions of smog-producing hydrocarbons and nitrogen oxides by about one-third, beginning with 1994 models. It also calls for 96 urban areas—currently in violation—to meet federal standards for ozone and carbon monoxide levels. Factories releasing any of 189 toxic chemicals into the air will have to cut those emissions by 90 per cent.

To reduce acid rain, hundreds of coal-burning electric power plants must cut emissions of sulfur dioxide by 9.1 million metric tons (10 million short tons) by the year 2000 and emissions of nitrogen oxides by 1.8 million metric tons (2 million short tons) by 2001. Drivers must also use cleaner-burning automotive fuels in the most polluted U.S. cities beginning in 1995. The Environmental Protection Agency (EPA) projects the new act will cost the nation about $22 billion per year when its provisions are fully carried out.

National Energy Strategy. The Bush Administration also released the National Energy Strategy in February 1991. The strategy is a broad guideline for the use and production of energy in the United States through the year 2010. It recommends sweeping measures to increase energy efficiency in the transportation industry, as well as in homes and businesses.

One of the benefits of energy efficiency is less air pollution. For example, electric power plants that burn coal produce great amounts of air pollution, and measures that reduce the need for electricity production will also reduce much of the pollution these plants emit.

Ozone Hole

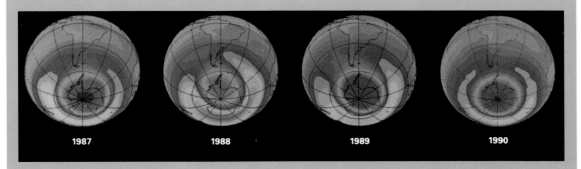

| 1987 | 1988 | 1989 | 1990 |

Measurements of ozone levels in the upper atmosphere above Antarctica show that in 1990, ozone concentrations dropped to the recorded lows of 1987 and 1989 for the second year in a row. (Heavier concentrations are represented by yellow and red and lighter by blue and violet.) Scientists believe chlorofluoro- carbons (CFC's), chemicals used widely in refrigeration and in- dustrial cleaning, destroy ozone in the upper atmosphere. This is of concern because the ozone layer protects life on Earth from the sun's damaging ultraviolet radiation.

Environment

Continued

Curbing carbon dioxide. Delegates from more than 100 nations met near Washington, D.C., in February 1991 to take up the task of crafting a treaty to curb emissions of carbon dioxide into the atmosphere. Carbon dioxide is one of the so-called "greenhouse gases" that trap heat and make Earth's surface warm enough to support life. Human activities, however, such as burning fossil fuels in cars, factories, and power plants, send excess amounts of carbon dioxide into the atmosphere. Some scientists fear that if the amount of carbon dioxide and other greenhouse gases in the atmosphere continues to increase, the global average tempera- ture may rise. This could produce widespread ecological problems, such as coastal flooding and a shift in crop- growing regions to areas farther north.

The United Nations General Assem- bly had asked the delegates to produce an agreement on principles in time for a June 1992 conference on the world environment. The talks, however, yielded only a decision on how to organize future climate negotiations.

Record temperature? Using ther- mometer measurements of tempera- tures on Earth's surface, U.S. and Brit- ish scientists from three agencies determined that the global average temperature in 1990 was 15.4 °C (59.8 °F). This was 0.05 Celsius degrees (0.09 Fahrenheit degrees) above the previ- ous record temperature set in 1988. The U.S. agencies conducting the meas- urements were the National Aeronau- tics and Space Administration (NASA) and the National Oceanic and Atmos- pheric Administration along with the British Meteorological Office.

The scientists were quick to caution that the high-temperature mark did not prove that human activities, such as burning fossil fuels, had set off a pattern of global warming. In fact, a separate NASA study based on satellite temperature recordings in Earth's lower atmosphere rated 1990 only the fourth-warmest year since 1979.

Antarctic ozone depletion. In Octo- ber 1990, scientists at NASA's Goddard Space Flight Center in Greenbelt, Md., found that ozone levels in the atmo-

Nature Loses in the Persian Gulf War

After the United States and 27 allied nations declared war on Iraq in January 1991, Iraqi President Saddam Hussein's troops were quickly ousted from Kuwait, the tiny oil-rich country they had invaded several months earlier. But the Iraqi military left in its wake a series of environmental horrors. Some scientists called the environmental damage disastrous, but widespread devastation throughout the war zone prevented scientists from immediately making an accurate assessment of the losses.

The first assault on the Persian Gulf environment occurred on or about Jan. 20, 1991, when Iraqi troops unleashed into the gulf a huge flow of oil from five supertankers docked at a Kuwaiti port. Iraqis also cut an underwater pipeline carrying oil from mainland storage tanks.

Estimates of the size of the spills varied widely, but a U.S. government report in April calculated that about 636 million liters (168 million gallons) of Kuwaiti oil had been released into the Persian Gulf. As of mid-May, another 477,000 liters (126,000 gallons) of oil was flowing daily into the gulf from damaged oil facilities. Based on these estimates, the spill was the largest in history.

Environmental consultant and expert on oil pollution Richard Golob reported to the U.S. Senate's Gulf Pollution Task Force on April 11 that oil continued to ravage the coastline of Kuwait and neighboring Saudi Arabia. He said the spill had killed marine mammals called *dugongs* and an estimated 20,000 to 40,000 birds. The gulf's fisheries also faced serious risks, he noted, because oil had damaged mangrove swamps, coral reefs, and other areas where many fish spawn.

In addition to releasing oil into the gulf, Iraqi troops set out to destroy Kuwait's oil production and storage areas. Another Senate task force witness testified that Iraqis had blown up or mined all of Kuwait's 1,000 oil wells. About 600 wells were still on fire, the witness reported in April, and another 80 were spewing oil. A lack of equipment initially hindered the progress of fire fighters. But imported gear and concentrated manpower had vanquished fires at 100 wells by mid-May. Fire fighters then predicted that they could put out at least half of the remaining 500 fires by summer's end and extinguish the others within a year.

Oil-thickened waters blacken shores in the Persian Gulf after Iraqi soldiers unleashed several million barrels of oil from Kuwaiti tankers, pipelines, and wells in January 1991.

Smoke billows from Kuwaiti oil wells set ablaze by Iraqi troops. Rising soot from an estimated 600 wells caused respiratory problems among many Kuwaitis and darkened skies more than 1,000 miles away.

Most scientists believe that the burning oil wells pose the most pressing threat to the environment and population. Perhaps burning up to 795 million liters (210 million gallons) of oil per day, these fires discharge dense clouds of black soot into the atmosphere and darken skies over regions as far as 1,600 kilometers (1,000 miles) away.

The Worldwatch Institute, an environmental organization in Washington, D.C., issued a report on March 1 describing the air pollution's effects. According to the report, the sooty air was causing respiratory problems among people in Kuwait and in people living as far as 320 kilometers (25 miles) away.

On April 3, the U.S. government dispatched to the Persian Gulf an investigative team from U.S. environmental, health, and military agencies. The group confirmed that the oil fires could worsen medical conditions such as asthma and lung disease. It added that the air pollution did not seem to present an immediate, life-threatening problem for healthy individuals, but that based on weather conditions the situation could change.

Some scientists were also concerned about the risk the pollution posed to the global climate. They worried that if the rising soot blocked too much sunlight over large regions, temperatures could decline, slowing crop growth and altering weather on a vast scale. But other analysts determined that smoke from the fires, though covering some 42,000 square kilometers (26,000 square miles), was not rising high enough to cause such widespread changes.

Many of the war's lingering environmental effects may have little to do with oil spills or fires. Worldwatch spokesmen noted that "the presence of more than 1 million soldiers with their immense arsenals has also placed severe strains on the already fragile desert ecology by compacting soil and destroying rare plants." Desert recovery from the invasion may take hundreds of years, they added.

Exhaust from more than 100,000 flights of allied jet fighters and bombers may also have added to the pollution. Unexploded mines, bombs, and missiles that litter Kuwait and Iraq could pose yet another threat to people and to the desert ecology.

Partly because of these scattered munitions, cleanup efforts in the gulf had progressed slowly by mid-1991. One report noted that less than 400 people were working to clear the oil spills, contrasted with some 40,000 workers on the 1989 *Exxon Valdez* spill in Alaska. And experts say that progress is further hampered because Middle Eastern environmental organizations lack the experience necessary to tackle many of these problems effectively.   [Janet Raloff]

Environment

Continued

sphere over Antarctica were the lowest since the previous record year, 1987. A layer of ozone-depleted air in Earth's *stratosphere* (upper atmosphere) has been detectable by satellite and instrument readings on the ground since the early 1980's. It usually appears over Antarctica in September, then changes shape and widens before breaking up two or three months later. But the 1990 depletion also lasted several weeks longer than previous occurrences. Because ozone filters out much of the sun's hazardous ultraviolet light, many scientists worry that if ozone depletion becomes substantial in the atmosphere above more populated regions, this could lead to a significant increase in the incidence of skin cancers. See also METEOROLOGY.

Scientists agree that increasing concentrations of chlorine and bromine in the stratosphere cause the breakdown of atmospheric ozone. Chlorine is found in *chlorofluorocarbons* (CFC's), gases most widely used in refrigeration and air-conditioning systems. Bromine is found in *halons* (chemicals used to extinguish fires). Most industrial nations have agreed to stop producing CFC's by the year 2000.

Oil spill cleanup. Spraying oiled-fouled beaches with high-pressure hot water to remove oil may do more harm than an oil spill itself, according to an April 1991 report. This was the conclusion of scientists from the National Oceanic and Atmospheric Administration who helped in the cleanup of the 1989 *Exxon Valdez* oil spill in Alaska's Prince William Sound. The scientists reported that the hot pressurized water used to clear beaches of oil damaged tidal pool marine life such as shellfish and sea grasses. It may have been best, the scientists said, to let the area recover naturally.

Electromagnetic controversy. Data reported in 1990 and 1991 concerning the possible health risks of electromagnetic "pollution" were far from clear. Electric and magnetic fields occur wherever there is electric power. For example, there are electromagnetic fields surrounding electric appliances when they are turned on.

Electromagnetic fields may be the cause of some cancers in humans, EPA scientists reported in December 1990,

though a final report was not due until late 1991. In February 1991, physician John Peters and his associates at the University of Southern California in Los Angeles reported that living close to electric transmission wires doubled the risk of childhood *leukemia*, a cancer of the blood.

But researchers at the National Institute of Occupational Safety and Health in Cincinnati concluded after a six-year study of telephone operators that use of video display terminals did not increase the risk of miscarriage. The researchers reported their results in March 1991. Female employees in some companies had attributed miscarriages that they suffered to harm from the electromagnetic field surrounding computer displays.

Sniffing out dirty cars. A special remote sensor can automatically determine whether car emissions of carbon monoxide are above government limits. Chemist Donald Stedman of the University of Denver invented the device. He tested the sensor in Denver and in England and reported his results in December 1990.

The device sends a beam of infrared radiation across a roadway, where a photovoltaic sensor converts it to a voltage reading. When a car passes, part of the infrared beam is absorbed by the carbon monoxide in the car's exhaust. This creates a drop in the voltage reading at the sensor. If the voltage drop is too large, the device then takes a picture of the offending car's license plate. The remote carbon monoxide "sniffer" could help cities meet new federal Clean Air Act emission standards.

Combating lead poisoning. An attack on lead contamination was launched in February 1991 by the heads of the EPA, Department of Health and Human Services, and the Department of Housing and Urban Development. The toxic heavy metal is found in older house paint, polluted urban soils, and sometimes in air, water, and food. The federal lead cleanup plan calls for reducing exposure to lead and for widespread screening of children under 6 years old for unsafe levels of lead in the blood.   [Robert Engelman]

In WORLD BOOK, see ENVIRONMENT; ENVIRONMENTAL POLLUTION.

Genetics

After years of preparation, the first human trial of *gene therapy*—giving a person new genes to correct a genetic defect or treat a disease—was begun in September 1990 at the National Institutes of Health in Bethesda, Md. The patient was a 4-year-old girl with a rare disease of the immune system. The NIH scientists in January 1991 began a second series of gene therapy tests, to treat advanced melanoma, a deadly form of skin cancer. See MEDICAL RESEARCH (Close-Up).

Genetically caused retardation. The discovery of a gene that causes the most common type of inherited mental retardation was announced in May 1991 by a team of researchers in the United States and the Netherlands. The identification of the gene is expected to lead to a prenatal test for the genetic defect. The scientists said it may eventually also be possible to treat individuals who inherit the defect to prevent their becoming retarded.

The gene underlies a condition called *fragile X syndrome,* so named because it is often associated with a break in the *X chromosome.* Chromosomes are tiny structures in the cell nucleus that carry the genes. The X chromosome is one of two chromosomes that determine a person's sex. Females have two X chromosomes in each cell; males have one X chromosome and one Y chromosome. Fragile X syndrome affects about 1 male in 1,500 and 1 female in 2,500, but the genetic defect causing it is more common than that. For reasons that have yet to be established, not everyone who carries the abnormal gene suffers from the syndrome.

The researchers—at Emory University in Atlanta, the Baylor College of Medicine in Houston, and the University of Rotterdam in the Netherlands—found the gene very close to the point on the X chromosome where the break always occurs. The gene is a faulty version of a normal gene that apparently is important in the development of the brain.

The investigators said that although they do not yet know the exact function of the gene, they have analyzed the

DNA magnified to reveal its atomic structure is the closest look ever at the molecule genes are made of. The image, showing DNA's double-helix structure, was made by researchers at the California Institute of Technology in Pasadena with a scanning tunneling microscope. The instrument probes the contours of a specimen with a stream of electrons emitted from an ultrafine needle.

protein that the gene codes for and found it to be very unusual. One segment of the protein contains 30 consecutive molecules of an *amino acid* called arginine. Amino acids, of which there are about 20 kinds, are the building blocks of proteins. The scientists said molecular biologists know of no other protein containing such a long string of that amino acid.

Now that the gene responsible for the syndrome has been located, researchers hope to learn how an abnormal version of the gene can disrupt brain development and what other effects it might have besides retardation. Neuroscientists suspect that fragile X may lie behind some other mental disorders such as autism, hyperactivity, and learning disabilities.

"Elephant man" gene found. The identification of the gene responsible for *neurofibromatosis* (NF), a potentially serious and often disfiguring disorder of the nervous system, was announced in July 1990 by researchers at the University of Michigan in Ann Arbor and the University of Utah in Salt Lake City. NF is also called the *elephant man's disease*. It gets this name from Joseph Merrick, an Englishman of the 1800's who was known as "the elephant man" because he was disfigured by huge benign tumors. Doctors now think, however, that Merrick was suffering not from NF but from a similar disorder called *Proteus syndrome*.

Affecting more than 100,000 people in the United States, NF is the most common genetically caused disorder of the nervous system. NF can cause a variety of symptoms, including large noncancerous tumors, learning disorders, and other problems with the nervous system.

Geneticists learned in the 1980's which chromosome held the defective gene. Chromosomes are tiny structures located in the cell nucleus that carry the genes. Most human cells have 46 chromosomes, arranged in 23 pairs. In 1987, scientists concluded that the NF gene was somewhere on chromosome number 17, and subsequent research narrowed the location to a particular portion of that chromosome. The race was then on to find the gene itself and to identify the *mutations* (changes) in it that are responsible for the disease.

The Michigan and Utah research groups both used the same strategy to locate the NF gene. Genes are sections of a complex molecule called *DNA* (deoxyribonucleic acid). The scientists extracted the DNA from the cells of healthy individuals and from those of NF sufferers. They compared the two groups' DNA from the region of chromosome 17 known to contain the gene, looking for mutations that would help them pinpoint the defective gene. Both of the two research groups were able to find the NF gene in this way, though each group discovered different mutations.

The NF gene turned out to be different from many other human genes. It is much bigger than most genes, and it contains three other, smaller genes.

In August 1990, the Utah and Michigan researchers announced that they had determined that the protein produced by the NF gene normally plays a role in preventing tumors. When the protein is faulty—the result of a mutated NF gene—abnormal cell growth results. But the scientists do not yet know why the effects of NF differ so widely among individuals.

Now that the NF gene has been identified, it should be possible to diagnose NF by analyzing a person's DNA. Also, as researchers learn more about the NF protein, they may be able to devise ways of counteracting its harmful effects on the body.

Genetic defect in cancer syndrome. The discovery of a rare abnormal gene that makes carriers of the gene highly susceptible to some forms of cancer was reported in November 1990 by scientists at the Massachusetts General Hospital Cancer Center in Boston. The genetic defect is responsible for a disorder known as *Li-Fraumeni syndrome*, which afflicts about 100 families around the world. Members of those families often develop cancer before age 30.

To track down the abnormal gene, the Boston researchers examined DNA from the cells of people in families with Li-Fraumeni syndrome. The scientists were especially interested in the DNA from a class of genes called *tumor suppressor genes*. In their normal state, these genes prevent cells from becoming cancerous. When tumor suppressor

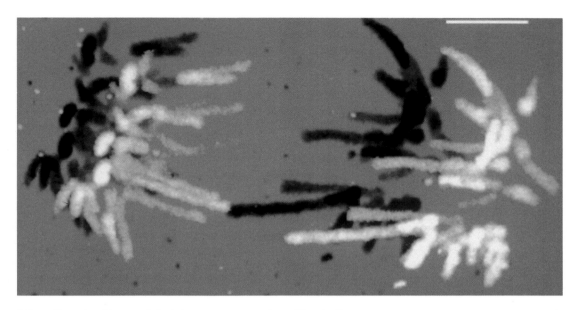

A three-dimensional image of plant chromosomes—carriers of the plant's genes—was made by British scientists using a new technique called *confocal laser scanning microscopy*. The researchers use a laser to make images of "slices" of the chromosomes, and a computer converts the data into the 3-D picture, which can be rotated and viewed from any angle.

Genetics

Continued

genes contain a defect, however, they are unable to carry out that function, and cancer may develop.

The investigators struck pay dirt when they looked at the DNA of a tumor suppressor gene known as *p53*. They found that in family members who had cancer, the gene always contained a particular mutation. Researchers hope that the discovery of the p53 defect will eventually lead to an improved understanding of how cancer develops.

Better way to cut chromosomes. A new method for cutting whole chromosomes into precise segments was reported in July 1990 by geneticists at the University of Wisconsin in Madison. The discovery will make it possible for researchers to cut chromosomes into a more manageable number of pieces than was previously possible.

Since the 1970's, geneticists have used various types of "chemical scissors," called *restriction enzymes*, to cut a DNA molecule apart. These enzymes make a cut wherever a certain sequence of molecular subunits called *bases* oc-

curs. Different restriction enzymes cut different sequences. One big problem, however, is that a particular sequence may occur more than 1,000 times in a chromosome. Thus, with the use of just one enzyme, the DNA in a chromosome may be cut into hundreds or even thousands of pieces. That can be an unwieldy assortment for many kinds of genetic research.

In the system devised by the Wisconsin scientists, a chromosome can be cut in as few places as desired—even at just a single spot. The researchers demonstrated this with yeast DNA. First, they inserted into a yeast chromosome a segment of bacterial DNA that contained a cutting site for a particular restriction enzyme. Using genetic engineering techniques, the scientists were able to insert the DNA segment exactly where they wished to make a single cut. They then added a bacterial protein called a *repressor*, which covered up the bacterial DNA segment containing the cutting site, thereby making it inaccessible to restriction enzymes.

Next, the researchers added a pro-

291

Turning One Gene into a Billion

Did Abraham Lincoln have Marfan syndrome? Lincoln's tall, gangly appearance has led physicians to suggest that he did indeed suffer from this genetic disorder, which causes the bones of the arms and legs to grow abnormally long. In most cases, the major artery leading from the heart is also abnormal and is likely to rupture. So even if Lincoln hadn't been shot by John Wilkes Booth, he might have died soon.

For years, the possibility that Lincoln was a Marfan victim was an interesting but unprovable theory. Now, however, geneticists have a remarkable tool called the *polymerase chain reaction* (PCR) that may enable them to settle the issue. But more importantly, PCR is a major new tool for researchers in molecular biology.

PCR enables investigators to make multiple copies of a gene. This can be valuable for confirming the presence of a particular gene in a mass of genetic material or for providing researchers with large numbers of a gene they wish to study.

The procedure has many applications. Not only can it be used to diagnose genetic diseases—even in a person long dead—but it is also valuable for analyzing small bits of blood or tissue left at crime scenes, for studying the genes of animals preserved in museums or in Arctic ice, and for many other kinds of genetic research. PCR will probably play a major role in a project now underway to map and decipher all the genetic material in a human cell.

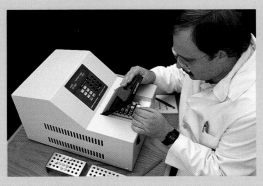

A researcher loads vials of DNA into a machine that automatically makes millions or even billions of copies of individual genes.

The proposed project to analyze Lincoln's genes shows the power of PCR. The National Museum of Health and Medicine in Washington, D.C., has in its possession fragments of Lincoln's skull, some strands of his hair, and pieces of his bloodstained shirt. Geneticists think that if the genetic material in those specimens is reasonably well preserved, PCR should make it possible to zero in on the suspected abnormal gene. A panel of scientists studying the ethical implications of the project gave its approval in May 1991, but the work is not expected to begin until mid-1992.

The creation of limitless copies of single genes was unheard-of before 1983, when the idea occurred to Kary B. Mullis, a chemist at the Cetus Corporation, a biotechnology company in Emeryville, Calif. Mullis realized in a flash of inspiration that it should be possible—fairly simple, in fact—to make a genetic "Xerox machine." The result of that revelation was the polymerase chain reaction.

To understand how PCR works, it is necessary to know how genes are constructed. Every gene is part of a long, complex molecule called *DNA* (deoxyribonucleic acid). DNA is composed of just four building blocks, called *nucleotides*, each of which contains a subunit known as a *base*. There are also four kinds of bases: *adenine* (A), *thymine* (T), *cytosine* (C), and *guanine* (G).

A molecule of DNA consists of two strands of nucleotides wrapped around each other to form a structure much like a twisted ladder. Each rung of the ladder is composed of two linked bases that are *complementary* to each other. That is, a certain kind of base always joins with only one other kind of base to form a complete rung: A always mates with T, and C with G.

When DNA *replicates* (reproduces), as it does whenever a cell divides, the two halves of the molecule split apart lengthwise like a zipper unzipping. Then, additional nucleotides manufactured by the cell attach to each single strand. Replication results in two complete double-stranded molecules, both of them identical to the original molecule.

The process of DNA replication, once the two strands have unzipped, is started by a piece of single-stranded DNA called a *primer*. When the primer attaches to the "starting point" at the end of a strand, it signals an enzyme called *DNA polymerase* to start adding nucleotides to the strand. The formation of a new double strand proceeds in one direction only from the primer.

The action of the primer is the key to PCR. It occurred to Mullis that if the sequence of bases on both sides of a particular gene were known, it would be a simple matter to prepare primers complementary to those sequences. In a batch of DNA that had been separated into single strands, the primers would attach to the targeted sequences, thereby establishing the boundaries of the DNA segment to be replicated. On each strand, replication would begin at the primer and proceed across the gene. Just the one gene, and a few adjoining bases on either side of it, would be reproduced. By repeating the replication cycle over and over, it should be possible to make any number of copies of a gene.

Mullis tested his idea, and it worked perfectly on the first try. Over the next few years, he and other Cetus researchers refined the process.

The PCR process takes place in a water bath in which the temperature can be controlled precisely over a range between about 60 °C and 98 °C (140 °F and 208 °F). The researcher adds DNA to the bath, along with the primers, nucleotide building blocks, and DNA polymerase, then brings the water to near-boiling temperatures. The DNA separates into single strands, and when the researcher lowers the temperature, the primers attach and replication of the targeted gene is carried out. Minutes later, the bath is reheated to start the cycle anew.

The process is called a *chain reaction* because it builds upon itself, doubling the number of copies of the gene in each cycle. After 20 cycles, there are about 1 million copies of the gene, and after 30 cycles the number has risen to about 1 billion. In most laboratories, PCR is now done with small machines that carry out the multiple cycles automatically.

PCR has been an incredible labor-saver for scientists. Previously, to make multiple copies of a gene, they had to rely on *cloning*, a complex and time-consuming procedure in which a gene is inserted into a microbe that replicates the gene along with its own DNA. Perhaps more important, PCR enables researchers and crime investigators to replicate genes from tissue samples so small or in such poor condition that they barely contain enough DNA to be examined.

The technique should also prove useful in medicine, particularly in diagnosing disease. For example, PCR could probably be used to multiply genetic material from the AIDS virus in a sample of blood. This would enable researchers to confirm the presence of the virus in the earliest stages of the infection, when too few viruses are present to be detected by other tests. PCR might also simplify the diagnosis of genetic diseases by enabling physicians to rapidly multiply a suspected faulty gene in a patient's DNA.

The value of PCR was recognized at once by the scientific community. In 1989, when the details of the procedure had been perfected, the American Association for the Advancement of Science honored PCR as the major scientific development of that year. [Robert H. Tamarin]

tein that inactivated all but one of the sites in the yeast DNA where a restriction enzyme would normally cut. Only the DNA segment covered by the bacterial repressor was shielded from the effects of this protein. Finally, the researchers added a chemical that removed the repressor, revealing the cutting site beneath it. A restriction enzyme could now cut the DNA in just that one place.

Cystic fibrosis defect corrected. Two groups of investigators in the United States reported in autumn 1990 that the genetic defect causing cystic fibrosis can be corrected in cell cultures in the laboratory. The research teams, at the University of Iowa in Iowa City and the University of Michigan in Ann Arbor, were following up on the 1989 discovery of the gene responsible for cystic fibrosis, a disorder marked primarily by a build-up of thick mucus in the lungs.

The mucus problem appears to be caused by the blockage of a channel that lung cells normally use to regulate the flow of *ions* (electrically charged atoms) into and out of the cell. The proper balance of sodium and chloride ions—the two parts of the salt molecule—inside the cell is essential to maintaining the moisture content of mucus outside the cell.

Research indicates that the channel is controlled by a protein called *cystic fibrosis transmembrane conductance regulator* (CFTR). Every lung cell has two copies of the gene that produces CFTR. If one or both copies of the gene are normal, the cell produces correctly functioning CFTR. But in people with cystic fibrosis, both genes are defective. As a result, the protein produced is faulty and does not properly control the flow of sodium and chloride ions. This causes water to be drawn into the cell rather than secreted into the mucus.

To see whether this defect could be corrected, the investigators inserted a copy of the normal CFTR gene into a virus that had been altered so it could not cause disease. Copies of the genetically engineered virus were then added to a culture of lung cells taken from a person with cystic fibrosis. The virus carried the gene into the cells and inserted the gene into the cells' DNA.

Cartoon by Brian Duffy. Reprinted with special permission of North American Syndicate, Inc.

Genetics

Continued

The cells then produced the correct CFTR protein, and the ion channel in the cells seemed to be working normally. Researchers will now try to learn whether the CFTR defect can be corrected in the bodies of cystic fibrosis patients, thereby curing them of the disease.

A major unanswered question is how best to get the normal CFTR gene into lung cells. One possibility being considered in 1991 was to package copies of the normal gene in tiny fat-coated bubbles that could penetrate cell membranes. The patient would most likely inhale an aerosol spray containing millions of the encapsulated genes.

Genes and Alzheimer's disease. The identification of a gene that may be involved in some cases of Alzheimer's disease was reported in February 1991 by researchers at St. Mary's Hospital Medical School in London. Alzheimer's disease is an incurable brain disorder that mainly afflicts people over age 60. Some kinds of brain cells in Alzheimer's patients become abnormal. Patients experience gradual mental dete-

rioration, sink into an infantlike state, and die. In some cases, the disease appears to be hereditary.

The British investigators studied a family in which several individuals in different generations had developed Alzheimer's disease. They looked at one particular gene called *APP*, which neuroscientists had long suspected of causing some cases of Alzheimer's.

The researchers found that in all the family members who had developed Alzheimer's, a mutation was present in the APP gene. They did not find the mutation in people without the disease. Moreover, they discovered the same mutation in members of an unrelated family with multiple cases of Alzheimer's disease.

If the mutation in the APP gene is confirmed as the cause of hereditary Alzheimer's disease, researchers might be able to develop an effective treatment for at least this form of the disease.   [David S. Haymer]

In the Special Reports section, see DRUG-BUG WARFARE. In WORLD BOOK, see CELL; GENETICS.

Geology

Two long-dormant volcanoes erupted in mid-1991. Lava, ash, gas, and superheated rock fragments erupted from Japan's Mount Unzen on June 3, 1991, killing at least 38 people and destroying several villages. The volcano, whose last major eruption occurred in 1792, is about 50 kilometers (30 miles) from Nagasaki on the southern island of Kyushu. The volcanic flow raced down the side of the mountain at speeds of up to 78 kilometers (125 miles) per hour. Also in June, Mount Pinatubo in the Philippines, which had been dormant for 600 years, erupted. The eruptions had killed almost 400 people by late June and forced the evacuation of nearby towns and a United States air force base. In the Special Reports section, see VOLCANO WATCHING.

Predicting earthquakes. Charting the number and location of moderate earthquakes in the San Francisco Bay area may enable geologists to predict when and where large earthquakes could occur. That conclusion was reported in December 1990 by seismologists Lynn R. Sykes and Steven C. Jaumé of the Lamont-Doherty Geological Observatory in Palisades, N.Y.

The scientists studied the level of earthquake activity preceding three major quakes in the bay area: the 1989 Loma Prieta earthquake, the great San Francisco earthquake of 1906, and a quake in 1868. The 1906 and 1989 quakes occurred along the San Andreas Fault, which runs west of San Francisco and San Francisco Bay. The 1868 earthquake struck along the Hayward Fault, which runs along the eastern side of San Francisco Bay.

For their study of activity before the 1989 quake, Sykes and Jaumé relied on data from *seismometers*—devices that record the motion of an earthquake. There were few seismometers in California until after the 1906 quake, however. For information about seismic activity before 1906, the scientists relied on newspaper reports. Geologists can roughly determine the *magnitude* (strength) of earthquakes from reports of the damage they caused.

Sykes and Jaumé found that moderate earthquakes—those with a magnitude greater than 5 but less than 7 on the Richter scale—frequently struck northern California from 1855 until 1868. Most of these quakes occurred on faults near the segment of the Hayward Fault that ruptured in 1868.

Seismic activity changes. After the 1868 quake, seismic activity in the bay area almost completely ceased until 1881. At that time, there was an increase in the number of moderate earthquakes along faults east and southeast of the bay. These faults lie near the segment of the San Andreas Fault that ruptured during the 1906 earthquake.

Sykes and Jaumé also found that after the 1906 earthquake, seismic activity in the bay area almost ceased once more. Earthquake activity began to increase in 1954. From 1954 until 1989, there was no movement on the San Andreas Fault itself. A number of moderate earthquakes, however, occurred around the south end of San Francisco Bay, on both sides of the segment of the San Andreas Fault that ruptured in the Loma Prieta quake.

Sykes and Jaumé theorize that in all three cases, the moderate earthquakes were precursors of the major earthquakes. They suggest that the moderate quakes released the geologic pressure that had been building on the smaller faults around the Hayward and San Andreas faults. The pressure released by these quakes, however, was transferred to nearby segments of the two larger faults. These segments of the faults then ruptured, producing major earthquakes.

Sykes and Jaumé predict three possibilities for future severe earthquakes in the area. First, if the number of moderate earthquakes in the bay area drops significantly, then geologists might conclude that a large shock is unlikely to occur for at least a decade. The drop could indicate that the Loma Prieta quake had relieved the stress on the segment of the San Andreas Fault running through the bay area.

The probability of another major quake in the bay area in the next few years would be high, however, if the frequency of moderate earthquakes remains as high as it was before the Loma Prieta quake. This could indicate that the Loma Prieta quake did not relieve the stress on the San Andreas Fault. The third possibility is that another large earthquake could occur before

Geology

geologists can determine whether the frequency of moderate earthquakes has declined.

"Grand Canyon" of British Columbia. Buried beneath Okanagan Lake in the Canadian province of British Columbia is a canyon deeper than the Grand Canyon in Arizona. That finding was reported in November 1990 by United States and Canadian geologists.

Lake Okanagan is a fiordlike lake 120 kilometers (75 miles) long and about 3.5 kilometers (2.2 miles) wide. The geologists studied Okanagan's lake bed using *seismic reflection surveying*. This technique involves sending sound waves into water and using underwater devices called *hydrophones* to detect echoes reflected from rock layers in the lake bed. The echoes reveal the number and thickness of the rock layers.

The seismic reflection profiles obtained by the geologists revealed a layer of sediment 790 meters (2,600 feet) thick beneath the lake. They report that this sediment layer covers the floor of a valley dug out by glaciers moving southward between about 1 million and 10,000 years ago. The valley was cut to a depth of more than 2 kilometers (1.2 miles) below a surrounding plateau. By comparison, the deepest parts of the Grand Canyon are 1.6 kilometers (1 mile) deep.

Shortly after the canyon was cut, the glaciers retreated. Within a few thousand years, the canyon was filled in, chiefly by sand and gravel that washed from the melting glaciers.

Asteroid impact in the Caribbean. An asteroid whose collision with Earth 65 million years ago may have led to the extinction of many plant and animal species—including the last of the dinosaurs—may have crashed in or around the Caribbean Sea. In 1990, geologists Alan R. Hildebrand and William V. Boynton of the University of Arizona in Tucson suggested two candidates for a Caribbean impact site.

A major piece of evidence supporting the theory that an asteroid collided with Earth is the presence of unusual material in a layer of rock, dated to 65 million years ago, that has been found in many places around the world. This

A towering plume of hot ash rises from Japan's Mount Unzen as it erupts in June 1991. At least 38 people died when lava and hot rocks swept down the side of the volcano. The last major eruption of Mount Unzen, which is on the southern island of Kyushu about 50 kilometers (30 miles) from Nagasaki, occurred in 1792.

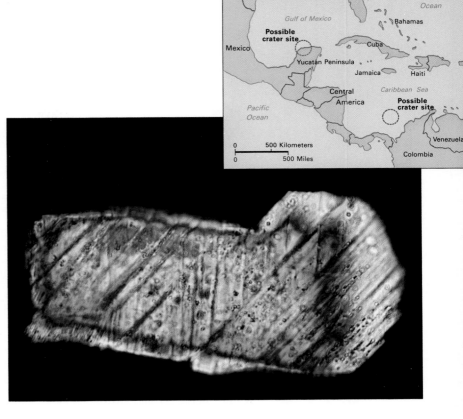

Tiny crystals cracked by the force of an asteroid impact, *right,* were discovered in 65-million-year-old rock in Haiti. This provided evidence that an asteroid crashed in or near the Caribbean Sea at that time. The impact may have caused the extinction of the last of the dinosaurs. In late 1990, scientists studying rock samples and other geologic evidence suggested that the impact site may be off the coast of Colombia or on the Yucatán Peninsula of Mexico, *far right.*

Geology

Continued

layer contains the element iridium, which is rare on Earth but relatively plentiful in asteroids.

While examining rock samples from Cuba and the western Caribbean region, Hildebrand and Boynton found another layer, about 2 centimeters (⅞ inch) thick, underlying the iridium layer. This second layer consists of clay that the scientists believe is crushed rock ejected from the impact site. In the layer, the scientists also found rocky debris similar to that typically deposited by *tsunamis* (huge tidal waves) as they pass through shallow water. (If the asteroid landed in the ocean, it would have created a tsunami that may have been several kilometers high.) This led the scientists to conclude that the asteroid landed in the Caribbean region.

While examining seismic reflection profiles of the Colombian Basin, an area off the northern coast of South America, Hildebrand and Boynton found a circular region 300 kilometers (185 miles) in diameter. The scientists speculated that this region, which they

believe was formed 65 million years ago, might be the impact site. In November, the scientists proposed another candidate for the site—the Chicxulub crater on the Yucatán Peninsula of Mexico.

Atmospheric oxygen. Geologists have long known that the amount of oxygen in the atmosphere has risen and fallen over the past 570 million years. But the reason for this fluctuation is unknown. In July 1990, Jennifer M. Robinson, a paleoclimatologist (scientist who studies ancient climates) at Pennsylvania State University in University Park, theorized that the variations may be related to the evolution of land plants and fungi.

Oxygen is released into the atmosphere by *photosynthesis.* In this process, plants remove carbon dioxide and water from the air and, using the energy of sunlight, convert these materials to food and give off oxygen. The decay or burning of dead plants, on the other hand, consumes atmospheric oxygen. If, however, dead plants become deeply buried without completely de-

Geology
Continued

caying—forming rock such as coal, for example—less atmospheric oxygen is consumed.

Robinson suggests that the burial of *lignin* may have played a special role in the fluctuations in the levels of atmospheric oxygen. Lignin is a woody substance in plants that decays slowly. It also inhibits the decay of other organic materials.

During the Late Paleozoic Era—570 million to 240 million years ago—*pteridophytes* (tree ferns) were the most common group of plants. Great forests of these plants, which contain lignin in large quantities, accumulated in vast swamps and bogs. The buried remains of these plants later formed large coal deposits. Robinson theorized that atmospheric oxygen levels in the Late Paleozoic were high because the large amount of lignin in the dead pteridophytes inhibited the decay of the plants.

During the Early Mesozoic Era—250 million to 180 million years ago—gymnosperms, the group to which the pines and firs belong, became the dominant land plants. Gymnosperms also produce large amounts of lignin. Robinson theorized, however, that the level of atmospheric oxygen dropped because Earth's climate changed from wet to dry. As a result, forested areas shrank, and the drier climate promoted the decay of plant remains.

During the Late Mesozoic Era—145 million to 65 million years ago—Earth's climate again became wetter and forested areas grew. Large quantities of plant remains were buried and formed rock. According to Robinson, the level of plant decay declined, and more oxygen accumulated in the atmosphere.

By the beginning of the Cenozoic Era, 65 million years ago, the angiosperms, which produce little lignin, had become the dominant land plants. In addition, fungi that can break down lignin had evolved. As a result, the decay rate increased, and the level of atmospheric oxygen declined to its present level. [William W. Hay]

In WORLD BOOK, see DINOSAUR; EARTHQUAKE; PLANTS.

Immunology

Human tests with a new AIDS vaccine indicate that the vaccine is safe and stimulates a response by the immune system, scientists at several research centers in the United States reported in January 1991. They said it was too soon to tell whether the vaccine would actually confer immunity to the human immunodeficiency virus (HIV), the virus that causes AIDS.

The vaccine is made from a surface protein of the virus called *gp160*. The vaccine is intended to stimulate the immune system to produce infection-fighting molecules called *antibodies* against the protein. The hope is that if an inoculated individual were later infected by HIV, the antibodies would immediately "recognize" the protein on the surface of the virus. The immune system would then attack and destroy the virus before it could cause disease.

But the vaccine would do this only for people vaccinated before they are exposed to HIV. It would not help people who are already infected, because the virus damages the immune system.

The experimental vaccine was tested in clinical trials at seven U.S. medical centers, beginning in early 1988. Participants in the tests were 72 healthy volunteers, aged 18 to 55. The researchers gave each of the volunteers four injections of the vaccine over a period of 18 months.

By the third or fourth dose, 91 per cent of the vaccinated individuals had developed antibodies to the protein. Furthermore, the vaccine seemed to be safe; only a few volunteers experienced side effects, and those were minor. Twelve to 18 months after the final injection, however, the volunteers' antibody levels dropped, so periodic revaccination might be necessary.

Unfortunately, scientists do not know whether the development of antibodies to the gp160 protein will prevent AIDS. It could be that a vaccine made from another part of the virus, or perhaps from the entire virus, would be required to produce immunity. Or, an even grimmer possibility, perhaps antibodies would be inadequate to fight off HIV infection.

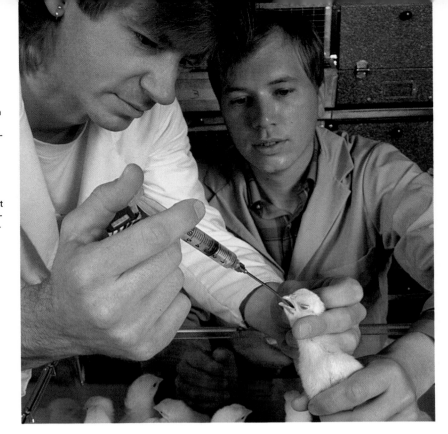

Researchers at the Agricultural Research Service laboratory in Beltsville, Md., inoculate chicks with an experimental vaccine against *coccidiosis,* a serious poultry disease caused by a parasite. In tests, the vaccine—made from parasites that have been weakened with X rays—was 100 per cent effective against coccidiosis. The vaccine must undergo further testing before it can be made available to farmers.

Immunology

Continued

Those questions remain to be answered. In the meantime, this study indicates that at least one of several AIDS vaccines under development is safe and able to stimulate an immune response.

Possible vaccine for Lyme disease. A newly developed vaccine against Lyme disease protects mice from the illness, scientists at Yale University in New Haven, Conn., reported in October 1990. Lyme disease—named for Lyme, Conn., where the first cases occurred in 1974—is an infection caused by a bacterium, *Borrelia burgdorferi,* that is transmitted through the bite of the deer tick.

Lyme disease has three stages. The first stage includes a rash and flulike symptoms. In the second phase, the disease can cause joint pain, an irregular heartbeat, and various neurological problems, including facial-nerve paralysis and disturbances of vision and memory. Finally, in the third stage, joint inflammation may increase to the point where the patient has arthritis.

If the disease is diagnosed early,

many of the later complications can be avoided or minimized with antibiotics. But in many cases, doctors fail to recognize the illness until it has progressed to the second or third stage. Thus, researchers have been trying to develop a vaccine to protect people from Lyme disease, particularly in areas of the United States, such as New England, where it is most common.

As with the AIDS virus, however, researchers have been unable to determine which part of the *Borrelia* microorganism would best confer immunity. Another problem is that there are numerous strains of *B. burgdorferi,* and immunity to one strain might not impart immunity to other strains.

The Yale scientists isolated the bacteria's gene that codes for the production of a surface protein called *OspA.* Because this protein is common to many strains of the bacteria, the investigators thought it might make an effective vaccine.

The researchers put the gene into another kind of bacterium; these bacteria served as tiny "factories," churn-

Telling White Blood Cells Where They're Needed
Researchers have learned that the cells lining blood vessels often insert special molecules, called *cell-adhesion molecules,* into the bloodstream to attract white blood cells needed to combat infections or heal tissue injuries. This process may also lead to inflammatory diseases such as rheumatoid arthritis.

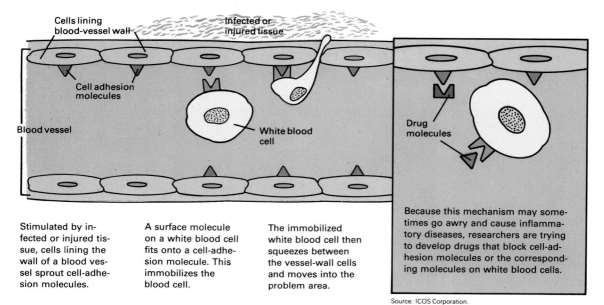

Cells lining blood-vessel wall

Infected or injured tissue

Cell adhesion molecules

Blood vessel

White blood cell

Drug molecules

Stimulated by infected or injured tissue, cells lining the wall of a blood vessel sprout cell-adhesion molecules.

A surface molecule on a white blood cell fits onto a cell-adhesion molecule. This immobilizes the blood cell.

The immobilized white blood cell then squeezes between the vessel-wall cells and moves into the problem area.

Because this mechanism may sometimes go awry and cause inflammatory diseases, researchers are trying to develop drugs that block cell-adhesion molecules or the corresponding molecules on white blood cells.

Source: ICOS Corporation.

Immunology
Continued

ing out large quantities of OspA. The scientists then inoculated mice with the protein and, later, infected the animals with different strains of *B. burgdorferi.* None of the mice, which ordinarily are highly vulnerable to the bacteria, developed Lyme disease. Moreover, antibodies taken from the mice's bodies protected other mice from infection without the need for the vaccine. This confirmed that the antibodies to OspA, and not some other factor, were producing the immunity.

Whether the OspA vaccine would be safe and effective as a human vaccine against Lyme disease remains to be seen; what works in animals does not always work in people. The Yale study offers hope, however, that Lyme disease may be preventable.

Gene therapy for immunodeficiency. In September 1990, researchers at the National Institutes of Health (NIH) in Bethesda, Md., used gene therapy to try to correct a rare genetic disorder of the immune system called *severe combined immunodeficiency* (SCID). This was the first approved use of human gene

therapy, a new approach to medical treatment in which patients are given new genes to correct a genetic defect or treat a disease.

Although the causes of SCID are not completely understood, in about 25 per cent of patients it results from the lack of a protein called *adenosine deaminase* (ADA). ADA apparently protects lymphocytes by breaking down harmful substances in the blood. The protein is missing because the gene that directs its production is abnormal.

In the laboratory, the NIH researchers inserted a normal ADA gene into harmless viruses and mixed them with lymphocytes taken from a 4-year-old girl with ADA deficiency. They then injected the virus-containing cells into the girl's body, where, they hoped, it would produce ADA. It was too early in mid-1991 to say whether the treatment was a success, but the NIH scientists reported that the girl seemed to be doing well. See also MEDICAL RESEARCH (Close-Up).   [Paul Katz]

In WORLD BOOK, see AIDS; IMMUNITY; LYME DISEASE.

Materials Science

In late 1990 and early 1991, researchers across the United States were creating and studying an intriguing form of carbon. This molecule, a hollow shell comprised of 60 carbon atoms, is named *buckminsterfullerene* because it is shaped like the geodesic dome popularized by the American architect R. Buckminster Fuller. The molecules are informally called *buckyballs*. Researchers reported a new technique for creating large amounts of buckyballs in September 1990. Scientists soon began to speculate that the material's properties might make it useful as a lubricant or semiconductor.

Making buckyballs. Richard E. Smalley, a physical chemist, made the first buckyballs at Rice University in Houston in 1985 by vaporizing graphite, a form of pure carbon, with powerful pulses of light from a light source called a *laser*. Careful study showed that some of the vaporized carbon atoms clustered to form sheets, which curled over to form hollow shells. Some shells were incomplete, but others were complete, containing 60 carbon atoms whose bonds formed 12 pentagons and 20 hexagons—the same pattern as the surface of a soccer ball. Scientists were intrigued by the material, but few could study it because only tiny quantities were available.

In September 1990, physicist Donald R. Huffman of the University of Arizona announced that scientists from Arizona and the Max Planck Institute for Nuclear Research in Heidelberg, Germany, had discovered how to make large quantities of buckyballs. The researchers passed a strong electric current between a pair of graphite electrodes in a chamber containing only a small amount of helium. As the current jumped between the electrodes, it created an arc of intense heat and light. The arc vaporized some carbon from the electrodes, forming soot that condensed on the chamber walls. The soot contained about 5 per cent 60-carbon-atom molecules (C_{60}), which could be isolated. Smalley's group at Rice University modified the process to make up to 10 grams (0.35 ounce) of buckyballs per day using an ordinary arc welder.

The electric arc process also forms other large, hollow carbon molecules—some containing 70 carbon atoms and others containing 84. Early experiments did not separate the larger, elongated C_{70} and C_{84} molecules from C_{60}. In November 1990, chemists Robert L. Whetten and François N. Diederich of the University of California at Los Angeles became the first to isolate C_{70} and C_{84} by passing the soot through a filter, which separated the molecules by size.

Buckyball behavior. With relatively large quantities of buckyballs available, researchers began studying their properties. In November 1990, Fred Wudl of the University of California at Santa Barbara showed that C_{60} and C_{70} molecules can each accept up to three extra electrons, making their electrical properties similar to semiconductors.

Research scientist Donald S. Bethune of the IBM Almaden Research Center in San Jose studied buckyballs with a scanning tunneling microscope, which uses electric current to sense objects as small as atoms. "They seem to be quite skittish and run around quite a lot on the surface," he reported at a meeting of the Materials Research Society held in Boston in November 1990. Bethune found what had previously been assumed: Because each carbon atom is stably bound to three others, C_{60} molecules are unreactive and do not stick to surfaces. For this reason, chemists think buckyballs might make a good lubricant.

In early 1991, scientists began adding other elements to buckyballs to change their properties. The addition of potassium, for example, made thin films of C_{60} molecules electrically conducting, a team at AT&T Bell Laboratories discovered. When cooled to -255 °C (-427 °F), the potassium-doped buckyballs become *superconducting*—able to conduct electricity without resistance. See also CHEMISTRY.

Optical amplification. The big news in telecommunications in 1990 and 1991 came from special optical fibers that can amplify as well as transmit light. The optical fiber, a triumph of modern materials science, is a strand of glass so pure and clear that it can transmit light signals up to 20 kilometers (12 miles) before half the light is lost. Such fibers are used in cables that carry telephone messages across Eu-

Manipulating Materials Atom by Atom

Using advanced microscopes, materials scientists manipulated atoms to create the patterns shown greatly enlarged below. With such techniques, they hope one day to build electronic devices on an atomic scale.

Seven xenon atoms, *right,* were strung together by a physicist at IBM's Almaden Research Center in San Jose. He used the electric current from the superfine tip of a scanning tunneling microscope (STM) to pick up and carry the atoms from one place to another.

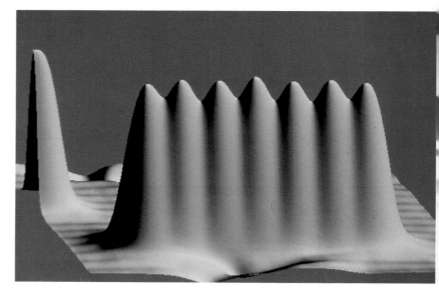

The letters *CU* for *Cornell University* and *NNF* for *National Nanofabrication Facility* were inscribed on a tiny silicon surface, *below* (bottom), by Cornell scientists using an STM-based technology. A layer of gold coating the silicon (top) was unchanged by the process.

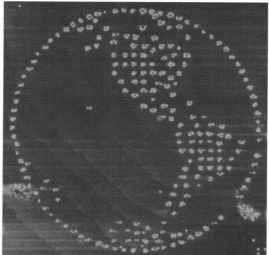

The world's smallest map, *above,* measures about 1/100 the width of a human hair in diameter. Each dot contains a few thousand gold atoms. Research scientists at IBM's Almaden Research Center used an STM to move the gold atoms into position.

Materials
Science
Continued

rope, North America, Australia, and the Atlantic and Pacific oceans. In the Science You Can Use section, see INFORMATION ON A LIGHT BEAM.

To make a fiber amplifier, scientists add a small amount of the rare earth element erbium to the glass of a conventional fiber. Light from a laser is used to energize the erbium atoms. The erbium atoms can then amplify a light signal at 1.54 micrometers, the wavelength at which optical fibers transmit light farthest.

In conventional fiber-optic systems, light signals become too weak to be reliably detected after passing through a hundred or so kilometers of fiber. To boost their strength, the signals are converted to electronic form and back to light before they travel through the next segment. This process is expensive and limits the amount of information the system can carry. The new fiber amplifiers eliminate the need to convert light to electronic signals.

New distance records for fiber amplifiers were reported in February 1991 by researchers at AT&T Bell Laboratories. The researchers sent data in the form of light pulses through a loop of optical fiber. They could send 5 billion *bits* (on/off pulses used to convey data) per second over a total distance of 9,000 kilometers (5,600 miles) with little distortion. When the researchers reduced the data load to 2.4 billion bits per second, the signals traveled without significant distortion through 21,000 kilometers (13,000 miles) of fiber, the equivalent of about half the distance around the world. By comparison, the first transatlantic fiber-optic cable, installed in 1988, carries 300 million bits per second.

The first use of fiber amplifiers is likely to be in long-distance communication systems. AT&T and the Japanese telecommunications firm Kokusai Denshin Denwa Limited plan to use such amplifiers in a 10,000-kilometer (6,200-mile) underwater telephone cable between the United States and Japan. The cable is scheduled to begin operation in 1996.   [Jeff Hecht]

In WORLD BOOK, see FIBER OPTICS; MATERIALS SCIENCE.

Medical
Research

Patients suffering from certain life-threatening infections may benefit from a new antibody developed by genetic engineering researchers at Stanford University in California and the University of California in San Diego. In February 1991, medical centers in the United States, Canada, and Europe reported that the substance, the HA-1A antibody, is a safe and effective treatment for patients with a serious blood infection.

Infections brought on when viruses or bacteria enter the bloodstream are a leading cause of death in hospitalized patients. The infections are especially dangerous if they are caused by certain bacteria that produce *toxins* (poisons) that can cause *shock* (a life-threatening condition that involves an extreme drop in blood pressure).

To treat these infections, doctors usually identify the bacterium responsible, then administer the proper antibiotic. But this approach often fails because by the time the bacterium is identified, the infection may be too advanced to treat successfully. Also, some bacteria have become resistant to many antibiotics. In the Special Reports section, see DRUG-BUG WARFARE.

The newly developed antibody treatment uses a different strategy. An antibody is a molecule that recognizes and helps destroy a foreign substance in the body. Rather than combating the bacteria directly, the HA-1A antibody attacks the bacterial toxin.

To test the safety and effectiveness of the HA-1A antibody, physicians at the medical centers studied 197 patients with severe infections caused by toxin-producing bacteria. The doctors gave 105 of the patients conventional antibiotic treatment and the HA-1A. The other 92 patients received only conventional antibiotics.

Within 28 days, 45 (49 per cent) of the 92 patients who did not receive HA-1A died. In contrast, only 32 (30 per cent) of the 105 patients who received HA-1A died. None of the patients treated with the new antibody suffered side effects. Thus, the researchers concluded that immediate HA-1A treatment might be a wise choice for all patients who appear to have bacterial blood infections.

Gall bladder surgery. In 1991, surgeons reported the results of the first large studies testing a new surgical technique for removing diseased gall bladders. Gallstone formation is a major cause of gall bladder problems.

The surgical technique, called *laparoscopy*, eliminates the large surgical scars and long recovery periods associated with conventional gall bladder surgery. Laparoscopy patients also tend to need relatively few painkillers after surgery and usually can leave the hospital within a day. Laparoscopy has also been used widely to detect and remove other diseased organs in the abdomen.

Three groups of surgeons independently reported high success rates when they removed gall bladders through laparoscopic surgery. This technique involves inserting into the body an instrument called a *laparoscope*, a tube with the diameter of a drinking straw. The laparoscope has a miniature video camera at one end that transmits to a television screen pictures of areas inside the body. This enables surgeons to see and work inside the body without opening it with a large incision.

Surgeons begin the operation by making an incision below the navel about 1 centimeter (⅓ inch) long. Through this slit, they insert a *trocar*, a narrow tube with a sharp pointed tip. Next they pump carbon dioxide into the abdomen through a hose in the trocar. This pushes the organs aside to create space for the surgeon's instruments. The trocar also is used to guide the laparoscope into the abdomen and to the gall bladder.

The surgeons make three more incisions, even tinier than the first, under the right ribs. Through these they insert other trocars that guide instruments for grasping and cutting.

Watching the images transmitted to the television screen, the surgeons locate the gall bladder and cut it away from the bile ducts and blood vessels to which it is attached. They stop the bleeding and seal off the ducts with heat generated by either an *electrocautery wand*, which uses electricity, or by a surgical *laser*, which creates an intense beam of light.

The surgeons then bring the gall bladder up to the incision at the navel. If the gall bladder is filled with gallstones, it can be quite large, and the surgeons can only pull the neck of the organ through the incision. When this is done, they make an opening in the gall bladder and remove the gallstones inside it. Then they pull the empty gall bladder out through the incision.

The surgeons repair incisions in muscles with a few *sutures* (stitches). But the incisions in the skin are so small they normally are simply covered with small bandages.

In January 1991, surgeons reported the results of two studies evaluating a combined total of 200 patients selected for laparoscopic surgery using electrocautery instruments. Only 9 patients were unsuitable for the technique and nearly all the laparoscopic patients went home from the hospital on the day after surgery. Most resumed all their usual activities within one week.

In March 1991, other surgeons published comparisons of 100 patients who had conventional gall bladder surgery and 100 similar patients who had laser laparoscopic surgery. They found that most laparoscopic patients stayed in the hospital one day, compared to four days for patients who had conventional surgery. Only 6 laparoscopic patients had complications after surgery, compared with 10 of the standard surgical patients.

Surgery to prevent stroke. In February 1991, the National Institute of Neurological Disorders and Stroke in Bethesda, Md., informed physicians involved in its national study of stroke patients that a surgical procedure, if expertly performed, may be better than aspirin therapy for preventing strokes in high-risk patients. Such patients have substantial deposits of cholesterol, fatty substances, calcium, and scar tissue on the inner walls of their *carotid arteries*, the main blood vessels carrying blood to the brain. If these deposits, also known as *plaque*, build up and cut off the blood supply, they can cause a stroke.

To perform the surgery, called a *carotid endarterectomy*, a surgeon makes small slits in the patient's neck, opens the carotid arteries, and removes the plaque. Although this operation had

New Gall Bladder Surgery
A procedure for removing gall bladders without creating large scars, *right,* was reported in 1990. Through tiny incisions, surgeons insert a cutting instrument, such as a laser, *bottom,* and a miniature video camera, called a *laparoscope,* which transmits a picture of the inside of the body to a monitor, *below.*

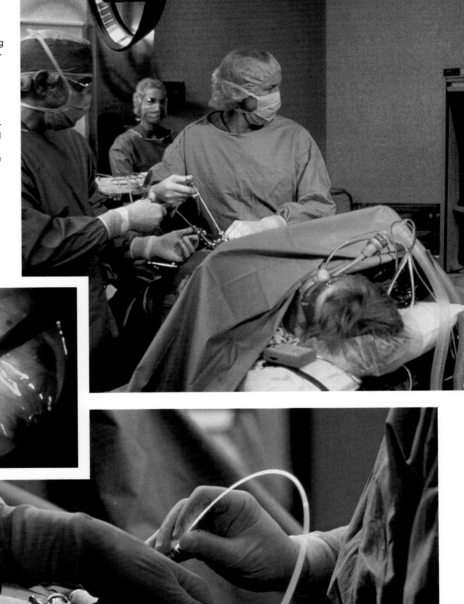

Replacing Defective Genes

A new era in medicine in the United States began on Sept. 14, 1990, when researchers at the National Institutes of Health (NIH) in Bethesda, Md., inserted a thin needle in the hand of a 4-year-old girl. While the child sipped chocolate milk, tubing connected to the needle carried 1 billion genetically altered white blood cells into her veins. The procedure lasted only about 30 minutes. When it was over, the child had become the first person to undergo a United States government-approved attempt at *gene therapy*. Gene therapy involves inserting healthy genes into a patient's cells in an effort to cure or treat hereditary illnesses and other types of disease.

The 4-year-old, whose name was not released to the public, has a rare and fatal inherited disorder called *severe combined immunodeficiency syndrome* (SCIDS). The cause of the disease is a defect in the gene that *codes for* (directs the production of) the enzyme *adenosine deaminase* (ADA). This enzyme is essential for helping the body fight infections. Until September, perhaps the most famous SCIDS patient was a child named David, often referred to as the "Bubble Boy." David, who died at age 12 in 1984, spent nearly all his life in a sterile plastic bubble.

Before her treatment with gene therapy, the 4-year-old girl had been able to live relatively normally at home, thanks to weekly injections of ADA. But the girl's doctors suspected that the ADA shots would provide only short-term protection. They feared that her immune system would eventually produce cells that would attack and destroy the supplementary ADA.

Weeks before the new genetic treatment began, researchers withdrew some of her blood and separated out the white blood cells, which were cultured in a laboratory to increase their number. The researchers chose white blood cells because they are the immune system cells most damaged by ADA deficiency.

Normal ADA genes obtained from a volunteer were also multiplied in the laboratory and then inserted into viruses that can infect human cells without damaging them. When the girl's white blood cells were mixed with the modified viruses, the viruses infected the cells and inserted normal ADA genes into the cells' chromosomes. Finally, the altered white blood cells were injected into the child.

The researchers conducting the test hoped that the altered white blood cells would multiply rapidly and produce the missing enzyme. Their hopes seem to have been well founded. In April 1991, genetic surgeon W. French Anderson, the leader of the NIH team, reported that the girl's altered white blood cells had multiplied and were producing measurable quantities of ADA.

The treatment is only a means of delivering ADA, however, not a cure for the disorder. The 4-year-old must return to Bethesda once a month to receive new transfusions of modified white blood cells because the cells are mature cells that, although they reproduce, die fairly quickly. The researchers supplement the genetic treatment with weekly ADA injections. They hope that eventually she will not need the weekly injections.

The 4-year-old is not the only patient currently undergoing gene therapy. Two other attempts began in January 1991. In the first, Anderson's team began treating another SCIDS patient, a 9-year-old girl. In the second, other NIH researchers began the first attempt to use gene therapy to treat cancer. Two patients suffering from advanced melanoma, a form of skin cancer that invades other organs, received transfusions of a special type of white blood cells that attack tumors. The cells were fortified with genes that code for a protein that destroys cancer cells.

Genetic specialists have dreamed of using gene therapy to treat and cure hereditary disorders since the early 1980's, when researchers first learned how to insert normal copies of defective genes into a cell's genetic material. But dreaming was one thing, and actually performing genetic therapy turned out to be another.

For most of the 1980's, gene therapy researchers focused on altering *stem cells*—immature cells in the bone marrow that become white and red blood cells. They reasoned that if they could correct a genetic defect in these cells, the treatment would be magnified a millionfold as the cells matured and reproduced. Moreover, because stem cells give rise to virtually endless generations of blood cells, the defect would, in essence, be cured.

There were two major stumbling blocks on this path, however. One was presented by stem cells themselves, which are difficult to distinguish from mature blood cells. Scientists had to transplant copies of the gene into millions of blood cells in the hope that a few of the cells would be stem cells. This hit-or-miss procedure had a very low success rate.

The diseases themselves presented another obstacle. Many common inherited diseases, such as muscular dystrophy and cystic fibrosis, involve disorders of the nervous system, the muscular and skeletal system, or body organs. Because transplanting genes into stem cells would affect

Replacing Defective Genes
In the first government-approved attempt at gene therapy, researchers gave copies of a normal gene to a young patient with a genetic defect that prevented her white blood cells from making an important enzyme. Scientists used viruses to insert into her cells normal copies of the gene obtained from another person's DNA.

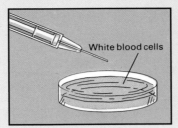

White cells removed from the patient's blood were grown in the laboratory.

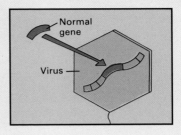

Normal human genes were inserted into harmless viruses.

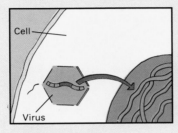

When the viruses and white cells were mixed, the viruses transferred copies of the normal gene to the cells.

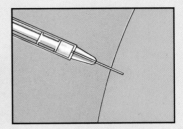

The white cells containing the normal gene were injected into the patient's bloodstream.

only the bloodstream, the procedure would have little effect on these conditions.

By 1988, Anderson and a number of other gene therapy researchers had changed their approach. They no longer viewed gene therapy as a means of curing hereditary disease. Instead, they came to see it as an efficient drug-delivery system, a way of providing temporary relief from a condition, just as medication can lower a patient's blood pressure without curing the underlying cause of the problem.

Some researchers foresee using gene therapy to treat a variety of nonhereditary diseases. For example, some have suggested using altered genes to prevent heart attacks. In this scenario, a gene that codes for a protein that dissolves blood clots could be inserted into copies of the cells that line blood vessels. Researchers theorize that the altered cells, seeded into vessels in heart patients, would provide a built-in defense against the blood clots that cause heart attacks.

Other researchers have suggested using gene therapy to boost the liver's ability to remove a harmful form of cholesterol from the blood. High levels of this fatty substance are a risk factor for heart disease. In this case, genes that code for liver proteins that filter the cholesterol

from the blood would be inserted into liver cells.

In April 1991, a team of American and French scientists reported on animal experiments that they believe could someday lead to a treatment for cystic fibrosis and a hereditary form of emphysema. The scientists inserted into the lungs of laboratory animals copies of a gene that, if defective, causes hereditary emphysema. The gene codes for a protein that protects the air sacs in the lungs against an enzyme that circulates in the blood. If the gene is defective, the lungs do not produce the protein, and the enzyme eventually destroys the air sacs.

The use of gene therapy has aroused debate about how far researchers should go in altering human genetic material. Most ethicists and scientists believe that tinkering with genes in human eggs, sperm, and embryos should be prohibited. The effects of gene therapy, they believe, should be limited to the patient. The therapy should not make changes that would be inherited by the patient's descendants. Nor should gene therapy be used to "improve" people—for example, to make them smarter. If such uses are avoided, they argue, gene therapy would not really be much different from other forms of medical treatment.   [Beverly Merz]

been thought to prevent strokes, no previous studies had shown that it actually worked. Moreover, 3 to 6 per cent of patients who had the surgery suffered strokes as the operation was being performed.

To determine whether the operation's benefits outweighed its risks, the national study was conducted at 50 medical centers known for their expertise in carotid endarterectomy. Each center evaluated patients aged 35 to 80 who had carotid artery blockage and had suffered prestroke symptoms or a mild stroke.

The patients were divided into two groups—those whose arteries were 30 to 69 per cent blocked, and those whose arteries were 70 to 99 per cent blocked. About half the people in each group received aspirin and other drugs to prevent blood clots and to lower cholesterol, blood pressure, or blood sugar. The others received the same drug treatment and also underwent endarterectomy.

For the group with more arterial blockage, researchers found that dur-

ing the first month, 3 per cent of the patients who received only drug treatment had strokes, while 5 per cent of those who had undergone surgery had strokes. However, after 18 months, 24 per cent of the patients who did not have surgery had had strokes, but only 7 per cent of the surgical patients suffered the same fate. This showed that the risk of stroke was reduced 17 per cent in the patients with severe blockages who underwent endarterectomy. Researchers were still evaluating patients with less severe blockage.

A drug to prevent stroke. Low doses of an *anticoagulant* (a drug that prevents or slows blood clotting) prevented stroke in one group of high-risk patients, according to a November 1990 study funded by the National Heart, Lung, and Blood Institute in Bethesda. Although physicians know that anticoagulants can prevent the type of stroke caused by blood clots, they also know that these drugs can cause another type of stroke by triggering bleeding in the brain. This study was designed to determine whether low

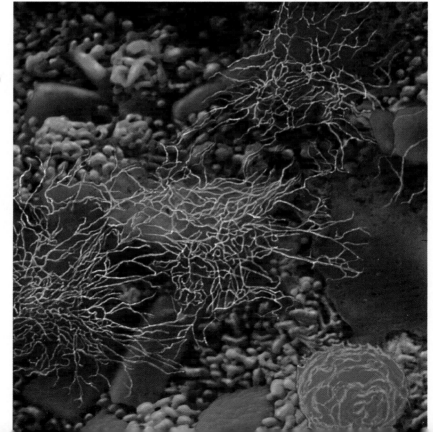

Seen through a microscope, bone marrow cells (purple) sprout branches after they are taken from a rat and placed on a piece of ceramic (green). When reimplanted into the rat, the cells build new bone tissue, according to researchers who developed the procedure at Case Western Reserve University in Cleveland. The technique might one day be used in human beings to replace bone destroyed by injury or disease.

doses of the anticoagulant warfarin could prevent blood clots without causing bleeding.

The researchers studied patients who had *atrial fibrillation*, a condition in which the contractions of the *atrium*, the upper chamber of the heart, are too rapid and weak to pump all the blood from the atrium into the heart's lower chamber. Because some blood collects in the atrium, it has a tendency to clot. If a clot leaves the atrium and lodges in a blood vessel leading to the brain, it can cause a stroke.

Of the 420 patients studied, 212 received low doses of warfarin. The other patients did not take warfarin, though some took regular doses of aspirin, another anticoagulant. During the two-year study, 13 people not taking warfarin suffered strokes, but only 2 of those who took warfarin had strokes. The researchers determined that warfarin had reduced the risk of stroke by 86 per cent.

Although 38 patients in the warfarin group and 21 in the other group had minor bleeding in the brain during the study, only 1 patient in each group had major bleeding. The investigators concluded that warfarin treatment, at low doses and under close supervision, can prevent strokes in people with atrial fibrillation.

Rectal cancer therapy. A combination of radiation and chemotherapy after surgery could increase the survival rates for some patients with rectal cancer, the National Cancer Institute (NCI) in Bethesda announced in March 1991. Rectal cancer is one of the more common cancers, affecting about 45,000 people in the United States each year. In about half of these patients, the cancer has progressed so far by the time of surgery that the patients are considered high-risk. About 55 per cent of these patients die within five years if treated only with surgery.

The NCI based its information on a study that evaluated 204 patients who had undergone surgery to remove the tumor. After surgery, 100 patients received only radiation therapy, and 104 patients received both radiation and chemotherapy. The chemotherapy consisted of standard cancer-fighting drugs as well as an experimental drug.

After seven years, 111 patients had died. Of these, 56 per cent had received only radiation therapy and 44 per cent had received the combined therapy. This outcome represented a 36 per cent reduction in cancer deaths among the combined-therapy patients, according to the researchers. These patients also showed 34 per cent fewer cancer recurrences than did those treated with radiation alone. However, like other cancer patients, those who underwent combined therapy suffered more side effects, such as nausea, vomiting, and diarrhea, from the drugs.

Partial-lung transplants. For the first time, doctors used part of the lung of one living donor to replace the full lung of a recipient in October 1990. Transplant surgeon Vaughn A. Starnes and his colleagues at Stanford University Medical Center performed this first living-donor lung transplant by removing a *lobe* (segment) from the right lung of a 46-year-old woman and using it to replace the entire right lung of her 12-year-old daughter. The daughter had suffered lung damage when she was an infant. As a result, she had high blood pressure and breathing difficulties.

To lessen the chance that the girl's body would reject the transplant, the surgeons decided to use the mother's lobe rather than the entire lung of an unrelated child who had died. Because the mother and daughter were close relatives, the daughter's body was less likely to attack the lobe as a foreign invader.

In a three-hour operation, the surgeons cut away the upper lobe of the mother's right lung, along with its major blood vessels and *bronchus*, the airway leading to that part of the lung. At the same time, another surgical team removed the daughter's entire right lung, leaving the bronchus and major blood vessels in place.

Starnes sutured the girl's bronchus and blood vessels to the bronchus and blood vessels attached to the lobe taken from the mother. Then he sutured the edges of the lobe together to create the new lung. The surgeons expect the partial lung to increase in size as the girl grows.

Two other partial-lung transplants performed at Stanford in 1991 were not successful. A 4-year-old boy who

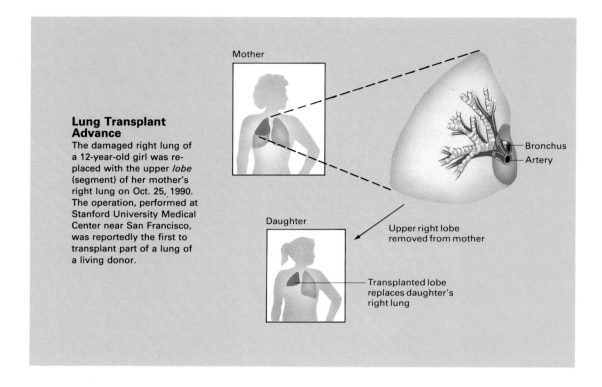

Lung Transplant Advance
The damaged right lung of a 12-year-old girl was replaced with the upper *lobe* (segment) of her mother's right lung on Oct. 25, 1990. The operation, performed at Stanford University Medical Center near San Francisco, was reportedly the first to transplant part of a lung of a living donor.

Mother

Bronchus

Artery

Daughter

Upper right lobe removed from mother

Transplanted lobe replaces daughter's right lung

Medical Research

Continued

received a lobe from his father died after it failed to function. A 1-month-old baby girl also died after her body rejected a lobe she received from a 2-year-old child who had died.

Pregnancy after menopause. When treated with hormones, women over age 40 who have stopped ovulating can become pregnant—using eggs from another woman—and deliver a normal baby. Researchers at the University of Southern California in Los Angeles reported this finding in October 1990. Until this study, scientists had no conclusive evidence about whether the uterus of a woman who had passed *menopause* (the time of a woman's life when menstruation ceases) could support a fetus.

The researchers studied seven married women aged 40 to 44 who had been unable to conceive because their ovaries could not produce eggs. Doctors gave each of the women hormones to stimulate the growth of the lining of the uterus, called the *endometrium*, which supports and helps nourish the growing fetus.

The doctors obtained eggs from fertile women donors aged 31 to 34. The eggs were fertilized in the laboratory with sperm donated by the recipient's husband. The embryos were then transferred through a thin tube into the uterus.

Six of the seven women became pregnant, one with twins. However, one woman later suffered a miscarriage, and another delivered an infant who was dead at birth.

The researchers compared these outcomes to studies using similar treatments with postmenopausal women under age 40. They found no significant differences between the groups in their ability either to become pregnant or to carry the fetus to term. Moreover, both the pregnancy rate and the birth rate were greater for women who used donor eggs than for another group of women aged 40 to 44 who became pregnant using their own eggs, which were removed, fertilized, and returned to the uterus. [Beverly Merz]

In WORLD BOOK, see ARTERIOSCLEROSIS; CANCER; IMMUNITY; STROKE.

Meteorology

On April 30, 1991, a cyclone battered heavily populated coastal districts of Bangladesh, including the port city of Chittagong and about a dozen islands in the Bay of Bengal. The storm killed at least 125,000 and perhaps as many as 500,000 people.

A cyclone is a tropical storm consisting of a spiral pattern of high winds and heavy rain. The Bangladesh storm generated wind speeds of up to 235 kilometers per hour (145 miles per hour) in the eye of the cyclone, according to meteorologists, with wind speeds of 81 to 130 kilometers per hour (50 to 80 miles per hour) outside the eye. It caused tidal waves up to 6 meters (20 feet) high. The cyclone's winds were stronger than the 224 kilometers per hour (138 miles per hour) winds of a 1970 cyclone that killed 500,000 people in the area. Fifty-five cyclones have hit what is now called Bangladesh since 1900.

Although climate experts agree the cyclone was a major storm, the density of the population in the coastal areas hit by the cyclone contributed to the high death toll. In addition, many people in the storm's path lived on extremely low-lying silt islands, which were especially susceptible to flooding.

Global warming debate. Controversy continued to rage in 1990 and 1991 over whether Earth's climate might change due to rising atmospheric levels of "greenhouse" gases. Greenhouse gases, chiefly carbon dioxide, methane, and water vapor, trap heat in Earth's atmosphere that would otherwise escape into space.

Although this so-called *greenhouse effect* warms Earth enough to support life, scientists fear that increased levels of greenhouse gases in the atmosphere may cause global warming and cause widespread crop failure and flooding. Greenhouse gases occur naturally, but human activities such as burning fossil fuels, including coal and oil, and the destruction of forests increase the concentration of greenhouse gases.

The debate over a so-called runaway greenhouse effect centers on several points: whether the climate is getting warmer as a result of increased greenhouse gases, how much of an increase in atmospheric carbon dioxide levels are needed to trigger global warming,

how much human activity may contribute to global warming, whether other natural processes will counteract the greenhouse effect, and whether increased carbon dioxide levels and global warming are good or bad for the world's ecosystems. For instance, some scientists claim that coral reefs, which are made of small animals called *polyps* and grow in tropical waters, will do well in warmer seas, but a panel of scientists told a United States Senate committee in October 1990 that warming seas are killing coral reefs.

Despite the scientific debate in other areas, there is firm agreement that levels of carbon dioxide have increased. In July 1990, scientists from Scripps Institution of Oceanography in La Jolla, Calif., reported that readings from the top of the volcanic mountain Mauna Loa on the island of Hawaii showed that the total amount of carbon dioxide in the atmosphere has risen sharply since the mid-1950's.

Inconclusive evidence. Evidence that Earth's climate is warming is not conclusive, according to most atmospheric scientists. Scientists at the University of East Anglia in Great Britain reported in January 1991 that 1990 was the warmest year since temperature recording began nearly 100 years ago. The British team found that the average surface temperature of the globe in 1990 was 0.05 Celsius degree (0.09 Fahrenheit degree) higher than in 1988, the previous warmest year.

Their findings are not universally accepted, however, because the researchers recorded many temperatures near cities, which are warmer than surrounding areas and may not accurately reflect average temperatures. In addition, scientists at the National Aeronautics and Space Administration's (NASA's) Marshall Space Flight Center in Huntsville, Ala., in January 1991 reported no definite warming trend since the late 1970's. The researchers used satellite temperature measurements to determine average temperatures around the globe.

Uncertainty about warming's effects. Scientists also disagreed about how global climate warming and increased levels of carbon dioxide in the atmosphere might affect plant and animal life. In November 1990, the Intergov-

Meteorology
Continued

Massive flooding resulted from a cyclone that struck Bangladesh on April 30, 1991, one of the worst storms ever to hit the nation. The cyclone and its aftermath killed at least 125,000 people and left thousands more homeless.

ernmental Panel on Climate Change (IPCC), a United Nations group, issued a report that lends support to some scientists' claim that increased carbon dioxide levels will benefit plants by promoting photosynthesis, the process by which plants use energy from sunlight to turn carbon dioxide and water into food. Although there is some evidence to support this claim, experts say that more research is needed to draw a final conclusion. See ECOLOGY.

Rate of future warming. In the same report, the IPCC predicted that global temperatures will rise about 0.3 Celsius degree (0.5 Fahrenheit degree) per decade for the next century if greenhouse gas production remains at the current level. Although this estimated temperature increase is half that of some previous predictions, it may be large enough to produce flooding in low-lying coastal areas as a result of polar ice melting, according to the group.

Evidence obtained by examining the growth cycles of glaciers and from examining remains of preserved plants shows that temperatures higher than those recorded in 1990 have occurred within the last 1,000 years. To some scientists this suggests that the Earth warms and cools in natural cycles and that any present appearance of global warming may not necessarily result from human activity.

Ozone "hole." NASA scientists found that seasonal thinning of the ozone layer above Antarctica in October 1990 tied that of 1987 and 1989, the worst years on record, for the second year in a row. Pollutants such as *chlorofluorocarbons* (CFC's) used in consumer products and refrigeration systems, are blamed for the ozone layer's deterioration. The ozone layer protects the Earth's surface from some of the damaging part of sunlight called *ultraviolet radiation.* (Ozone, a form of oxygen, is also found in the lower atmosphere, but there it is the result of chemical reactions between sunlight and pollutants. In the lower atmosphere, ozone can be dangerous to human health, causing respiratory problems.)

Meteorology
Continued

The NASA findings surprised scientists, whose observations of yearly fluctuations in the extent of the thinning led them to expect ozone levels to increase above Antarctica during 1990. The thinning has resulted in a "hole" in the region's ozone layer, in which nearly all the ozone in the upper atmosphere has been destroyed. In September 1990, NASA scientists also reported partial depletion of the ozone layer above the Arctic.

In April 1991, the EPA announced that ozone levels over the United States had decreased much faster than expected during the previous 12 years. Because ozone protects the skin from the sun's damaging ultraviolet radiation, the extra decrease could cause as many as 200,000 more skin cancer deaths than expected by 2041, according to the EPA.

Unlike the link between greenhouse gases and global climate warming, the relationship between CFC production and ozone depletion is fairly clear. CFC's have a long lifetime, and their ozone-destroying effects are expected to last for at least 50 years. Most industrial nations agreed in June 1990 at a meeting in London to stop producing CFC's by the year 2000.

New weather detection system. The National Weather Service began tests of new radar wind-detection systems in the Great Plains in October 1990. The new detection systems are installed on the ground but can read wind speeds up to 9,144 meters (30,000 feet) above the Earth's surface by sending radio waves into the air. By measuring the change in frequency of radio waves reflected from moving raindrops and ice particles, the radar systems can calculate wind speed.

The new wind detectors are designed as part of a broader, more advanced weather detection system planned by the National Weather Service to go into service during the 1990's. The system will include new surface observation stations, satellites, and advanced computers that will increase the accuracy and speed of weather forecasts. [Douglas K. Lilly]

In WORLD BOOK, see METEOROLOGY.

Neuroscience

A possible means for blocking two addictive effects of *opiate drugs* was reported in January 1991 by neuroscientists Keith Trujillo and Huda Akil of the Mental Health Research Institute at the University of Michigan in Ann Arbor. Opiate drugs, which include morphine and heroin, are derived from the opium poppy.

Morphine is frequently prescribed by doctors, particularly to relieve pain. Repeated doses of the drug produce *tolerance*, in which the body gradually adjusts to the drug. When this occurs, the patient must take larger doses of morphine to obtain the same amount of pain relief.

Prolonged morphine use leads to an additional effect, called *dependence*. In this condition, the body has adjusted itself to receiving morphine on a daily basis. When use of the drug is stopped, the patient suffers *withdrawal sickness*, a reaction that can include such symptoms as nausea, vomiting, chills, and diarrhea.

Trujillo and Akil studied the effects of repeated doses of morphine on laboratory rats. After each administration of morphine, the scientists measured the rats' reactions to a painful stimulus to learn how much pain relief the animals obtained from the drug.

The researchers also treated some of the rats with a chemical substance called *MK-801*. MK-801 blocks the effect of certain *neurotransmitters*, chemicals in the brain that transmit signals between *neurons* (nerve cells).

Rats that were treated with morphine alone became tolerant to the drug, as indicated by a steadily decreasing ability of the drug to ease their pain. In contrast, rats that received MK-801 along with constant-sized doses of morphine experienced a high level of pain relief throughout the experiment. This result indicated that the MK-801 had prevented the tolerance effect.

The investigators also tested the ability of MK-801 to prevent dependence. They found that rats receiving MK-801 developed much less physical need for morphine than rats that were given just morphine.

Further research on MK-801's ability to inhibit tolerance and dependence may help explain how these effects occur. The studies may also lead to ways of using opiate drugs for controlling pain in human patients without producing addictive effects.

Easier Alzheimer's diagnosis? The discovery of an unusual form of a brain chemical that might help physicians diagnose Alzheimer's disease was reported in February 1991 by a researcher in England. A. David Smith, a *neuropharmacologist* (a scientist who studies the effects of drugs on the nervous system) at Oxford University, said the altered chemical seems unique to Alzheimer's patients. It thus might be useful as a *marker*, or telltale sign, confirming the presence of the disease.

Alzheimer's disease, which affects mostly people over age 60, is an incurable disorder of unknown cause that destroys certain groups of neurons in the brain. As the disease progresses, the patient gradually loses mental abilities and finally dies.

Diagnosing Alzheimer's disease, especially in its early stages, can be very difficult. That is because other conditions, such as stroke or depression, can produce many of the same symptoms. Even when other possible health problems are ruled out, the physician may not be reasonably sure a patient has Alzheimer's until the person's mental deterioration has progressed to an advanced stage.

Smith and his colleagues examined the *cerebrospinal fluid* (fluid that bathes the brain and spinal cord) of 61 people who had died of various causes, including 23 who had died of Alzheimer's. The researchers found that 19 of the Alzheimer's victims had a previously unknown form of a brain chemical called *acetylcholinesterase* in their cerebrospinal fluid. The cerebrospinal fluid of the people who had not suffered from Alzheimer's did not contain the unusual form of the chemical. In its normal form, acetylcholinesterase acts to break down *acetylcholine*, an important neurotransmitter.

The neurons that are most affected by Alzheimer's disease all use acetylcholine to communicate, so researchers have long suspected that acetylcholine and acetylcholinesterase are strongly involved in the disease. The finding of the unusual form of acetylcholinesterase seems to confirm that theory. As well as serving as a possible diagnostic aid, the unusual chemical may shed light on the exact role of acetylcholinesterase in Alzheimer's disease. Such an insight could lead to an understanding of what causes the disease.

AIDS and the brain. New findings on how AIDS harms the brain were reported in December 1990 by neuroscientist Dana Giulian and co-workers at the Baylor College of Medicine in Houston. They reported that a *toxin* (poison) secreted by certain cells in the nervous system in AIDS patients may damage neurons.

AIDS can have a very destructive effect on the brain. More than half of all AIDS patients experience memory loss, confusion, or even paralysis at some stage in their illness. In some cases, the loss of brain function advances to the point of full-blown *dementia*, a severe deterioration of personality and intellectual ability.

Autopsies on the brains of AIDS patients who suffered brain damage from the disease have found extensive damage to neurons. The studies have shown, however, that the cells themselves are not infected with the human immunodeficiency virus (HIV), the virus that causes AIDS. Rather, the neurons seemed to have been damaged by a toxin secreted by three kinds of *phagocytes* (scavenger cells) infected with HIV: brain cells called *microglia* and immune-system cells called *macrophages* and *macrophagelike cells*.

The Baylor researchers exposed macrophagelike cells to HIV and found that the infected cells secreted a toxin. When they exposed neurons to the toxin, the neurons began dying within 10 hours. After 48 hours, about 60 per cent of the neurons were dead. The toxin behaved much like the toxins that are often created in the brain after a stroke or head injury.

Scientists plan further studies of the HIV-induced toxin. If they can find a way to block its effects, that knowledge might be applicable not only to AIDS but also to other brain conditions involving neuron-killing toxins.

Brain clues to suicide. People who commit suicide may have a brain chem-

Pictures of Thought Patterns

"Shadows of thoughts" are revealed with MANSCAN, an imaging technique developed at EEG Systems Laboratory in San Francisco. MANSCAN joins *electroencephalography* (EEG), a measurement of the brain's electrical activity, with a scanning method called *magnetic resonance imaging* (MRI) to produce 10 or more "snapshots" of the brain each second.

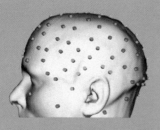

EEG data is collected with 124 electrodes placed at various points on the head.

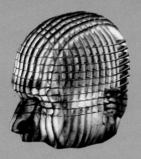

The three-dimensional MRI scan divides the brain into vertical and horizontal "slices."

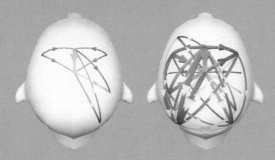

The combined EEG-MRI "snapshots" show electrical patterns during a series of moments. Activity is much higher during a memory task, *right,* than during a test requiring less concentration, *left.*

istry different from that of other people, according to research reported in November 1990 and February 1991 by scientists in Israel and the United States.

The study was conducted by neuroscientists Anat Biegon of the New York University School of Medicine in New York City and Ruth Gross-Isserof of the Weizmann Institute in Rehovot, Israel. The researchers compared the brains of 12 people who had committed suicide with the brains of 12 people of similar ages who had died of other causes. They found that the neurons of the suicide victims' brains had many more *opioid receptors* than the neurons of the other group's brains. Opioid receptors are molecular "doorways" on neurons that enable *opioids*—natural opiatelike substances in the brain—to enter the cells. Opioids are involved in the perception of pleasure and pain.

Researchers had long theorized that some sort of biochemical abnormality in the pleasure-pain centers of the brain might contribute to the feelings of deep depression experienced by many individuals, including a large percentage of those who commit suicide. A greater number of opioid receptors in the brain might make a person more prone to depression—and thus to committing suicide—than most other people.

Neuron-killing genes. The nematode, a tiny roundworm, may provide clues to why certain diseases of the nervous system, such as multiple sclerosis, cause nerve cells to die. Neuroscientist Martin Chalfie and his co-workers at Columbia University in New York City reported in November 1990 and February 1991 that they had found *mutations* (changes) in two genes of the nematode that account for neuron death in that simple organism. The investigators speculated that similar genes might affect human nerve cells.

The mutated genes cause the production of abnormal proteins. The researchers named these proteins *degenerins* because they have a degenerating effect on the nematode's neurons, causing them to swell and die.

By analyzing the nematode degenerins, the researchers hope to learn how the proteins are able to destroy nerve cells and how their action might be

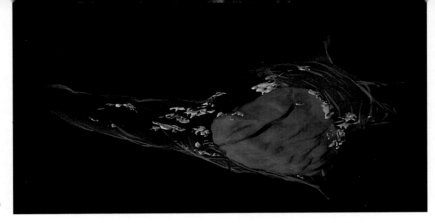

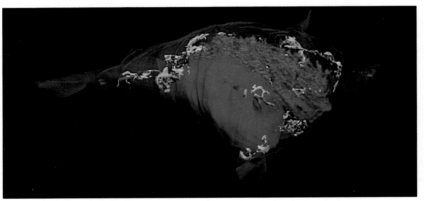

A Close-Up Look at Alzheimer's Disease
A brain cell from an Alzheimer's disease patient, *bottom,* contains abnormal fibers (orange) that are absent from a normal brain cell, *top.* From an analysis of the images, researchers speculate that mental decline in Alzheimer's may result when the fibers displace the cell nucleus (purple) and other structures. Scientists at the University of California at San Diego used a computer to assemble data from photomicrographs of cell slices into the three-dimensional images.

Neuroscience

Continued

blocked. There are fundamental similarities in the way all nervous systems develop and function, and many of the nematode's neurotransmitters are identical to ones in the human nervous system. Thus, studying the nematode may help solve the mysteries of human nervous-system diseases.

Sluggish brain, hyperactive behavior. New findings on the possible cause of hyperactivity were reported in February 1991 by neuroscientist Alan J. Zametkin and his colleagues at the National Institute of Mental Health in Bethesda, Md. Hyperactivity, also called *attention deficit hyperactivity disorder* (ADHD), affects as many as 4 per cent of school-age children, mostly boys. These children have difficulty controlling their impulses and focusing their attention. The disorder sometimes continues into adulthood.

Doctors often prescribe drugs called *amphetamines* to counteract hyperactive behavior. Amphetamines act as stimulants when taken by normal adults, but small doses have a calming effect in hyperactive children.

Zametkin and his associates used an imaging technique called *positron emission tomography* (PET) to compare the brains of normal adults with the brains of hyperactive adults who were parents of hyperactive children. PET uses radioactive *positrons* (positively charged electrons) to observe activity in the brain.

The researchers found that, compared with the normal subjects, the hyperactive individuals had a low level of activity in the brain areas that control mental concentration and body movement. This finding indicated that the cause of ADHD is physical, not psychological. It also explained why amphetamines counteract hyperactivity: The drugs apparently increase the activity of the brain areas that the PET scans showed were idling, enabling children to sit still and concentrate on mental tasks. But why those brain areas do not function at a normal level in some people must still be learned. See also PSYCHOLOGY. [George Adelman]

In WORLD BOOK, see BRAIN; NERVOUS SYSTEM.

Nobel Prizes

United States and Canadian scientists made a clean sweep of Nobel Prizes in the sciences in October 1990. The Royal Swedish Academy of Sciences in Stockholm, Sweden, awarded the Nobel Prize in chemistry to a U.S. organic chemist and the Nobel Prize in physics to one Canadian and two U.S. physicists. The Karolinska Institute, also in Stockholm, gave the Nobel Prize for physiology or medicine to two U.S. physicians. Each prize carried a cash award of about $700,000, which the recipients divided if there was more than one winner.

The chemistry prize went to Elias James Corey of Harvard University in Cambridge, Mass., for his pioneering work in *synthesizing* (creating laboratory duplicates of) complex molecules ordinarily found only in nature. In the mid-1960's, Corey carried out the first synthesis of *prostaglandins*, hormonelike compounds used to treat digestive ulcers, heart disease, and other illnesses. Before he developed synthetic prostaglandins, the drugs had to be extracted in tiny amounts from the pros-

tate glands of sheep and other animals. Corey and his assistants also synthesized more than 100 other important chemicals.

Corey developed a technique called *retrosynthetic analysis* that is now the standard method used in the drug and chemical industries to synthesize biological molecules. Using this technique, a chemist analyzes the structure of the desired compound and attempts to break it down into its components before trying to duplicate the original compound by assembling smaller units.

Corey was also one of the first to use computers to help identify the simplest way of synthesizing organic compounds. Many chemical and pharmaceutical laboratories use computer programs that he wrote.

The physics prize was shared by Richard E. Taylor, a Canadian-born physicist working at Stanford University in California, and Jerome I. Friedman and Henry W. Kendall, both of the Massachusetts Institute of Technology in Cambridge. The Nobel committee honored the three physicists for

Elias James Corey of Harvard University, winner of the 1990 Nobel Prize in chemistry, chats with Sweden's Queen Silvia at the Nobel Prize ceremonies in Stockholm, Sweden, in December 1990.

providing the first experimental evidence confirming the existence of subatomic particles called *quarks.*

Scientists once believed that particles called electrons, protons, and neutrons were the smallest building blocks of matter. In a famous series of experiments at the Stanford Linear Accelerator Center from 1967 to 1973, Friedman, Kendall, and Taylor fired a beam of electrons at a target containing protons and neutrons. The way the electrons scattered after hitting the target suggested that the protons and neutrons were not uniformly dense but were made up of pointlike objects, later identified as quarks.

The physiology or medicine prize was divided between two transplant pioneers, surgeon Joseph E. Murray of Brigham and Women's Hospital in Boston and *oncologist* (cancer specialist) E. Donnall Thomas of the Fred Hutchinson Cancer Research Center in Seattle. Murray performed the first successful human organ transplant in 1954, giving a man dying of kidney failure a healthy kidney from the man's identical twin brother. Murray later experimented with drugs that made it possible to transplant kidneys from unrelated donors. The drugs suppressed the patient's immune system and prevented it from rejecting the donated organ.

Thomas performed the first human bone-marrow transplant in 1956, also between identical twins. Bone marrow is a soft, blood-forming tissue that fills the cavities of many bones. Eventually, Thomas found improved tissue-matching techniques and antirejection drugs that made possible bone-marrow transplants between unrelated individuals.

Thomas pioneered a technique by which patients with leukemia, a form of blood cancer, receive a healthy new supply of bone marrow after all their own marrow has been destroyed by powerful drugs or radiation. The bone-marrow transplant procedure is now a standard treatment for leukemia, enabling doctors to cure many patients who would otherwise have died.   [Sara Dreyfuss]

In WORLD BOOK, see NOBEL PRIZES.

Nutrition

A study published in 1990 shed light on the question of whether calcium supplements can prevent bone loss in women. Another report revealed a connection between eating red meat and developing colon cancer. Other research supported the theory that the nutrient beta-carotene protects against heart disease, cancer, and infection.

Calcium reduces bone loss. Calcium supplements can help reduce bone loss, called *osteoporosis,* in some women past the age of *menopause* (the time in a woman's life when menstruation ceases). This finding was made by researchers at the U.S. Department of Agriculture (USDA) Human Nutrition Research Center on Aging at Tufts University in Medford, Mass.

Osteoporosis particularly affects postmenopausal women because the disease is linked to decreased levels of the hormone estrogen. This in turn can lead to depletion of calcium from the bones.

Calcium is naturally found in dairy foods, sardines, salmon, legumes such as soybeans, and leafy, green vegetables. Although researchers have known that adequate dietary calcium intake is important for building and maintaining strong bones, they have not known whether postmenopausal women would benefit from consuming extra calcium. Earlier studies have found that low levels of calcium maintained throughout life are associated with an increased risk of osteoporosis. Other reports have shown that calcium supplements slow the loss of bone calcium that leads to osteoporosis. But some surveys, equally well designed, have shown no such benefit.

During a two-year study, the USDA researchers evaluated the effects of calcium supplements taken by 361 women aged 40 to 70. Before the study began, half the women had normally consumed less than 400 milligrams of calcium per day. The others had a daily calcium intake of 400 to 650 milligrams. Seven women had regularly taken more than 650 milligrams of calcium per day.

Women who had reached menopause less than five years before the

Nutrition

Continued

study began showed rapid bone loss unaffected by extra calcium. But women who had experienced menopause at least six years before the study, and whose calcium was boosted from less than 400 milligrams per day to 800 milligrams per day, showed a significant decrease in bone loss. Other older postmenopausal women whose diets already included adequate amounts of calcium did not benefit from consuming calcium supplements. These findings reflect a long-standing belief among nutritionists: increasing low amounts of nutrients to adequate levels can be beneficial, but consuming more than what is needed provides no added gain.

Red meat and cancer. People who eat large amounts of animal fat are at increased risk for developing colon cancer, according to a December 1990 report by researchers at Harvard Medical School and Brigham and Women's Hospital in Boston. In the United States, cancerous tumors of the colon and rectum are the second leading cause of death from cancer.

Epidemiologist Walter C. Willett and his colleagues found that women who ate red meat, such as beef, pork, or lamb, as a main dish every day had nearly two-and-one-half times the risk of developing colon cancer as a similar group of women who ate red meat less than once a month. Neither vegetable fat nor the number of calories consumed were associated with increased cancer rates, but consuming liver and processed meats, such as packaged cold cuts, further increased the risk of developing colon cancer.

The findings were based on a study of the eating habits of 88,751 nurses aged 34 to 59. Of these, 150 developed colon cancer. Although the study was confined to women, other reviews of men's diets have shown similar connections between animal fat and cancer, according to the researchers. The conclusions supported established recommendations to replace red meat with chicken, fish, or other types of protein.

Clearing arteries with beta-carotene. Beta-carotene, a nutrient the human body converts to vitamin A, may help

A rhesus monkey eats a low-calorie meal as part of a nutrition study at the University of Wisconsin-Madison. Researchers there announced in November 1990 that decreased food consumption seemed to slow the aging process in the animals—a potentially important finding because rhesus monkeys and human beings are subject to similar age-related diseases.

Nutrition

Continued

prevent heart attacks and strokes in people with clogged arteries. Harvard Medical School researchers reported this at an American Heart Association meeting in November 1990.

The researchers studied 333 men who had symptoms of heart disease. Of this group, 160 men took supplements of beta-carotene for six years and 173 took no supplements. The group that took the supplements had only half as many heart attacks and strokes as did the group that did not.

The scientists believe beta-carotene prevents a form of blood cholesterol called low-density lipoprotein (LDL) from combining with oxygen, a process called *oxidation*, and changing into a harmful substance. According to the report, oxidized LDL's can damage artery walls and promote a build-up of deposits in them. The deposits restrict blood flow and can lead to heart attack or stroke. Until recently, the theory that beta-carotene and other antioxidants could help prevent heart disease has been supported primarily by animal research.

Another beta-carotene study showed that supplements increased the number of certain immune-system cells that protect against cancer and viral and bacterial infections. The research, published in January 1991 by scientists at the University of Arizona in Tucson, evaluated 60 men and women who took up to 60 milligrams of beta-carotene per day. The number of immune cells in the bodies of people who took only half this dose also increased appreciably.

The average American obtains about 1.5 milligrams of beta-carotene in the daily diet. People who are known to be at increased risk for developing cancer may want to take extra beta-carotene supplements, which are not harmful, said immunology researcher and coauthor of the study Ronald R. Watson. Other people could safely increase their levels of beta-carotene by eating more food that contains the nutrient. Such foods include carrots, yellow squash, sweet potatoes, and leafy, green vegetables.   [Robert Barnett]

In WORLD BOOK, see NUTRITION.

Oceanography

In July 1990, three paleontologists from the United States reported finding for the first time several prehistoric whale skeletons with functional foot bones and pelvic limbs, features the scientists believe reveal how the animals made the transition from land to sea. Although they live in the sea, whales belong to a group of aquatic mammals called *cetaceans* that evolved from hoofed land animals.

Philip D. Gingerich and B. Holly Smith of the University of Michigan in Ann Arbor, Mich., and Elwyn L. Simons of Duke University in Durham, N.C., uncovered more than 300 partial skeletons of ancient ancestors of modern whales during the late 1980's. They also unearthed several nearly complete 40-million-year-old skeletons of *Basilosaurus isis* in sandstone deposits about 95 miles southwest of Cairo, Egypt. *Basilosaurus isis* was a serpentlike whale approximately 16 meters (50 feet) long. These skeletons were the first of the cetacean family to be found with pelvic limbs and foot bones.

The well-formed limbs and three-toed feet were too small, however, to have been much use for swimming in the shallow seas that once covered northern Egypt. They were almost certainly not strong enough to support the whales on land, either. The scientists speculated that the hind limbs may have helped stabilize *Basilosaurus isis* for activities such as mating, a difficult task for a serpentine animal in shallow, offshore waters. They may also have helped *Basilosaurus isis* free itself from bottom mud. See also PALEONTOLOGY.

Phytoplankton linked to monsoons. Microscopic ocean plants called *phytoplankton* may contribute to the formation of monsoons in the Arabian Sea by raising sea surface temperatures above the level caused by normal summer warming. A team of oceanographers led by Shubha Sathyendranath at Dalhousie University in Halifax, Canada, reported this finding in January 1991. The scientists used satellite observation of specific types of electromagnetic radiation reflected from the sea surface to determine approximate phytoplankton concentrations. They used these

Tracking a Huge Iceberg

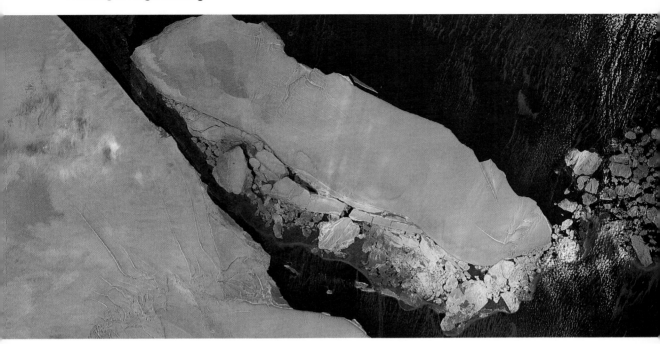

In late 1990, scientists reported satellite observations of the movement of a 154-kilometer-long (96-mile-long) iceberg, *above,* which broke off from the Ross Ice Shelf in Antarctica in 1987. By tracking the iceberg's path, *right,* the researchers identified a complex system of currents along the Antarctic coast.

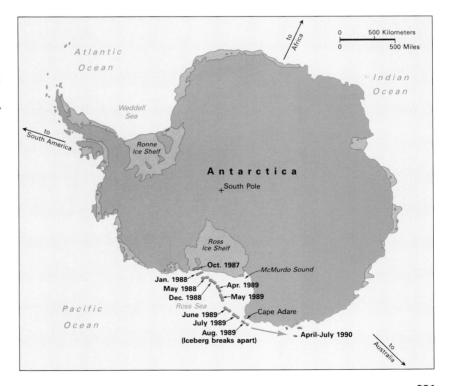

Oceanography

Continued

observations and a computer model to compare surface temperatures with different concentrations of phytoplankton and to calculate the temperature of surface waters when no phytoplankton was present. They found sea surface temperatures were between 1 and 4 Celsius degrees (1.8 and 7 Fahrenheit degrees) higher from August to September, when phytoplankton levels are higher than other times of the year.

In a process called *photosynthesis*, phytoplankton use the energy from sunlight to convert water and carbon dioxide into sugar. During this process, phytoplankton absorb sunlight and heat the surrounding water. The amount of phytoplankton on the surface varies depending on the presence of nutrient-bearing currents from deeper water. Monsoons often contribute to this process by drawing these currents to the surface, according to the researchers.

Because warm ocean water often contributes to the formation of monsoons and other tropical storms, Sathyendranath suggested that weather forecasters can use phytoplankton growth as a forecasting tool.

Ocean stagnation. One feature of worldwide ocean circulation has nearly stopped, according to a March 1991 report by oceanographer Peter Schlosser and his colleagues at Columbia University's Lamont-Doherty Geological Observatory in Palisades, N.Y. The oceanographers reported that the sinking of dense, cold ocean water near Greenland nearly stopped between 1979 and 1989. Using water samples taken from different depths, Schlosser and his team measured circulation below 1,500 meters (4,900 feet) at various sites east of Greenland in the central Greenland Sea.

Most of the water below 1,000 meters (3,280 feet) in the North Atlantic Ocean comes from the Arctic Ocean. First, this dense, cold water enters the Norwegian Sea and Greenland Sea. From there, it flows over ridgelike geologic formations on the ocean floor and sinks into the North Atlantic.

According to Schlosser, Arctic waters sank to the bottom of the Greenland Sea in the 1960's and 1970's at a rate that renewed the bottom water there approximately every 34 years. These waters sink because they are slightly saltier and colder—and thus more dense—than the Greenland and Norwegian waters, according to Schlosser.

Schlosser estimated that the rate of sinking slowed by about 80 per cent sometime between 1978 and 1982, however, and continued to slow through the latest tests in 1989. The team estimated that at the slower rate, it would take 170 years to renew Greenland Sea bottom water, making the sea nearly stagnant.

This finding is important because the circulation of deep water in the Greenland Sea is a key link in a global process that trades heat and gases such as carbon dioxide between the oceans and Earth's atmosphere. This process works like a conveyor belt to carry warm water from the equator to the poles, where the water gives up its heat to the atmosphere by *convection* (the transfer of heat from one place to another). The water then cools, sinks, and travels toward the equator, where the cycle begins again. A disruption in this process could affect global climate. Although an exact cause for the change in the Greenland Sea circulation is uncertain, a decrease in water *salinity* (saltiness) may play a role, according to Schlosser. In the Special Reports section, see CURRENTS AND CLIMATE.

Young reef. Australia's *Great Barrier Reef*, the largest structure made by living organisms, may be younger than previously supposed, according to a November 1990 report. The Great Barrier Reef consists of various kinds of *coral*, a stony substance made of the skeletons of small animals called *polyps*. It covers an area about the size of Utah, approximately 200,000 square kilometers (80,000 square miles), and stretches 2,000 kilometers (1,200 miles) along Australia's northeastern coast.

In the early 1970's, researchers judged that the reef was 20 million years old. In November 1990, oceanographers aboard the drillship *JOIDES Resolution* reported that the reef is much younger, however. By studying fossils contained in samples taken from 5,000 meters (3 miles) below the reef, the scientists determined that the reef is between 500,000 and 1 million years old.   [Lauriston R. King]

In WORLD BOOK, see OCEAN.

Paleontology

A new analysis of a spectacular collection of fossils dating from 520 million to 530 million years ago has provided dramatic evidence that the development of complex life forms was more sudden and widespread than scientists had believed. The analysis, published in May 1991, was conducted by paleontologists from Sweden and China.

The fossils, which were found in China in 1984, date from the Cambrian Period. During this geologic period, which lasted from 570 million years ago to about 500 million years ago, life forms became increasingly numerous and complex. Before the Cambrian "explosion," life forms consisted mainly of one-celled organisms, such as bacteria and algae.

The fossils found in China represent 70 species of marine animals, including worms, sponges, and trilobites. They were found on what once was a muddy seabed. The creatures were apparently buried in mud stirred up from the sea floor by a violent storm. The fossils are unusually well preserved because a lack of oxygen in the mud prevented decay.

Many of the species found in China resemble those found in the Burgess Shale, a famous fossil bed in the Canadian Rockies that dates from 530 million years ago. The Burgess fossils had been the main source of information about the life forms that existed during the Cambrian Period. The similarity between the two groups of fossils suggests that the explosion of life during the Cambrian Period was more widespread and earlier than scientists had believed.

One of the most significant of the Chinese fossils is an armor-plated, wormlike animal that was a type of onychophoran. An analysis of this fossil has helped clear up mysteries surrounding two other fossils. Scientists discovered that small, porous plates previously believed to represent a separate organism actually were part of the onychophoran's armor. They also found that the Chinese onychophoran was a close relative of *Hallucigenia*, a weird fossil from the Burgess Shale. Long considered a unique life form, *Hallucigenia* now appears to have been

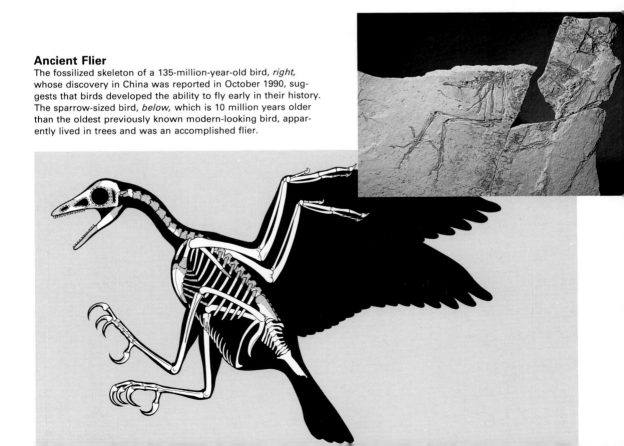

Ancient Flier
The fossilized skeleton of a 135-million-year-old bird, *right,* whose discovery in China was reported in October 1990, suggests that birds developed the ability to fly early in their history. The sparrow-sized bird, *below,* which is 10 million years older than the oldest previously known modern-looking bird, apparently lived in trees and was an accomplished flier.

A New Look at *T. Rex*

Paleontologist Jack Horner of the Museum of the Rockies in Bozeman, Mont., and his team examine the fossilized skeleton of a *Tyrannosaurus rex, below,* found in Montana. The June 1990 discovery included the first complete examples of the dinosaur's tiny arm bones.

Contracted

Relaxed

Some scientists think that the arms, *above,* long considered weak, were powerful pincers capable of holding about 195 kilograms (425 pounds) of prey. They suggest that *T. rex* may have been a hunter rather than a scavenger.

Paleontology

Continued

Oldest land animals. Well-explored fossil sites may sometimes yield new discoveries. In October 1990, a team of British scientists reported finding fossils from the oldest known land-dwelling animals in a section of rock in England that has been famous for its fossils since the early 1800's. The newly discovered fossils are from the late Silurian Period, about 414 million years ago. They are 14 million years older than the oldest previously known land animals.

The scientists found the fossilized remains of three types of *arthropods* (joint-legged animals). They include two types of centipede and a trigonotarbid arachnid, an early relative of spiders. The fossils consist of tough outer coatings from the bodies of these ancient animals.

The British scientists noted that the ancient arthropods were meat-eaters. This suggests that these animals were part of an ecosystem at the site that was well established by 414 million years ago and so they must have moved onto the land even earlier than that.

The discovery of the arthropods also suggests that animals emerged from the ocean soon after plants started to colonize the land, about 470 million years ago. Some scientists have argued that plants were well established on land long before the first animals emerged from the ocean.

Early amphibians. Descriptions and illustrations of early amphibian fossils, published in September 1990 by zoologists at the University of Cambridge in England, challenged some long-held views about these creatures. Except for some highly specialized forms, nearly all modern *tetrapods* (land-dwelling vertebrates with four legs) have five toes or five fingers on each limb. Paleontologists have long assumed that this five-digit pattern evolved with the first tetrapods—amphibians that appeared about 360 million years ago. But the British zoologists' discovery of the first well-preserved fossilized limbs of these early amphibians has called this assumption into question.

The scientists reported that *Ichthyostega*, a fishlike amphibian, had seven digits on its hind limbs. Another equally ancient amphibian called *Acanthostega* had eight digits on its front legs. The extra digits would correspond to fingers or toes extending from the outside of the thumb or big toe. The discovery indicates that the five-digit pattern must have developed later in tetrapod evolution.

Whales with hind legs. The discovery of well-preserved fossilized skeletons of primitive whales has provided the first direct evidence that these animals had functional hind legs and feet. The discovery was reported in July 1990 by a team of scientists headed by paleontologist Philip D. Gingerich. Paleontologists have long known that modern whales evolved from land-dwelling mammals that walked on four legs.

The fossils, which date from the Eocene Period, about 45 million years ago, were found in north-central Egypt. They belong to a species of whale called *Basilosaurus*, a large serpentlike creature that lived about 10 million years after whales first appear in the fossil record. The skeletons show that the animals had short, permanently flexed legs with three toes. Gingerich and his colleagues concluded that the hind legs were too small to have been used for walking on land. They speculate that *Basilosaurus* may have used the limbs as guides or "stabilizers" during mating. See also OCEANOGRAPHY.

Oldest mushroom. The rare discovery of a well-preserved fossilized mushroom was reported in June 1990 by biologist George Poinar, Jr., of the University of California at Berkeley and botanist Ralph Finger of the Field Museum of Natural History in Chicago. Because mushrooms decay rapidly, few mushroom fossils have been found.

Poinar and Finger found the fossilized mushroom in a lump of *amber* (hardened resin from coniferous trees) in 20-million-year-old rocks. According to the scientists, the fossil mushroom has several modern features, including "gills" on the underside. The modern appearance of the fossilized mushroom suggests that mushrooms probably evolved much earlier than 20 million years ago.   [Carlton E. Brett]

In WORLD BOOK, see ARTHROPOD; PALEONTOLOGY; WHALE.

Physics, Fluids and Solids

Physicists in 1990 and 1991 continued to explore the properties of materials cooled to extremely low temperatures. At ultralow temperatures, solids and liquids often exhibit unusual properties. Physicists have already discovered that very cold solids may become *superconducting*—able to conduct electricity without resistance. And supercooled liquids, called *superfluids*, flow without friction.

Supercooling metals. In January 1991, physicist Bernard Vinet and his co-workers at the University of Grenoble in France reported that they had cooled molten tungsten and rhenium almost 1,000 Celsius degrees below their melting points without the metals' solidifying. These elements have higher melting points than other metals: Tungsten's is 3417 °C (6182 °F) and rhenium's is 3177 °C (5751 °F).

For some years, physicists have been investigating the mechanisms by which liquids change to solids as they cool. They have found that when a liquid is cooled to its freezing point, solidification sets in at some points before others. First, a few atoms group together. As other atoms settle on the tiny solid area, it grows rapidly in a process called *nucleation*.

One kind of nucleation, *homogeneous nucleation*, occurs when some atoms stick together randomly as the liquid cools. Another kind of nucleation, called *heterogeneous nucleation*, is caused by the presence of tiny impurities, such as dust. Solidification occurs as the atoms or molecules of the liquid stick to the impurities rather than to one another. Heterogeneous nucleation occurs at higher temperatures than homogeneous nucleation and is the most common cause of freezing.

Water, for example, usually freezes at exactly 0 °C (32 °F), either because it contains impurities or because nucleation sets in where the water comes into contact with the walls of its container. But when extremely pure water is cooled very slowly, it can remain liquid below 0 °C. The process of cooling a liquid beyond its normal freezing point without its solidifying is called *supercooling* or *undercooling*.

New Bonding Technique

At Argonne National Laboratory near Chicago, a scientist demonstrates a process for applying a thin metal coating to ceramic surfaces, *below*. As atoms of molten metal rise in a vacuum chamber, a beam of *ions* (charged particles) bonds the atoms to the ceramic, *right*. The process may be used in making ceramic engines.

Ceramic surface

Ion beam

Metal atoms

Molten metal

Molten metals can also be undercooled significantly when kept away from an impurity or other material that might bring about heterogeneous nucleation. The metal thus cannot sit in a container for undercooling to occur. The scientists at Grenoble solved this problem by letting drops of liquid metal fall down a tube 48 meters (160 feet) long. All the air was pumped out of the tube to prevent contamination.

To create the drops, the researchers melted the tips of a tungsten wire and a rhenium wire with a beam of electrons. Each drop of molten metal reached a temperature about 150 Celsius degrees (270 Fahrenheit degrees) above its normal melting point, then cooled while falling down the tube. Sensors on the tube measured the temperature of the drops as they passed. A sudden slight increase in temperature indicated that the drops had become solid.

The tungsten drops solidified at 2887 °C (5229 °F), which is 530 Celsius degrees below tungsten's melting point. The rhenium drops showed even greater undercooling, solidifying at 2202 °C (3996 °F), or 975 Celsius degrees below rhenium's melting point. Because all the drops of each metal solidified at almost exactly the same temperature, the scientists at Grenoble believe they observed the result of true homogeneous nucleation. If nucleation had been caused by impurities, the drops would have solidified over a range of temperatures.

Approaching absolute zero. The lowest temperatures to date, one- or two-millionths of one degree above absolute zero, were recorded in August and September 1990. Absolute zero is believed to be the lowest attainable temperature—equal to −273.15 °C (−459.67 °F). Scientists use the Kelvin scale to express extremely low temperatures. In this scale, absolute zero corresponds to 0 Kelvin. At this temperature, atoms and molecules have the least possible energy. Physicists theorize that it is impossible to reach a temperature of precisely absolute zero, though it is possible to come very close.

In August, a group of scientists at the École Normale Supérieure (ENS) in Paris reported that they had cooled cesium atoms to a temperature of 2.5 microkelvin. (One microkelvin equals one-millionth of one degree Kelvin.) In September, a team at the University of Colorado in Boulder reported cooling atoms to 1.1 microkelvin.

The low temperature records were achieved by using a laser-cooling technique developed in the 1980's. In this technique, beams of light from several lasers are directed at cesium gas atoms in a vacuum.

Both the French and American teams trapped the atoms in what is known as an *optical molasses*. The "molasses" is a region of intense light where six beams of laser light intersect. *Photons* (light particles) from the lasers interact with the atoms in such a way as to slow the atoms' natural vibrations. The motion of atoms and molecules produces heat energy. The greater the motion, the greater the heat produced. So slowing this motion lowers the temperature of the atoms.

In the French experiment, a beam of cesium atoms was released in a tabletop vacuum chamber at a velocity of about 300 meters (980 feet) per second, which corresponds to a temperature of 100 °C. Each time an atom in the chamber collided with a photon from a laser beam, its speed dropped by about 3 millimeters (0.1 inch) per second. Over a distance of 2 meters (6.5 feet), the atoms collided with about 100,000 photons and slowed down to a few meters per second. When these slow atoms reached the optical molasses, their motion was further reduced to about 1 centimeter per second.

The physicists used the speed of the atoms to determine their temperature. To do this, they switched off the six laser beams. Some of the atoms then dropped into the beam of another laser. This laser caused the atoms to *fluoresce* (emit light), and the light given off could be studied by the researchers. The patterns of the light revealed how far apart the atoms had spread in the time they fell and thus how fast they were moving.

The Colorado team, led by physicist Carl Wieman, used a magnetic field in addition to an optical molasses to trap the gas atoms. The magnetic trap helped hold the atoms in the laser beam trap and cooled them to 1.1 microkelvin.   [Alexander Hellemans]

In WORLD BOOK, see PHYSICS.

Matter and antimatter have the same mass, according to a measurement accurate to 1 part in 25 million reported in June 1990. Antimatter is made up of elementary particles that are exactly like the elementary particles that compose ordinary matter except for their electric charge, which is the opposite. For example, the antimatter counterpart of the electron, which has a negative charge, is the positron, which has a positive charge.

The exceptionally precise experiment, which was comparable to measuring the weight of two automobiles to within the weight of a grain of rice, was the work of a team of physicists from Harvard University in Cambridge, Mass.; the University of Washington in Seattle; and the University of Mainz in Germany. The team, headed by Harvard's Gerald Gabrielse, carried out the experiment at the European Organization for Nuclear Research (CERN) near Geneva, Switzerland. The particles measured were the proton and its antimatter counterpart, the antiproton.

That particles and their antiparticles must have exactly equal masses is predicted by two fundamental theories of physics—the theory of relativity developed by German-born physicist Albert Einstein and the quantum theory of matter. All ideas about the nature of subatomic matter use these two theories as their framework. Finding a difference in mass between matter and antimatter particles would imply that one or both of the theories is seriously flawed.

Measurements of comparable accuracy have been carried out with electrons and positrons. Physicists did not know, however, if similar measurements would be found with protons and antiprotons. These particles are subject to one force that electrons are insensitive to—the strong nuclear force, which holds *quarks* (fundamental building blocks of matter) together inside protons and neutrons. This force accounts for most of the mass of protons and antiprotons.

Producing antiprotons. Physicists find it extremely difficult to work with antimatter. If antiprotons—or any other antimatter particle—come in contact with ordinary matter, they are annihilated in a flash of energy. The experimenters had to produce antiprotons in a particle accelerator, a device that hurls subatomic particles together in violent collisions. The physicists then had to slow the antiprotons to about $\frac{1}{100}$ of the speed at which they were produced and store them in a vacuum in a device called a *Penning Trap*. The trap uses a combination of electric and magnetic fields to hold particles in circular orbits. Although millions of antiprotons were produced in the accelerator, it took many hours to capture and store as many as 10,000 in a Penning Trap.

To keep the antiprotons from straying from orbit, the scientists cooled them to a temperature of 4 degrees above absolute zero—the lowest temperature possible, about -273 °C (-459 °F). By measuring the time required for the antiprotons to complete each orbital revolution in the Penning Trap, the scientists were able to calculate a precise estimate of their mass. The measurement was then repeated using protons instead of antiprotons.

Solar neutrinos. A new detector that scientists hoped would shed light on the mystery of "missing" solar neutrinos yielded surprising results in 1991. Solar neutrinos are elementary particles produced as a result of nuclear reactions inside the core of the sun. The theory of how nuclear reactions occur in the sun predicts that a certain number of neutrinos are produced each second. But scientists who set up previous neutrino detectors, beginning in the late 1960's, had observed only one-third to one-half the predicted number.

The new detector, which is called the Soviet-American Gallium Experiment (SAGE), was a joint project of scientists from the Soviet Union and the United States. It was designed to be more sensitive than earlier instruments. As of June 1991, however, this device had not detected a single neutrino that could definitely be traced to the sun, thereby deepening the solar neutrino mystery.

Neutrinos easily penetrate matter, passing right through Earth with little chance of being absorbed. They can even escape the hot dense core of the sun, where energy is produced in nuclear fusion reactions. These reactions

The Continuing Neutrino Mystery

Physicists in 1991 continued searching for electron neutrinos, subatomic particles that are produced by the sun and other stars and radiated into space.

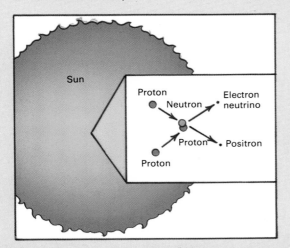

Many nuclear reactions in the sun eventually cause four protons to join and form a helium nucleus. The most common first step toward this is a reaction in which two protons collide. One proton is converted into a neutron and gives off an electron neutrino and a positron.

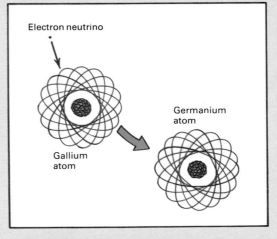

Electron neutrinos have almost no mass, so they pass through Earth without disturbing anything. But occasionally, an electron neutrino will collide with the nucleus of a large atom, such as gallium, changing a neutron in the atom's nucleus into a proton. This converts the gallium atom to a germanium atom.

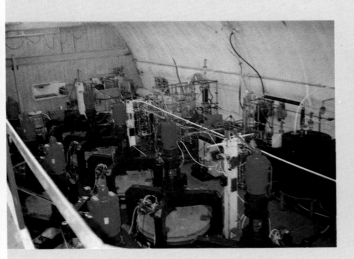

The most sensitive solar neutrino detector yet devised, the Soviet-American Gallium Experiment, consists of large, gallium-filled tanks underground in the Caucasus Mountains. Instruments there can detect the conversion of gallium atoms to germanium, and thus the presence of electron neutrinos. But no conversions that can definitely be attributed to solar neutrinos had been detected by June 1991.

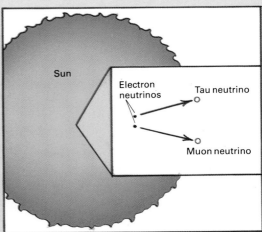

In trying to solve the puzzle of the missing neutrinos, some physicists reason that electron neutrinos are converted to other types of neutrinos—called *tau* or *muon*—on their way from the sun's core to Earth. These neutrinos are even more difficult to detect than electron neutrinos.

fuse, or combine, hydrogen nuclei to form helium nuclei. The nucleus of most hydrogen atoms consists of a single proton. The nucleus of a helium atom, however, contains two protons and two neutrons. When hydrogen nuclei fuse to form helium, two protons are converted into neutrons, a process that always leads to the emission of a neutrino.

Knowing the rate at which nuclear reactions occur in the sun and knowing that neutrinos can escape from the sun's core, scientists can calculate how many neutrinos should reach Earth. They estimate that about 70 billion neutrinos pass through each square centimeter of Earth every second.

Early neutrino detectors. The oldest neutrino detector on Earth has been operating since 1968 deep underground in South Dakota's Homestake gold mine. The detector uses a tank of *perchloroethylene*. The nuclei of chlorine atoms in perchloroethylene occasionally absorb a neutrino. When this happens, chlorine nuclei are converted to radioactive argon nuclei, which can be detected with a radiation counter. At Homestake, fewer than one neutrino per day is detected—less than one-third the expected number.

Since 1987, solar neutrinos also have been monitored in a tank of water called the Kamiokande detector, which is located in a Japanese lead mine. When neutrinos collide with electrons in the water, the electrons give off tiny flashes of light as they move through the water. Electronic sensors on the wall of the tank can detect these flashes.

The Kamiokande detector sees less than one-half the neutrinos expected. Neither the Homestake nor the Kamiokande detector is sensitive to the sun's principal form of fusion, called the *proton-proton chain*, or *pp reaction*, that produces more than 98 per cent of solar neutrinos. Neutrinos from the pp reaction have a maximum energy of 0.42 million electronvolts (0.42 MeV). (An electronvolt is the amount of energy an electron gains when it moves across an electric potential of 1 volt.) Homestake can detect only neutrinos with an energy above 0.83 MeV, and Kamiokande can detect only neutrinos above 7.5 MeV. These more energetic neutrinos come from rare nuclear re-

actions in the sun that produce less than 2 per cent of all solar neutrinos.

The SAGE detector uses the rare metal gallium, which can be transformed into radioactive germanium by neutrinos with as little as 0.23 MeV of energy. Nearly half of the pp neutrinos have this much energy. SAGE consists of several tanks of gallium in an underground laboratory in the Soviet Union.

The first data from SAGE were reported in August 1990. Scientists observed that 20 gallium nuclei were converted to radioactive germanium during five months of operation. But this was the number expected from the effects of background radiation alone, which comes from the radioactive decay of rocks. To account for the sun's energy production, scientists would have had to observe 40 conversions.

Many scientists believe that the most likely explanation for these results is that neutrinos are being generated in the sun at the expected rate, but that something happens to them before they reach Earth. Three types of neutrinos exist, but only one, the electron neutrino, is produced in the sun.

Some scientists believe that electron neutrinos are being converted to one or both of the other types, either spontaneously or through interactions with matter in the sun. The Homestake and SAGE detectors are sensitive only to electron neutrinos. Kamiokande can detect the other two varieties but it is not very sensitive to them.

Solar neutrinos, therefore, might not be "missing." Instead, they may have been changed into other types of neutrinos known as *muon* and *tau*.

One way or another, these experiments are telling physicists something important, either about the sun or about neutrinos. New, more sensitive detectors now on the drawing boards may help settle the question.

The t quark. Physicists continued their search for the elusive *t quark* during 1990 and 1991 but without success. Quarks, the fundamental particles that make up protons and neutrons in the atomic nucleus, are among 12 fundamental building blocks of matter. Four of the 12 particles—the u quark, d quark, electron, and electron neutrino—dominate the universe today. But in the first moments of the creation

"I always get it confused. Was that
an example of fusion or fission?"

Physics,
Subatomic

Continued

of our universe, eight other elementary
particles had important roles to play.
Most of these particles can be observed
in particle accelerator collisions.

According to the theory that describes the 12 fundamental particles,
the heaviest of all should be the t quark,
which has so far eluded detection. Only
the world's most powerful particle accelerator, the Tevatron at Fermilab
near Batavia, Ill., has sufficient energy
to produce t quarks in quantity. Inside
the Tevatron, beams of protons and
antiprotons travel in opposite directions. When they collide and annihi-
late, they release as much as 3.6 trillion
electronvolts (3.6 TeV) of energy. Each
collision produces dozens of particles,
and on rare occasions one of these
should be a t quark.

Physicists believe the t quark is a
highly unstable particle that breaks up
too quickly to be observed directly. But
its disintegration will set off a telltale
sequence of particle reactions, one of
which will release an unusually energetic electron or a *muon*. (A muon is an
elementary particle that closely resem-

bles an electron but has a greater mass.)

Physicists at Fermilab have been
searching for examples of this reaction
with a massive apparatus called the
Colliding Detector Facility. As of June
1991, their search was unsuccessful.
The Fermilab physicists calculated that
the t quark would have been found if it
had a mass equivalent to less than 90
billion electronvolts (90 GeV). (Physicists often state the mass of a particle in
terms of its equivalent energy.)

Theoretical estimates, however,
place the mass of the t quark in the
range of 120 to 200 GeV. This mass
would make the production of t quarks
too rare to have been seen to date.
However, planned improvements in
the strength of the proton and antiproton beams that collide with each other
at Tevatron will permit a search for
rarer collisions, including those that
produce particles with masses up to
140 GeV.   [Robert H. March]

In the Special Reports section, see
QUESTIONS OF GRAVITY. In WORLD
BOOK, see NEUTRINO; PARTICLE PHYSICS;
QUARK.

Psychology

The effectiveness of audiotapes that carry *subliminal messages*, words or phrases recorded at volumes so low or speeds so fast they cannot be consciously heard, was called into question by a study released in August 1990. Manufacturers of these tapes claim that listening to them produces such benefits as improved memory.

Psychologist Anthony G. Greenwald and his colleagues at the University of Washington in Seattle gave commercially available subliminal tapes to 237 adult volunteers. The tapes aimed to boost memory or self-esteem by subliminal messages recorded with audible sounds of ocean waves. Half the tapes used in the study carried an accurate label, while the remainder were falsely labeled, so that some of the subjects who thought they were given memory tapes actually received self-esteem tapes and vice versa.

After one month, the researchers administered tests to measure changes in the volunteers' self-esteem or ability to remember. People who listened to memory tapes displayed no more memory improvement than those who listened to self-esteem tapes. Likewise, volunteers who used self-esteem tapes showed no more increase in self-worth than those who heard memory tapes.

But the perception of some volunteers differed from the tapes' intent. For example, people who used self-esteem tapes labeled as memory enhancers reported that their memory but not their self-esteem had improved.

Language processing. The human brain uses different mechanisms for processing written and spoken words of different grammatical classes, such as verbs and nouns, according to a March 1991 report. The researchers, neuropsychologists Alfonso Caramazza of Johns Hopkins University and Argye E. Hillis of HealthSouth Rehabilitation Corporation, both in Baltimore, studied how different brain regions control thought and behavior. They reported their findings after examining two women who had suffered strokes damaging small areas on the left side of the brain.

On a series of tests, the women made frequent errors pronouncing or writing verbs but not nouns. One woman made errors only when pronouncing verbs, while the other had problems only when writing verbs.

The same pattern extended to words that convey different meanings as nouns or verbs, but retain the same sound and spelling. For example, the word *crack* can serve as either a noun ("There's a crack in the mirror") or as a verb ("Don't crack the nuts here."). The first woman had difficulty only with reading aloud such words used as verbs, while the second did poorly only when trying to write them.

Mathematics memory. A study relevant to education concluded in December 1990 that people who take college courses in calculus or more advanced mathematics retain most of what they had learned in high school algebra or geometry classes. The report showed that if students take classes spread over several years that expand on previously learned material, their memory of that prior material is significantly boosted.

Psychologist Harry P. Bahrick and colleague Lynda K. Hall of Ohio Wesleyan University in Delaware, Ohio, gave an algebra or geometry test to 1,524 volunteers who had taken their last algebra or geometry class several months to 50 years earlier.

Those who took college calculus, which builds on the principles of high school mathematics, answered at least 80 per cent of the test questions correctly, even if they had graduated from high school 50 years earlier. Volunteers who took no college calculus scored poorly.

Mathematics aptitude played no role in the results. People with the same high school math grades displayed great differences in their ability to remember math 50 years later, depending on whether they took college calculus. In addition, few of the volunteers reported using algebra or geometry in their daily lives. Bahrick suggested that this and similar surveys indicate that memory for many school subjects might be improved if classes met weekly for one or two years, rather than daily for a few months.

Academic acceleration. Contrary to the fears of many parents and teachers, intellectually advanced teen-agers may be able to skip a grade or take college-level courses without suffering social

Positron emission tomography (PET) scans published in November 1990 by government researchers in Bethesda, Md., show less neurological activity in the brain of a hyperactive person (right) than in that of a person without the disorder. Activity (white, orange, and red) is decreased most in areas of the brain that control movement and attention. The PET scans suggest that hyperactivity may stem from a neurological disorder rather than from psychosocial problems.

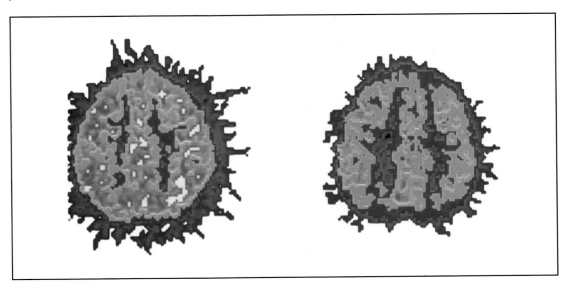

Psychology

Continued

and emotional maladjustment. This finding was published in September 1990 by psychologists Teri M. Richardson and Camilla P. Benbow of Iowa State University in Ames.

The psychologists studied 1,247 students ages 12 to 14 who had scored in the top 1 per cent on a national academic achievement test. The students had the verbal and math abilities of pupils four to five years older. About half the students later entered some type of accelerated academic program.

When surveyed at ages 18 and 23, the young adults generally reported feeling good about themselves and in control of their lives. Even those who had skipped the most grades or taken the most college courses reported no difficulties in adjusting or making friends. In fact, young women said academic acceleration slightly improved their social lives.

Anxiety and pregnancy. Emotional distress and anxiety during pregnancy contribute to premature births and low birth weights among newborns, regardless of the mother's medical condi-

tion. This conclusion was announced in August 1990 by psychologist Marci Lobel of the State University of New York at Stony Brook. The finding was significant because babies weighing less than 2.5 kilograms (5.5 pounds) may face life-threatening risks, including breathing and digestive problems, in the first months of life.

Lobel's research team studied 130 women receiving prenatal care at a Los Angeles medical center. In addition to checking the women's medical histories, the researchers monitored anxious feelings and distressing events reported by each woman during her pregnancy. Women reporting the most daily anxiety throughout pregnancy proved most likely to deliver premature and low-birth-weight babies. All pregnant women experience some anxiety, often without effects on the fetus, Lobel observed. But the study suggests that markedly distressed women may need help to ease their emotional burden to safeguard their unborn children.   [Bruce Bower]

In WORLD BOOK, see PSYCHOLOGY.

A dentist with AIDS (acquired immune deficiency syndrome) probably infected at least five of his patients, according to reports in 1990 and 1991 from the United States Centers for Disease Control (CDC) in Atlanta, Ga. The information stirred concern and controversy among health care workers, many of whom perform procedures that might leave patients vulnerable to infection. In response, the American Dental Association called for dentists infected with the AIDS-causing human immunodeficiency virus (HIV) either to not perform invasive procedures or to disclose their infection to their patients.

A CDC report noted that the Florida dentist could have transmitted the AIDS virus through cuts or needlestick injuries he experienced while treating his patients. The patients may have become infected if blood from such cuts came into contact with open wounds caused by procedures such as tooth extractions.

Infectious disease specialists do not know the exact number of patients the dentist treated after he became infected. When the state health department tested 732 of the dentist's patients, it found 2 infected with the AIDS virus. It identified another by comparing patients' names with the state's AIDS records.

The CDC reminded all health care workers, including dentists, of precautions they should take to avoid blood contact between themselves and their patients. These included wearing latex gloves and properly cleaning and sterilizing equipment and instruments. Although the Florida dentist practiced some safety measures, lapses occurred, according to investigators. Instead of using a new pair of latex gloves for each patient, he and his staff sometimes washed and reused the gloves. The dental equipment also was not always cleaned according to recommendations, investigators reported.

AIDS death toll surpasses 100,000. Since efforts began in 1981 to track the AIDS epidemic, more than 100,000 people in the United States have died from the illness, and almost one-third of these deaths were reported in 1990. If the trend continues, AIDS could rank among the top five causes of death for the U.S. population in 1991.

Of those who had died from the disease by January 1991, 59 per cent were homosexual and bisexual men, and 21 per cent were intravenous drug users. Nearly three-fourths of those who died were adults between 25 and 44 years of age.

By 1991, AIDS had claimed many children's lives as well. In New York state, AIDS was the leading cause of death among Hispanic children aged 1 to 4 and the second leading killer of black children in the same age group.

AIDS in China. In Yunnan Province, a remote area of rural China, nearly 4 of every 500 men are infected with the AIDS virus, a rate similar to that in the United States. The Chinese Ministry of Health released this information in September 1990. Most of the 385 infected people were exposed to the virus through intravenous drug abuse.

Although relatively few of China's more than 1 billion residents carry the AIDS virus, Chinese officials are greatly concerned about further infection. Because disposable needles and sterilization equipment are not readily available in China, authorities fear that doctors may unintentionally spread the virus by using unsterilized needles. The Chinese government has reacted by promoting widespread AIDS education and requesting hundreds of thousands of disposable needles from the World Health Organization.

Blacks' life expectancy. A black person born in the United States in 1988 can expect to live 69.2 years, while a white person born in the same year can expect to live 75.6 years, according to the U.S. National Center for Health Statistics. The difference in projections reflects, in part, a greater occurrence of heart disease, cancer, and stroke among blacks. But homicide, not illness, is the leading cause of death among black adults, especially young black men.

The CDC reported that homicides in 1987 (the latest year for which figures were available) accounted for 42 per cent of deaths among young black males aged 15 to 24. The same year, murder rates for young black men were nearly 5 times greater than for young black women, 8 times greater than for young white men, and 22 times

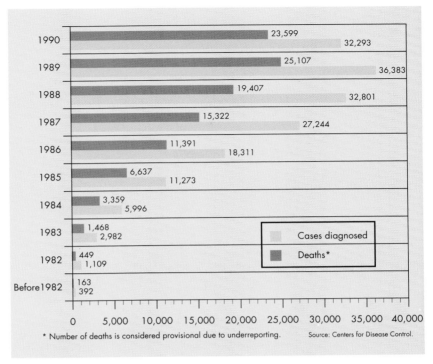

The Toll of AIDS
Of 168,784 people in the United States diagnosed with AIDS since 1981, 106,902 had died by the end of 1990, according to statistics released in May 1991 by the Centers for Disease Control in Atlanta, Ga. Several thousand more cases may eventually be recorded for 1990, and AIDS may rank among the five leading causes of death by the end of 1991.

Year	Deaths*	Cases diagnosed
1990	23,599	32,293
1989	25,107	36,383
1988	19,407	32,801
1987	15,322	27,244
1986	11,391	18,311
1985	6,637	11,273
1984	3,359	5,996
1983	1,468	2,982
1982	449	1,109
Before 1982	163	392

* Number of deaths is considered provisional due to underreporting.   Source: Centers for Disease Control.

Public Health

Continued

greater than for young white women.

Firearms were the most common weapon used in the murders. From 1978 to 1987, 78 per cent of the killings of black males aged 15 to 24 were carried out with guns, as were 83 per cent of the murders of black males between the ages of 15 and 19. According to the report, firearm availability, alcohol and drug abuse, drug trafficking, poverty, and racial discrimination contributed to these deaths.

Motorcyclists and head injuries. Researchers reported in November 1990 that 28,749 people died in motorcycle accidents in the United States between 1979 and 1986, and more than half of those deaths were associated with head injuries. The risk of death from head injuries was twice as high in states that did not require helmets as in those that did.

Riders who lost control of their motorcycles accounted for 40 per cent of all deaths. White males aged 15 to 34 years comprised 69 per cent of those who died. The deaths represent nearly 600,000 years of potential life lost,

according to epidemiologists at the CDC's Division of Injury Control.

Smokeless tobacco and cancer. Baseball and smokeless tobacco: the two have gone together for a long time. But epidemiologists at the University of California, San Francisco, reported in July 1990 that of 1,109 baseball players who used smokeless tobacco, 46 per cent had *oral leukoplakia*. This condition, which is marked by smooth, white patches on the tongue or cheek, leads to cancer in about 5 per cent of those who have it.

Although many baseball teams have banned the use of smokeless tobacco, nearly 40 per cent of players in the minor and major leagues surveyed during spring training reported using chewing tobacco. Most players said they knew the habit could be harmful. Some said they switched from chewing tobacco to chewing gum because they—like public health experts—were concerned that their tobacco habit might negatively influence young fans.   [Deborah Kowal]

In WORLD BOOK, see PUBLIC HEALTH.

Science Student Awards

Winners in the 50th annual Westinghouse Science Talent Search were announced on March 4, 1991, and winners of the 42nd annual International Science and Engineering Fair were named on May 10. Science Service, a nonprofit organization in Washington, D.C., conducts both competitions.

Other science student competitions included international olympiads in chemistry, mathematics, and physics, all held in July 1990.

Science Talent Search. The 40 finalists were chosen from 1,573 entrants from high schools throughout the United States. The top 10 finalists received scholarships totaling $175,000 provided by the Westinghouse Electric Corporation of Pittsburgh, Pa.

First place and a $40,000 scholarship went to 17-year-old Ashley M. Reiter of the North Carolina School of Science and Mathematics in Durham. She submitted a mathematics project involving *fractals,* complex, repeating geometric figures that resemble the irregular shapes found in nature. In her project, Reiter determined the dimensions of fractals generated by certain number sequences.

Second place and a $30,000 scholarship were awarded to Denis A. Lazarev, 17, of Elmwood Park Memorial High School in Elmwood Park, N.J. He did a project in molecular genetics in which he analyzed how a certain regulatory protein helps control gene expression.

Third place and a $20,000 scholarship went to William Ching, 17, of Riverdale Country School in New York City. He discovered that the optic nerve contains a chemical receptor called GABA-B, which is associated with the transmission of nerve impulses.

Fourth place and a $15,000 scholarship were awarded to Dean R. Chung, 16, of Mountain Lakes High School in Mountain Lakes, N.J.

Fifth place and a $15,000 scholarship were awarded to Ciamac Moallemi, 15, of Benjamin N. Cardozo High School in Bayside, N.Y.

Sixth place and a $15,000 scholarship went to 17-year-old Tessa L. Walters of San Gabriel High School in San Gabriel, Calif.

Seventh place and $10,000 were awarded to 17-year-old Debby Ann Lin of Stuyvesant High School in Elmhurst, N.Y.

Eighth place and $10,000 went to Yves J. Jeanty, 16, a classmate of Lin's at Stuyvesant.

Ninth place and $10,000 were awarded to Jim Way Cheung, 17, of Bronx High School of Science in New York City.

Tenth place and $10,000 went to Ragashree Ramachandran, 15, of Rio Americano High School in Sacramento, Calif.

Ashley M. Reiter displays the project that won her first place in the Westinghouse Science Talent Search in March 1991. She found the dimensions of figures generated by *Pascal's triangle,* a triangular arrangement of numbers in which each number is the sum of the numbers to the right and the left of it in the row above.

Science Student Awards

Continued

Science fair. The 42nd annual International Science and Engineering Fair took place May 5 to 11 in Orlando, Fla. The 748 contestants were chosen from finalists at science fairs in the United States and other countries.

Two students, judged the best of the 748 finalists, won a trip to the Nobel Prize ceremonies in Stockholm, Sweden, in December 1991. The winners were Raj Chakrabarti, 16, of Upper St. Clair High School in Upper St. Clair, Pa., and Tatiana Schnur, 17, of Robinson Secondary School in Fairfax, Va. The 33 First Award winners of $500 each were:

Behavioral and social sciences. Tatiana Schnur.

Biochemistry. Ivan O. Rivera-Torres, 18, University Gardens High School, Rio Piedras, Puerto Rico; Jonathan D. Schiff, 18, Paul D. Schreiber High School, Port Washington, N.Y.; Tessa L. Walters, 17, San Gabriel High School.

Botany. Matthew D. Litwin, 17, Nova High School, Davie, Fla.; Chelsea A. Morroni, 17, The Canterbury School, Fort Myers, Fla.; Michael A. Schenkel, 16, Indiana Academy for Science, Mathematics, and Humanities, Muncie, Ind.

Chemistry. Wade William Butin, 18, Klein High School, Spring, Tex.; Raj Chakrabarti.

Computer science. Daniel A. Grossman, 16, Bloomingdale Senior High School, Valrico, Fla.; Derek W. Holland, 16, Niceville Senior High School, Niceville, Fla.

Earth and space sciences. Blake W. Thomas, 16, Moriarty High School, Moriarty, N. Mex.; Tim Vislocky, 17, Satellite High School, Satellite Beach, Fla.

Engineering. Hugh Greene, Jr., 18, Brewer High School, Somerville, Ala.; Darin Marriott, 16, Dayton Christian High School, Dayton, Ohio; Mate Sztipanovits, 16, Hume Fogg Academic High School, Nashville, Tenn.

Environmental sciences. Robert Danley, 19, Glynn Academy, Brunswick, Ga.; Erik J. Edoff, 16, Athens High School, Troy, Mich.; Sam Houston, 17, Decatur High School, Decatur, Ala.; Edward D. Melillo, 17, Falmouth Academy, Falmouth, Mass.; Barbara D. Saatkamp, 17, A&M Consolidated High School, College Station, Tex.

Mathematics. Andrew Dittmer, 16, Thomas Jefferson High School for Science and Technology, Alexandria, Va.; Matthew A. Neimark, 18, Montgomery Blair High School, Silver Spring, Md.

Medicine and health. Morgan B. Gandee, 17, Parkersburg South High School, Parkersburg, W. Va.; Nina Lin, 18, Thomas Wootton High School, Rockville, Md.; Benjamin C. Preisner III, 17, Hilton Head Prepatory School, Hilton Head, S.C.

Microbiology. Anil A. Dhople, 15, Satellite High School, Satellite Beach, Fla.; Evelyn M. Figueroa, 17, Von Steuben Metropolitan Science Center, Chicago; Matt Grafenberg, 17, Winona Senior High School, Winona, Minn.

Physics. Mark W. Decker, 17, Sherman E. Burroughs High School, Ridgecrest, Calif.; Greg B. Thompson, 18, Camden High School, Camden, Ark.

Zoology. Kelly R. Lindauer, 18, John F. Kennedy High School, Denver; Paul J. Plummer, 15, Central Bucks West High School, Doylestown, Pa.

Chemistry Olympiad. The 22nd annual International Chemistry Olympiad was held in Paris. Four-member teams from 28 nations took part in the competition, which included written tests and laboratory experiments.

China won first place, Poland second, and West Germany third. The United States team placed fourth, the highest finish a U.S. team had ever achieved in that competition.

Thirteen gold, 21 silver, and 33 bronze medals were awarded. Four U.S. team members won medals. Wayne Whitney of Medfield High School in Medfield, Mass., won a gold. Silver medals went to Marc Dionne of La Jolla High School in La Jolla, Calif.; Roger Moore of Thompson Valley High School in Loveland, Colo.; and Steven Gubser of Cherry Creek High School in Englewood, Colo.

Math Olympiad. The 31st annual International Mathematical Olympiad took place in Beijing, China. Fifty-four nations sent teams that competed on six challenging math problems. First, second, and third place went to China, the Soviet Union, and the United States, respectively. Two U.S. team members, Kiran Kedlaya of Silver Spring, Md., and Jeffrey Vanderkam of Raleigh, N.C., won gold medals. Silver medals went to Royce Yung-Tze Peng of Rancho Palos Verdes, Calif.; Avinoam Freedman of Teaneck, N.J.; and Joel Rosenberg of Hartford, Conn.

Physics Olympiad. The 21st annual International Physics Olympiad took place in Groningen, the Netherlands. Five-member teams from 32 nations took examinations testing their experimental skills and understanding of theoretical physics. Dylan Thurston of Princeton, N.J., and Jonathan Higa of Honolulu, Hawaii, won bronze medals.

[Sara Dreyfuss]

Space Technology

The United States in 1990 and 1991 achieved success with several new space science missions. The Soviet Union continued to average more than one unmanned launch per week and kept at least two cosmonauts continuously aloft in the *Mir* space station. There were also problems, however. The U.S. National Aeronautics and Space Administration (NASA) was forced to make significant changes to the design of its planned space station. Cosmonauts were twice threatened by emergency situations in space. And hydrogen leaks in the propulsion systems of two U.S. orbiters forced a five-month grounding of the U.S. shuttle fleet beginning in late June 1990.

Shuttle flights resumed on October 6 with the launch of *Discovery*, which carried the European Space Agency's (ESA's) *Ulysses* spacecraft in its cargo bay. *Ulysses* will transmit data on the polar areas of the sun, regions that cannot be viewed well from Earth and where no other spacecraft has gone.

The spacecraft was mounted atop a large booster rocket when deployed from the shuttle. The booster and one other solid propellant rocket stage were then fired to accelerate the spacecraft on a path to the planet Jupiter. In February 1992, *Ulysses* will fly by the giant planet, using Jupiter's gravity to gain enough momentum to move out of the plane of the solar system on a path back toward the sun. *Ulysses* will travel past the south pole of the sun during summer 1994 and over the north solar pole in 1995.

Astronomy mission. The shuttle orbiter *Columbia* was launched on December 2 on a space astronomy mission, carrying a $150-million array of three ultraviolet telescopes and one X-ray telescope. The four telescopes remained attached to the shuttle payload bay, where they were pointed at objects in deep space by ground controllers and *Columbia*'s seven astronauts.

Early in the flight, however, the failure of two on-board monitors used to help control the telescopes threatened the mission. Ground controllers at NASA's Johnson Space Center in Houston and the Marshall Space Flight

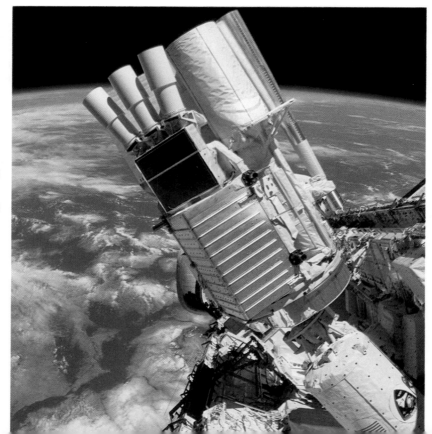

The Astro observatory, consisting of three ultraviolet telescopes and an X-ray telescope, peers at the heavens from the cargo bay of the shuttle *Columbia* in December 1990. The astronomy mission appeared to be in jeopardy when monitors that help control the telescopes failed, but, working with ground controllers, astronauts were able to point the telescopes at 135 deep-space objects.

Center in Huntsville, Ala., devised new procedures so that the astronauts, working with ground control, could continue to point the telescopes at celestial objects.

The mission, commanded by veteran astronaut Vance D. Brand, obtained unique high-resolution images and data from objects in space that give off most of their radiation at ultraviolet and X-ray wavelengths, which cannot penetrate Earth's atmosphere and so can be observed only from space.

A spacewalk had to be made by astronauts on the first shuttle mission of 1991 to carry out repairs on another payload important to astronomy and astrophysics. The orbiter *Atlantis* was launched on April 5, carrying the *Gamma Ray Observatory* (*GRO*). This spacecraft, along with the *Hubble Space Telescope*, is part of NASA's Great Observatory program, which is expected to launch a total of four orbiting observatories. The *GRO* is designed to detect extremely short, high-frequency *gamma rays*. Many astronomers believe gamma rays are associated with the intense radiation given off by matter being pulled toward *black holes*, objects so dense and massive not even light can escape the gravitational field at their surface.

The astronauts on *Atlantis* had to give *GRO* the equivalent of a swift kick to fix a critical antenna that initially failed to open on the satellite. The antenna's 5-meter (16-foot) boom was to have unfolded from the side of the spacecraft as *GRO* was being held by the shuttle's 15-meter (50-foot) manipulator arm. The arm is used to lift satellites out of the cargo bay. When multiple commands from ground control at the Goddard Space Flight Center in Greenbelt, Md., failed to open the device, Air Force Lieutenant Colonel Jerry Ross and civilian astronaut Jerome Apt donned their space suits and went outside the shuttle to free the antenna manually.

Crawling atop the $617-million spacecraft, Ross first banged on the antenna, then gently lifted it into place. *GRO* was then released from the shuttle arm and began returning data on gamma rays to Earth.

It was the first spacewalk by U.S. astronauts since 1986. Ross and Apt

had been scheduled to make a spacewalk on the flight anyway, and one day after they repaired *GRO*, the two astronauts again donned space suits and floated into the *Atlantis* payload bay. On this spacewalk, they tested devices that would be used to move parts of the framework of the planned U.S. space station, *Freedom*.

U.S. unmanned launches. Between June 1990 and April 1991, the United States launched 17 unmanned space missions from Cape Canaveral, Fla., and Vandenberg Air Force Base in Vandenberg, Calif. The only failure during the period occurred on June 23, when a commercial Titan rocket launched an *Intelsat* spacecraft. The spacecraft failed to reach its target altitude of 35,890 kilometers (22,300 miles), where it would have orbited in unison with Earth's rotation in what is called a *geosynchronous orbit*.

The launch of *Intelsat* went normally, but once the satellite was placed in a temporary low-altitude orbit, it could not be properly separated from the Titan's upper stage. This left the satellite stranded in a useless orbit. A space shuttle mission planned for May 1992 will retrieve the satellite so that it can be boosted to the correct orbit.

Other space developments. NASA launched the space shuttle *Atlantis* on a mission for the U.S. Department of Defense on Nov. 15, 1990. The shuttle's five-member crew deployed a large military satellite during the flight, but the Defense Department kept the purpose of the satellite secret.

The *Magellan* spacecraft, which had been launched in 1989, reached Venus in August 1990 and began taking radar images of Venus' surface through the planet's total cloud cover. In the Special Reports section, see EXPLORING THE SURFACE OF VENUS.

Another major event in the U.S. space program was a significant change in the size and complexity of *Freedom*. In March 1991, NASA and the White House approved a new design that would shorten the width of the station's main framework structure from 150 meters (493 feet) to 108 meters (353 feet) and use smaller structural units.

The Soviet space program remained the most active of all national space efforts during 1990 and 1991. Between

Tackling Hubble's Troubles

The launch of the *Hubble Space Telescope* on April 24, 1990, by the National Aeronautics and Space Administration (NASA) was supposed to usher in an exciting new era of astronomical discoveries. By orbiting above Earth's atmosphere—which blurs visible light and blocks much other radiation from space—the telescope was intended to see the universe with vastly greater clarity and finer detail than can ground-based observatories.

But after the *Space Telescope* was launched, astronomers were horrified to discover that something was seriously wrong with the observatory's optical system. Instead of showing stars as needle-sharp points of light, the telescope smeared the starlight into diffuse streaks and smudges. "It's as if the telescope were looking through waxed paper," astronomer James Westphal of the California Institute of Techology in Pasadena described the situation. The fuzzy images meant that many observations planned years beforehand were now impossible and that many others would be of lesser quality.

Project engineers diagnosed the optical problem by making carefully controlled images of specific distant objects and painstakingly analyzing the results. By early July, they were convinced that the telescope's main mirror, the most precise optical surface ever created, had a tiny error in its curvature. Officials then turned their attention to discovering how this error had occurred.

To investigate exactly what had gone wrong, NASA appointed a panel led by Lew Allen, then director of the Jet Propulsion Laboratory in Pasadena. Panel members questioned the firm that had manufactured the telescope's mirrors, Hughes-Danbury Optical Systems Incorporated (formerly the Perkin-Elmer Corporation) in Danbury, Conn. On Nov. 27, 1990, the panel announced that the firm's opticians had indeed shaped the mirror incorrectly and had relied on flawed testing equipment. When other tests suggested a possible flaw, the panel said those results had been ignored.

NASA concluded that it would be too expensive to send up a space shuttle to bring the telescope back for a new mirror. Instead, the agency plans to send astronauts to make repairs to the telescope in late 1993 or early 1994. The astronauts will replace one of the orbiting observatory's two cameras with a version outfitted

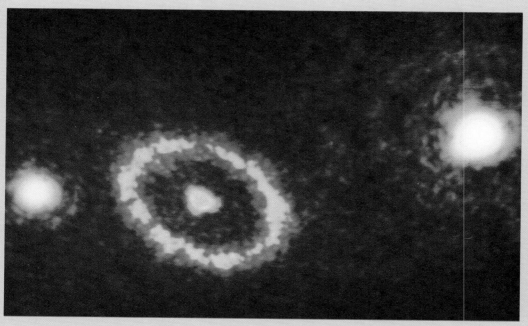

A photograph taken using the *Hubble Space Telescope* in August 1990 reveals a ring of glowing gas surrounding the remains of the star that exploded as Supernova 1987A. Two other stars appear as white objects.

with corrective lenses—much like prescription eyeglasses—to compensate for the mirror's flaw. A second camera and two *spectrographs*—instruments that help scientists analyze light—may get corrective optics as well.

The astronauts will also install a replacement gyroscope to help keep the spacecraft pointed steadily and replace the telescope's solar-cell panels, which vibrate and cause the cameras to shake. Only after these repairs have been made can the telescope function as originally designed.

Even though the orbiting observatory is somewhat nearsighted, it has provided a wealth of observations. All the instruments on board are operating well, and the project's astronomers have been carefully, patiently learning how best to overcome the telescope's optical handicap. Computer programs have helped to compensate for the mirror's distortion and produce much sharper images than obtainable on the ground.

Some of the *Space Telescope*'s earliest targets were planets in our solar system. In May 1990, it recorded an image of the distant planet Pluto and its moon Charon. From observatories based on Earth, the two appear too close together to be distinguished individually, but the *Space Telescope* showed them clearly as distinct objects. Further observations are expected to provide data on their composition. In November, the observatory's cameras captured a violent storm on Saturn. These images should help astronomers gain a better understanding of Saturn's atmosphere. In December, the *Space Telescope* provided a very detailed portrait of Mars. By May 1991, it had swung around to take a picture of Jupiter.

The observatory has also peered deeper into space, looking into the heart of a huge cluster of stars called M15 in the constellation Pegasus. Astronomers had thought the stars might be swarming around a massive yet invisible black hole at M15's center. But images from the *Space Telescope* revealed that the stars had not coalesced into a black hole. Another image showed that a "cannibal" star in the constellation Aquarius is sucking material off a neighboring star and then, like a cosmic burp, spewing a huge jet of matter into space.

The telescope's spectrographs have been busy, too. One observation shows that a star in the constellation Pictor is drawing in dust and gas from a disk surrounding it. Astronomers believe this proves that the star, known as Beta Pictoris, is creating a solar system of its own.

Because the *Space Telescope* has an anticipated lifetime of 15 to 20 years, astronomers expect it to make many more observations. And a successful repair mission should enable the orbiting observatory to live up to its billing as "astronomy's discovery machine."　　[J. Kelly Beatty]

June 1990 and mid-April 1991, the Soviet Union launched 62 space missions, carrying a total of 83 spacecraft into orbit—more than all other nations combined during the same period.

Cosmonaut operations aboard *Mir* continued to be the most spectacular of Soviet space activities. On June 10, a large new unmanned module carrying scientific instruments docked with *Mir*. The new module brought the total number of such modules docked at the station to three, enlarging the space station to three times its original size.

Cosmonaut spacewalk. The main highlight of the mission, however, was the need for the crew—cosmonauts Anatoly Solovyev and Alexander Balandin—to conduct a spacewalk to repair loose insulation on the exterior of their *Soyuz* spacecraft, the vehicle that ferries cosmonauts between the station and Earth. The insulation, which had accidentally ripped loose, might have interfered with sensors needed to orient the craft for reentry into Earth's atmosphere.

The spacewalk ran into problems immediately. The crew accidentally opened a *Mir* hatch when there was some air pressure still in their air lock. The pressure blew the hatch open, damaging its hinges. The cosmonauts had difficulty making their way to the damaged area of the *Soyuz*, which was docked with the space station, and then took longer than expected to repair the insulation.

Concerned about the cosmonaut's diminishing oxygen supply, Soviet ground controllers ordered the cosmonauts back inside *Mir* before they had a chance to retrieve two ladders they had taken with them to reach the damaged area. By the time they reached the hatch to reenter the station, their space suits were running out of oxygen. And then they could not close the broken hatch and had to use another hatch to enter *Mir*, just in time to renew their oxygen supply.

Repairing repair problems. Although the crew had corrected the insulation problem, they had created two other problems in doing so—breaking a *Mir* hatch necessary for full station operations and leaving ladders outside, where they could affect future station operations. The cosmonauts made a

A fantastic display of light called the *aurora australis* (Southern lights) extends lengthwise for hundreds of kilometers above the ocean near Antarctica. Cameras aboard the space shuttle *Discovery* photographed the aurora to collect data on how auroras could affect a space-based weapons system. Auroras occur when electrically charged particles from the sun, trapped by Earth's magnetic field, strike atoms and molecules in Earth's atmosphere.

Space Technology

Continued

second spacewalk to correct the situation on July 26. The crew found they could not repair the hatch but were able to close it with brute force. They also safely secured the ladders on the station's exterior.

A new crew consisting of cosmonauts Gennadiy Manakov and Gennadiy Strekalov were launched to the *Mir* on August 1, and Solovyev and Balandin returned to Earth safely on August 9 in their repaired *Soyuz*. The new crew made a spacewalk on October 29 in a second attempt to repair the hatch, but they found it severely damaged.

Journalist in space. This crew was joined by cosmonauts Viktor Afanasyev and Musa Manarov on December 2. Accompanying them into orbit was Japanese television reporter Toyohiro Akiyama of the Tokyo Broadcast System.

The Japanese broadcasting company paid the Soviet Union several million dollars to allow Akiyama to become the first journalist in space. After several days in orbit, Akiyama returned to Earth with Manakov and Strekalov.

Another near disaster. Cosmonauts Afanasyev and Manarov narrowly escaped disaster on March 23, 1991, when an unmanned resupply vehicle named *Progress* nearly collided with the station during an automatic docking attempt. The incident was "a near catastrophe" that could have resulted in the death of the cosmonauts, Soviet space officials said.

Initial analysis indicated that the cosmonauts, while working outside the station earlier, may have accidentally bumped and misaligned a critical *Mir* docking system antenna. A ground controller at the Soviet Kaliningrad manned flight control center noted that the vehicle was misaligned with the station and instead of docking with *Mir* was going to crash into it. He transmitted commands for *Progress* to veer away, which it did, missing the station by only about 12 meters (40 feet). After the cosmonauts made several adjustments, *Progress* docked successfully on March 28, providing the crew with new supplies. [Craig P. Covault]

In WORLD BOOK, see SPACE TRAVEL.

Zoology

The first discovery of a new whale species in 28 years—*Mesoplodon peruvianus*—was reported in February 1991 by zoologists James G. Mead of the Smithsonian Institution in Washington, D.C., and Koen Van Waerebeek of the Peruvian Center for Cetalogic Studies in Lima, Peru. The gray whale lives in the Pacific Ocean off the coast of Peru, but its exact range and population are not yet known. The whale grows to 3.7 meters (12 feet) in length—making it the smallest member of the *Mesoplodon* group—and has a dolphinlike snout. It probably feeds on squid.

The scientists based their identification on 10 dead specimens found since the mid-1970's. Mead speculated that the species appeared now because the whales have moved closer to shore, where they are caught in fishing nets or wash up on beaches after dying.

Newly hatched sea turtles — both leatherback and green sea turtles—use different environmental cues to find water and determine which direction to swim, according to research reported in October 1990. The turtles crawl from nests high on a beach down to the water's edge, and then they swim out to sea. Researchers have wondered how baby turtles know where the water is, and, once the turtles are in the water, how they know which direction to swim. Biologists at the University of Illinois in Urbana-Champaign reported that they had discovered answers to these questions.

On the beach, the researchers said, the turtles look for and move toward bright, open horizons. Once in the water, they swim toward approaching waves and swells.

For this experiment, the biologists removed 45 newly hatched green turtles and 48 leatherbacks from their nests before they had a chance to wander on the sand. They then harnessed them to special buoys that allowed them to swim freely, but which could be monitored from a boat. The young turtles continually swam into the waves, even when out of sight of land. When placed in water-filled tanks, the turtles swam into mechanically generated waves. Their behavior suggests that waves are cues for the long-distance migration of adult turtles.

How bats find food. The greater horseshoe bat uses radar to determine the size of its prey, according to a July 1990 report by zoologist Gareth Jones of Bristol University in England. Zoologists have long known that bats use a natural form of radar when searching for prey: They make sounds and then listen for the echoes to bounce off insects. Jones reported that the horseshoe bat sends out two kinds of sounds—pulses of varying tones sandwiched between long, constant tones. The pulses tell the bat how far away the insect is. The long signal helps the bat know how fast the insect is flying, how fast its wings are beating, and consequently how big the insect is.

Jones showed that the bats prefer relatively large moths and beetles and home in on smaller insects only when larger prey is unavailable.

Parasitic wasps look for a different kind of signal in their search for prey. These tiny insects eat caterpillars and locate them by detecting odors from corn leaves these caterpillars eat.

In a series of experiments reported in November 1990, T. C. J. Turlings, a scientist with the United States Department of Agriculture in Gainesville, Fla., showed that the wasp was attracted more to the chemicals released by damaged corn leaves than to odors from the caterpillar or its wastes. When Turlings sliced the leaf with a razor blade to injure it, the leaf did not emit as much of the chemical as it did when being chewed. Turlings concluded that the plant seems to defend itself against being eaten by caterpillars by giving off odors that attract predators of the caterpillar.

Thump in the "night." Mole rats do not react to sound but to the vibrations the sound makes in the ground, according to a report from Israeli biologists in February 1991. The mole rat, a small mammal that lives underground, communicates by thumping its head against the top of its burrow. In the dark, underground environment where eyes cannot see, a mole rat thumps its head in specific rhythms to interact with its neighbors.

Eviatar Nevo from the University of Haifa and two colleagues monitored electrical impulses from the brains of 27 mole rats under different condi-

The Vanishing-Amphibian Riddle

By 1991, scientists worldwide had become seriously concerned about frogs—and toads and salamanders and other amphibians. Since the mid-1970's, individual researchers have noticed that some of the species of amphibians they studied had begun to disappear. When these biologists gathered at an international meeting in England in September 1989, they learned that the phenomenon might be quite widespread. Since then, more and more scientists have become alarmed, because amphibian disappearances could be an early warning of problems for other animals as well as plants. An amphibian's thin skin easily allows harmful substances to pass through it. Furthermore, its dual existence— *amphi* means *both*, and *bios* means *life*—of living both in water and on land puts it at risk from pollution in both environments.

Scientists have discovered amphibians on every continent except Antarctica, and they have identified about 3,000 species. Amphibians are cold-blooded animals with backbones and soft, scaleless skin. They lay eggs that lack shells and require a moist place to incubate and hatch. After hatching, the young have gills that allow them to live in water. While maturing, most amphibians undergo dramatic changes that enable them to live their adult lives on land. They lose their gills and develop lungs and legs, but they return to the water to mate and produce young. Like other animals, amphibians cannot survive if their habitats change too much, either through natural events or human activity.

When a forest is cleared, for example, soil may wash into streams, making the water muddy and less suitable for amphibians. As ponds are drained or water is diverted, marshes dry up, depriving amphibians of wet places to lay their eggs and to provide nurseries for their young. Many other ecological changes can threaten the creatures as well.

After the 1989 meeting in England, salamander expert David Wake of the University of California at Berkeley began compiling a "missing amphibians" list. For the United States, he listed the Yosemite toad, Colorado western toad, Sierra and foothill yellow-legged frogs, Oregon's cascade frog, and Colorado's tiger salamander. Other researchers have noted missing species or reduced populations around the world.

Drought may be the most likely cause of frogs disappearing in Australia. According to zoologist Michael J. Tyler of the University of Adelaide in Australia, the populations of 20 species—10 per cent of Australia's total number—have declined during the past 10 to 20 years. Two species, including a frog that broods its young in its stomach, have disappeared altogether.

Researchers count the masses of eggs laid by wood frogs in a pond in Colorado's Rocky Mountain National Park. Dwindling numbers of these frogs caused the state to declare the species "threatened" in 1989.

Colorado's tiger salamander, *left,* and Costa Rica's golden toad, *right,* are among the amphibian species that are mysteriously disappearing from their usual habitats.

Biologist Marc Hayes of the University of Miami at Coral Gables, Fla., says that in Costa Rica, golden toads once seemed to blanket the forest floor. But recently he had to give up studying them because they had become so scarce. Experts speculate that substances spewed from a nearby volcano may be the culprits harming this toad species.

In the Rocky Mountains of Colorado, Paul S. Corn, a U.S. Fish and Wildlife biologist, observed leopard frogs in just 4 of the 33 locations where it is usually found, and the boreal toad is missing from 49 of 59 of its traditional haunts. Biologists John Harte and Erika Hoffman of the University of California at Berkeley counted salamanders in Colorado mountain ponds each summer from 1982 through 1986. The number of adults and young declined by 65 per cent, perhaps because of acidic snowfall in the region. Air pollutants such as sulfur dioxide can cause snow to become acidic. When such snow melts in the spring, the acidic water flows into ponds where salamanders lay their eggs. Harte and Hoffman have discovered that these eggs are harmed by acidic conditions. Salamanders that survive do not grow as large as expected.

Environmental scientist David Bradford of the University of California in Los Angeles reported that in the 1970's, each of several ponds in the High Sierra typically contained 800 adult yellow-legged frogs and twice that number of tadpoles. In summer 1989, Bradford searched 38 ponds, all remote from human activity, and found frogs in only one pond. He blamed airborne dust from pesticides used on distant farm fields.

From 1979 until 1989, biologists Laurie J. Vitt and Janalee P. Caldwell of the University of California in Los Angeles surveyed amphibians living near the Savannah River around Aiken, S.C. This forested area has remained undisturbed by people for 40 years. Nevertheless, the scientists say that during 1988 and 1989, the number of amphibians declined drastically. Biologists speculate that drought, causing some ponds and marshes to dry up, may be one reason. But so might rising levels of carbon dioxide and methane in the air. Depletion of Earth's protective ozone layer in the upper atmosphere might be another explanation. The layer blocks some of the sun's harmful ultraviolet radiation—so its depletion could expose amphibian eggs floating on the water's surface to this damaging form of sunlight.

Is nature or is human activity diminishing amphibian populations? Solving the riddle is complicated by the fact that the animals' numbers fluctuate naturally. In a few places, scientists are finding more amphibians than ever before. Enough animals are missing, however, to warrant investigation. [Elizabeth J. Pennisi]

Zoology

Continued

tions. The animals reacted to a tapping sound, but only if it created sound waves that vibrated the ground. Deafened mole rats also reacted to sounds that created ground vibrations.

Mouse menaces the monarch. Usually, even a hungry animal will not nibble on a monarch butterfly because it is poisonous. But one type of mouse has discovered a way to thrive on monarchs when the butterflies are plentiful in their mountainous winter home, reported biologists Lincoln Brower and John Glendinning of the University of Florida in Gainesville in November 1990.

The scientists first noticed these mice—the species *Peromyscus melanotis*—while studying monarchs that gather in Mexico each year between November and April. The mice migrate to the same place at the same time. Chilled by cool mountain air, the monarchs, which attach themselves to trees, sometimes stiffen and fall to the ground, becoming easy prey. The mice feast on the butterflies by peeling away the insects' tough outer skin, where most of the poison is concentrated.

Guppies adapt. A July 1990 report of an 11-year study of guppies provided the first demonstration of evolution among animals outside the laboratory. Three biologists reported that descendants of guppies introduced to a new predator reacted to the predator's habit of eating young, small fish by having fewer, larger offspring.

For the experiment, David A. Reznick and his colleagues from the University of California in Riverside changed the environment of 200 guppies in 1976. They moved the fish from one river in Trinidad, where they were typically attacked by predators that ate adult guppies, to a stream that fed into the river. The only predator there was the killifish, which eats young, small guppies. After 30 to 60 generations, the guppies had begun to grow bigger and wait longer before producing young. The fish also gave birth to fewer and larger offspring than did earlier generations.

The guppies matured more slowly because they devoted more energy to

An arctic tern offers shrimp to a tern decoy, one of 33 decoys that researchers placed on Eastern Egg Rock off the coast of Maine to attract terns back to the island. In the early 1900's, hunters killed off the island's tern population. By 1991, the decoy colony had attracted more than 1,200 nesting pairs.

Rediscovered Butterfly
Fender's blue butterfly, *right,* a rare species thought to be extinct since 1937, was rediscovered in autumn 1990 near Corvallis, Ore., and in five other sites in the Willamette Valley, *below* (black dots). The species lives on a wildflower that grows almost exclusively in the valley.

Washington

Pacific Ocean

Portland
Salem
Corvallis
Eugene

Oregon

Idaho

Former habitat of Fender's blue butterfly

0   100 Kilometers
0   100 Miles

California

Nevada

Zoology

Continued

surviving when they were young. By producing bigger babies, they gave the young a head start in growing too big for the killifish.

A crossed bill works best. A bird with a crossed bill has helped teach scientists how evolution works. In February 1991, Craig W. Benkman and Anna K. Lindholm, zoologists at the University of British Columbia in Vancouver, Canada, reported that the peculiar beak of the red crossbill enabled the bird to break open pine cones and lift out seeds easily.

The zoologists compared seed consumption among three red crossbills with their bills intact and four other crossbills whose bills were trimmed so that the top and bottom parts no longer overlapped. (Like fingernails, the bills grow back in a few weeks.)

The zoologists found that the birds with the trimmed bills took less and less time to extract seeds as their bills grew back. At first, they needed more than five seconds to extract each seed. A month later, they took only about two seconds. This growth represents what

happened through evolution, the zoologists suggested. The gradual improvement in the red crossbills' ability to extract and eat seeds faster showed how a trait provides advantages even as it evolves.

Polar hostage. A tiny, shrimplike animal called the *amphipod* has developed an unusual way to defend itself from predators, according to an August 1990 report. This orange plankton is no bigger than a grain of rice, yet by kidnapping a smaller, foul-tasting snaillike creature called the *pteropod,* the amphipod avoids being eaten by fish. James B. McClintock, a biologist at the University of Alabama in Birmingham, and John Janssen, a biologist at Loyola University in Chicago, reported this finding.

Common heritage. Even though they look and act very differently, some fish are actually quite closely related, molecular biologists at the University of California in Berkeley reported in October 1990. The scientists studied 14 of about 200 types of fish, called *cichlids,* that live in Lake Victoria in Africa, and

Zoology
Continued

23 other types of African fish. Often sold in pet stores, these fish seem remarkable to biologists because they have such varied behavior, eating habits, and shapes even though they originate from the same lake.

To find out whether all these varieties evolved from a single ancestral fish, the scientists studied genetic material from the *mitochondria*, tiny parts of a cell that generate energy. This genetic material, known as *mitochondrial DNA* (mtDNA), is different from the genetic material in the nucleus of cells in that it is usually passed directly from mother to offspring. Most genes are inherited from both mother and father. But, because mtDNA comes only from the mother, it changes less over time and can be used to evaluate how closely related similar species are.

In the case of the cichlid varieties, there was less variation in mtDNA than is usually evident between members of the same species. The researchers concluded that these fish did have a common ancestor and that their great variety is the result of very rapid evolution.

Pesky pelican chicks. Unhatched pelican chicks cheep inside the egg to tell their parents if they are too hot or too cold, according to biologist Roger Evans of the University of Manitoba in Winnipeg, Canada. Pelicans have a clutch of two eggs, which parents monitor very carefully, standing up to shade them and sitting on them to keep them warm.

When the chick in the first egg begins to hatch, a process that takes two or three days, it pecks a small hole in the shell and calls to the parents. An adult then keeps this egg between its legs until it hatches, leaving the second egg unattended and in danger of cooling down or broiling in the sun. Evans found that both in the laboratory and in the wild, pelican parents respond to the unhatched chick's persistent chirps by restoring the egg to its normal temperature.   [Elizabeth J. Pennisi and Thomas R. Tobin]

In the Special Reports section, see How Smart Are Dolphins? In World Book, see Adaptation; Animal; Evolution; Zoology.

Science You Can Use

In areas selected for their current interest, *Science Year* presents information that the reader as a consumer can use in understanding everyday technology or in making decisions—from buying products to caring for personal health and well-being.

Cash by Computer: Automated Teller Machines

In 1990, automated teller machines (ATM's) across the United States handled 6 billion banking transactions—a threefold increase from the early 1980's. Customers used the country's more than 80,000 banking machines primarily to withdraw cash, make deposits, check account balances, and transfer funds between savings and checking accounts.

The popularity of ATM's has increased dramatically since the early 1970's, when Citibank of New York City and Banc One of Ohio became the first financial institutions to install ATM's on a large scale. At the time, the banks hoped simply to reduce their operating costs by replacing human tellers with machines, little suspecting that the cash machines would become so successful. But as more banks added round-the-clock automated service through ATM's, their competitors scrambled to keep pace and the machines proliferated.

By the late 1970's, banks realized that they would save more money—and could provide service at many more locations—by electronically linking ATM's in networks. Today, nearly all large banks in the United States belong to one of 85 regional networks.

A regional network may encompass a metropolitan area; a state; or, in a few cases, several neighboring states. Regional networks typically operate ATM's at hundreds of locations, thereby enabling customers to get cash not only at banks but also at airports, office buildings, shopping malls, supermarkets, and other sites.

The largest regional networks include New York Cash Exchange (NYCE) in New York, Star System in California, Money Access Service in Philadelphia, and MOST in Washington, D.C. Only Banc One and a few other banks that pioneered ATM's continue to operate their own networks.

In addition to a regional network, most large banks belong to one of the two large international networks—Cirrus System Incorporated, headquartered near Chicago, or Plus System Incorporated, based in Denver. These networks enable customers to use ATM's when traveling in the United States or in more than 20 countries abroad. Both systems convert foreign currency withdrawals to dollars at the day's exchange rate and subtract the amount from a savings or checking account back home.

To use an ATM, all you need is a plastic cash card issued by your bank. The cardholder and the issuing bank are identified both by lettering and by embossed numbers on the card. In addition, a cash card carries the name of the regional network the bank belongs to, such as NYCE or Star System. The card works in any machine in that network. A card bearing a Cirrus or Plus System logo can be used in all machines in those networks as well.

Your bank may also offer ATM service through a credit card, such as MasterCard or Visa. MasterCard International owns Cirrus, and Visa International owns about a third of Plus System. In addition, agreements between the American Express Company and several regional networks enable American Express cardholders to use machines in those networks.

On the back of the cash card, a magnetic strip carries coded data, including the cardholder's personal identification number, bank account number, and a number that identifies the issuing bank. The strip is made of plastic coated with metallic particles magnetized to form a pattern that stores the card's numerical data. Magnetic strips on some cards also carry the cardholder's name, enabling ATM's to address customers by name.

To begin a transaction, the customer inserts the card into an ATM and punches in a personal identification number on the machine's keypad. This personal ID number, which typically consists of four digits, prevents anyone else from using the card.

The ATM next flashes instructions on its display screen for carrying out transactions. To get cash, for example, the customer presses buttons that indicate whether the money should be withdrawn from a checking or a savings account and the amount to be withdrawn. This request is then displayed on the screen. After the customer presses a button to verify that the information is correct, the ATM goes to work on the request.

Inside the machine, an electromagnetic device called a *card reader* has already scanned the magnetic strip on the card and converted the data coded on it into electrical signals. These signals and electrical signals representing the cardholder's request travel together to a series of computers that check the information, route it to the next computer, and authorize the transaction. The information nearly always travels through the system by telephone lines, even though the computers that process transaction requests may be hundreds of miles apart. A few banks, which have branches in neighboring states, find it cheaper to relay requests by satellite instead.

The request first reaches the computer that drives the ATM. This computer checks the numbers on the customer's card to determine whether the customer's bank belongs to the same regional network as the ATM. If so, the computer routes the request to the regional network's central computer, called the *switch*. If not, the computer routes the request to a national switch belonging to Cirrus or Plus System for identification of the regional network. The national switch then routes the request to the proper regional network switch.

The switch lies at the hub of an ATM network. It acts as a traffic officer, directing requests from thousands of

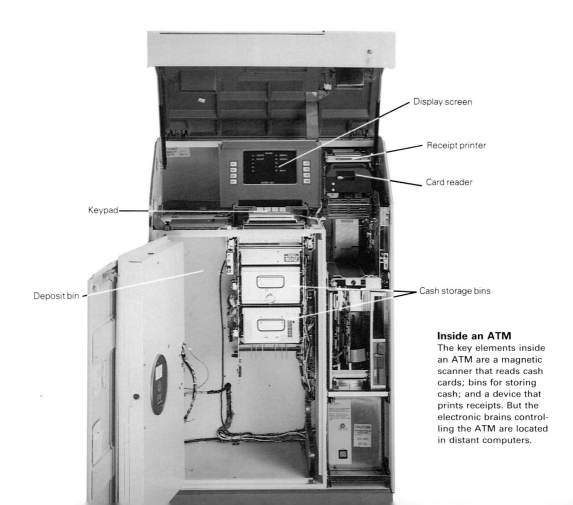

Display screen

Receipt printer

Card reader

Keypad

Deposit bin

Cash storage bins

Inside an ATM
The key elements inside an ATM are a magnetic scanner that reads cash cards; bins for storing cash; and a device that prints receipts. But the electronic brains controlling the ATM are located in distant computers.

ATM's to the proper banks. The switch stores identification numbers for all the banks that share the regional network. By checking the data received from the ATM against numerical tables stored in its memory, the switch can identify the customer's bank and direct the request to it.

The bank's computers process the request in two stages. One computer stores personal ID numbers and bank account numbers in its memory. It identifies the customer and verifies that the personal ID number keyed in at the ATM matches the ID number on the card. If the numbers do not match, a message comes back to the ATM informing the customer that he or she has entered an invalid ID number.

If the ID numbers do match, the computer forwards the request for cash to a computer that stores records of customers' accounts. After this com-

puter receives the request, it checks how much money is in the customer's account, and—if there are sufficient funds—subtracts the cash requested from the balance. The computer then sends a signal approving the transaction. If the account does not contain enough money, the computer sends a denial of the request.

The approval or denial travels back to the ATM via the same series of computers. An approval arrives with signals that instruct the machine's cash-storage bins to extract and dispense the correct number of bills. Although various methods have been developed for delivering cash, most machines use rollers or suction devices to count and spit out the precise number of bills.

The ATM's printer then makes out a receipt indicating the amount of the transaction and its date and time. Many receipts also note the new balance in

From ATM to Bank and Back

Nationwide computer networks make it possible for an ATM cardholder to withdraw cash in one state from a bank account in another state. The request for a withdrawal travels electronically over telephone lines to a series of computers that process the transaction within seconds. Even a request initiated in the customer's hometown is likely to travel to a computer in another state.

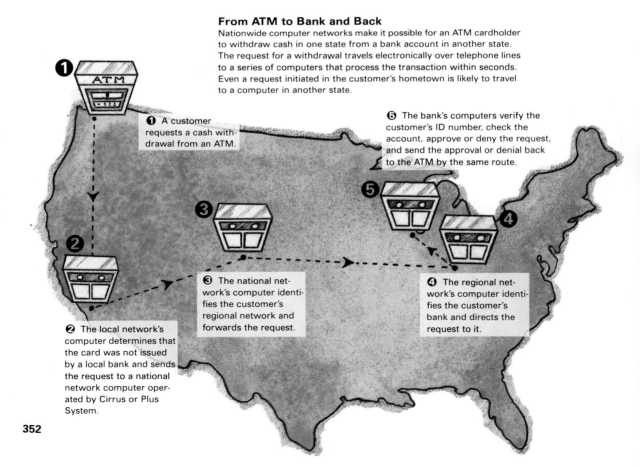

❶ A customer requests a cash withdrawal from an ATM.

❷ The local network's computer determines that the card was not issued by a local bank and sends the request to a national network computer operated by Cirrus or Plus System.

❸ The national network's computer identifies the customer's regional network and forwards the request.

❹ The regional network's computer identifies the customer's bank and directs the request to it.

❺ The bank's computers verify the customer's ID number, check the account, approve or deny the request, and send the approval or denial back to the ATM by the same route.

the cardholder's bank account.

Deposits and other transactions are handled by the system in much the same way as withdrawals. But deposits must be placed in an envelope and inserted into a slot in the ATM. The envelope is collected and sent to the bank by people who service the machine. For this reason, it can take three or four days from the time of an ATM deposit until the funds are available for withdrawal. To limit the delay in entering deposits, some banks allow customers to make ATM deposits only in machines at the bank.

Machines in busy locations receive daily service visits to remove deposit envelopes and restock them with cash. Less active machines may be serviced only weekly or monthly. An ATM may be stocked with as much as $80,000 and typically handles about 5,000 transactions—including deposits and transfers of funds—before needing a refill. Cash withdrawals are the most common transactions, and the average withdrawal is $55.

How safe is banking by ATM? The personal ID number is meant to prevent anyone from using a cash card without authorization. If someone enters the wrong identification number for a card, a message on the ATM's screen will ask the user to try again. If three attempts fail to produce the correct number, most machines keep the card. This safeguard prevents anyone who might find a card from trying to crack the identification code by trial and error. As another precaution against card theft, the bank generally limits the amount that may be withdrawn by cash card in a single day, in most cases to $200.

The ID number and account number magnetically coded on the card are kept confidential during transmission by a process of scrambling called *encryption*. A coding device inside the ATM scrambles the numbers before they are sent to the switch. The switch and the other computers along the way unscramble the information to read it, then scramble it again before relaying it. Finally, the computer with the bank's records unscrambles the information once more before gaining access to an account. Encryption prevents someone from electronically tapping into an ATM network and stealing money. In addition, all the information on a cash card's magnetic strip is also encrypted so that someone finding a card cannot learn the cardholder's personal ID number or bank account number.

What happens if you make a mistake in entering information? If you deposit a check for $1,000 but press buttons indicating a deposit of only $100, the mistake will be caught once the envelope with the check arrives at the bank. The additional $900 will then be credited to your account. As another safeguard, a computer tape inside the machine records each transaction and the number and denomination of the bills dispensed.

ATM technology has changed little since the early 1970's, though today's machines operate with much greater speed and reliability and perform a wider variety of operations. An entire transaction, from inserting the card to receiving the cash and printed receipt, now takes as little as 10 seconds, even though the request may have gone to computers in several different states.

ATM's may perform more operations in the future. A pilot system in Philadelphia, for example, allows ATM customers to cash paychecks for exact amounts, make installment payments on loans, reorder checks, and print bank statements. Access to some ATM's can be adjusted at the touch of a button to accommodate people in wheelchairs or in automobiles.

The U.S. government even plans to deliver welfare benefits through ATM's and has instituted pilot programs in Baltimore, Houston, and several other cities. Under these programs, welfare recipients receive cash cards, which they use to withdraw funds from a monthly deposit made by the government.

By 1991, banks had issued more than 190 million cash cards. Holders of these cards will one day be able to use almost any machine in the United States, Canada, Mexico, or overseas, as regional networks hook up with the international networks.

ATM's have already transformed America's banking habits. As more financial transactions are performed electronically, the role of ATM's will become even larger.   [Mark Brohan]

Antilock Brakes: A Potential Lifesaver

The avoidance of automobile driving accidents has always depended on two principal factors: the skill of the driver and the design of the vehicle. These days, however, some of the stress is being taken off the driver as automotive engineers strive to incorporate a greater degree of safety into their designs. And in the avoidance of one of the most dangerous driving situations of all—uncontrollable skids—the engineers have developed a system that makes even the slickest roads less threatening: antilock brakes.

Skids occur when the steering or braking forces on a car's tires exceed the traction the tires have with the road. The car then behaves more like a sled than a wheeled vehicle because the driver has almost no steering control.

Skids can happen during braking if the driver brakes too hard, causing the wheels to slow down too quickly and *lock up*, or stop turning. But even though the wheels are locked, the car continues to move because of its own momentum. During wheel lockup, the car often keeps traveling in the original direction it had been heading, no matter how the driver turns the steering wheel.

Although it is possible to lock the wheels on a dry road surface if the brake pedal is hit hard enough, lockup is much more likely to occur when roads are slick. That is because tires have much less traction on wet or icy surfaces than on dry ones—as much as 95 per cent less on ice.

To avoid lockup when driving in treacherous conditions, drivers have traditionally been advised to pump the

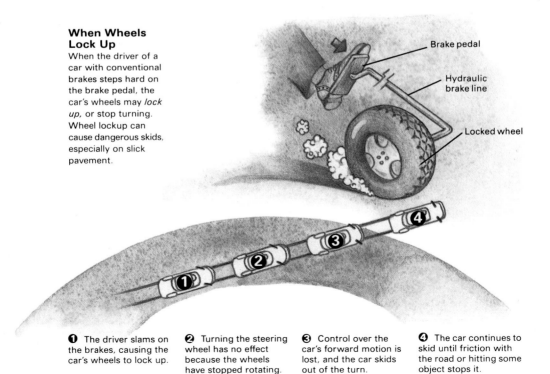

When Wheels Lock Up
When the driver of a car with conventional brakes steps hard on the brake pedal, the car's wheels may *lock up*, or stop turning. Wheel lockup can cause dangerous skids, especially on slick pavement.

Brake pedal

Hydraulic brake line

Locked wheel

❶ The driver slams on the brakes, causing the car's wheels to lock up.

❷ Turning the steering wheel has no effect because the wheels have stopped rotating.

❸ Control over the car's forward motion is lost, and the car skids out of the turn.

❹ The car continues to skid until friction with the road or hitting some object stops it.

brakes, rather than apply them with consistent force. The action of alternately pressing and easing up on the brake pedal slows the car while also allowing the wheels to keep turning until the vehicle comes to a safe stop. In an emergency situation, however, such advice is not so easy to follow. The driver's instinct is to slam on the brakes, and the result may be a fatal skid.

The importance of brakes to safe motoring in general, and to the avoidance of skidding in particular, has long been recognized. Nonetheless, there have been few advances in automotive braking systems since the mid-1930's, when *hydraulic* (fluid-activated) brakes came into widespread use. In a hydraulic braking system, the pressure of a thick fluid—brake fluid—is used to activate braking mechanisms at the four wheels. The mechanisms produce friction at the wheels to absorb the energy of motion, thereby slowing and stopping the car.

At the heart of a hydraulic braking system is a small pump called the *master cylinder*, which contains the car's central reservoir of brake fluid. The master cylinder is connected to each wheel by small tubes called *brake lines*, which are also filled with brake fluid. When the driver pushes the brake pedal, the master cylinder pressurizes the fluid in the system, and that pressure is immediately translated into braking force at the wheels.

There are two basic kinds of hydraulic brakes: *drum brakes* and *disk brakes*. The drum brake was the first mass-produced brake, and it is still widely used by car manufacturers, though mostly just on the rear wheels. Disk brakes were first installed mainly on sports cars, but in recent years they have become standard on many other kinds of vehicles as well.

To grasp the essence of how drum brakes work, imagine pressing the backs of your hands against the curved inside surface of a round cookie tin. Corresponding to the cookie tin on the brake is a cast-iron *drum*, which is attached to the inside of the wheel and rotates with it. The action of a drum brake begins when the master cylinder pressurizes fluid in a *wheel cylinder* on the brake. The pressure forces two

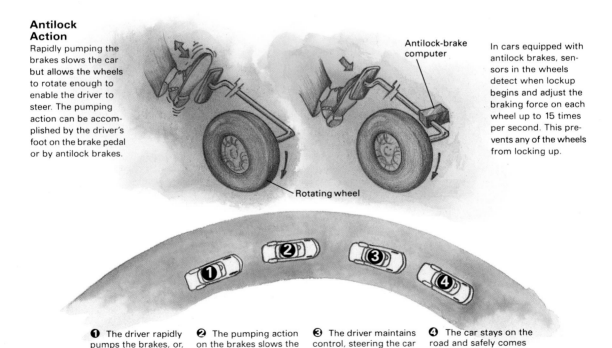

Antilock Action

Rapidly pumping the brakes slows the car but allows the wheels to rotate enough to enable the driver to steer. The pumping action can be accomplished by the driver's foot on the brake pedal or by antilock brakes.

Antilock-brake computer

Rotating wheel

In cars equipped with antilock brakes, sensors in the wheels detect when lockup begins and adjust the braking force on each wheel up to 15 times per second. This prevents any of the wheels from locking up.

❶ The driver rapidly pumps the brakes, or, with antilock brakes, hits the pedal hard.

❷ The pumping action on the brakes slows the car but allows the wheels to turn.

❸ The driver maintains control, steering the car around a curve.

❹ The car stays on the road and safely comes to a stop.

curved linings, called *shoes*, against the inner wall of the drum, slowing it—and thus the wheel.

The main advantage of drum brakes is that they are *self-energizing*—that is, when the brakes are activated, the vehicle's momentum forces the forward shoe of each wheel into the drum, increasing braking power. Drum brakes are also relatively inexpensive—about $100 less per wheel than disk brakes.

The major shortcoming of the drum brake is that with repeated braking, the drum gets hot and expands. The shoes must then travel farther to contact the drum, and so the driver must depress the brake pedal harder and farther to slow the car.

A disk brake consists of a *caliper*—a hydraulically activated clamp—that fits over the edge of a disklike *rotor* that turns with the wheel. If you were to stop a spinning plate by grasping it between your thumb and fingers, you would be applying the same principle used in disk brakes.

The disk brake's caliper contains two linings called *pads*, one on each side of the rotor. When the driver steps on the brake, the caliper causes the pads to grip the rotor, slowing it down.

Disk brakes are superior to drum brakes in high-speed stops because the gripping action on the rotors provides more stability than the pressure of shoes on drums. Disk brakes provide safer, surer stops in almost all situations than drum brakes do.

More than 80 per cent of the cars being built today are equipped with disk brakes on the front wheels and drums on the rear. The reason for that arrangement has to do with both braking effectiveness and cost. When braking, the weight of the car is concentrated on the front wheels, which means the front brakes must work harder than the rear brakes. Engineers have found that a safe, economical braking system can be achieved by combining disk brakes in the front with lower-cost drum brakes in the rear.

Some sports and luxury cars, for which economy is less of a consideration, are equipped with disk brakes on all four wheels. Four-wheel disk brakes provide the maximum in stopping power and control.

The antilock braking system was developed to make braking even surer, especially in wet and icy driving conditions. Antilock brakes provide optimum braking by preventing wheel lockup and skidding regardless of how hard the brake pedal is pressed. In fact, with antilock brakes the driver is supposed to apply hard, steady pressure on the brakes when making an emergency stop.

The heart of a typical antilock braking system is a small computer, which is attached to the normal hydraulic braking system. During braking, a sensor on each wheel feeds a continuous stream of data about the wheel's movement to the computer. If the computer detects that a wheel is locking up, it activates a small, electrically powered valve to momentarily reduce the fluid pressure to that wheel, allowing it to continue turning. These adjustments are repeated in quick succession—as often as 15 times a second with some antilock systems. With many systems, the driver can feel the rapid opening and closing of the valves as a shuddering in the brake pedal. The adjustments continue until the tire regains traction or the brake pedal is released.

Although antilock brakes are of most benefit on slick roads, they can also provide an advantage in normal driving conditions. In emergency stops made by test drivers, antilock brakes shortened braking distances on dry surfaces by 5 to 20 per cent.

Antilock brakes are expensive; they add about $800 to the price of a car. Because of their high cost, antilock systems are offered only as optional equipment on most automobiles, and fewer than 10 per cent of new-car buyers in the United States ordered them in 1991.

Nonetheless, antilock brakes offer such an obvious safety advantage that automotive experts predict that by the mid-1990's, more than 50 per cent of new cars sold in the United States will be equipped with antilock braking systems. As more and more drivers are protected by this feature, we may see the rate of automobile accidents and highway deaths drop significantly. If so, perhaps someday we'll wonder how we ever got along without antilock brakes.   [Don Schroeder]

Sunglasses Wear
New Rating Labels

The sunglasses you buy to match your new bathing suit should also shield your eyes against harmful solar radiation. But not all sunglasses provide the same protection. How can you decide which ones are the best?

The Sunglass Association of America, cooperating with the United States Food and Drug Administration (FDA), adopted a voluntary program in summer 1990 for labeling sunglasses to indicate how much radiation they transmit. To understand the new labels, you need to understand how the sun's rays can harm your eyes.

Our eyes enable us to perceive sizes, shapes, dimensions, and colors by collecting and focusing light. Light passes first through the *cornea*, the transparent membrane that covers the colored iris and the pupil, then through the *crystalline lens* in the middle of the eye, and finally to the *retina*, a layer of light-sensitive cells lining the inner wall of the eyeball. From the retina, signals travel along the optic nerve to the brain, where they are interpreted as visual images.

The cornea, lens, and retina can be damaged by overexposure to one of the many components of sunlight. Visible sunlight appears white but actually contains every color. This is apparent in a rainbow, for example, where sunlight has passed through raindrops and divided into different colors. Light

Sunglasses come in a dazzling array, *below.* But style and high price do not necessarily indicate good eye protection against solar rays.

travels in waves, like ripples on a lake. The distance from the top of one wave to the top of the next wave is called a *wavelength*, and we perceive light of different wavelengths as different colors. Red has the longest wavelength we can see and violet the shortest.

Light contains rays of even shorter wavelengths than violet, called *ultraviolet* (UV) radiation, that are invisible to the human eye. It is these wavelengths that can cause sunburn, skin cancer, and eye damage.

Scientists have classified UV radiation into three types according to wavelength. These wavelengths are very short and measured in *nanometers*. (A nanometer is one-billionth of a meter or about 0.00000004 inch.) UV-A has the longest UV wavelengths, and UV-C, the shortest.

Any of the three types can cause eye damage, and the shorter the wavelength, the more damaging the rays. Fortunately, UV-C from the sun is absorbed by ozone in the upper atmosphere and does not reach us. If the ozone layer is damaged by pollution, UV-C could become a health risk. But, for now, the greatest risk comes from UV-A and UV-B.

Eye damage can be caused by exposure to large amounts of UV-A or UV-B over a short period of time or by repeated exposure to small amounts over a long period of time. Since the longer wavelengths of UV-A are the least damaging, scientists regard UV-B as posing the greater risk to the cornea, the crystalline lens, and the retina.

The cornea and surrounding outside parts of the eye can become inflamed when exposed to UV rays. The cornea is usually able to repair itself quickly. But intense exposure—for example, to UV rays reflected from sand or water—may produce corneal burn, or *photokeratitis*. Repeated intense expo-

sure may painfully damage, and even kill, cornea cells, impairing the cornea's ability to transmit light.

The crystalline lens may become hazy or cloudy when exposed to UV rays over long periods. This haziness is called a *cataract*. Many studies have found that people living near the equator, where UV rays are most intense, are more likely to have cataracts than people living farther away from this region. A cataract scatters light as it passes through the eye and can eventually cause partial or total blindness.

If the lens containing the cataract is surgically removed without implanting an artificial lens, the retina is directly exposed to damaging UV rays. UV rays damage special cells in the retina called rods and cones, without which we cannot see. Because UV rays striking the retina do not cause pain, the rods and cones can become irreversibly damaged without any warning.

Eye doctors highly recommend that all people protect their eyes from the damaging effects of UV rays, especially when outdoors between 9 a.m. and 4 p.m., when the sun's radiation is most intense. Medical conditions put some people at special risk for UV damage. In particular, people with such eye diseases as cataracts or retina degeneration need good eye protection.

Patients taking certain medicines, such as oral contraceptives, certain antibiotics, antiacne medications, and the diuretic chlorothiazide also need UV protection. These medications may be *photosensitizing*. They make the skin more sensitive to light and can be absorbed readily by the eye, increasing its susceptibility to UV damage.

Finally, experts say that children who play outside for long periods during the day should wear UV-blocking sunglasses. Because years of exposure to UV rays may cause cataracts and other

Ultraviolet (UV) radiation is part of the electromagnetic spectrum, which includes X rays, visible light, and *infrared* (heat) radiation. UV rays, which are invisible, are divided into three types, A, B, and C. Fortunately, most UV-C rays, which are the most dangerous type of UV radiation, are absorbed by the ozone layer in Earth's upper atmosphere.

| X rays | Ultraviolet radiation | Visible light | Infrared (heat) radiation |

C B A

eye problems, it is likely that this damage is preventable by starting UV protection during childhood.

Glass lenses that block UV rays are produced by adding metal oxides to the lens material itself or to a coating applied to lens surfaces. The metal oxides absorb most or all of the UV radiation. The darkness of the tint has relatively little to do with blocking UV radiation. Untreated plastic lenses will offer some degree of protection from the most damaging part of the UV spectrum.

Some sunglasses now sold over the counter carry a label with ratings developed by the American National Standards Institute (ANSI). The label should state that the sunglasses meet or exceed ANSI regulation number Z80.3, and a rating should be marked on, or at-

tached to, the sunglasses. There are three ANSI classes—*cosmetic, general purpose*, and *special purpose*—based on how much UV radiation the lenses absorb. Sunglasses classified for cosmetic use may transmit 40 per cent or more of the UV-A that strikes the lens and 20 to 30 per cent of UV-B. Sunglasses classified as general purpose may transmit 8 to 40 per cent of UV-A and 4 to 5 per cent of UV-B. Under ANSI specifications for special purpose sunglasses, the transmission of UV-A varies proportionately with the amount of visible light transmitted through the lens. These glasses may transmit up to 1 per cent of UV-B. In addition, sunglasses available only from eye doctors and opticians transmit no UV-A or UV-B.

Because the labeling program is vol-

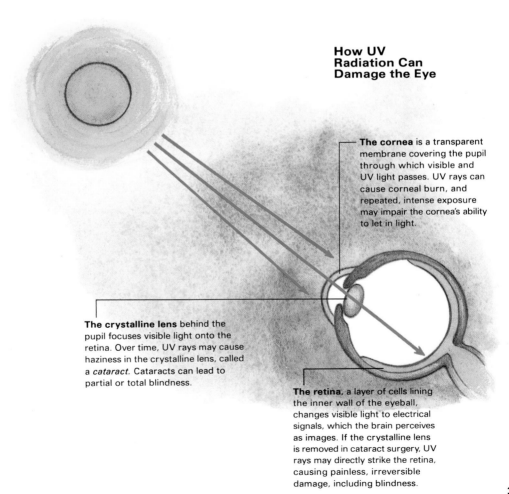

How UV Radiation Can Damage the Eye

The cornea is a transparent membrane covering the pupil through which visible and UV light passes. UV rays can cause corneal burn, and repeated, intense exposure may impair the cornea's ability to let in light.

The crystalline lens behind the pupil focuses visible light onto the retina. Over time, UV rays may cause haziness in the crystalline lens, called a *cataract*. Cataracts can lead to partial or total blindness.

The retina, a layer of cells lining the inner wall of the eyeball, changes visible light to electrical signals, which the brain perceives as images. If the crystalline lens is removed in cataract surgery, UV rays may directly strike the retina, causing painless, irreversible damage, including blindness.

What the Labels Mean

Sunglasses	Classification	Transmits		
		Visible light	UV-A	UV-B
Purchased over the counter	Cosmetic	More than 40%	40% or more	20% to 30%
	General purpose	8% to 40%	8% to 40%	4% to 5%
	Special purpose	3% or more	1.5% or more	1% or less
Purchased through eye doctors	UV-400	Varies	0%	0%

Under a new voluntary rating system, sunglasses purchased over the counter may carry labels indicating how much protection they provide against UV radiation. Sunglasses marked *special purpose* afford the most protection among glasses available in stores. Eye-care professionals can provide sunglasses that block all UV radiation.

untary, some manufacturers may not provide UV-blocking information with their sunglasses, and some labels may make misleading claims. For example, a label could claim that the sunglasses "provide 100 per cent protection" or "transmit 0 per cent of harmful UV rays," when in fact the lenses only provide the protection required for the cosmetic standard. Ideally, the label should state which ANSI rating class the glasses belong to and what percentage of UV-A and UV-B radiation is transmitted.

Special types of sunglasses vary in their ability to block UV radiation. *Reflective lenses*, those with mirrored finishes, can block some UV rays, but how much depends on the mirrored coating and how it is applied. Usually, these lenses both reflect and absorb UV rays. But the finish is easily scratched, allowing sunlight to reach the eye.

Photochromic lenses darken or lighten in response to UV intensity. Indoors, they lighten in about five minutes, and outdoors, they darken in about 30 seconds. These lenses are temperature-sensitive and darken more in cold conditions than in hot. The lenses absorb some UV radiation, but they may not meet the special purpose or general purpose standards.

Polarized lenses have a filtering layer that absorbs sunlight reflecting off pavement, water, sand, or snow. These lenses are designed to cut intense glare rather than UV rays, however.

UV protection is not the only important feature of sunglasses, of course. Although the color or darkness of the lens tint may not affect the UV-protect-ing ability of sunglasses, it does affect the amount of visible light transmitted. Reducing intense visible light reduces eye fatigue and squinting. Many eye doctors recommend that sunglasses reduce the visible light transmission to between 10 and 20 per cent.

The health value of amber-colored lenses that block visible blue light is controversial among eye specialists. Blue light has some of the shortest wavelengths of visible light. It is not considered as dangerous to the eye as UV radiation, but some experts think that overexposure to blue light can cause retina damage. Other specialists say it is unnecessary to block all blue light and that enough protection is provided by sunglasses that absorb at least 75 per cent of visible light.

Some glasses carry labels describing the amount of visible light transmitted. You can also tell if a tint is dark enough by trying the glasses on in front of a mirror. You should not be able to see your eyes through the lenses. If you can, the lenses transmit too much visible light to be comfortable on bright days. Medium or dark gray is the best tint color because it does not distort natural colors. The lens material should also be free from distortions, which can cause headaches.

Finally, the frames of sunglasses should be strong and fit comfortably. Frames that wrap around the head give the best protection because they block some light coming from the side.

The variety of sunglasses seems endless. But the pair that is fun and fashionable should also safeguard your sight. [Robert N. Kleinstein]

Information on a Light Beam

Hair-thin fibers made of very clear glass, plastic, or other materials are being used in a growing variety of applications that affect our everyday lives. These *optical fibers* were developed in the 1960's as a result of research in a branch of physics called *fiber optics*, the study of how such fibers carry waves of light.

Optical fibers are now used widely to transmit telephone conversations and computer data as pulses of light. They are also used in a variety of medical and surgical instruments. Optical fibers have revolutionized a number of surgical and diagnostic procedures by allowing the surgeon to insert instruments through veins and arteries or a tiny incision, rather than having to make a large incision. And now they promise to usher in a new era in the way information is exchanged in homes as well as businesses.

A beam of light can travel through optical fibers for distances as great as 160 kilometers (100 miles) before the light beam has lost too much intensity and needs to be amplified. This is one of the reasons optical fibers have begun to replace copper wires for telephone communications. Electrical signals traveling over copper wires require more amplifiers than optical fibers to cover the same distance.

Optical fibers have also replaced copper wiring in telecommunications be-

Pulses of light sent through hair-thin optical fibers, *left,* can efficiently transmit information. A single optical fiber, *above,* can carry many times more information than a much larger cable of copper wires.

cause they can carry more information and take up less space. Optical fibers can be made extremely small, measuring less than 0.004 millimeter (0.00015 inch) in diameter. A telephone optical cable measuring 12 millimeters (0.5 inch) in diameter and containing about 96 individual fibers can carry more than 1 million telephone calls at one time. By comparison, about 27 standard cables, each measuring 76.2 millimeters (3 inches) in diameter and each consisting of 7,200 copper wires, would be needed to carry the same number of calls at one time.

Optical fibers consist of a transparent core of glass or plastic surrounded by a covering called a *cladding* through which no light can escape. Light from a laser or some other source enters the core at one end. As light waves travel along the fiber, some strike the cladding at an angle. Rather than "leaking" out, they are reflected inward by the cladding and continue traveling along the core. While in free space, light travels in straight lines. But because light traveling through an optical fiber is confined within the core and clad-

ding, the light will follow curves in the fiber.

In long-distance telephone communications, a special type of fiber known as a *single-mode fiber* is required to guide pulses of light over long distances. In the single mode fiber, the core is only about 0.01 millimeter (0.0004 inch) in diameter. Because the core is so small, a beam of light can travel through the fiber only along the fiber axis (an imaginary line running through the center of the fiber). This requires the use of a high-speed laser to inject a narrow light beam into the fiber. Single mode optical fibers can transmit light signals over distances as great as hundreds of kilometers.

Telephone conversations are carried over optical fibers by a method called *digital transmission*. Sound waves are first converted into electrical signals, which are sampled by an encoder. The encoder assigns each electrical signal a digital code—a series of 0's and 1's. The 1's may be represented by a pulse of light from the laser, and the 0's, by the absence of a pulse. Or the 1's may be represented by a high level of light

Communicating on Light

As pulses of light travel along optical fibers, they transmit information such as telephone conversations. A cladding material around the fiber keeps the light from "leaking" out.

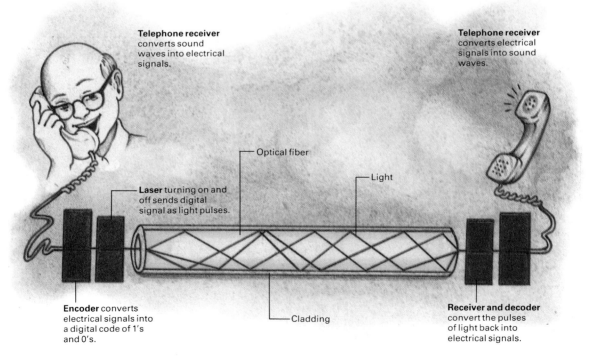

Telephone receiver converts sound waves into electrical signals.

Telephone receiver converts electrical signals into sound waves.

Optical fiber

Light

Laser turning on and off sends digital signal as light pulses.

Encoder converts electrical signals into a digital code of 1's and 0's.

Cladding

Receiver and decoder convert the pulses of light back into electrical signals.

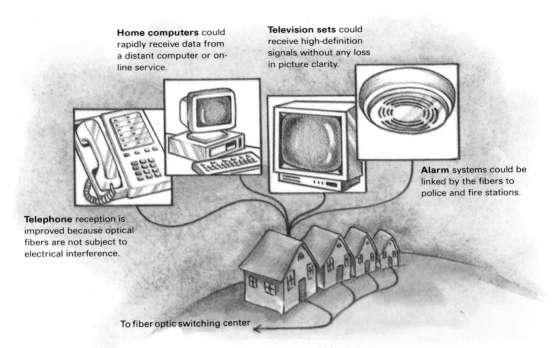

Home computers could rapidly receive data from a distant computer or on-line service.

Television sets could receive high-definition signals without any loss in picture clarity.

Alarm systems could be linked by the fibers to police and fire stations.

Telephone reception is improved because optical fibers are not subject to electrical interference.

To fiber optic switching center

and the 0's, by a low level of light. When the light pulses reach their destination, a decoder converts the digital code back into an electrical signal that is then converted to a sound wave coming out of the receiver.

This method of long-distance communication has been so successful that more than 16 million kilometers (10 million miles) of optical fibers have been installed throughout the world. Cables of optical fibers carry long-distance calls between cities in North America and—via underwater cables that cross the Atlantic and Pacific oceans—between North America, Europe, and Asia. But optical fibers have not yet replaced the copper wiring that runs into individual homes.

Telephone companies in Europe, Japan, and the United States are currently testing optical fiber connections that carry new communication services to homes. The prospect of bringing optical fibers into residential neighborhoods has raised the possibility that computer data could be transmitted by optical fibers to home computers. Optical fibers could also bring television signals into the home.

For example, Bell Communications Research—the research and engineering branch of the seven regional Bell Telephone Companies—in Morristown, N.J., has demonstrated a method of sending high-definition television (HDTV) signals with optical fibers. An HDTV picture contains much more detail than a conventional TV picture. Optical fibers can send the HDTV signals to a home television set without any change in image quality, because these signals are converted into digital codes. As a result, they represent an exact copy of the original scene picked up by the television camera.

In addition to telecommunications and medicine, optical fibers also have a number of industrial uses. The fibers can be used to make gyroscopes without mechanical parts. Such devices help guide airplanes and spacecraft through air or space. Optical fibers are also used in industry to measure electric current. Consumers may not directly encounter the latest advances in optical technology in their everyday lives, but optical fibers are beginning to have a dramatic impact on the way we live.   [Nathan M. Denkin]

Optical Fibers in the Home

An optical fiber can carry tremendous amounts of information because thousands of light rays can travel through it at any given time. If optical fibers proved economically feasible to replace the copper wiring that serves a neighborhood, many residents could receive and transmit information through a single pair of fibers.

The Biology
of a Compost Heap

If you have a pile of autumn leaves, grass clippings, and twigs in a far corner of your backyard, you have a working compost heap. Given a little water, air, and warmth, the pile of yard waste will eventually turn into compost.

This dark, crumbly material is useful as a mulch to spread over the soil to control weeds and protect the roots of garden plants. Compost can also be tilled into soil to boost both the content of its organic matter and its growing power.

You can purchase special bins and chemicals for making compost, but the essential machinery of a compost heap is free—the natural process of decay. Through decay, the nutrients that were once locked up in the complex carbohydrate and protein compounds that make up leaves, twigs, and other types of organic matter are transformed into simpler molecules that living plants can use.

The process begins when nature's workers move into a pile of biological waste and set up shop. Bacteria, fungi, worms, and other tiny creatures feed on dead plant and animal matter. They multiply rapidly in the midst of such a banquet. In fact, some bacteria double their numbers every few minutes. Soon the compost heap becomes a universe in miniature—dark, silent, moist, and teeming with microscopic life.

Some of the creatures that live in the heap are chemical decomposers. They produce chemicals called *enzymes* to digest the waste. Other organisms are physical decomposers. They chew or tear the material into small pieces that the chemical decomposers can more easily attack. They also digest some organic material directly.

The most important chemical decomposers are oxygen-consuming, or *aerobic*, bacteria. These bacteria produce enzymes that break down complex molecules into simpler ones. The bacteria use the carbon, nitrogen,

Composters Large and Small

Gardeners and recyclers make compost heaps by assembling a pile of organic waste, *right.* The heap decomposes as bacteria and fungi secrete enzymes that break down complex molecules in the garbage. Earthworms and other larger creatures digest some of the material or tear it into small pieces.

Bacteria

phosphorus, and other elements in these simple compounds for growth and energy. This chemical transformation produces heat—so much so that in the center of a compost heap, the temperature may soon exceed 55 °C (131 °F).

In the outer, and cooler, fringes of the heap live microbes that specialize in chemically digesting the tough stuff— such as woody plant fibers. Among them are microscopic fungi and a type of bacteria that look like fungi called *actinomycetes*. The actinomycetes produce enzymes that give decaying leaves their characteristically frosty, cotton-candy look.

Physical decomposers play a secondary role in the silent laboratory of the compost heap. Mites, beetles, and tiny roundworms are important physical decomposers. So is the springtail, a minute insect with a forked springing organ on its abdomen that enables it to jump into the air. Spiders, centipedes, and insects are also likely to be found in the compost heap, where they feed upon the physical decomposers.

One of the most beneficial larger creatures in the heap is the earthworm. These long, segmented worms tunnel deep into the pile to feed on organic matter during the day; at night, some squirm out again to mate. Their tunnels enable water and air to filter into the heap, helping fuel the growth of aerobic bacteria. The earthworms also directly help the process of decomposition, eating raw compost, digesting it, and leaving behind fecal nuggets rich in nitrogen. This is important because most of the matter in compost heaps is nitrogen-poor.

Eventually, the earthworms and other creatures decompose so much of the material that their food supply becomes depleted. The bacteria and fungi die off, and the once-warm pile cools. The waste has become black and crumbly.

When decomposition occurs in nature—on the floor of a forest, for example—several months may pass before leaves, twigs, and animal droppings are partially decayed. With a compost heap, you create excellent conditions for the growth of decomposers, and the process can take as little as 21 days.

It's important to remember that, like other creatures, the decomposers need food, water, and air. The most important foods for the microbes are carbohydrates, generally found in plant material. Thus, any items that were once part of plants—from potato peelings to grass clippings—are suitable for the pile. Weeds can be thrown on the heap, but if they contain seeds the compost may promote the growth of new weed plants.

Newspapers, which are made of

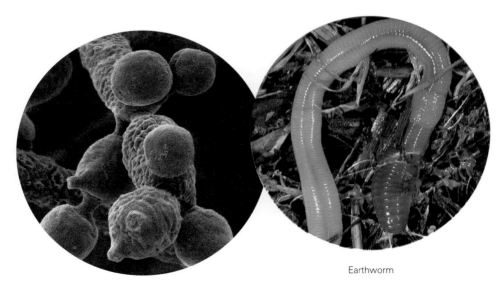

Fungi

Earthworm

Building a Compost Heap:

What to Add	What to Avoid
☐ Plant waste (such as grass clippings and leaves)	☐ Grease or oil
☐ Nonmeat kitchen waste (such as eggshells, tea bags, coffee grounds, and potato peelings)	☐ Pesticides or plant waste treated with pesticides
☐ Biodegradable packages	☐ Human feces
☐ Shredded newspaper	
☐ Steer manure	

woody plant fibers, are also fine, as are cardboard packages marked "biodegradable." Shredding paper products will make them easier to decompose and speed up the process.

The bacteria also need small amounts of nitrogen, phosphorus, and other nutrients. Protein-containing table scraps such as meat or cheese are rich sources of nitrogen. But they are also liable to attract dogs, cats, and rodents.

To discourage pests, it's best to use a nitrogen source that animals find far less desirable—commercial fertilizer or manure. Steer manure is readily available at garden centers, but you can also use pet litter or the droppings of horses, chickens, or other farm animals. Human feces, however, should never be placed in compost heaps because it might contain organisms that cause disease.

You should also avoid adding diseased plants or those treated with pesticides. Any pesticide or toxin is likely to kill beneficial decomposing microbes. It might also yield compost that would add dangerous chemicals to the soil.

Many novice composters become turned off when they discover that their compost heap smells like rotten eggs rather than newly plowed soil. The culprits are bacteria that live in the absence of oxygen. These bacteria, called *anaerobic*, can decompose waste, but they do so slowly and inefficiently, and they create foul-smelling gases as by-products. By occasionally turning the pile, you can keep the growth of these bacteria in check.

Use a shovel or pitchfork to mix the contents of the heap. Doing so distributes oxygen, keeping the aerobic bacteria alive, and hindering the growth of types of bacteria that do not use oxygen. The compost dwellers also need moisture, so it's a good idea to sprinkle water on the compost heap during dry spells.

Warmth is the only other requirement for composting, and the speed of the process depends on the climate. A compost heap started in late summer may produce compost within a few weeks. One begun in late autumn may not be complete until spring.

Eventually, of course, your backyard heap will be transformed. But some experts think it's a shame to leave composting to the backyard when the process could be done on a large scale. Every year, people in the United States dump millions of tons of leaves, grass clippings, and other organic materials into trash cans. Municipalities that collect the trash place it in incinerators or landfills, where its nutrients are never reclaimed.

Some experts believe that cities, counties, and states should adopt programs to compost this biological trash instead of discarding it. Under proper conditions, the wasted tons of organic material could be turned into mountains of mulch or soil additive easily and at low cost. After all, in this method of recycling, nature does virtually all of the work.   [Cecil E. Johnson]

World Book Supplement

Five new or revised articles reprinted from the 1991
edition of *The World Book Encyclopedia*.

Pontiac Division, GMC

Strong, lightweight plastics make up the body of this van.

Amoco Chemical Company

Durable polyester fabrics are made of plastic fibers.

WORLD BOOK photo by Ralph J. Brunke

Plastics are used to package a variety of items.

Plastics have special properties that allow them to be used in a wide variety of products. The photographs above illustrate some of the many uses of plastics.

Plastics

Plastics are man-made materials that can be shaped into almost any form. They are one of the most useful materials ever created. Our homes, schools, and businesses are filled with plastic products. Engineers have developed plastics that are as rigid as steel or as soft as cotton. They can make plastics that are any color of the rainbow—or as clear and colorless as crystal. Plastics can be rubbery or rigid, and they can be shaped into an endless variety of objects, ranging from automobile fenders to squeezable bottles to soft fabrics. Plastic products, especially those used by industries, often have a useful life of many years.

Plastics consist of long chains of molecules called

The contributors of this article are all members of the staff of the Polymer Processing Institute (PPI) at Stevens Institute of Technology. They are Joseph A. Biesenberger, President of PPI and Professor of Chemical Engineering; Paul G. Kelleher, Associate Manager of PPI's New Jersey Polymer Extension Center; and Marino Xanthos, Research Director of PPI and Research Professor of Chemical Engineering.

polymers. These chains are made of repeating patterns of smaller molecules. Each of the smaller molecules forms a "link" in the polymer's chain. In some plastics, the chains are rigid and are lined up like logs flowing down a river. In others, they are flexible and tangled like spaghetti on a plate. These different structures give plastics their most notable characteristic, the ability to be shaped. In fact, the word *plastics* comes from the Greek word *plastikos,* which means *able to be shaped.*

As useful as they are, plastics do have drawbacks. The biggest problem is that most plastics take a very long time to *decompose* (break down into simple compounds). Figuring out how to dispose of plastic wastes has become a major environmental concern.

How plastics are used

Engineers have created hundreds of different plastics, each with its own properties. They have developed plastics that can replace metals, natural fibers, paper, wood and stone, and glass and ceramics. Manufacturers use these plastics to make products stronger, lighter, longer lasting, easier to maintain, or less expensive to make. In addition, inventors have used plastics to create items that could be made with no other materials.

To replace metals. Plastics are used to replace metals in a variety of products. Automakers commonly use plastic bumpers, fenders, and wheel covers in their products. In some cars, the entire body is made of plastics. Plastic auto parts do not rust, nor do they dent as easily as metal ones. They are easier and often less expensive to repair. Replacing metal parts with plastic ones also reduces the weight of a vehicle, resulting in more efficient fuel use. Airplane manufacturers use plastic wing and body assemblies for many of these same reasons. These large, seamless parts also create less wind resistance than do riveted metal sections.

Plastics have also replaced metals in many building construction materials, such as pipe and home siding. Plastic siding does not dent as easily as that made from aluminum. Pipe made from plastics is lightweight and easy to cut and join. Moreover, it does not corrode like metal pipe.

Surgeons mend broken bones with plastic parts rather than metal ones, because the plastics are less likely to trigger a harmful reaction. Dentists often use plastic fillings because—unlike metal fillings—the plastic ones can match the patient's tooth color.

To replace natural fibers and hides. The textile industry uses plastics to replace such natural fibers as cotton, ramie, silk, and wool. Plastic fibers may have such qualities as strength, durability, and resistance to stains and wrinkling. Some plastic fibers are tough enough to be used for automobile safety belts or bulletproof vests. Others are delicate enough to be made into sheer hosiery. Durability and resistance to stains make plastic fibers an excellent material for clothing, carpeting, and furniture coverings. Manufacturers can also treat plastic fibers to make them more difficult to burn. Plastic fibers are often mixed with natural fibers to produce fabrics with qualities similar to an all-natural fabric but with added durability.

Plastics are also used to create synthetic leathers, suedes, and furs. Spun plastic fibers replace down or feathers in insulated jackets and pillows.

To replace paper. Plastics have replaced paper in many packaging applications. Plastic-foam packing materials provide more protection for boxed products than crushed paper does. Many products, particularly delicate electronic equipment, are packed in foamed plastic inserts that fit the shape of the item exactly. Many fast-food restaurants use foamed plastic containers that help keep foods warm.

Plastic wraps have many uses. They preserve foods longer than paper wraps can. Plastic wrap can stretch to form a seal around the opening of a container. Many items that are sold in cardboard packages, such as jigsaw puzzles and record albums, are sealed in clear plastic wrap. Such hardware items as nuts and bolts are packaged in clear plastic boxes that allow a buyer to see the product.

To replace wood and stone. Plastics have replaced wood and stone in many applications. Laminated plastic countertops come in a variety of patterns. Some look like marble. Laminated countertops are lighter, less expensive, and easier to install than marble ones. They also resist marring and stains.

Furniture makers use plastics to produce cabinet doors and tabletops that look like wood but are easier

to clean and do not warp. Plastics have also replaced wood in boat hulls. Plastic boats are stronger than wooden ones and require less maintenance. Unlike wooden hulls, plastic hulls can be constructed easily in one piece. These smooth, one-piece hulls can be shaped to cut through water with less resistance.

To replace glass and ceramics. Because they are lighter and far less likely to break, plastics have replaced glass or ceramics in a variety of products. Plastic wall tiles, bathtubs, and sinks are cheaper and easier to install than ceramic ones. Airplane windows made of acrylic plastics are lighter and less brittle than glass. Safety and comfort have made lightweight, shatterproof plastic eyeglass lenses a popular substitute for glass lenses. Plastic bottles are also shatterproof, and they have replaced glass ones in packaging milk, ketchup, household cleaners, and many other foods and household goods. Plastic bottles also weigh much less than glass ones and so help cut down shipping costs.

To provide new characteristics. Plastics are used in many ways that would not be possible for other materials. They have many medical applications because they are not harmful to the body and can be formed into any shape. Parts made from plastics can replace damaged hip, knee, and finger joints. Plastic pieces are used to rebuild facial structures damaged by accidents. Sometimes, plastic parts are used to replace faulty heart valves.

Plastics are also used to make insulating foam that blocks the flow of heat and sound. The foam can be blown into the walls of a home through a small hole. Integrated circuits, which hold thousands of transistors that control the flow of electricity, are sealed in plastics. The plastics protect the delicate transistors without interrupting the flow of electricity.

Types of plastics

Although there are hundreds of different plastics, all of them belong to one of two basic types, based on how they behave when heated. These types are (1) thermosetting plastics and (2) thermoplastics.

Thermosetting plastics—or thermosets, for short—can be heated and set only once. They cannot be remelted or reshaped. When a thermoset is heated, it undergoes a chemical reaction called *crosslinking,* which binds its polymer chains together. This reaction is similar to the hardening of an egg when it is boiled. Once it has hardened, it cannot become a liquid again. Because thermosets cannot be remelted, engineers use them in applications that require high resistance to heat. Products made from thermosetting plastics include pot handles and trays for sterilizing medical instruments.

Thermoplastics can be melted and re-formed again and again. Their polymer chains do not form crosslinks. Thus, the chains can move freely each time the plastics material is heated.

Thermoplastics are used much more widely than are thermosets. Manufacturers prefer thermoplastics because they are easier to handle. They also require less time to set—as little as 10 seconds, compared to as long as 5 minutes for thermosets. And unlike thermosets, most thermoplastics can be dispersed in liquids to produce durable, high-gloss paints and lacquers. Because their molecules can slide slowly past one another, some

Kinds of plastics

All plastics are classified as *thermosetting* or *thermoplastic,* depending on the way they act when heated. This table lists 20 common thermosetting and thermoplastic materials according to their chemical names. Each kind includes hundreds of compounds formed by adding chemicals to the basic material.

Thermosetting materials

Allylic: strong, resists heat and weather. Used for electronics parts, coatings for moisture protection.
Epoxy: resists water and weather, hardens quickly, has high bonding strength. Used for adhesives, casting compounds, reinforced plastics, protective coatings, tools.
Melamine- and urea-formaldehyde: easily colored, resists heat, odorless, tasteless. Used for dinnerware, lampshades, adhesives, buttons, tabletops, electrical parts, plywood binders.
Phenolic: resists heat and cold. Used for adhesives, appliance handles, electrical devices, surface coatings.
Polyester: strong, hardens quickly, molds under low pressure. Used for boats, luggage, swimming pools, automobile bodies, chairs.
Polyurethane: tough, resists chemicals. Used for electrical insulation, structural parts, insulation foam, foam seat cushions, fabrics with elastic qualities.
Silicone: resists weather, has high elasticity and good electrical qualities. Used for oven gaskets, electrical insulation, greases and other lubricants, waterproof materials.

Thermoplastic materials

ABS (acrylonitrile-butadiene-styrene): strong, long wearing, resists stains and chemicals. Used for telephones, wheels, handles, appliance parts, luggage, piping.
Acetal: tough, stiff, keeps its shape under pressure, has high melting point. Used for refrigerator and washing machine parts, cams, wheels.
Acrylic: resists weather and chemicals, easily colored, has high clarity. Used for optical lenses, airplane canopies, signs, displays, automobile tail lights, fabrics, paints.
Cellulose acetate: tough, transparent. Used for toys, novelties, handles, packaging, photographic film, machine guards.
Cellulose acetate butyrate: tough, resists water. Used for steering wheels, pipe, tool handles, industrial parts.
Nylon: strong, springy, resists abrasion, has good electrical qualities. Used for fabrics, gears, bearings, hardware, brush bristles, electrical appliances, carpeting.
Polycarbonate: resists heat, has high impact strength. Used for business machine parts, electrical connectors, coil forms, light diffusers, windows, eyeglass safety lenses, airplane canopies.
Polyethylene: lightweight, flexible, has waxlike feel. Used for bottles, packaging, electrical insulation.
Polypropylene: lightweight, resists heat and chemicals. Used for rope, packaging, automobile parts, baby bottles, appliance parts, carpeting.
Polystyrene: lightweight, tasteless, odorless. Used for housewares, toys, electrical insulation, radio cabinets, packaging.
Polytetrafluoroethylene: resists heat and chemicals, slides easily. Used for cable insulation, bearings, valve seats, gaskets, frypan coatings, slides and cams.
Polyvinyl chloride: strong, easily colored, rigid or flexible, resists abrasion. Used for imitation leather, phonograph records, packaging, pipe, electrical insulation, flooring.
Polyvinylidene chloride: crystal clear, tough. Used for packages for meat and other foods.

thermoplastics tend to lose their shape when exposed to constant pressure over a long period of time. For this reason, manufacturers prefer to use thermosets for such products as plastic seats on buses.

How plastics are made

The substances used to make plastic products are called *synthetic resins.* These resins are made primarily from petroleum, but some come from such other natural sources as coal, natural gas, cotton, and wood. Chemical manufacturers produce the resins and sell them to companies that make plastic products.

The chemistry of plastics. To understand how plastics are made, it is helpful to know something about the chemistry of polymers. The polymers in plastics are made up of small molecules called *monomers.* Most of these molecules are composed of carbon, hydrogen, nitrogen, and oxygen atoms. Some include chlorine, fluorine, silicon, or sulfur atoms. A polymer chain consists of hundreds, thousands, or even millions of monomer links. In some polymers, these links are made up of the same kind of monomer, repeated over and over. Others are composed of two or more kinds of monomers, which may be linked randomly or in alternating sequences. In some polymers, blocks of one kind of monomer are joined to blocks of another kind.

Polymer chains may or may not have branches. A chain may have branches on only one side or alternating from one side to the other. The chains may pack together in straight rows to make a stiff, crystalline solid. Or they may remain tangled and spread out, to make a soft, rubbery material. The properties of plastics depend on the types of monomers in their polymer chains, the lengths of the chains, and the arrangement of the chains.

Different kinds of polymer molecules can be mixed together to form *polymeric alloys,* or *blends.* Alloys are often easier to create than new synthetic polymers. They may have properties that lie between those of their component polymers, or they may have properties that are better than either. Polymer scientists can engineer plastics blends with the ideal properties for nearly any task. Alloys are used in products that range from packaging films to automobile body parts.

Making synthetic resins. Resin manufacturers make polymers by combining chemical compounds. These range from familiar chemicals like ammonia and benzene to compounds with tongue-twisting names such as hexamethylenediamine. When a manufacturer combines appropriate compounds, chemical reactions cause atoms to cluster together to form monomers. Further reactions cause the monomers to *polymerize*—that is, to form long chains of molecules. Polymerization produces the synthetic resin.

The steps in polymer building can be illustrated by the production of polystyrene resin. To make polystyrene, a chemical manufacturer begins with the liquid benzene and the gas ethylene, two chemicals derived from petroleum. The manufacturer bubbles the ethylene through the benzene. During this process, the compounds react to form the liquid *ethylbenzene.*

The chemical manufacturer uses the ethylbenzene to make liquid styrene by heating ethylbenzene gas to a high temperature and bringing it into contact with certain metal oxides. This process removes some hydrogen atoms from the ethylbenzene. The remaining atoms form molecules of styrene.

Finally, the manufacturer polymerizes the styrene to make solid polystyrene. One way this can be done is by suspending the styrene in water, adding chemicals, and heating it. A chemical reaction causes the styrene molecules to link together and form chainlike molecules of polystyrene. The manufacturer then forms the solid polystyrene into grainlike particles. These particles are the raw material used to mold polystyrene products.

Manufacturers frequently use *additives* to change the properties of a plastics resin. Common additives include (1) reinforcements, (2) fillers, (3) plasticizers, and (4) pigments.

Resin makers use such reinforcements as glass fibers or carbon fibers to give plastics extra strength or rigidity. The resulting mix, called a *composite* or a *reinforced plastic,* may contain from 10 to as much as 80 per cent reinforcement. Composites are lightweight and can replace metals in missiles, aircraft, and automobiles.

Resin manufacturers may use fillers to improve the quality of plastics or to extend an expensive resin. Common fillers include powdered wood, talc, and clay.

Manufacturers add plasticizers to certain synthetic resins to make them softer, more flexible, and easier to shape. Plasticizers overcome the attractive forces between the polymer chains and separate them to prevent intermeshing.

Pigments change the color of plastics. Resin makers use pigments to produce unlimited varieties of color.

Additives enable resin manufacturers to make plastics even more useful. For example, vinyl plastics are naturally clear and rigid. But thanks to additives, vinyl plastics can be made into products ranging from rigid, gray pipe to slightly flexible, black phonograph records to soft, transparent windows for convertible automobile tops.

Making plastic products. Manufacturers use seven main processes to shape plastics into products. These processes are (1) molding, (2) casting, (3) extrusion, (4) calendering, (5) laminating, (6) foaming, and (7) thermoforming.

Molding. There are a variety of molding processes, including compression, injection, blow, and rotational molding. In all these processes, force is applied to the plastic material during and after it enters the mold. Once the product has hardened, it is released from the mold.

Compression molding is the most common method of molding thermosetting plastics. Compression-molded products include automobile hoods and fenders, electrical switches, and handles for cooking utensils and irons. In compression molding, resin powder is put into a mold. The manufacturer then heats the mold and, at the same time, applies pressure. After the plastics have set, the mold is opened and the product is released. The mold can then be refilled.

Injection molding is the most widely used method of molding thermoplastics. Injection-molded products include telephones, computer housings, automobile steering wheels, and a variety of other items. In injection molding, resin pellets fall from a hopper into a heated, horizontal barrel, where they melt. A plunger or revolving screw inside the barrel pushes the liquid resin under pressure into a mold. Most injection-molded products take only 10 to 30 seconds to harden. The mold is opened, and ejector pins push the formed product out of the mold. The mold is then closed and refilled.

Blow molding is used to make bottles and other hollow objects. In this process, a tube of molten resin, called a *parison,* is inserted into a mold. Compressed

How plastic resins are made

Plastic resins are made primarily from chemicals that come from petroleum. This diagram shows how ethylene, a gas derived from petroleum, is polymerized to form polyethylene plastic resins.

WORLD BOOK diagram by Tony Gibbons, Bernard Thornton Artists

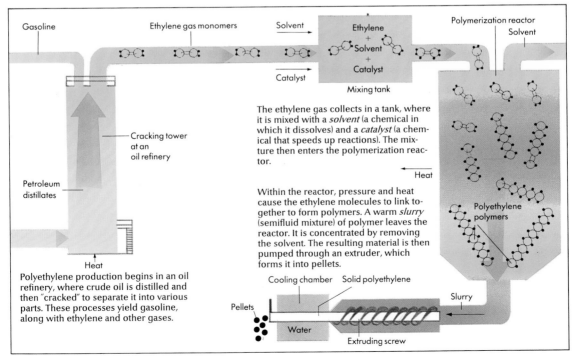

Gasoline

Ethylene gas monomers

Solvent

Ethylene + Solvent + Catalyst

Polymerization reactor

Solvent

Catalyst

Mixing tank

Cracking tower at an oil refinery

The ethylene gas collects in a tank, where it is mixed with a *solvent* (a chemical in which it dissolves) and a *catalyst* (a chemical that speeds up reactions). The mixture then enters the polymerization reactor.

Heat

Petroleum distillates

Within the reactor, pressure and heat cause the ethylene molecules to link together to form polymers. A warm *slurry* (semifluid mixture) of polymer leaves the reactor. It is concentrated by removing the solvent. The resulting material is then pumped through an extruder, which forms it into pellets.

Polyethylene polymers

Heat

Polyethylene production begins in an oil refinery, where crude oil is distilled and then "cracked" to separate it into various parts. These processes yield gasoline, along with ethylene and other gases.

Cooling chamber   Solid polyethylene

Pellets

Slurry

Water

Extruding screw

How plastic products are made

Manufacturers make plastic products from plastic resins, which melt into a syrupy liquid when heated. The products are shaped by several methods, as shown in these illustrations.

WORLD BOOK illustrations by Paul D. Turnbaugh

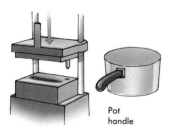

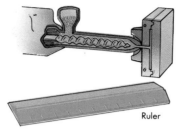

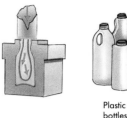

Pot handle

Ruler

Plastic bottles

Compression molding uses heat and pressure to shape plastics. The process is commonly used to mold thermosetting plastics.

Injection molding shoots molten plastic material under pressure into a mold. It is the most widely used method of molding thermoplastics.

Blow molding produces hollow objects. It uses air or steam to expand a tube of molten resin, forcing the material against a mold's walls.

Nylon gear

Garden hose

Casting does not depend on any external pressure to shape the plastics. In the casting process, melted resin is simply poured into a mold. Manufacturers use casting to produce thick, solid objects.

Extrusion is used to produce such continuous forms as pipe, rods, fibers, and wire coatings. Rotating screws force the plastics through a heated barrel, in which they melt, then force them out through a specially shaped die.

air or steam then is forced into the parison, which expands much like a balloon being inflated. This action forces the resin against the walls of the mold, where it is held until it hardens.

Rotational molding also forms hollow objects, such as soccer balls, dolls, and automobile fuel tanks. In this process, a mold is partly filled with powdered resin. The mold is then heated while a motor spins it rapidly, creating a centrifugal force. This force pushes the melting resin against the mold walls and holds it there as the mold is cooled and the object solidifies.

Casting, unlike molding, does not depend on any external pressure to shape the plastics. Manufacturers use this method to shape both thermoplastics and thermosetting plastics. To cast thermosets, they pour a liquid resin containing chemicals into a mold and harden it by applying heat. For thermoplastics, the molten resin is poured into a mold and cooled until it sets. Processors employ casting to make thick plastic panels and to produce gears, paperweights, and other solid objects.

Extrusion is used to produce pipe, rods, fibers, wire coatings, and other products that have the same shape along their entire length. Solid thermoplastics particles from a hopper enter a stationary, heated barrel. One or more rotating screws force the particles through the barrel, where they melt as they are pushed along. The molten material is forced out through a shaping die.

Calendering produces a continuous plastic sheet or film by pressing molten plastics between pairs of polished, heated rollers. Manufacturers feed fabric, paper, or metal foil through the rollers to produce such items as plastic-coated playing cards and tablecloths.

Laminating uses plastics to bind together stacks of glass-fiber, wood, paper, cloth, or metal-foil sheets. The sheets are coated or soaked with a resin. They are then placed one on top of the other. A machine squeezes the sheets together and heats them until the resin has joined them firmly. Laminating produces strong materials with a wide range of thicknesses for such products as plywood, electronic circuit boards, and tabletops.

Foaming refers to any of several methods that produce plastic foams. All these methods involve introducing a gas into heated plastic resins. The gas expands and creates bubbles in the cooling resin. The resulting material is lightweight plastic foam, which is sometimes called *cellular plastic*. Depending on the resins and the method, plastic foams can be stiff and strong, such as those used in home insulation and fast-food packaging. Others can be soft and rubbery, such as the foams in furniture cushions and pillows.

Thermoforming is an inexpensive process used to mold items from sheets of plastics. In this process, workers clamp a plastic sheet over a mold. They then heat the sheet until it becomes soft. Next, a pump sucks

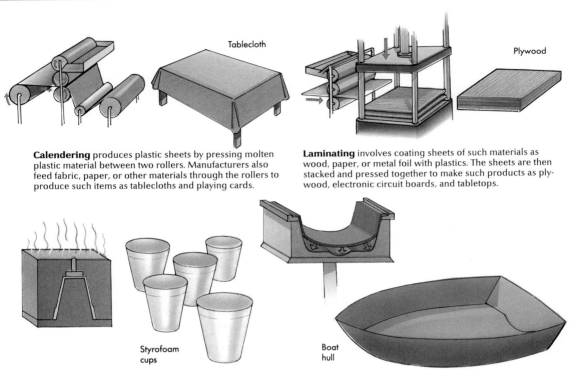

Calendering produces plastic sheets by pressing molten plastic material between two rollers. Manufacturers also feed fabric, paper, or other materials through the rollers to produce such items as tablecloths and playing cards.

Laminating involves coating sheets of such materials as wood, paper, or metal foil with plastics. The sheets are then stacked and pressed together to make such products as plywood, electronic circuit boards, and tabletops.

Foaming is any of several methods that produce solid plastics filled with air spaces. To make styrofoam, for example, manufacturers use beads of thermoplastic resin containing a chemical that forms a gas when heated during molding.

Thermoforming is used to mold items from sheets of plastics. A sheet is clamped over a mold and heated until it becomes soft. A vacuum pump sucks air out through tiny holes in the mold, drawing the sheet into the mold.

air out through tiny holes in the mold. This creates a vacuum that pulls the soft plastic sheet down until it covers the surface of the mold. There it cools and hardens in the shape of the mold. Manufacturers use thermoforming to produce such objects as bathtubs, shower bases, and yogurt containers.

Development of plastics

For thousands of years, people used natural gums and resins with properties similar to plastics. For example, the ancient Greeks and Romans created decorative objects from *amber,* a fossil resin. During the Middle Ages, Europeans used the natural resin *lac,* and its purified form, *shellac,* to coat objects.

By the mid-1800's, the commercial molding of plasticslike natural substances had developed. Manufacturers molded items from lac, *gutta-percha* (a tree resin), and other substances obtained from animal, vegetable, and mineral sources. Products made from these natural "plastics" included brush handles, knobs, electrical insulation, phonograph records, and novelty items. Museums and collectors treasure the beautiful molded objects created during the late 1800's and early 1900's.

Despite their beauty, these natural molding materials had several disadvantages. Manufacturers often had difficulty obtaining the raw materials. Some materials

proved difficult to mold, and many of the finished products turned brittle and broke easily.

The invention of Celluloid. In the late 1860's, John W. Hyatt, a printer from Albany, N.Y., developed a material to replace the scarce ivory used to make billiard balls. In 1870, he and his brother Isaiah received a patent for the material, which they later named *Celluloid.* Celluloid was the first synthetic plastic material to receive wide commercial use.

Hyatt made Celluloid by first treating *cellulose,* a substance found in cotton, with nitric acid. He then combined the resulting substance, *pyroxylin,* with the solvent *camphor.* The end product, Celluloid, was a hard, stiff material that could be shaped under heat and pressure to form useful items.

Celluloid was used for years to make such products as combs, dentures, and photographic films. But it was highly flammable. During the early 1900's, researchers produced a similar, but less flammable, material called *cellulose acetate.* Today, manufacturers use cellulose acetate to make films, fibers, and molded objects. Celluloid itself is still used to make ping-pong balls.

The invention of Bakelite. During the early 1900's, Leo Baekeland, a chemist from New York City, attempted to make a synthetic shellac by combining the chemicals carbolic acid (also known as phenol) and formaldehyde. Chemists had experimented with combining these chemicals for several years, but the reaction had been too violent to contain. Baekeland succeeded in controlling the reaction, which created *phenolic resin.*

The resin did not turn out to be the synthetic shellac that Baekeland had sought. But his research was hardly a failure, for he had created the first completely synthetic resin and the first of the thermosetting plastics. He patented it in 1909 and named it *Bakelite,* after his own name. Bakelite soon became widely used to make such items as telephones and handles for pots and irons. It continues to be used today in the electrical and automotive industries.

Growth of the plastics industry. The introduction of Bakelite in 1909 gave scientists a better understanding of polymer chemistry. The plastics industry expanded steadily throughout the next three decades. Scientists in the United States, Great Britain, and Germany conducted a great deal of research in plastics, shedding new light on their structures.

The most dramatic developments occurred in the 1930's. Four important thermoplastics—acrylics, nylon, polystyrene, and polyvinyl chloride (PVC or vinyl)—came into commercial use. Acrylics are strong and clear. They became widely used for airplane windows. Nylon was used to make women's hosiery and, later, such molded products as bearings and gears. Manufacturers used polystyrene in many products, including clock and radio housings, toys, wall tile, and food containers. PVC, too, had numerous applications, finding its way into such diverse products as garden hoses, raincoats, wire insulation, and electric plugs. The introduction of specialized machinery to form and mold plastics into useful items also helped the growth of the industry.

Important thermosetting plastics called polyesters were introduced commercially in the 1940's. Important thermoplastics developed during the 1940's included polyethylene, silicones, and epoxy resins. All of these plastics found new uses during the early 1950's. Polyethylene proved an excellent material for dishes, squeezable bottles, plastic bags, artificial flowers, and other products. Manufacturers used silicones in lubricants and electrical insulation, and physicians used them in body implants. Epoxy resins gained wide use as strong adhesives. Manufacturers used polyesters to make boat hulls. In 1953, the General Motors Corporation introduced the Chevrolet Corvette—a sports car with a body made of polyester reinforced by glass fibers. The Corvette rolled into history as the first mass-produced automobile with a plastic body.

The uses of plastics continued to grow during the late 1950's and the 1960's. This growth corresponded directly to the growth of the petrochemical industry, the major producer of the raw materials for plastics. Engineers found new uses for plastics in medicine, nuclear and space research, industry, and architecture. Polymer chemists developed several new plastics that are especially resistant to chemicals and extreme heat.

Throughout the 1970's and 1980's, plastics continued to find new applications, appearing in such products as microwave cookware, personal computer housings, and compact discs. Aerospace engineers used heat-resistant polyurethane foam to cover the external fuel tanks of the United States space shuttles. This plastic foam acts as heat insulation to prevent loss of fuel by evaporation. During the late 1980's, scientists developed the first practical *conductive plastics,* which—unlike other plastics—can carry an electric current. Conductive plastics have possible uses in batteries, wiring, and static-resistant fabrics.

The plastics industry

The United States, Japan, and other industrialized nations lead the world in plastics production. The plastics industry continues to grow rapidly in these countries. The growth of the industry in any country depends on a plentiful supply of petroleum.

Plastics companies may be divided into three general groups: *resin manufacturers* (mostly chemical companies) who make and supply resins; *processors* who shape the resins into products; and *finishers and assemblers* who make products by cutting, drilling, decorating, and assembling plastic parts. Most resin manufacturers are located in regions that allow easy access to great supplies of petroleum. Most processors, finishers, and assemblers operate in areas where they can serve many industries.

The plastics industry offers a variety of job opportunities, including careers in research, design, machine operation, quality control, and sales. For information about careers in plastics, write to the Society of Plastics Engineers, 14 Fairfield Drive, Brookfield, CT 06804.

Plastics and the environment

As more and more plastic packaging materials are used by consumers, more plastic waste is generated. Because most plastics do not readily break down, this waste contributes significantly to environmental pollution.

Recycling has emerged as one method of combating the problem of plastics waste. Industries that produce or use large amounts of plastics have recycled their wastes for years. Usually they clean and separate the plastics by type. They recycle the thermoplastics by remelting and re-forming them into new products. Thermosets are either ground into fine powders or shredded. The powders are used as fillers. The shreds can be used as insulation in such products as quilted jackets and sleeping bags.

In the 1980's, many cities and towns turned to recycling to help dispose of consumer plastics waste. These communities require citizens to sort certain plastic items—such as polyester soft drink bottles and polyethylene milk bottles—from other waste materials. These plastics can be reused in the same manner as industrial plastics waste.

Some communities do not separate the plastics but instead burn the mixed municipal waste. This process yields energy that can be used for electricity or heating. It requires, however, sophisticated incinerators that remove the acid gases produced by the burning of PVC and other plastics.

Another approach to the disposal problem is to design plastics that can be broken down by nature and time. In the 1970's, chemists introduced *biodegradable* plastics that break down through the actions of microorganisms. In products made from these plastics, molecules of starches or cellulose separate the polymer chains of the plastics. Microorganisms attack and consume the starches and then cause the products to deteriorate. Scientists also created *photodegradable* plastics that break down through long exposure to sunlight. The polymers in these plastics are decomposed by a chemical additive that breaks down when exposed to sunlight.

In the mid-1980's, manufacturers began using degradable plastics to make trash bags, foam cups, and other disposable products. But such plastics have come under fire from environmental groups and even members of the plastics industry. These critics argue that even under the best conditions, degradable plastics products leave plastics residue behind, and that the products will not break down at all when buried in landfills. They are also concerned that the additives used to enable plastics to degrade also make the plastics unfit for recycling.

Joseph A. Beisenberger, Paul G. Kelleher, and Marino Xanthos

Related articles in *World Book* include:

Acrylic	Fiber	Polymerization
Bottle	Fiberglass	Resin, Synthetic
Cast and casting	Glass (Specialty	Silicone
Cellophane	glasses)	Strength of
Die and diemaking	Laminating	materials
Du Pont Company	Nylon	Styrofoam
Environmental pol-	Packaging	Synthetics
lution (Techno-	Petrochemicals	Theater (Costumes
logical causes)	Polarized light	and makeup)
Extrusion	Polyester	Vinyl

Outline

I. **How plastics are used**
   A. To replace metals
   B. To replace natural fibers and hides
   C. To replace paper
   D. To replace wood and stone
   E. To replace glass and ceramics
   F. To provide new characteristics
II. **Types of plastics**
III. **How plastics are made**
   A. The chemistry of plastics
   B. Making synthetic resins
   C. Making plastic products
IV. **Development of plastics**
   A. The invention of Celluloid
   B. The invention of Bakelite
   C. Growth of the plastics industry
V. **The plastics industry**
VI. **Plastics and the environment**

Questions

What are the leading plastics-producing countries?
What are some metal products that plastics can replace?
How does casting differ from molding?
What is a *filler*? A *plasticizer*?
How do thermoplastics differ from thermosetting plastics?
What is the chief source of chemicals for the production of synthetic plastics?
What was the first synthetic plastic material to receive wide commercial use?
What is a polymer?
What are some methods for controlling plastic waste?
What types of new applications did plastics find during the 1970's and 1980's?

Additional resources

Dineen, Jacqueline. *Plastics.* Enslow, 1986. For younger readers.
Richardson, Terry L. *Industrial Plastics: Theory and Application.* 2nd ed. Delmar Pubs., 1989.
Whyman, Kathryn. *Plastics.* Gloucester Pr., 1988. For younger readers.
Working with Plastics. Time-Life Bks., 1982.

Crustacean, *kruhs TAY shuhn,* is an invertebrate animal with many jointed legs and a hard external shell. A crustacean has no bones. The external shell, called an *exoskeleton,* covers and protects the body. Crabs, crayfishes, lobsters, and shrimp are crustaceans, as are barnacles, water fleas, and wood lice.

There are more than 42,000 species of crustaceans. The largest species, the giant spider crab of Japan, measures up to 12 feet (3.7 meters) long between its outstretched claws. The smallest crustaceans, such as copepods and water fleas, may be less than $\frac{1}{24}$ inch (1 millimeter) long. Most crustaceans live in salt water, but some inhabit fresh water. A few species, including certain crabs and wood lice, live on land.

Crustaceans play a major role in *aquatic* (water) ecology. In most aquatic environments, small, floating organisms that make up the *phytoplankton* are the basic food producers. These organisms produce food from light by means of photosynthesis. Many small crustaceans feed on phytoplankton. These crustaceans then are eaten by larger crustaceans, fish, and even baleen whales. Crustaceans thus form an important link between the small food-producing organisms and the larger animals in the aquatic food chain.

People in many parts of the world eat lobsters, shrimp, and other crustaceans. On the other hand, some kinds of crustaceans cause problems for people. For example, certain aquatic wood lice burrow into, and eventually destroy, wooden wharves. Barnacles attach themselves to the hulls of ships and greatly reduce the vessels' speed. In some tropical regions where farms are near the sea, certain crabs and other crustaceans harm crops by burrowing into and damaging dikes that surround the fields or by eating the young plants.

The body of a crustacean

Outer body. The body of an adult crustacean typically has three main parts, each of which consists of many segments. These three parts are (1) the head, (2) the thorax, and (3) the abdomen.

The head of a crustacean has two pairs of antennae, a pair of eyes, and three pairs of accessory mouthparts. The eyes may be level with the surface of the exoskeleton or at the ends of stalks. The head also includes the mouth and a pair of jaws.

Each segment of the thorax has a pair of legs. The two pairs of legs closest to the head have *pincers* (claws), which are used for catching food and bringing it to the mouth, for fighting, and for other activities. Crustaceans use their other legs mainly for walking or swimming. In some crustaceans, gills for breathing develop at the base of the legs.

The abdomen of a crustacean varies greatly in size and appearance, depending on the species. The abdomen of a lobster is large and muscular and extends from the thorax like a tail. The abdomen of a crab, on the other hand, is thin and is folded beneath the thorax. Some species of crustaceans, such as lobsters and shrimp, have leglike appendages on their abdomen. These appendages usually are tiny, and the animal uses them primarily in swimming. A crustacean's abdomen ends in a flattened, taillike structure called a *telson.* Some crustaceans snap the telson rapidly to swim backward.

Giant spider crab

Orion Press from Bruce Coleman Ltd.

Spiny lobster

© Edward S. Ross

© F. Stuart Westmorland,
Tom Stack & Assoc.

Goose barnacles

© Paulette Brunner,
Tom Stack & Assoc.

Copepod

Crustaceans are invertebrate animals with an external shell. There are more than 42,000 species of crustaceans. Most of them live in salt water. The above photographs suggest the great variety of types of crustaceans.

Internal organs. In large crustaceans, a heart pumps blood throughout the body. Arteries carry blood away from the heart. The blood drains into cavities in the lower parts of the body and then returns to the heart through special openings. Some of the smaller crustaceans, such as certain copepods, have no heart. Their body movements promote circulation of the blood.

A crustacean's digestive system has three main parts: (1) the foregut, (2) the midgut, and (3) the hindgut. A crustacean has no teeth, and so it cannot chew. Instead, plates and spikes of shell in the foregut grind up food. The food is then directed to the midgut or the hindgut. The midgut produces enzymes and other substances that help digest the food. The hindgut stores undigested materials until they are eliminated from the body through an opening called the *anus.*

Crustaceans have a simple brain. It is connected to a nerve cord that extends along the underside of the body. Branches from the nerve cord enter each body segment and control various activities.

Most crustaceans breathe through gills. However, many small species have no gills. They breathe through their skin.

Senses. Most adult crustaceans have a pair of *compound eyes.* These eyes consist of many separate simple eyes. The entire group of eyes provides the crustacean with a mosaic image and can detect movement. Adult copepods and a few other species of crustaceans have only *simple eyes,* which sense light but do not form an image.

Tiny hairlike *setae* cover various parts of the exoskeleton. Certain of them are sensitive to taste and touch. These sensory setae are concentrated on the antennae, mouthparts, and pincers.

The life of a crustacean

Reproduction. Among crustaceans, a new individual is created when a sperm of the male fertilizes the egg of a female. The male may deposit sperm on the female's shell or into sperm receptacles on her abdomen. The sperm then fertilize the eggs as the female lays them. The number of eggs produced at one time varies tremendously among species. The crayfish lays from about 50 to 150 eggs. The Chinese wool-handed crab produces as many as 900,000 eggs at a time. In most species of crustacean, the female carries the eggs on the abdomen and protects them until they hatch.

The body of a crustacean

A crustacean's body has three main parts: head, thorax, and abdomen. The animal's hard shell, called the *exoskeleton,* protects the body. The crustacean pictured below is a shrimp.

WORLD BOOK diagram by Patricia J. Wynne

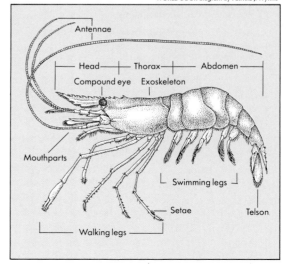

Interesting facts about crustaceans

WORLD BOOK illustrations by James Teason

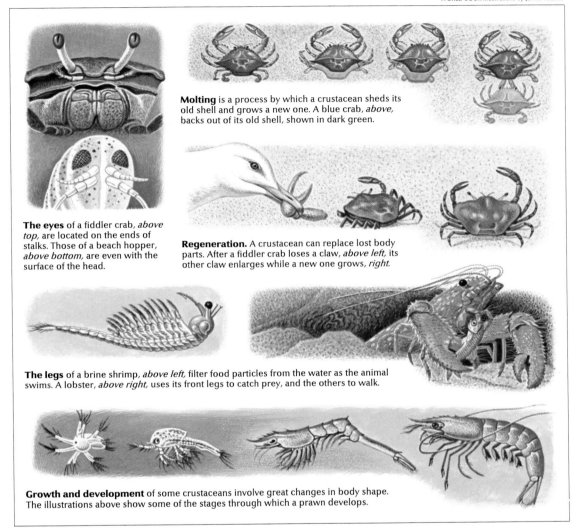

Molting is a process by which a crustacean sheds its old shell and grows a new one. A blue crab, *above,* backs out of its old shell, shown in dark green.

The eyes of a fiddler crab, *above top,* are located on the ends of stalks. Those of a beach hopper, *above bottom,* are even with the surface of the head.

Regeneration. A crustacean can replace lost body parts. After a fiddler crab loses a claw, *above left,* its other claw enlarges while a new one grows, *right.*

The legs of a brine shrimp, *above left,* filter food particles from the water as the animal swims. A lobster, *above right,* uses its front legs to catch prey, and the others to walk.

Growth and development of some crustaceans involve great changes in body shape. The illustrations above show some of the stages through which a prawn develops.

Growth and development. Most crustaceans hatch from the egg in an immature form known as a *larva.* At first, the larva does not look at all like the adult animal. The larva swims weakly in the sea for several weeks. During this time, it gradually changes form, adding new body segments and appendages until it looks like its parents. A few species of crustaceans, including beach hoppers and wood lice, have no larval stage. The young of these species hatch as miniature adults.

A crustacean's exoskeleton does not expand, and so the growing animal repeatedly sheds its old shell and grows a new, larger one. The shedding process is called *molting.* Many species of crustaceans continue to molt throughout life, but others stop after reaching maturity. Before molting begins, the crustacean absorbs some of the nutrients from its old shell. It uses these nutrients to form a soft, thin new exoskeleton beneath the old shell. The old exoskeleton then splits, and the animal works its

way out of it. The crustacean takes in water and swells to a larger size before the new shell hardens. A crustacean's muscles are connected to its shell. During molting, muscle attachments to the old shell are broken, and the animal has difficulty moving about. Until the new shell hardens, the animal often hides in a crevice or a small underwater cave.

If certain parts of a crustacean's body are damaged or lost, they may be repaired or replaced through a process called *regeneration.* The replacement part may appear during the next molt in a reduced size and then gradually enlarge to full size with successive molts. Some crustaceans, such as crabs and lobsters, can voluntarily detach a limb that has been caught by an enemy.

Food and habits. A few species of crustaceans live as parasites on other animals. Other species, including crabs, crayfishes, and lobsters, prey on various water creatures or eat the remains of animals and plants. Certain species, such as copepods and water fleas, as well as many crustacean larvae, drift through the water and feed on floating microorganisms. In turn, these crustaceans are eaten by barnacles, krill, and other crustaceans, and by many kinds of fish. Krill, in turn, are eaten by baleen whales, fish, and birds. Various other crustaceans become the prey of birds and land mammals.

Crustaceans live in a wide variety of habitats. Some drift continuously in the water as part of the plankton. Others prowl along the shore of a body of water and hide among rocks or weeds. Some find shelter in a sponge or coral, or inside an abandoned shell of a snail. Crabs and some other crustaceans burrow into mud or sand for safety. Barnacles attach themselves to rocks along the seashore as well as to turtles, whales, ships, and wharves. Most land crustaceans live under rocks or in burrows, rotting wood, or other damp places.

Scientific classification. Crustaceans make up the subphylum Crustacea in the phylum Arthropoda. Crabs, crayfishes, lobsters, shrimp, and wood lice belong to the class Malacostraca. Barnacles make up the class Cirripedia. Copepods make up the class Copepoda. Water fleas belong to the class Branchiopoda.

Jonathan Green

Cosmic rays are high-energy particles that originate in outer space. Scientists believe these rays fill the Milky Way and other galaxies as well. Cosmic rays consist of subatomic particles that carry an electric charge, such as protons, electrons, and the nuclei of atoms. In outer space, they travel at nearly the speed of light, which is 186,282 miles (299,792 kilometers) per second.

Physicists measure the energy of cosmic rays in units called *electronvolts* (eV). Most cosmic rays have energies that range from a few million electronvolts (MeV) to a few billion electronvolts (GeV). A billion electronvolts would light a flashlight bulb for only about one ten-billionth of a second. However, when a cosmic ray proton carries that amount of energy, it can travel through an iron plate nearly 2 feet (60 centimeters) thick.

Cosmic rays originate from many sources in space. Scientists believe that exploding stars called *supernovae* and very dense stars known as *pulsars* produce great quantities of cosmic rays. Some cosmic rays come from the sun. Only cosmic rays with very high energies can penetrate the earth's atmosphere. Fewer than one in a million of those reach the earth's surface without colliding with an atom in the air. These collisions destroy both the cosmic ray and the atom, producing showers of high-energy subatomic particles. Some of these particles do reach the surface and even penetrate deep underground. The cosmic rays in outer space are called *primary cosmic rays.* The showers produced in the atmosphere are *secondary cosmic rays.*

Scientists study cosmic rays because these particles provide samples of matter that has traveled through millions of *light-years* of space. A light-year is the distance light travels in one year—about 5.88 trillion miles (9.46 trillion kilometers). Cosmic-ray research has enabled scientists to learn much about the physical conditions in regions far from the solar system.

Primary cosmic rays

Primary cosmic rays, also called *primaries,* are cosmic-ray particles that originate in space. There are two main types of primaries—*galactic* and *solar.*

Galactic cosmic rays come from outside the solar system. They make up most of the primaries. During periods of low activity on the sun, an average of about six galactic cosmic rays strike each square inch (6 square centimeters) of the top of the atmosphere each second.

About 98 per cent of galactic cosmic rays are atomic nuclei. The other 2 per cent consist of electrons and *positrons* (electrons with a positive charge). Of the nuclei, about 87 per cent are *protons* (hydrogen nuclei) and 12 per cent are helium nuclei. The rest of the nuclei include those of all the elements heavier than helium.

Physicists believe that most galactic cosmic rays are accelerated to their high energies by shock waves from supernovae or by strong magnetic fields around pulsars. Galactic cosmic rays can also gain energy from collisions with moving kinks in the weak magnetic fields in *interstellar space* (space between the stars). A magnetic field can be thought of as a set of imaginary lines of magnetic force extending through space. Like beads on a string, the particles move easily along these *field lines* but have difficulty cutting across the lines. When a field line moves, some of the energy of its motion is transferred to the particles traveling along it.

Once accelerated, the galactic cosmic rays in the earth's galaxy travel randomly in the galaxy's magnetic fields for an average of about 10 million years. They eventually either escape from the galaxy or are slowed down by collisions with interstellar matter.

Some galactic cosmic rays are kept out of the solar system by the *solar wind.* The solar wind consists of electrically charged atoms that flow outward from the sun throughout the solar system. The solar wind carries a magnetic field, which excludes many galactic cosmic rays from the solar system, especially during periods of high activity on the sun's surface. Thus, the concentration of galactic cosmic rays near the earth decreases as solar activity increases in an 11-year cycle called the *sunspot cycle.*

Solar cosmic rays are produced by the sun during *solar flares.* Solar flares are spectacular eruptions at the sun's surface that occur mainly during periods of high activity in the sunspot cycle. The particles released in these flares typically have energies of only a few MeV, but particles with energies of up to a few GeV may be produced in large flares. Most solar cosmic rays are protons. Others consist of heavier nuclei or electrons.

Other high-energy particles in space. Some particles are accelerated to energies of many MeV in the earth's *magnetosphere.* A magnetosphere is the region of space filled by a planet's magnetic field. Jupiter, Saturn, Uranus, and Neptune also have magnetospheres in which particles are accelerated to energies of many MeV. Most particles stay trapped in the magnetospheres and form belts of radiation around the planets.

In addition, particles are accelerated to energies of a few MeV by shock waves in the solar wind. These shock waves are produced by solar flares or by fast streams in the solar wind that behave like gusts or jets.

Secondary cosmic rays

Secondary cosmic rays, or *secondaries,* are produced when primary cosmic rays collide with atomic nuclei high in the earth's atmosphere. In these collisions, the

How cosmic rays penetrate the earth's magnetic field

Primary cosmic-ray particles, even those with low energies, can enter the earth's atmosphere near the poles by traveling along the field lines of the magnetic field. Only particles with extremely high energies can cut across the field lines and reach the atmosphere near the equator. The magnetic field there reflects most particles, including many with high energies. Secondary cosmic rays are created in the atmosphere by collisions between the primary rays and atomic nuclei.

WORLD BOOK diagram

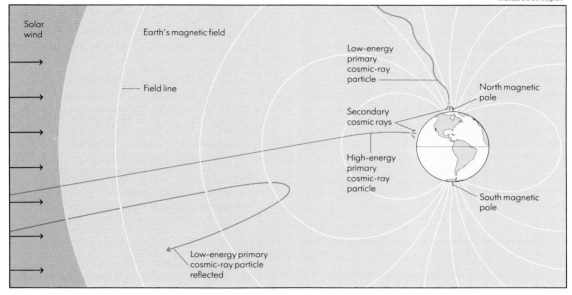

primaries break up, and some of their energy takes the form of subatomic particles. A number of the new particles collide with other nuclei in the atmosphere, producing even more particles. Such successive collisions produce a shower of secondaries that includes all types of subatomic particles. Secondaries occur from the upper atmosphere to the deepest mines in the earth.

Secondaries slow down in the atmosphere, and so only a small fraction of them reach the earth. Every minute, an average of about six particles strike each square inch of the earth's surface. Most of these particles are subatomic particles called *muons.*

The concentration of secondaries in the atmosphere is affected by the earth's magnetic field. The lines of this field curve from the earth's north magnetic pole to the south magnetic pole. Only primaries with extremely high energies can penetrate the magnetic field near the equator because they must cut across the field lines. Near the poles, even primaries with low energies can travel along the field lines and strike the atmosphere. Thus, the concentration of secondaries is lowest at the equator and increases toward the poles.

Effects of cosmic rays

The level of radiation produced on the earth by cosmic rays is far too low to harm living things. Scientists measure radiation in units called *rads.* Long-term exposure to more than a few rads a year is considered unsafe. At sea level, the dose from secondary cosmic rays is less than 0.04 rad per year. Even beyond the atmosphere, the dose from galactic cosmic rays is less than 10 rads per year. However, the level of radiation in the earth's radiation belts can endanger astronauts and damage instruments, as can radiation anywhere above

the atmosphere after large solar flares. As a result, spacecraft that may encounter such radiation must carry shielding against it. Manned space missions try to avoid the radiation belts and large solar-flare events.

Problems have resulted on some spacecraft from the effects of galactic cosmic rays on the crafts' electronic circuits. A single cosmic ray that penetrates a tiny circuit chip can change the information stored on the chip. The high energy of galactic cosmic rays makes it almost impossible to shield against them. Therefore, scientists and engineers have had to develop circuit components that are less sensitive to cosmic-ray effects.

One useful effect of cosmic rays comes from a reaction of secondaries with nitrogen nuclei in the earth's atmosphere. This reaction produces a radioactive form of carbon, called *radiocarbon.* Living things continuously incorporate carbon—including radiocarbon—into their cells. Because radiocarbon breaks down at a constant rate, the amount of it left in once-living material can tell scientists the material's age (see **Radiocarbon**).

Cosmic-ray research

Early studies. During the late 1800's, physicists used instruments called *electroscopes* in the study of radioactivity. Even when shielded from the most powerful radioactive rays, the instruments continued to react as if an unknown form of penetrating radiation were present. In 1912, the Austrian physicist Victor F. Hess took electroscopes along on a balloon flight. They indicated that radiation increases with altitude, and so Hess concluded that the radiation must originate in the atmosphere or beyond. In 1936, Hess received the Nobel Prize for physics for discovering cosmic rays.

Physicists originally thought that cosmic rays were

gamma rays (see **Gamma rays**). In the late 1920's, scientists discovered that cosmic rays, unlike gamma rays, are affected by magnetic fields. This effect indicated that the rays must be charged particles. In the late 1940's, the photographic study of cosmic rays revealed that primaries consist mainly of hydrogen nuclei and helium nuclei. In the 1950's, physicists studied the effects of the sun on cosmic rays. In 1961, they first observed electrons among primaries. Since the 1960's, spacecraft have enabled scientists to study primaries outside the earth's atmosphere and magnetic field.

Research today. Much cosmic-ray research today involves the physical nature of the stars and other objects that make up galaxies. If, as scientists believe, cosmic rays are accelerated by supernovae and pulsars, the particles provide samples of matter from places near these objects. Studying such cosmic rays helps scientists learn about the nuclear processes that occur when a star explodes as a supernova and about conditions near a pulsar. Cosmic-ray research also uncovers clues about the structure and distribution of the matter and magnetic fields that primaries encounter in interstellar space.

New instruments are being designed that will provide more detailed information about the origin, acceleration, and travel of the most energetic cosmic rays. These devices also will permit closer examination of the nuclear composition of lower-energy primaries.

Secondary cosmic rays were once the main source of subatomic particles used in research. From the 1930's through the 1950's, physicists discovered many new subatomic particles among secondaries. Today, physicists use machines called *particle accelerators* for most particle research. However, the study of cosmic rays may reveal new kinds of subatomic particles that exist only at energies much higher than accelerators can produce.   R. B. McKibben

Air pollution occurs when wastes dirty the air. People produce most of the wastes that cause air pollution. Such wastes can be in the form of gases or *particulates* (particles of solid or liquid matter). These substances result chiefly from burning fuel to power motor vehicles and to heat buildings. Industrial processes and the burning of garbage also contribute to air pollution. Natural *pollutants* (impurities) include dust, pollen, soil particles, and naturally occurring gases.

The rapid growth of population and industry, and the increased use of automobiles and airplanes, have made air pollution a serious problem. The air we breathe has become so filled with pollutants that it can cause health problems. Polluted air also harms plants, animals, building materials, and fabrics. In addition, it causes damage by altering the earth's atmosphere.

The damage caused by air pollution costs the people of the United States billions of dollars each year. This includes money spent for health care and increased maintenance of buildings. Air pollution also causes damage to the environment that cannot be reversed.

Chief sources of air pollution

People depend on the atmosphere to dilute and remove pollutants as they are produced. But weather conditions called *thermal inversions* can trap the pollutants over a certain area until they build up to dangerous levels. A thermal inversion occurs when a layer of warm air

settles over a layer of cool air that lies near the ground. This condition traps the impurities and prevents them from rising until rain or wind breaks up the layer of stationary warm air.

Forms of transportation, such as automobiles, airplanes, ships, and trains, are the leading source of air pollution in the United States, Canada, and most other industrial nations. The major pollutants produced by these sources are carbon monoxide gas, carbon dioxide gas, *hydrocarbons* (compounds of carbon and hydrogen), *nitrogen oxides* (compounds of nitrogen and oxygen), *sulfur oxides* (compounds of sulfur and oxygen), and soot. Nitrogen oxides can react with hydrocarbons in the presence of sunlight to produce a form of oxygen called *ozone*. Ozone is the chief component of photochemical smog, a common form of air pollution.

Fuel combustion for heating and cooling homes, office buildings, and factories contributes significantly to air pollution. Electric power plants that burn coal or oil also release pollutants into the atmosphere. The major pollutants from these sources are nitrogen oxides, sulfur oxides, particulates, and carbon dioxide.

Industrial processes produce a wide range of pollutants. Oil refineries discharge ammonia, hydrocarbons, organic acids, and sulfur oxides. Metal smelting plants give off large amounts of sulfur oxides and particulates containing lead and other metals. Plants that make aluminum expel fluoride dust. Plants that produce plastic foams are a major source of *chlorofluorocarbons* (CFC's), which are compounds of chlorine, fluorine, and carbon.

Burning of solid wastes often creates a very visible form of air pollution—thick, black smoke. The burning of garbage, leaves, and other refuse is banned in most parts of the United States and Canada.

© Joe Sterling, Click/Chicago

Air pollution is a serious problem in many of the world's large cities. Heavy concentrations of air pollutants, which are often in the form of smog, settle over a city, creating a health hazard for its people.

Other sources of pollution include chemical sprays and organic chemicals used to start fires on charcoal grills. Forest fires and structural fires also contribute to air pollution. In rural areas and in developing countries, the burning of forests and grasslands to clear areas for farming is a major source of air pollution.

Natural sources also contribute to air pollution. Volcanoes emit large amounts of sulfur oxides and particulates. Microbes in the guts of cattle and in rice paddies break down plant materials and release an odorless gas called *methane,* a type of hydrocarbon.

Indoor air pollution occurs when energy-efficient houses and office buildings trap pollutants inside. As a result, some pollutants found outdoors are found indoors in even higher concentrations. Some plastic products, processed wood products, paints, and adhesives can give off hydrocarbons. Many cleaning products emit poisonous gases such as ammonia and chlorine. An odorless gas called *radon* is released into the atmosphere from soil and rocks. It enters buildings through cracks in the foundation.

Effects of air pollution

Health. When people breathe polluted air, the impurities can irritate their air passages and their lungs. Particulates often remain in the lungs and can worsen such respiratory ailments as asthma and bronchitis. Radon can cause lung cancer if inhaled in large quantities. Certain chemicals contribute to the formation of cancer, pneumonia, and emphysema. In addition, carbon monoxide decreases the ability of the blood to take up oxygen in the lungs.

In London in 1952, about 4,000 people died of respiratory diseases during a "killer smog." More than 600 people died as a result of thermal inversions that occurred in New York City in 1953 and 1963. Today, such extreme events are rare because of government *emission standards,* which limit pollutants released by factories and other sources. However, air pollution still contributes to a large number of deaths each year.

Agriculture. Air pollutants can stunt the growth of crops, harm livestock, and destroy crops as well. Such damage costs the United States millions of dollars each year. Forests also have been damaged by air pollution.

Atmosphere. Some pollutants are not poisonous themselves but can cause damage by altering the earth's atmosphere. For example, the amount of carbon dioxide in the atmosphere has been increasing since the late 1800's, chiefly as a result of the burning of coal, oil, and other carbon-containing fuels. Carbon dioxide allows

Major air pollutants and their sources Most air pollution is caused by artificially created wastes in the form of gases and tiny particles of liquid and solid matter. The five principal sources of these pollutants are shown below at the left. The charts show the approximate percentage of each kind of pollutant that these sources contributed to air pollution in the United States.

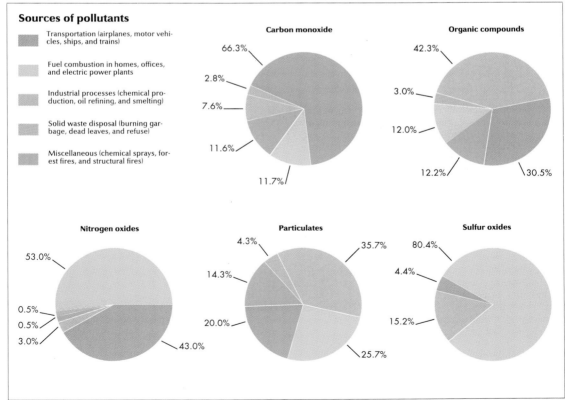

Sources of pollutants

- Transportation (airplanes, motor vehicles, ships, and trains)
- Fuel combustion in homes, offices, and electric power plants
- Industrial processes (chemical production, oil refining, and smelting)
- Solid waste disposal (burning garbage, dead leaves, and refuse)
- Miscellaneous (chemical sprays, forest fires, and structural fires)

Carbon monoxide — 66.3%, 2.8%, 7.6%, 11.6%, 11.7%

Organic compounds — 42.3%, 3.0%, 12.0%, 12.2%, 30.5%

Nitrogen oxides — 53.0%, 0.5%, 0.5%, 3.0%, 43.0%

Particulates — 4.3%, 35.7%, 14.3%, 20.0%, 25.7%

Sulfur oxides — 80.4%, 4.4%, 15.2%

Figures are for 1987. Source: U.S. Environmental Protection Agency.

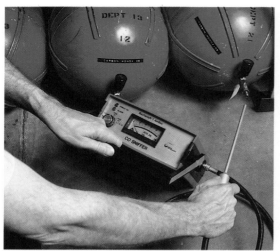

© Peter Vadnai, The Stock Market

A carbon monoxide detector is used in manufacturing facilities to test for leakage from tanks that store the gas. Carbon monoxide has many uses in industry, but it is a deadly poison.

© Chris Jones, The Stock Market

A platinum catalyst pollution scrubber removes pollutants from industrial smokestacks before they are released into the atmosphere. It is similar to catalytic converters in cars.

sunlight to reach the earth and warm its surface, but it also prevents some surface heat from escaping out of the atmosphere. This *greenhouse effect* may produce significant climatic changes, which could, in turn, destroy many kinds of plants and animals.

Chlorofluorocarbons break down the layer of ozone in the earth's upper atmosphere. This layer protects plants and animals from harmful ultraviolet rays.

Other effects. Most materials deteriorate faster when exposed to the pollutants present in the air. Concrete and stone are dissolved by air pollutants. Metals corrode faster than usual. Plastics, rubber, and fabrics are also damaged by air pollutants.

Air pollution is closely related to other forms of environmental pollution. Sulfur dioxide and nitrogen oxides can react with water droplets in the air to produce acid rain. Acid rain pollutes lakes and streams and damages the fertility of the soil.

Control of air pollution

In the United States, all levels of government—federal, state, and local—have passed laws designed to control pollution. Congress passed the Air Quality Act in 1967. Under this act, the federal government sets goals called *air quality standards* for achieving cleaner air. The states must enforce air pollution controls to meet the goals. When states fail to enforce the regulations, the federal government can act against the polluters by imposing fines. However, the lack of funding to enforce these regulations has allowed some polluters to continue releasing harmful pollutants for years.

States may set stricter air standards than the federal government requires. Since 1970, California has set the strictest standards for motor-vehicle emissions. Stricter nationwide standards for emissions have been repeatedly postponed because of opposition from automobile industry groups.

Pollution from automobiles has been reduced by

changes in motor vehicles. Since 1975, most American-made cars have been equipped with pollution-control devices called *catalytic converters.* Devices called *scrubbers* have been installed in many electric power plants, factories, and incinerators, to remove sulfur oxides and some other pollutants before they reach the air. Pollution can also be reduced by increasing energy efficiency and burning less fuel. In addition, recycling reuses some wastes that otherwise might have been burned.

Efforts to control air pollution in the United States have had some success. But many urban areas fail to meet federal air quality standards. Since 1970, emissions of sulfur oxide, carbon monoxide, hydrocarbon, and lead have decreased by about 30 per cent. Nitrogen oxide emissions have only dropped about 10 per cent.

In 1990, the U.S. Congress amended the Clean Air Act of 1970. The amendments set stricter standards for air quality and emissions, require the sale of cleaner burning fuels, and call for cuts in sulfur dioxide emissions from power plants to reduce acid rain. Also in 1990, a plan took effect to help the Los Angeles area meet federal air quality standards by 2007.

In other countries. The lack of controls on automobile emissions in Western Europe has contributed to extensive damage to forests there. Countries in Eastern Europe have lacked pollution controls altogether and have suffered enormous environmental damage as a result. Protecting the environment will require international cooperation.   David E. Henderson

Endangered species are living things threatened with *extinction*—that is, the dying off of all individuals of their kind. Thousands of species of animals and plants are endangered, and the number increases each year. Endangered animals include blue whales, some kinds of crocodiles, orangutans, rhinoceroses, snow leopards, tigers, and whooping cranes. Endangered plants include running buffalo clover, Santa Cruz cypress, snakeroot, and many species of cactuses.

© Zig Leszczynski, Animals Animals

© Allison Leete, Los Angeles Zoo

© Peggy Olwell, The Center for Plant Conservation

Endangered species include some of the earth's most marvelous living things, such as the tiger, *top left*, the California condor, *left*, and the Knowlton cactus, *above*. These photographs suggest the variety of animal and plant species around the world that are in danger of extinction.

Each species of plant and animal plays a part in the delicate balance of all living systems. Thus, the extinction of large numbers of species threatens the survival of other living things, including human beings. As more and more species have become endangered, people have increased their efforts to protect them.

Most biologists consider a species endangered if they expect it to die off completely in less than 20 years without special efforts to protect it. Some species have small populations, but they are not endangered because their population is not decreasing or threatened.

Until the last few centuries, species became rare or died out entirely chiefly because of natural causes. For example, changes in the earth's climate during the Ice Age probably caused mass extinctions of plants and animals. Today, species become endangered primarily as a result of the activities of human beings. The chief reasons that species become endangered include (1) destruction of habitat, (2) wildlife trade, (3) overhunting, and (4) competition with domestic animals.

Destruction of habitat poses the greatest threat to the survival of wild species. Most animals and plants are specially adapted to live and reproduce in a specific environment or habitat and cannot survive when it is destroyed. People damage many types of wildlife habitats when they provide space for settlement, farming, and industry. Clearing land for development and harvesting trees for lumber have destroyed vast amounts of forest

habitats. In some parts of the world, grasslands have become barren because people have allowed their livestock to overgraze land. Coastal marshlands have been filled in with land for housing and commercial buildings. Coral reefs have sometimes been dynamited to obtain species of coral and tropical fish that are valued by collectors.

Tropical rain forests contain the greatest variety of animal and plant life on earth, and they are being destroyed more rapidly than any other type of wild habitat. Many scientists believe that as many as 50 million acres (20 million hectares) of tropical rain forests are burned or cleared each year. If the current rate of clearing continues, almost all the rain forests—and the species they support—will be eliminated in less than 30 years.

Wildlife trade includes the capture of animals for pets, zoos, and research and the killing of animals for their fur or other body parts. The capture of wild animals for commercial use has endangered many species. For example, Spix's macaw, a colorful parrot of Brazil, is nearly extinct in the wild because people have captured so many of the birds for private bird collectors. Many species of primates, including the orangutan, have become endangered because so many individuals have been captured for zoos and for pets.

Other animals have been killed in such large numbers for their fur, hides, tusks, or horns that they are nearly extinct. Such animals include cheetahs, rhinoceroses, and snow leopards. Although these animals are now protected by law in the countries where they live, they are still *poached* (hunted illegally). Poaching also has seriously reduced the number of African elephants.

Overhunting has brought many species to the brink of extinction. These animals include the Caribbean manatee, the dugong, and many species of pheasants. A growing number of sea birds and sea mammals, including certain dolphins, have become endangered by commercial fishing. Each year, fisheries unintentionally entrap and kill thousands of such animals in their nets.

Competition with domestic animals. On many islands, native birds, mammals, and reptiles have become endangered after people introduced domestic animals, which compete with native species for living space. Sheep, goats, and cattle overgraze vegetation, eliminating habitat. Domestic cats prey on birds and small mammals. Rats escape from the holds of visiting ships and infest islands, killing small birds and their eggs.

Protecting endangered species. Laws and conservation programs are helping to reduce endangerment worldwide. In the United States, the Endangered Species Act of 1973 protects endangered wildlife against hunting, collecting, and other activities that might harm them or their habitats. Since this law was enacted, the numbers of certain endangered animals—including alligators, bald eagles, and peregrine falcons—have increased in some areas.

Many wild species are protected by the international Convention on International Trade in Endangered Species (CITES). This agreement, originally signed by 10 nations in July 1975, aims to control trade in wildlife and wildlife products. For example, CITES bans the trade of furs of such endangered species as leopards and cheetahs. It also forbids the import or export of ivory obtained from the tusks of elephants. By 1990, more than 100 nations had signed CITES.

Various organizations publish lists of endangered species to bring these species to the attention of lawmakers, conservationists, and the public. The International Union for the Conservation of Nature and Natural Resources (IUCN) compiles lists of endangered plants and animals worldwide. The U.S. Fish and Wildlife Service, many state governments, and various organizations also maintain such lists. These organizations do not always agree about which species should be listed as endangered.

A growing number of animal species have become extinct in the wild and live only in captivity. Some zoos and animal research centers conduct programs that breed such animals with the hope of returning their offspring to the wild. In some cases, the offspring must be trained to survive in the wild. These captive-breeding programs have greatly improved the outlook for such endangered species as the black-footed ferret, the California condor, and the whooping crane.   Greta Nilsson

Some endangered species of animals and plants

Common name Animals	Scientific name	Distribution	Survival problems
American crocodile	*Crocodylus acutus*	Florida, Mexico, Central and South America, Caribbean islands	Overhunted for its hide; habitat destruction
Asiatic lion	*Panthera leo persica*	India	Habitat destruction; overhunted for sport
Black-footed ferret	*Mustela nigripes*	Known only in captivity	Poisoning of prairie dogs, its chief prey
Black rhinoceros	*Diceros bicornis*	South of Sahara in Africa	Habitat destruction; overhunted for its horn
Blue whale	*Balaenoptera musculus*	All oceans	Overhunted for its blubber, for food, and for whale oil
Brown pelican	*Pelecanus occidentalis*	North Carolina to Texas, California, West Indies, coastal Central and South America	Contamination of food supply with pesticides
California condor	*Gymnogyps californianus*	Known only in captivity	Habitat destruction; hunted for sport; overcollection of eggs for food
Devils Hole pupfish	*Cyprinodon diabolis*	Nevada	Habitat destruction
Imperial parrot	*Amazona imperialis*	West Indies, Dominica	Habitat destruction; illegal capture for pets
Ivory-billed woodpecker	*Campephilus principalis*	South-central and Southeastern United States, Cuba	Habitat destruction; overcollection for museums
Kemp's ridley sea turtle	*Lepidochelys kempii*	Tropical and temperate parts of the Atlantic	Overhunted for its leather; overcollection of eggs
Orangutan	*Pongo pygmaeus*	Borneo, Sumatra	Habitat destruction; overcollection of young for zoos
Red wolf	*Canis rufus*	Southeastern United States to central Texas	Habitat destruction; hunted, trapped, and poisoned because people consider it a pest
Snow leopard	*Panthera unica*	Central Asia	Overhunted for its fur
Tiger	*Panthera tigris*	Temperate and tropical Asia	Habitat destruction; overhunted for sport
Plants			
Floating sorrel	*Oxalis natans*	South Africa	Habitat destruction
Green pitcher plant	*Sarracenia oreophila*	Alabama, Georgia	Overcollection; habitat destruction
Knowlton cactus	*Pediocactus knowltonii*	New Mexico, Colorado	Habitat destruction
Santa Cruz cypress	*Cupressus abramsiana*	California	Difficulty reproducing because of habitat conditions
Running buffalo clover	*Trifolium stoloniferum*	Central United States	Unknown
Snakeroot	*Eryngium coneifolium*	Florida	Habitat destruction

Index

How to use the index

This index covers the contents of the 1990, 1991, and 1992 editions
of *Science Year*, The World Book Science Annual.

Each index entry gives the last two digits of the edition year, followed by a colon and the page number or numbers. For example, this entry means that information on a Bangladesh cyclone may be found on page 311 of the 1992 *Science Year*.

The "see" and "see also" cross references indicate that references to the topic are listed under another entry in the index.

When there are many references to a topic, they are grouped alphabetically by clue words under the main topic. For example, the clue words under **Black holes** group the references to that topic under five subtopics.

An entry in all capital letters indicates that there is a Science News Update article with that name in at least one of the three volumes covered in this index. References to the topic in other articles may also be listed in the entry.

An entry that only begins with a capital letter indicates that there are no Science News Update articles with that title but that information on the topic can be found in the editions and on the pages listed.

The indication (il.) after a page number means that the reference is to an illustration only.

Index

A

Index

Index

391

Index

393

Index

Index

Index

Acknowledgments

The publishers of *Science Year* gratefully acknowledge the courtesy of the following artists, photographers, publishers, institutions, agencies, and corporations for the illustrations in this volume. Credits should read from top to bottom, left to right on their respective pages. All entries marked with an asterisk (*) denote illustrations created exclusively for *Science Year*. All maps, charts, and diagrams were prepared by the *Science Year* staff unless otherwise noted.

Cover J. D. Griggs, USGS

2   Jet Propulsion Laboratory; Boise Interagency Fire Center; © V. Ivleva, Magnum

3   NASA; NASA; © Jose Nicolas, Sipa Press; Noboru Hashimoto, Sygma

4   *Christopher Columbus* (1519) by Sebastiano del Piombo; Scott Lopez, Hawaii Volcanoes National Park; © Alain Nogues, Sygma

5   U.S. Department of Agriculture; NASA; © Dan Cheatman, DRK

10   Ocean Images from Image Bank; © Warren Morgan

11   © Hank Morgan, Rainbow; Jet Propulsion Laboratory

12   *Christopher Columbus* (1519) by Sebastiano del Piombo; Metropolitan Museum of Art, Gift of J. Pierpont Morgan; Granger Collection (4)

13   © Jay M. Pasachoff; © Gian Berto Vanni, Art Resource

16   The Three Central Figures of the Lord of Southern Dipper, Yuan Dynasty (1379 to 1468) fresco by an unknown artist; Royal Ontario Museum

17   Bettmann

18   Luann Roberts*

19   Granger Collection; Luann Roberts*

21   Luann Roberts*; Granger Collection; Luann Roberts*

22   © Gian Berto Vanni, Art Resource; Historical Pictures Service

23   Jay M. Pasachoff; Derek Bayes, Aspect Picture Library; Le Conte's *Voyage to China* (1698)

24   Granger Collection

28   *Galileo Dictating to His Son Discorsi Solle Due Nuove Scienze,* oil on canvas by Tito Lessi; Instituto e Museo di Storia della Scienza di Firenze

30   Ocean Images from Image Bank

33   © Joseph A. Thompson, Seavision Productions

34   Guy Wolek*

35   Marion Pahl*

38   © Ed Kashi

39   © Lawrence Migdale; © Lawrence Migdale; Diana Reiss; © Lawrence Migdale

40   © Dolphin Biology Research Institute

41   © Dolphin Biology Research Institute; Rachel Smolker

42   © C. Allan Morgan from Peter Arnold

44   Jet Propulsion Laboratory

47   Adaptation by Roberta Polfus*; Joann Harling*

48   TASS from Sovfoto

49   NASA; U.S. Geological Survey; Joann Harling*

50-51   Jet Propulsion Laboratory

52   Roberta Polfus*

54-55   Jet Propulsion Laboratory

58   Nathan Green*

62   Nathan Green*; © Warren Morgan

64   Denver Museum of Natural History

65   Joe Rogers*

66   Tom Dillehay; John Adovasio; Ruth Gruhn Bryan

69   Christy G. Turner II

72   J. D. Griggs, USGS

76   Superstock; Oxford Illustrators Limited*; © Kraft, Explorer/SS from Photo Researchers; Oxford Illustrators Limited*

77   Oxford Illustrators Limited*; Camera Hawaii; Pacific Marine Environmental Lab, NOAA; Pacific Marine Environmental Lab, NOAA; Hawaii Volcanoes National Park

80   J. D. Griggs, USGS (3); Oxford Illustrators Limited*

82   Oxford Illustrators Limited*; J. D. Griggs, USGS

83   Scott Lopez, Hawaii Volcanoes National Park; Christina Heliker, USGS; T. J. Takahashi, USGS

84   J. D. Griggs, USGS

85   Royal Society of London

86   © Robert Winslow, Tom Stack & Assoc.

88   Rhode Island Solid Waste Management—Collage by Gail Greenwood, designed by Betsy Bowersock, and photographed by Josh Edenbaum

91   Trudy Rogers*

92   Waste Management, Inc.; © Woodallen, Browning-Ferris Industries

93   Institute of Scrap Recycling Industries, Inc.; Browning-Ferris Industries; © Ira Wexler, Reynolds Metals Company; Reynolds Metals Company

95   NSWMA; NSWMA; Garden State Paper Company, Inc.

97   © Hank Morgan, Rainbow; Mayfran International; OSCAR

99   Wellman, Inc.; Wellman, Inc.; © Susan Lapides

102   © Ray Ng

104   Ken Abbott*

106   © Ray Ng

107   © Ray Ng; © Ray Ng; Ken Abbott*

109   Ken Abbott*

110   © Robert T. Bakker; Ken Abbott*; © Robert T. Bakker

113-118   Ken Abbott*

121   © Comstock; Don Wilson*

124   Don Wilson*

126   © Alain Nogues, Sygma; Don Wilson*

128   Westinghouse Electric Corporation; Argonne National Laboratory

129   General Electric

130   Don Wilson*

134   TreePeople

137   Nancy Lee Walter*

138   © Randall Hyman, Stock, Boston

139   Illinois State Natural History Survey

140   Linda King, National Arbor Day Foundation

141   Nancy Lee Walter*

142   National Arbor Day Foundation

143   James R. Clark, University of Washington

146-150   Catherine Twomey*

151   © Andrew McClenaghan/SPL from Photo Researchers; © J. Burgess/SPL from Photo Researchers

152-158   Catherine Twomey*

160   Boise Interagency Fire Center; Michael S. Quinton; Jim Peaco, Yellowstone National Park; © Alan and Sandy Carey

165   Tom Herzberg*

166   Jeff Henry; © *Seattle Times* from Gamma/Liaison

168   © Alan and Sandy Carey; Michael S. Quinton

170   Jim Peaco, Yellowstone National Park; Tom Herzberg*; Charlie Ott, Photo Researchers; Tom Herzberg*

171   Michael S. Quinton; © Alan and Sandy Carey; Tom Herzberg*

173   Jeff Henry

174   Jane Bock

176   © Peter Menzel, Stock, Boston

179   Berkeley Sensor and Actuator Center (3); NovaSensor

180-183   Tom Herzberg*

184   © Peter Menzel, Stock, Boston; University of Wisconsin at Madison

186   © Peter Menzel, Stock, Boston

187   Tom Herzberg*

190   Jet Propulsion Laboratory

193   U.S. WOCE

196   University of Miami

197   Oxford Illustrators Limited*

198   NASA; Oxford Illustrators Limited*

199   Oxford Illustrators Limited*

201   U.S. WOCE

204   *World Book* illustration by Anne Norcia

World Book Encyclopedia, Inc., provides high-quality educational and reference products for the family and school. They include THE WORLD BOOK MEDICAL ENCYCLOPEDIA, a 1,040-page fully illustrated family health reference; THE WORLD BOOK OF SPACE EXPLORATION, a two-volume review of the major developments in space since man first walked on the moon; and the STUDENT INFORMATION FINDER and HOW TO STUDY, a fast-paced video presentation of key study skills with information students need to succeed in school. For further information, write WORLD BOOK ENCYCLOPEDIA, INC., P.O. Box 3073, Evanston, IL 60204-9974.